New Face of the Church
in Latin America

The *American Society of Missiology Series*, in collaboration with Orbis Books, seeks to publish scholarly works of high merit and wide interest on numerous aspects of missiology — the study of mission. Able presentations on new and creative approaches to the practice and understanding of mission will receive close attention.

Previously published in
The American Society of Missiology Series

American Society of Missiology Series, No. 18

NEW FACE
OF THE CHURCH
IN LATIN AMERICA

Between Tradition and Change

**Edited by
Guillermo Cook**

ORBIS BOOKS

Maryknoll, New York 10545

The Catholic Foreign Mission Society of America (Maryknoll) recruits and trains people for overseas missionary service. Through Orbis Books, Maryknoll aims to foster the international dialogue that is essential to mission. The books published, however, reflect the opinions of their authors and are not meant to represent the official position of the society.

Library of Congress Cataloging-in-Publication Data

New face of the Church in Latin America: between tradition and change
    /edited by Guillermo Cook.
        p.   cm. — (American Society of Missiology series; no. 18)
    Includes bibliographical references.
    ISBN 0-88344-937-4
    1. Christianity — Latin America — 20th century. 2. Protestant
churches — Latin America — 20th century. 3. Latin America — Religious
life and customs. I. Cook, Guillermo. II. Series.
BR600.N49   1994
278'.082 — dc20
                                                                94-2812
                                                                   CIP

Contents

Part Four

AREA STUDIES

Part Five

THE FUTURE OF THE LATIN AMERICAN CHURCH

Preface to the Series

The purpose of the ASM Series is to publish—without regard for disciplinary, national, or denominational boundaries—scholarly works of high quality and wide interest on missiological themes from the entire spectrum of scholarly pursuits relevant to Christian mission, which is always the focus of books in the Series.

By "mission" is meant a passage over the boundary between faith in Jesus Christ and its absence. In this understanding of mission, the basic functions of Christian proclamation, dialogue, witness, service, worship, and nurture are of special concern. And in that context, how does the transition from one cultural context to another influence the shape and interaction between these dynamic functions, especially in regard to the cultural and religious plurality that comprise the global mission context of mission?

The promotion of scholarly dialogue among missiologists and among missiologists and scholars in other fields of inquiry may involve the publication of views that some missiologists cannot accept, and with which members of the Editorial Committee do not agree. Manuscripts published in the Series reflect the opinions of their authors and are not understood to represent the position of the American Society of Missiology or of the Editorial Committee. The Committee's selection is guided by such criteria as intrinsic worth, readability and accessibility to a range of interested persons and not merely to experts or specialists.

The ASM Series Editorial Committee
James A. Scherer, Chair
Mary Motte, FMM
Charles Taber

Introduction

The Changing Face of the Church in Latin America

Guillermo Cook

It took less than a century for Spain and Portugal to "Christianize" the population of Latin America.[1] For the next four hundred years the Roman Catholic Christendom model of society reigned supreme. Protestantism, at first ethnic and extraneous, then testimonial and compassionate,[2] remained at the margins of Latin American society. Roman catholicism was a given — socioculturally and politically — a religious force to be reckoned with. Even after the political influence of the Catholic Church began to wane in countries like Brazil, Uruguay, Chile, México, and Guatemala, cultural catholicism reigned supreme. Until the 1960s, the pageantry and the color of traditional catholicism attracted the attention of foreign visitors who were rarely aware of the existence of Protestant churches.

Students of Latin American religious phenomenology in Latin America did not at first consider protestantism to be a significant factor in society. The attention of Catholic, secular, and a handful of Protestant students was directed to renewal movements within catholicism — the Charismatic Renewal, the Base Ecclesial Communities (BECs), and Latin American (or Liberation) Theology. Evangelical missiologists were, by and large, excited by signs of accelerating Protestant growth in the region. Now, in the 1990s, the scholarly spotlight focuses mainly upon the "explosive" growth of protestantism. The various dimensions of this latest phenomenon have been studied from a number of methodological perspectives by scholars in North America and Europe. Latin American social scientists of various religious and ideological persuasions are also analyzing the growth of protestantism with new understanding. Unfortunately, much of this valuable research is unavailable to English readers.[3] This book, in its emphasis upon protestantism, is a reflection of this new focus.

The change in focus began in the late 1960s and accelerated in the 1970s and 1980s. Today, in the 1990s, it is affirmed that "in Brazil, on any given Sunday, more Christians attend [Protestant] worship than attend worship at Roman Catholic churches." And that "in certain nations of Central America there is ample evidence that within the next few years, evangelicalism will have swept into a position where it is the faith of the majority of the population" (Berg and Pretiz 1992, 8). Although this last statement may be somewhat exaggerated on both quantitative and qualitative grounds, it nonetheless suggests the beginning of a startling reversal in religious roles. What has happened to bring this about? We need to look for the causes in both catholicism and protestantism, in broad historical perspective. Two ground-breaking studies deal with the social and religious factors in Protestant growth. Although the premises may not be valid in every respect, we need to take them into consideration (Martin 1990 and Stoll 1990). It may be helpful to review their main thesis before reading the chapters in this book.

FACTORS IN ROMAN CATHOLIC DECLINE

The Failure of Imperial Strategies

David Martin, a British sociologist, analyzes the phenomenon from a macro-historical perspective. He sees the phenomenon of Pentecostal growth as a contemporary expression of the centuries-old clash of two imperial worldviews. Anglo-American-type voluntarism, rooted in popular dissent, appears to be besting the Vatican, the heir of imperial Rome, in its last great bastion of power, Latin America. For five hundred years the Church of Rome has attempted three strategies to defend its interests in Latin America: (1) The Christendom church-state symbiosis (sixteenth through eighteenth century); (2) political alignments and aggressive indoctrination (nineteenth to mid-twentieth century), as a form of social control; and (3) liberation theology and the base church communities (late twentieth century). In the end, none of these strategies has worked, Martin says (1990, 25). Rome is now attempting a fourth strategy, the "new evangelization" of Latin America (*Lumen 2000*). It was announced by Pope John Paul II and affirmed at the Santo Domingo Conference of Bishops (CELAM IV) in October 1992 (Cook 1993c).

Vatican Conservatism

Anthropologist David Stoll points the finger in another direction: present Protestant history which he analyzes micro-socially. He suggests that the impressive Protestant growth is in part a result of the growing conservatism of Rome. As Latin American Catholics find less and less room for freedom of the spirit, they are turning to other alternatives, including to Evangelical protestantism (1990, xvi, 33-35).[4] This perception seems to be supported by a study done by an ecumenical agency in Brazil, where Catholic base community members may be joining Pentecostal churches in mass (CEDI 1990, 8-11).

Liberationist Radicalism

Both Martin and Stoll comment on the greater success of Pentecostals, vis-à-vis mainline Protestants and Catholic liberationists, at attending to the felt needs of the poor. Stoll wonders why conservative protestantism is more successful at attracting the masses than a theology that is so explicitly concerned with the liberation of the masses. By way of a tentative reply, he insists that "evangelicals provided an ideology, not just of political resignation, as so often noted, but of personal improvement." Indeed, evangelical conversion may have become for the masses a more peaceful outlet for revolutionary fervor than the political message of liberation. Liberation theology, while raising the consciousness of segments of the very poor, has also raised expectations beyond the capacity of the base communities to deliver. Meanwhile, Pentecostal churches and Protestant relief agencies seemed to deliver more tangible material results — without setting off violent confrontations (Stoll 1990, 308, 310-314).[5]

FACTORS IN PROTESTANT GROWTH

Protestantism grows in Latin America largely at the expense of catholicism. Factors in Protestant growth have something to do with Catholic decline. The hypotheses of both Martin and Stoll are worthy of consideration.

Workplace versus Home

Stoll, alluding to Lalive d'Epinay's groundbreaking studies of Chilean pentecostalism (1968 and 1969), points to a growth factor that Martin also emphasizes. Liberation theology (using marxist analysis) focuses upon the workplace, whereas the locus of Protestant growth and social involvement is the family (Stoll 1990, 317-318; cp. Martin 1990, 181, 220, 229). This insight may offer one explanation for the short "shelf life" of the base communities, when compared to the permanence and numerical increase of Protestant congregations. When the goals of their struggle seem to be within reach, the base communities often experience a crisis of identity. During periods of political openness and seeming democratization, the social issues tend to blur. The family orientation of the Evangelical churches may be one cause of their longterm stability. Extended family networks provide linkages for continued growth. If this is true, it is important to ask what might happen to Latin American protestantism now that family structures may be gradually beginning to disintegrate under the onslaught of modernization.

Church versus Sect

It became fashionable during the 1980s for left-of-center Christians to blame the extraordinary Protestant growth in Latin America on a U.S. right-wing conspiracy. "Pinning the gringo label on the growth of protestantism can't change the fact that the Catholic Church is losing its appeal" to the masses in Latin America "at the very moment when the whole society is caught up in the confusion and transformation involved in economic development" (Marcom 1990, 57). Rome echoed the complaint, conveniently forgetting that in earlier years it had attempted to relate Protestant inroads to a communist conspiracy.

Stoll's answer to this critique of pentecostalism is apt. To blame Evangelical growth on extraneous influences of this kind implies a profound distrust of the poor and of their ability to "turn an imported religion to their own purposes." He insists, correctly, that the impressive Protestant growth cannot be ascribed entirely to the right-wing sects. The reasons, as several of the contributors to this book will argue, are more complex (Stoll 1990, xvi, 33-35).

At one level, there is nothing wrong with being a sect because often it means going back to our religious roots. This is true theologically.

> The church is never more true to itself than when it remembers its origin as a sect, as a minority opinion, countercultural and antiestablishment. Questioning the rightness of things as they are has again and again been the spark of the church's renewal and the hallmark of its faithfulness to the gospel. (Reinsberger 1989)

Church history can also enlighten us. Sectarian movements are not always introverted. Prophetic challenge and denunciation has often been one of their hallmarks. As Martin aptly points out, many of the ideals — women's rights, the peace movement, rejection of capital punishment — that are espoused by "radical" groups today were incubated within the sectarian confines of religious groups such as the Bohemian Brethren, Mennonites, Quakers, and Swedenborgians, in the seventeenth and eighteenth centuries (Martin 1990, 235-237).

At another level, the meaning of "sect" needs to be clearly defined. Official catholicism has a quite different understanding of the term than do Protestants. Any Protestant church that evangelizes or proselytizes Catholics is for many bishops a sect, whereas sects are for Protestants only those groups that have a low christology (e.g., Mormons, Moonies, Jehovah's Witnesses, and Christian Scientists). Chapters 11 and 12 address this issue.[6]

NEW RELIGIOUS ACTORS — NEW CHALLENGES

This book was originally meant to be the work of one author. But the rapidly changing religious reality in Latin America is of such complexity that the analysis of a single "expert" would seem to be unnecessarily limiting. Reflecting this fact, several works have begun to appear in which a small number of specialists present different aspects of the current Latin American religious phenomena.[7] The editor has chosen another route. He has brought together a selection of papers and articles by people who have been closely involved in some aspect of the life of the Latin American churches. The content is about evenly divided between unpublished papers, translated articles, and papers that have appeared in specialized journals. The twenty-one chapters, of varying lengths, have been divided into four sections. The distribution, which may seem at times arbitrary and at times repetitive, was nonetheless unavoidable, given the loosely structured nature of this book. The contributors represent the wide variety of new actors in Latin American Christianity: Liberation Catholicism, Ecumenical, and Evangelical[8] Protestantism. The authors are Latin Americans, and also North Americans who have closely identified with Latin America.

The variety of responses to Latin American reality was reflected in the five major gatherings of Christians that took place during the second half of 1992: The Ecumenical Encounter of the Latin American Council of Churches (CLAI) in Cochabamba, Bolivia; the Fourth Conference of Indigenous Evangelicals (CIEL) in Otavalo, Ecuador; the Third Latin American Congress on Evangelization (CLADE III) and the base community Assembly of the People of God, both in Quito, Ecuador; and the Fourth General Conference of Latin American Bishops (CELAM IV) in Santo Domingo, Dominican Republic. The historical catalyst in each case was the five centuries of Iberian Catholic presence and the implications for mission today.

It is important to consider the past before considering the present in order to begin looking to the future. The first section of the book (chapters 1-3) deals with the *Five Hundred Years of Christianity*. The articles were written on the eve of 1992 by representatives of the Protestant, Evangelical, and Ecumenical traditions. The three contributors share more than a preoccupation with the past. Each is concerned about the ongoing legacy of Colonialism and its implications for the life and mission of the Church today. To illuminate the *dynamics of change* in the Latin American religious sphere in recent decades, we have brought together, in chapters 4-8, articles by persons who are closely acquainted with socioreligious change in Latin America, whether as actors or participant observers. Five chapters (9-13) deal with the positive and negative dimensions of *popular religion*. This was long thought to be the exclusive province of Roman catholicism, but popular religiosity is a growing phenomenon in protestantism as well. However, the socioreligious context and the responses of the churches are not the same in every country. We must avoid generalizations. The five *case studies* (chapters 14-18) can help us to comprehend the dynamics of change in particular countries and regions. These chapters deal with Christian witness in the midst of violence and ideological polarization in Central America, and with the institutionalization of the base communities and variety of responses to the crisis in Latin America by Protestant "parachurch agencies" in Brazil. In the final section, two distinguished Latin American theologians discuss *the future of the Church* from ecumenical Protestant and liberationist Catholic perspectives. The Conclusion attempts to draw some missiological lessons, by an Evangelical, from the content of the book.

THE SCOPE OF THE BOOK

That this book is more about protestantism than about catholicism is because "the new face of the church in Latin America" is largely a Protestant story. But there is also a Catholic story to tell — a story of the struggles of "the church of the poor" to be obedient to God in contexts of political violence and hierarchical domination. There is a paucity of women and of native Americans among the contributors. Unfortunately, two important contributions, by a Peruvian woman and a Mayan Indian, did not reach us in time for publication. The countries represented, either by author or focus, are Argentina, Brazil, Costa Rica, Chile, El Salvador, Guatemala, Hispanic United States, Nicaragua, and Perú. They represent five major areas of conflict and change in Hispanic America: North and Middle America, the Andean Region, Brazil, and the Southern Cone. Because of the limitations of space and of available publications, the nations of the Caribbean basin do not appear. If Central America and Brazil seem to occupy a disproportionate space in this book, it is for three reasons. Both regions present significant examples of the tension between tradition and change; much has been written in Spanish and Portuguese about these regions; and, last but not least, the editor has maintained long-term relationships with both regions. Our hope is that the contributors have presented their cases with sufficient breadth, as well as depth, to encompass problems that go far beyond their own interests and particular fields of service in the Reign of God. Our prayer is that the many faces of Christianity may someday become one, in obedience to our Lord who prayed that we all "become one that the world might believe . . . that the glory of the Lord may cover the earth as the waters cover the sea."

NOTES

1. This happened both by imposition and by genocide. At the time of the "discovery" it is variously estimated that there were between 80 and 100 million inhabitants in the "New World." Seventy-two years later, there were only 10 to 12 million native Americans left, most of them superficially baptized into the Church. The rest had died off through warfare, alienation, and above all disease (Prien 1985, 77-78; cp. Thornton 1987, 22-25; see also Rivera 1992, 173, and Wright 1992, 14).

2. The compassion of early Protestant missions led to the founding of hospitals, orphanages, and other assistance services.

3. Three such studies are dealt with by Samuel Escobar in chapter 10. See also chapter 17 by José Comblin. The bibliography in David Martin (1990, 320-343) is a fair illustration of the abundance of material available in Spanish, Portuguese, and English on Protestant phenomenology in Latin America. See the Bibliography at the end of this book for more recent works.

4. Stoll suggests that spiritism, secularism, eastern religions, and satanism are probably a greater threat to Catholicism than is Protestantism (1990, 114).

5. Stoll further observes that liberation theology has been implicitly "equated with the Protestant Reformation, while Evangelical protestantism is assigned the reactionary Catholic role of Counter-Reformation." He postulates that this may no longer be true (1990, 22).

6. Although the Santo Domingo Document does, at one point, recognize this difference, it levels the same criticisms at all "sects."

7. E.g. Edward L. Cleary and Hannah Stewart-Gambino (1992) and a scheduled follow-up by the same editors. The Calvin Center for Christian Scholarship of Grand Rapids, Michigan, has published the papers of a symposium entitled *The Church in Latin America* (1993).

8. The term *evangélico* has encompassed virtually the entire spectrum of Latin American Protestantism. However, North American theological categories increasingly prevail. For this reason, I have chosen to use the terms "Ecumenical" and "Evangelical." While they are not mutually exclusive, they denote in general terms those Protestants who do or do not identify with the ecumenical movement.

PART ONE

1492-1992:
CHANGE AND CONTINUITY

1

Voices of Compassion Yesterday and Today

Justo L. González

A Hispanic Presbyterian holds up the prophetic role of Spanish priests in the defense of the native Americans as a challenge to mission today. In North America the natives were not treated any better by the early settlers because of the work of Protestant churches. Though "supposedly freer from state and civil intervention than the Spanish church, no voice arose possessing the prophetic character of that of Las Casas." Dr. González is Director of the Hispanic Summer Program of the Fund for Theological Education and the author of numerous books and articles on historical theology. His article is reprinted with permission by *Missiology: An International Review*, vol. xx, no. 2 (April 1992).

In writing this article, I have no desire or inclination to minimize the many cruelties perpetrated by my Spanish ancestors against my native American ancestors by dwelling on the positive figures among missionaries. On the contrary, I am convinced that the so-called "encounter" between two hemispheres led to one of the greatest tragedies in human history, and one of the worst blots on Christian history. The death of millions upon millions of human beings, the disappearance of entire civilizations and peoples, and the subjugation of others for five hundred years should not be obscured nor minimized. The cries of trampled and destroyed generations still rise to heaven, and justice still remains to be done.

However, it is precisely that context of greed and wanton cruelty that makes the phenomenon of the "voices of compassion" even more remarkable. In the midst of a church wholly supported by the state, in a nation proud of its power and religious unity, there arose voices of missionaries whose solidarity with their flock was such that they dared oppose the most powerful authorities and structures of their time in order to make their protest heard.

The best known among those who protested the abuses perpetrated by the Spanish conquistadores and settlers is the Dominican Friar Bartolomé de Las Casas. His fame is justly deserved, for he spent an entire — and very long —

lifetime seeking justice for the original inhabitants of these lands. It was not an easy or a popular task, and for that he deserves such credit. Unfortunately, however, the main reason why he is so well known among the English-speaking public is that his writings have been used for a purpose entirely different from his own: to show that Roman Catholic expansion in general, and Spanish colonization in particular, were exceptionally cruel with original inhabitants of the Western Hemisphere. By implication, British colonization and missions were purer, milder, less cruel, more Christian.

In this regard, I find it necessary to point out that the British colonial and missionary enterprise, and the work of the churches and the settlers who came to North America, did not result in any better treatment for the natives than was the case in Spanish and Portuguese America. The same is true after the independence of the United States. What is remarkable is that, in a church that was supposedly freer from state and civil intervention than was the Spanish church, no voice arose possessing the prophetic character of that of Las Casas. In this, the "voices of compassion" of the Iberian conquest are unique, not only for their prophetic stance vis-à-vis the abuses that were being committed against the aboriginal population of this Hemisphere, but also because at a time of increasing nationalism — indeed, at the very apex of Spanish power — they took a critical stance toward their nation and its policies of expansion.

It is also important to point out that Las Casas, far from being the sole or even one of a few "voices of compassion" in Spanish America, was simply the best-known representative of a host who took similar positions in favor of the native inhabitants of these lands. A few names and events should suffice to prove this point. First of all, even before Las Casas began his protest, it appears that all the Dominicans in Hispaniola held the views that later became associated with his name. The Dominicans and other friars in Chile, following the leadership of Gil González de San Nicolás, declared that wars against the natives were unjust, and that those who profited from them could receive no absolution until they made restitution (Mires 1987, pp. 68–70). Although he was silenced, his views and work were later taken up by the Jesuit Luis de Valdivia (ibid., pp. 70–79). The story of the Jesuit missions in Paraguay and their resistance to encroaching forces of slavery is well known. St. Luis Beltrán, the first of the missionaries to the Western Hemisphere to be canonized, was well known for his defense of the natives. One of the miracles attributed to him in his canonization process took place when Beltrán was sitting at the table of an *encomendero* (see p. 5). His host took offense at Beltrán's comment, that the Spanish were living off Indian blood, and to prove his point Beltrán took a tortilla and squeezed blood from it. Furthermore, most of these people were not isolated defenders of the natives, but rather formed part of a vast network that kept in touch through correspondence and other means. It is for this reason that, rather than concentrating on Las Casas and his work, I have decided to deal with other, lesser-known figures, and to draw some general conclusions regarding the entire movement.

The first recorded protest against the treatment given to the natives was a sermon by the Dominican Friar Antón (or Antonio) de Montesinos, delivered in

Santo Domingo on a Sunday shortly before Christmas, 1911. Las Casas quotes part of the sermon:

> In order to make your sins known to you I have mounted this pulpit, I who as the voice of Christ crying in the wilderness of this island; and therefore it behooves you to listen to me, not with indifference but with all your heart and senses; for this voice will be the strangest, the harshest and hardest, the most terrifying that you ever heard or expected to hear.
>
> This voice declares that you are in mortal sin, and live and die therein by reason of the cruelty and tyranny that you practice on these innocent people. Tell me, by what right do you wage such detestable wars on these people who lived mildly and peacefully in their own lands, where you have consumed infinite numbers of them with unheard-of murders and desolations? Why do you so greatly oppress and fatigue them, not giving them enough to eat or caring for them when they fall ill from excessive labors, so that they die or rather are slain by you, so that you may extract and acquire gold every day? And what care do you take that they receive religious instruction and come to know their God and creator, or that they be baptized, hear mass, or observe holidays and Sundays?
>
> Are they not men? Do they not have rational souls? Are you not bound to love them as you love yourselves? How can you lie in such profound and lethargic slumber? Be sure that in your present state you can no more be saved than the Moors or Turks who do not have and do not want the faith of Jesus Christ. (Quoted in Goodpasture 1989, pp. 11–12)

In order to appreciate the import of this sermon, it is necessary to understand the system of *encomiendas*, and also Montesinos's purpose in preaching it.

The *encomiendas* [trusteeships] were a system begun by Columbus, whereby a number of "Indians" were "entrusted" — *encomendados* — to a Spaniard so that they could be taught the Christian faith. The Spaniard was to feed them and care for them, and in exchange they would work for him. Technically, such natives were not the property of the Spaniard, as a slave was, and therefore they could not be sold. Yet, in some ways this system proved to be worse than slavery, for the Spaniard who had been entrusted with a group of natives had no economic investment in them. An *encomienda* was a temporary grant. If some of the natives given in *encomienda* died, others could be had simply by requesting them from the authorities. On the other hand, if they procreated, their offspring did not belong to the *encomendero* — the trust-holder. Therefore the *encomenderos* had no financial interest in preserving the life and health of those entrusted to them, and tended to exploit and underfeed them to the point that they became ill and died, the women miscarried regularly, and stillbirths became quite common.

It was for these reasons, and still within the accepted context of the *encomiendas*, that Montesinos said to the *encomenderos* such things as, "Why do you so greatly oppress and fatigue them, not giving them enough to eat or caring for them when they fall ill from excessive labors, so that they die or rather are slain by you, so that you may extract and acquire gold every day? And what care do you take that they receive religious instruction and come to know their God and creator, or that they be baptized, hear mass, or observe holidays and Sundays?" His point is that they are not even fulfilling the requirements of the *encomienda*.

Justo L. González

The settlers, however, were satisfied with the *encomienda* system. For them, this was quite acceptable as a way of obtaining what amounted to slave labor. The Crown had forbidden the enslavement of the natives, except those who were cannibals or who were taken in war. Thus it was in the interest of the Spaniards to promote wars where natives could be made captive, and then shipped to Spain to pay for goods. Given the practice of the *encomiendas*, and the quarterly tributes in gold or other goods which the Spaniards had imposed on the natives, it was not difficult to provoke them to rebellion and thus to start a war against them. This is why Montesinos asks: "Tell me, by what right do you wage such detestable wars on these people who lived mildly and peacefully in their own lands, where you have consumed infinite numbers of them with unheard-of murders and desolations?"

This was the context in which the sermon was preached. Therefore, what Montesinos was saying was that the *encomenderos* were not really fulfilling the terms of their *encomiendas* and that they were making war on the Indians with no justification.

Yet the purpose of the sermon went far beyond the exhortation of a single preacher on a particular Sunday morning. It was part of a carefully conceived and developed plan to bring the treatment of the Indians to the foreground, and to provoke the Crown to issue legislation protecting the natives from the abuse practiced by Spanish settlers. Montesinos himself had been chosen by the Dominican vicar, Friar Pedro de Córdoba, to preach a sermon challenging the practices of the Spaniards, and the other Dominicans in Hispaniola signed it in order to signify that this particular sermon was not the whim of a fanatical preacher, but the considered view of all of them.

Córdoba himself seems to have been the driving force behind Montesinos's protest. His theological rationale for his position is worth noting. In a letter, which unfortunately cannot be exactly dated, he declared that what had taken place in Hispaniola was such that the natives had been "destroyed in body and soul," and that "they can neither be Christians nor even live." The result of the entire colonial enterprise is negative, as far as the Christianization of the natives goes, and therefore it would be preferable to let them return to their original state. If that were done, even though "they would have no gain in their souls, at least they would gain their lives . . . which is better than losing all" (Gutiérrez 1981, p. 507). In other words, the natives are not really being given a chance to become true Christians, nor are they allowed to continue their own peaceful and productive way of living. They lose the material, and do not gain the spiritual. "It would be less evil for the Indians to remain on their lands as they are, than that they have the name of Christ blasphemed as is now the case" (Gutiérrez 1981, p. 508). Since the justification of the *encomienda* system, and indeed of much of the Spanish enterprise in the Western Hemisphere, was the notion that the natives were being offered the great gift of Christianity, Córdoba's argument undermined the very foundation of that enterprise.

Furthermore, as far as we can tell, Córdoba was the first to turn the cast of characters of Exodus in such a way as to identify the Spanish Christians, not with the Israelites, but with Pharaoh: "Even Pharaoh and the Egyptians were not so cruel with the people of God" (ibid.). As we shall see, this was a rather common theme among those who took upon themselves the defense of the native inhabitants of the Western Hemisphere.

In any case, Montesinos's sermon, grounded as it was on the theological outlook of Córdoba and apparently of the rest of the Dominicans on the island, was part of a much larger plan whose purpose was not so much the conversion of the Spanish *encomenderos* as the amelioration of conditions for the natives, on the basis of political action. The text of the sermon was made available in written form and was widely circulated — which in itself was part of a strategy on the part of the Dominicans to make certain that their protest reached the Spanish court. In response, the *encomenderos* sent Franciscan Friar Alonso de Espinar to protest before the Crown.[1]

The representations of the *encomenderos* at court led to an order that the Dominicans in Hispaniola should recant, and that if they refused to do so they should be sent to Spain for trial. Apparently this was precisely what the Dominicans sought, for Montesinos refused to recant, and thus gained an audience before the King. This audience took place in the form of a debate between Montesinos and Espinar, the Franciscan who had been sent from Hispaniola to defend the *encomiendas*. The debate proved inconclusive, and led to the "Junta de burgos," where a group of jurists and others would establish the principles and laws by which the natives should be treated in the future. The result was a very partial triumph for the Dominicans, for the Junta limited the abuse of the *encomiendas*, but this in itself was a confirmation of the system.[2]

The Laws of Burgos were never obeyed, and repeatedly were modified. Yet the point of my argument here is not so much the result obtained by the Dominicans as the manner in which they proceeded, for it is clear that their protest was both theological and structural. Their protest, born out of their solidarity with the suffering natives, was grounded on an understanding of the gospel and of Scripture, but it also took the form of carefully planned political action.

These are the three elements that appear repeatedly in the "voices of compassion" of Spanish America: solidarity with the suffering native masses, political action, and a theological grounding. In this, they were forerunners of similar voices being raised today in the same lands.

The point of departure which separated these "voices of compassion" from the rest of the church and of society was their solidarity with the native population. This was a solidarity born out of direct experience and personal contact. It is no coincidence that the first protesters against the abuses that were taking place were Dominicans, Jesuits, and some Franciscans — missionaries whose vows of poverty made it possible for them to live in close contact with the native population. It was out of this close contact that the protest arose. Many Spaniards — including the vast majority of the diocesan clergy — had very little idea of the suffering that the process of "Christianizing" the colonies was causing. All they could see was cities and churches being built, "Indians" being taught the Christian faith and learning European customs, and vast wealth being accumulated.

They did not see, as did the missionaries who related more directly with the natives, the broken families and traditions, the growing sense of hopelessness, and the many deaths that were the price for such "progress."

A second characteristic of the "voices of compassion" is that they were more than voices. They spoke for an entire plan of political action and economic restructure. Pedro de Córdoba was already proposing, in lieu of the military conquest, an "evangelical conquest." This has been deemed unrealistic by many modern writers; and indeed the very fact that it did not produce the desired outcome gives grounds for such judgment. Yet the project of an "evangelical conquest" was not as politically naive as has often been suggested.

The struggle was not only between the *encomenderos* on the one side and the friars on the other. In between and above both of these parties stood the Crown. It too had a stake in the debate, and its decision would be guided by its own interests. On some points, those interests coincided with those of the *encomenderos* and other settlers. Above all, the Crown needed the continued income from the nascent colonies, and the only way to produce such income was with the labor of the natives. On the other hand, the Crown also had reason to fear the growing power of the *conquistadores*. For generations, the rulers of the various Spanish kingdoms had seen their authority questioned by powerful magnates who derived their power from the possession and exploitation of vast lands. Isabella's father had been repeatedly humiliated by such magnates. It was only recently, under Isabella and Ferdinand, that their power had finally been placed under the control of the Crown. Now, in the distant "Indies," a new class of wealthy Spanish magnates threatened to be born. The basis for their power was the exploitation of mines and lands through native labor. Therefore, although the Spanish court realized that it needed the product of the work of the natives, it also feared that the *encomenderos* and other settlers would also grow so powerful on the basis of that very labor, that eventually they would come to challenge the authority of the Crown, as had been the case in Spain itself a generation earlier.[3] It was for this reason, for instance, that those who drafted the Laws of Burgos had no difficulty in following the suggestions of the friars, that the size of the *encomiendas* be limited to a hundred natives each.

The proposed "evangelical conquest" of the friars took the interests of the Crown into account. What was envisioned was not the Christianization of the native population in such a way that all Spaniards would cease deriving income from their work. It was not simply a matter of converting the "Indians" by peaceful means, and then leaving them to their own devices, without any benefit to the Crown. Such a proposal would have been entirely unacceptable to the Crown, and anyone making such a suggestion would have been promptly silenced. The "evangelical conquest" was a much more modest proposal, but a more realistic one. What the friars were suggesting was "an alternative mode of conquest which, while retaining the specific privileges of the monarchy, would do away with *encomiendas* and in general with any form of 'distribution' of the natives [among the settlers] and which, for that very reason, would push the military to the background, and lift the clergy to the fore. . . . What they proposed was a sort of displacement in the hegemony over the guidance of the process. Nothing more" (Mires 1987, p. 60). Obviously, this "displacement in the hegemony" had a number of concrete elements, which Las Casas and others outlined. The *encomiendas* would be abolished — at least in those areas set aside for such "evangelical conquest." Instead, the natives would be encouraged, through peaceful means, to gather in villages, to hear the Gospel and to practice it.[4] In these villages, the native chiefs would still hold under their authority, under that of the Crown — and, although not always explicitly stated, also under the authority of the friars. Mining, which was one of the principal reasons why the *encomenderos* needed abundant native labor, should be generally supplanted by agriculture and animal husbandry, whose products, although less valuable than gold, would still enrich Spain without all the disruptive effects which the enormous inflow of precious metals was having on the national economy. These were the essential points Las Casas proposed to Cardinal Francisco Jiménez de Cisneros, who was Regent after the death of Ferdinand. They were also the main points that had appeared from earlier times in a series of proposals for a different mode of colonization and Christianization.

There certainly was much in the proposal that was inordinately utopian and idealistic. Yet, there was enough in it to attract the attention of the Spanish Crown, if not as a system to be implanted throughout all the colonies, at least as an alternative that could be used to curb the power of the settlers. It was for that reason that this proposal for an evangelical conquest was tried with significant success in an number of places — and not only, as historians sometimes imply, in the failed project of Las Casas in Cusaná. Already in the very early years of the conquest, under the direction of Pedro de Córdoba, several missionary initiatives were undertaken, many with significant success, following the model of an "evangelical conquest." Slightly later, a royal decree granted the Hieronimites of Hispaniola the right to set aside a vast portion of the mainland in order to pursue such a peaceful conquest, and to forbid any other Spaniard from entering such territories without the express permission of the Crown. And ten years later, in 1516, Charles V issued instructions to the effect that the captain of any expedition could not land in a new place, make war on the natives, or force them to work, without the authorization of the missionaries assigned to the expedition. Although these regulations — as well as most others — were never fully obeyed, they are an indication that the proposal of the friars was not entirely lacking in political viability.

Therefore it is correct to say of Las Casas that what he proposed was a form of colonization more strictly controlled by the state, in contrast with the manner in which it was being conducted, almost as a private enterprise, that this control was to be employed for the benefit of both the state and the natives — and to the detriment of the *encomenderos* — and that it would be exercised mostly through the friars. It is for this reason that, in contrast to all the descriptions of Las Casas as a dreamy visionary, Mires says that he was "above all, a politician, that is, someone who seeks the actualization of his principles in view of the various constellations of forces that appear successively" (Mires 1987, p. 85).

In this, Las Casas was simply continuing the traditions begun by the Dominicans of Hispaniola, of making their defense of the natives a matter not only to be preached from the pulpit, but also to be defended in political planning and negotiation. If they failed, it was not because they did not take political matters into account, but because they overestimated the power of the Crown to have its laws obeyed across the Atlantic.

A final characteristic of these "voices of compassion" is that they were informed, not only by solidarity with the oppressed and the resulting compassion, but also by a theological outlook that combined much that was traditional with a unique perspective born out of the suffering they had witnessed. Most "voices of compassion" — Montesinos, Las Casas, Francisco de Vitoria, among others — were Dominicans, and made ample use of Thomistic notions of natural law in order to defend their positions. Most of them had been educated at the University of Salamanca, and were part of a theological tradition whose main representative was Francisco de Vitoria. Indeed, Vitoria's lectures *On the Indies* both reflected much that he had learned from the "voices of compassion" and provided further theological ammunition for such voices.[5] What thus took place was a mutual enrichment between the traditional academic theology of Salamanca and the experience and reflection of the missionaries in the Western Hemisphere — a mutual enrichment made easier because many of the participants in this dialogue were joined by a common bond in the Dominican order.

Together with other Spaniards of the time, these "voices of compassion" had a providentialist understanding of the events of their time. According to that understanding, Spain had been raised by God to fulfill a historic task, and this consisted primarily in bringing Catholic Christianity to these lands, as Casas even saw in Columbus' first name, Christóforo, a sign that he had been set aside to be *Christum ferens*, that is, bearer of Christ to these remote lands. After quoting Las Casas's rivals to the effect that the "discovery" was an act determined by divine providence, historian Luis Rivera Pagán goes on to affirm that "Las Casas has a missionary and providential sense similar to that of his rivals. Also, for the great Dominican friar, the discovery of the Indies by the Spaniards is the result of divine providence, of the history of human redemption planned and arranged by God" (Rivera 1992, p. 58).

Within this providentialist framework, however, the "voices of compassion" saw things very differently than did the defenders of armed conquest. The latter saw the *conquistadores* as instruments of God to bring Christianity to the Indies. The Franciscan Friar Gerónimo de Mendieta, for instance, declared that Hernán Cortez was born the same day as Martin Luther, a day in which the Aztecs sacrificed more than 80,000 people. Thus he made Cortez into an anti-Luther, a providential figure whose role was to counteract in the New World the evil that Luther had done in the old. According to Mendieta, Cortez was even a new Moses whose task has been to bring the people of God to the land of the Canaanites (ibid., pp. 92–93).

By contrast, the "voices of compassion" saw things in the opposite way. Rather than identifying the Spanish with Moses and his companions, and the natives with Canaanites, they identified the natives with the children of Israel, and the Spanish with Pharaoh. I have already quoted Pedro de Córdoba to the effect that "Even Pharaoh and the Egyptians were not so cruel with the people of God." Similar phrases appear throughout the writings of those who undertook the task of defending the natives of these lands against the depredations of those who exploited them under the guise of evangelization. Even as late as 1699, at the very eve of the eighteenth century, Friar Diego de Humanzoro, Bishop of Santiago in Chile, declared:

> The personal service of these Indians has been, and still is, more intolerable than that of the children of Israel in Egypt and Babylon; their slavery was very mild and gentle in comparison with what these miserable Indians endured and still endure. . . . In the slavery and tyranny of the Pharaohs of Egypt . . . they fell far short of exhaustion and death.
>
> In four hundred years of captivity . . . the Hebrews increased in numbers and did not die. But our Indians in their own land, ever since the Spaniards entered it, have been wasted away in hundreds of millions by the harassment and tyranny they suffer, and by the severity of the personal service, which is greater and more terrible than that exacted by the Pharaohs of Egypt. (Salinas 1990, pp. 106-107)

What we have here, and in dozens of other texts that could be cited referring to the Spanish colonial enterprise as Pharaoh, as Babylon or as Nineveh (see Salinas 1990, pp. 104–107), is a reversal of the cast of characters in the reading of Scriptural history. The *conquistadores* and their supporters read the biblical narrative placing themselves in the role of the people of God and its leaders. The "voice of compassion" read the same narratives placing the exploited natives in that role, and thereby leaving the *conquistadores* — and in some cases almost Spain herself — in the role of Pharaoh, Babylon, and Nineveh.

Thus out of a single nation and a single theological tradition two very different positions arose, and two contrasting readings of Scripture. One simply continued the ideology that had been developed around the *Reconquista* against the Moors, which saw Spain as having a divinely appointed task to take the land from the infidel and establish orthodox Catholic Christianity. The other, while sharing most of the theological tradition of the former, reversed that ideology, calling Spain and her representatives to repentance. And all of this happened at a time when the emerging nations of Europe, intoxicated with their newly-found identity, produced very little in the way of self-criticism.

How could this happen? How could it be that a nation in which the power of the Inquisition was constantly growing, a nation that had recently expelled its Jewish population and was trying to get rid of the last vestiges of Moorish presence in its midst, could produce "voices of compassion" which not only critiqued the nation's greatest moment in history, but also provided an alternative theological understanding of what was taking place? The answer, though simple, is difficult to follow. These "voices of compassion" spoke as they did because they had themselves heard a different Voice. And they had not heard it in the great pulpits or the famous chairs of theology. They had heard it in sharing their lives in solidarity with the oppressed natives of these lands.

The lessons for today should be obvious.

NOTES

1. Although eventually many Franciscans joined the movement which the Dominicans had begun, in the early stages of the conquest a number of them took the side of the *encomenderos*. This was partly because they served as chaplains to the Spanish settlers, and partly due to the traditional rivalry between Dominicans and Franciscans, which in sixteenth-century Spain sometimes became quite bitter.

2. The Junta de Burgos established seven propositions on which all legislation regarding the "Indies" should be based: (1) The Indians are free and should be treated as such; (2) Their conversion should be sought with all diligence; (3) The King has the right to order that they be put to work, provided that such work does not impede their learning the Christian faith, and is beneficial both to them and the commonwealth; (4) such work should be bearable, and must include times of rest; (5) the natives should have their own house and land, and the time to tend to them; (6) they should have contacts with the settlers so that they can improve and receive Christian instruction; (7) they must be remunerated for their work, not in money, but in kind (Lopetegui and Zubillaga 1965, p. 258). On the basis of these principles, thirty-five laws were promulgated the following year. They provided a minimum number of days of rest for the natives, regulated the work of children and pregnant women, limited the number of natives to be granted to a single *encomienda*, etc. In general, the purpose of these laws was to improve the conditions of the natives (Mires 1987, p. 46).

3. Such rebellions did take place after the settlers had time to become entrenched in their power. Most notable was the case of Perú, where there was open rebellion against the Crown and war among the Spanish.

4. The details as to how this was to be done varied. At first Las Casas proposed bringing in Spanish rural laborers to live together with the natives. Later he became convinced that the native villages ought to be closed to all Spanish except the missionaries. That became the most common practice in many places where the "evangelical conquest" was implemented.

5. On Francisco de Vitoria and his lectures *On the Indies*, which there is no space to discuss here, but which provides a unique example of a scholar's critique of his nation's colonial and missionary policies, see González 1987, pp. 210–213. It is true that in the end Vitoria justifies the colonial enterprise. Yet, in the process of arriving at that conclusion he raises a number of questions that undermine many of the presuppositions of that enterprise.

2

Even Today What Began Five Hundred Years Ago

Lydia Hernández

When the Europeans came, they named and catalogued what they saw, in this way establishing their dominion over the native Americans. Things have changed little since then. "White is better than dark; European is better than indigenous. Culture refers to what is European, folkways refer to what is indigenous; theology is European religion, while superstition is what indigenous people believe." Lydia Hernández, who serves on the national staff of the Presbyterian Church (U.S.A.) in Atlanta, is a graduate of Austin Presbyterian Theological Seminary. This article appeared in *Church and Society*, January/February, 1992, Louisville, Presbyterian Church U.S.A. It is used with permission.

I was six years old when I entered school in a small rural town in south Texas. My father was the pastor of the Mexican Presbyterian Church, which had an *escuelita* [small school] where we learned about how God made everything and everything was good — except when we human beings decided to do bad.

It was because of the *escuelita* that I got into trouble right away. First I couldn't stay in the same class with my Mexican friends from my church and neighborhood because I could speak English. The teacher, a Mexican, insisted that I be transferred to the white section of the school, which was separate from the Mexicans. She told my parents that I might cause problems because not only could I speak English, but I could read and write. My parents did not agree with the teacher, but I was still transferred.

WHO NAMES WHOM?

I didn't like being with the whites: they called me a "smart aleck" — and other names, I am sure, even if not to my face! They felt that I was always answering the teacher's questions, and in their eyes I shouldn't have known so much, because I was Mexican. I missed my friends and felt very lonely, but luckily for me we had playtime once a day during which I would run and play with my Mexican friends. At first this was difficult because they thought I was being "uppity." Then they accused me of changing the spelling of my first name from a Spanish to an English spelling.

I went home crying. My father took out my birth certificate so that I could take it to school, and he explained to me what had happened. I had been born at home in a one-room shack with a dirt floor; it was next to the church. When he went to register me at the County Courthouse the white clerk took the name from him and told my dad that my name was spelled Lydia, not Lidia. My dad obviously lost the argument, because when the birth certificate came back from the State Registry of Births my name was spelled Lydia. Until his death in 1983 my dad always spelled my name Lidia.

This traumatic event when I was six was my first experience with imperialism. Linguistic imperialism is a well-studied problem, and I am sure it has made megabucks for some university professors, but to a six-year-old it is not a problem, it is a dehumanizing experience. Even today what began five hundred years ago — the elimination of indigenous languages — is still happening with, for example, the English-Only movement in the United States; in Latin America indigenous people speak what is known as a "dialect," not a language.

THE TWO CULTURES

Growing up in a household that was a mixture of two cultures — my father was an Indian from Mexico, and my mother was also from Mexico but with Italian ancestry — made for an interesting and lively childhood. I was always conspiring with my father against my mother, whom he would occasionally refer to as *la gringa* because of her light skin. Before eating our meals he would have me quietly remove all the silverware, which she would not notice until we were saying grace, at which time she would get angry and say, "JoeHernandez" as if it were one word, *"deja que Lidia ponga los fierros en la mesa!"* [Have Lydia put the silverware on the table!] And he would reply, "Before your people came with your silverware we didn't starve." He would go on and on, saying how before her people came fences did not exist, hard shoes did not create sores on their feet (he wore soft *huaraches*), and how they could live in the *selva* [jungle] with very little.

The one way she would bring him to a halt would be to remind him that he would not be able to read if her people had not come. Because he loved to read he would turn to me and say, "She may have a point — one point!" This may not in fact be true, since the Indian people were literate in their own language, but my father only spoke Spanish. He was probably referring to the fact that, being so poor, he might not have had the opportunity to continue in school.

ON BEING BROWN

Until the Christmas before he died my father would always dance the traditional Indian dances, and my mother would call him *viejo indecente* — literally, "indecent old man." While she said this in a joking manner, it points to the discrimination against Indians that still exists today: white is better than dark; European is better than indigenous. "Culture" refers to what is European, "folk-ways" refers to what is indigenous; theology is European religion, while super-stition is what indigenous people believe. My own people have internalized this kind of discriminatory ideology, so that being light-skinned puts you in positions of authority and prominence, and being dark-skinned means that you stay at the bottom of society.

I guess one reason I so identify with my father is that I am dark-skinned like him. He used to tell me that I should wake up every morning and give thanks to God for being brown, because that way I would never forget my people. He told me that while my sister Tavita was light-skinned with green eyes, this might prove to be a disadvantage, as she might be tempted to pass for white. But he said, "Remember, she may dress like them, look like them, speak like them, but one day should they happen to be talking about her in her absence, one of them will ask, 'Which Tavita?' And the answer will be, 'You know, the Mexican!'"

Cherrie Moraga, a Chicana lesbian writer, who is one of the emerging group of Chicana/o writers of the 1990s, in *Loving in the War Years* talks about being *güera*, light-skinned. Her family saw this as a way out of her poverty because she could pass for white. However, in the process of leaving behind all that was associated with being poor and Chicana, she became marginalized within her own community. In this way she links color to class and economics — as it has been since Columbus arrived.

THE RACE AND CLASS CONNECTION

When I was eight, my father took a pastorate in San Marcos, Texas. The neighborhood school was a block away from my house and all of us kids from the *barrio*, the poor neighborhood, went there. The whites lived on the other side of town and had their own school. Our school was in a poor neighborhood and we received a lower standard of education. While school officials gave us milk every day, assuming that we needed it, they did not provide the money for new textbooks. My parents and other parents petitioned the school board for im-provements in the buildings and more money for materials. The board refused, saying that if we wanted better facilities and resources we could join the whites in their school. My mother was very opposed to that idea; she felt that we would be exposed to a culture that she did not think would necessarily be good for us, especially after her negative experience with the all-white school board.

This is when I realized the connection between race and class. The fight in Texas today is how to distribute the money evenly among the schools, because the rich school districts do not want to share their money. As in Columbus's day, the people with the money make the rules.

I also got a different view of school bussing. Because our parents lost the school-board fight, we ended up going to the school on "the hill," which is how we referred to the white school. My father had observed that a school bus went by our house. So sure enough my father took my brother David and me to wait for the bus in front of the church. The bus did stop, but when the bus driver found out that we wanted to get on the bus he was insulted that Mexicans would even think of getting on the bus: "Don't you know you had to walk?" It was difficult walking to the white school because the white store owners and the white kids would insult us, calling us bad names — "greasers" and "dirty Mexicans."

The whites never thought we would actually go up the hill, but after we did they started making improvements in the local schools, not because they wanted to but because they didn't want us with them. If it wasn't that a classmate of my mother's had become a legislator, we would not have even succeeded in getting a hearing from the local school board. But the local Mexican community had been successful in their school board fight also because they were organized and united in this effort. As has been proven over and over since the arrival of Columbus, being poor and brown is fine until you become organized. Then you become a threat. All of a sudden the wonderful celebration of diversity becomes a problem of plurality.

THE FREE TRADE AGREEMENT: LINKING THE POLITICAL
TO THE SPIRITUAL

I guess these early experiences in my own life make it hard for me to accept the concept that some people believe that the political is separate from the spiritual and that the spiritual is separate from the personal.

Recently I was asked to speak to a church group about the issues concerning the border between Mexico and the United States. I told the group that I wanted to address the Free Trade Agreement, and a member of the planning committee asked me to be cautious when speaking about this issue, for I would be seen as just another flaming radical, since they were not able to link the political with the spiritual. Needless to say, I spoke about it anyway.

I was concerned then, and still am, that the two entities which will be most affected by the agreement, poor people and the environment, will not be represented at the negotiating table. I was challenging the church to advocate space at the table for the hearing of these voices. A friend asked, "Why did you waste your breath? The church — and no one else, for that matter — is not going to do anything about it." For me the issue is not what others are going to do about it, but what did I do? I had to speak on this issue because I felt that I was representing the church, and it is my belief that the church needs to be involved in the Free Trade Agreement, protecting those who are most vulnerable. Lest we forget, in the five hundred years following the Conquest there have always been those in the church who stood on the side of the defenseless.

Former Governor Babbitt of Arizona, in a conference speech, emphasized the importance of protecting the environment in the Free Trade Agreement, but in the excerpt that was printed in the *Christian Science Monitor* there was no mention of the thousands of poverty-stricken people who live along the border and who suffer the negative consequences of twin plants, *maquiladoras* [plants that hire immigrant labor]. Much of the blame for the poor conditions found along the border has fallen on México, which does hold part of the responsibility. But those of us on the United States side must pressure the government to take corrective steps for our share of the problem. The blame on México must be turned into a question of why there is so much poverty in México, and the role of the United States in that poverty.

THE BORDERLANDS

The Free Trade Agreement brings to mind the whole question of borderlands. Just as my dad reminded my mother that fences did not exist before her people came, as Christians who believe in the unity of all — humankind and nature — we need to be able to cross borders and understand those who live on the other side. And as Christians we are called to erase human-made borders that are unjust and harmful.

For many Mexicans (Mexican Americans, Mexican nationals, and Chicanos/as) the México-United States border does not exist, because most of the southwestern part of the United States was actually part of México from the Conquest until 1848. The Treaty of Guadalupe gave land rights to Mexicans living in what is now the United States. This treaty was not adhered to, so the land was taken by incoming Anglos, creating tension that still exists today. This is just a continuation of the process that has been going on since the original conquest — promises that the "winners" never intended to keep. Therefore, violent means are often used to keep the "losers" from fighting against injustice.

In a newspaper report on two recent deaths of Mexicans along the border, Margarito G. Rodríguez, president of the Mexican-American Bar Association, said,

> The recent deaths caused by the Border Patrol's use of deadly force have raised the specter of fear and dread in El Paso and have reinforced the perception that we are under siege by the very agents that are supposed to protect us.

But the borderland is more than just a geographical area. Gloria Anzaldua in her book, *Borderlands: Fronteras*, gives a definition of borderland that includes the psychological, sexual, and spiritual borderlands: "Borderlands are physically present wherever two or more cultures edge each other, where people of different races occupy the same territory, where under, lower, middle, and upper classes touch, where the space between two individuals shrinks with intimacy."

In one of Anzaldua's poems, "To live in the borderlands means you," she describes how we should live in the borderlands: "To survive the Borderlands you must live *sin fronteras* [without borders], be a crossroads." When I read this poem I was reminded of the vision John gives us of the unity of all people in God's Kingdom where they will hunger no more and God will wipe away every tear from their eyes (Rev. 7:9-17). How theological of Anzaldua! God in Christ came to break down all barriers that stand between human beings and between human beings and God. As instruments of God we should work to break down these barriers so that the Kingdom may come.

THE INDIGENOUS PEOPLE'S RESISTANCE

In the summer of 1990, I did an independent study in southern México where a large number of indigenous people live. The study also provided me with the opportunity to learn about the Guatemalan refugee camps that exist between the México-Guatemala border. I read about the resistance of the indigenous people to colonialization — and I saw present-day efforts of the same resistance.

As a child I remember being told, *Pareces pura india* [You look completely Indian], and it was said as an insult. Lucky for me that I had the dad that I had; he always seemed to promote a nationalistic attitude, which annoyed the integrationists among us. I too have always been proud of my Indian heritage while at the same time not denying the other heritage. It is important for us as Chicanas/os to rediscover our dual heritage. For example, Guatemalan refugees can give us important insights into our own situation in the context of five hundred years.

At the same time, we need to be aware of the continuation of the destructive elements of the Conquest, which result in indigenous people being refugees from their own homelands. We can learn from indigenous people how they have survived and what we can do to support and advocate their causes. This is especially true because as Chicanas/os we may inadvertently support United States government policies that are contrary to the liberation of the people in Guatemala and Mexico — and therefore our own liberation as people of color in the United States.

I believe recovering our European as well as indigenous roots is important in order to make sense out of the present and be able to project a liberationist future for Chicanas/os. The God of the Exodus continues to act in the present, and as a Christian one lives in the hope of God's liberating action.

THE WORLDWIDE BORDERS

In this latter struggle for our own liberation, the borders that we must cross are worldwide borders. We must support the students in their efforts for democracy and unification in Korea, support Nelson Mandela and other African National Congress leaders in South Africa to demolish *apartheid*, support the efforts to stop the genocidal policies against Gypsies in Europe, support the efforts of liberation struggles in the Philippines, and support the efforts of refugee women and children throughout the world to stop conditions that make fleeing a necessity. We must fight against war, hunger, poverty, and unequal trade agreements such as the Free Trade Agreement between Mexico and the United States and the General Trade and Tariff Agreement (GATT) All of these are a continuation of five hundred years-plus of worldwide conquest and colonization — an internal and external process.

THE *MACHISMO* FACTOR

Internal contradictions are found in all cultures, and they are usually the hardest ones to surface and change. In a culture that gave expression to the term *machismo* or "male chauvinism," change will be slow — but at least sexism is finally being publicly debated in my community.

I wanted to learn how to drive a car, but my two brothers were trying to talk my father into denying me permission to practice in the family car. They were arguing that as a woman I would be too emotional and could easily lose my composure, so it might not be the safest thing for me to drive. I had watched my father and brothers drive the automatic car, and it didn't seem like such a big deal to me. During one meal when such a discussion was going on, I decided to take the matter into my own hands. I left the table quietly, got the car keys, and began pulling the car out of the driveway, at which point my family came running out, shouting at me to please stop the car. I did — but only after they chased me around the block. After that the family decided it would be best to teach me how to drive: otherwise I would become a menace to the community.

That was not the last time that I had to go against what was considered normal for a woman in my community. Years later, as the only woman at a Hispanic staff church meeting, the men were teasing me about being a feminist because I challenged them about the way they were talking about women. Obviously their teasing did not change my behavior, since I had grown up in this type of environment. Instead of becoming oblivious to sexist behavior, I became more and more sensitive to it. I have always been thankful for my mother and other women who serve as living testimonies to the feminine aspect of God. My mother struggled for all her daughters to have the opportunity of a formal education, even though she was often told that her daughters were only going to get married, so why waste this type of effort and money on them?

Columbus's arrival brought a new economic system that also changed the sociocultural organization of the indigenous people. The Indian women were no longer equal to the men; they were raped and taken as objects of possession by the colonizers as a means to subjugate the population. The church allowed only men as the leaders of religion, and only pure white Spanish men at that; not even the colonizers' own mixed-blood offspring were acceptable as servants of God. So it is not surprising that even today — five hundred years later — women are still submissive to men. Obstacles exist even in the Protestant church, which is supposed to be open to women as leaders. I know of only five ordained Mexican-American Presbyterian women, and none of them are pastors in predominately Hispanic churches. The church needs to be a promoter of women, fighting against sexism, instead of upholding *machismo* as a necessary historical element of the church.

It is ironic that after five hundred years, the European theology of "pure-blood" still exists. Of the thirty members of the United States Christopher Columbus Quincentenary Jubilee Commission, eleven are Italian American, four are Hispanic, and none of them are Mexican American. It is ironic because without the European invasion Mexican Americans as a race would not exist, and Mexican Americans comprise more than half of all "Hispanics" in the United States.

THE GOOD NEWS

It seems that I have been crossing borders all my life — social, racial, economic, political, light-skinned versus dark-skinned, male versus female, poor versus rich, old versus young, capitalist versus communist. Always striving for the whole, for pluralism and inclusiveness, I realized that all things don't have to be the same to belong to one whole.

Thanks be to God that, in spite of the five hundred years, the good news comes through the living human flesh of Jesus of Nazareth who walks among the peoples of the earth. I have come to believe that spirituality is not experienced in isolation from the world. It is not liturgy nor is it heavenly focused but earthly centered. It is one's conscious decision to seek the truth as a way of life found in the God of justice. It is the ongoing process that keeps changing and moving us toward a solidarity with all of life, seeking the oneness in all God's creation. It is commitment to the love of God with all the passion of one's heart and loving all God's creation with the same passion. So that ultimately to do is to be.

3

The Church in Latin America after Five Hundred Years: An Evangelical Missiological Perspective

J. Samuel Escobar

After five hundred years of Christian presence, should Latin America be considered a mission field or a mission base, "from which missionaries go as messengers of Jesus Christ to plant Christianity in other continents of the world?" The author, professor of Hispanic and Missions Studies at Eastern Baptist Theological Seminary, explodes "Black Legends" about both Catholic and Protestant expansion. This paper was presented at the Overseas Ministries Study Center, New Haven, Connecticut, 24-25 April, 1992.

With what kind of attitude do we remember the five hundred years of Christian presence in the Americas? As Emilio Castro has commented, we hesitate between a festive "Te Deum" in order to celebrate or a solemn "Requiem" in order to lament (1990, 147). The bitter controversy about this issue evidences how difficult it is to be objective about the history of Christianity, especially in Latin America. This is even more difficult for a person who was born here and who happens to be an Evangelical. Therefore, these reflections are presented in a rather tentative way, in the hope that discussion will help all of us to see some things more clearly.

UNDERSTANDING HISTORY

I shall focus in this chapter on key points of interpretation from a missiological perspective. I consider that a missiological approach has to be systematic and critical, but also born out of an authentic concern for the fulfillment of the mission of the church, which is yet an unfinished business. In the case of Latin America two factors add urgency to the need for a correct understanding of the past. On the one hand, from both Protestant and Catholic sources there are now movements committed to the mobilization of Latin American resources — especially resources of personnel — for Christian mission in other parts of the world in the coming century. On the other hand, Latin America is at present the part of the world to which proportionately more missionaries are being sent from other continents by both Catholics and Protestants. This raises the question: Is Latin America still to be considered a *mission field* into which the churches from North America and Europe pour human, technical, and financial resources for missionary purposes? The question could also be posed in totally different terms. With its five hundred years of Christian presence, shouldn't Latin America be considered rather as a *mission base*, from which missionaries go as messengers of Jesus Christ to plant Christianity in other continents of the world?

Three points of clarification are necessary; they will help us to understand the history of Christianity in the Americas.[1] First is the question of the "Black Legend." Evangelicals must acknowledge that the Iberian conquest and evangelization of the Americas in the sixteenth century has frequently been perceived in Great Britain and North America through a highly critical and even hostile lens. The vast amount of literature produced from this negative perspective has been labeled a "Black Legend" by the defenders of Spain and Portugal.[2] It is considered legend and not history because it exaggerates some facts and it does not give a good account of others.

The first duty of Evangelical missionaries and missiologists in the light of 1992 will be to get acquainted with facts, to get beyond the "Black Legend" and its "White" counterpart. Historical research in recent years has contributed an incredible amount of data to help us understand the process of Catholic missions within the frame of conquest and colonial domination that followed Columbus's arrival. There are classic studies about missionary methodologies, such as those of Robert Ricard (1986) and Lewis Hanke (1949), and more recent valuable additions such as those by Manuel Marzal (1983; 1985), and the Franciscan Pedro Borges (1960; 1987). All these scholarly studies are filled with lessons for the contemporary reader interested in the practice and theory of mission. Historians, such as Enrique Dussel (1981), working from the perspective of liberation theology have contributed some clarification by their emphasis on the interaction of religious history with socioeconomic factors, and their commitment to look at the history of the church from the perspective of the poor (*IBMR* 1990, 14:3, 105-108). However, in some cases the use of marxist presuppositions and categories of analysis may limit our understanding of events like the sixteenth-century evangelization to little more than the religious cover-up for military conquest and political domination. A missiological approach should look for balance.

Another important reason for stressing the urgent need for balance is the fact that some Catholic and marxist historiography about the Protestant missionary work of the last two centuries has developed a new "Black Legend" — this time against Protestants, and especially against Evangelicals.[3] It is not uncommon to find publications from conservative Catholic or marxist sources that concur in presenting Latin American Protestant growth as a CIA-inspired plot against liberation theologians, or as an effort of large American corporations to manipulate the poor of Latin America. Almost daily, uninformed journalism and mass media repeat these generalizations *ad nauseam*. Let us hope that Evangelical missiologists will avoid using the same simplistic approach to their analysis of Catholic missions. Better informed Evangelicals can now give a fair treatment to both the Roman Catholic mission history of the sixteenth century and the Protestant mission history of the last two centuries.[4]

A second observation, once the exaggerations of the Black Legend are corrected, is that influential scholars today believe that a key to understanding the religious history of the Americas is the larger framework of the Iberian-Anglo-Saxon confrontation. In his recent book about Pentecostal growth in Latin America, David Martin called that confrontation "one of the longest running of all wars." He refers to "The four hundred year clash between the Hispanic imperium and the Anglo-Saxon imperium. On the one side are all the successor states of the Iberian Peninsula; on the other side are England and its mightiest successor state — the U.S.A." (Martin 1990, 9). Catholic missiologist Virgilio Elizondo uses this same framework in his study about the history and identity of Hispanics in the United States. In the introductory chapter of his study and at several other points, he evokes that confrontation which took a dramatic turn in the history of the expansion of the United States into Mexican territory. Elizondo sets the modern events within the frame of that centuries-long war in which, as he says, "[Queen] Elizabeth and Cromwell had already established a policy that stealing from Catholic Spain was a noble endeavor in favor of liberation and civilization" (Elizondo 1983, 14).

However, taking into consideration this larger historical frame of reference, one clarification is necessary. I think that we have to debate the validity of the idea that Roman Catholicism is an essential part of the identity of Ibero-Americans, to the degree that those who embrace protestantism are consequently losing their identity and are taking sides with the enemy. Within the Iberian experience there is a long tradition of an evangelical stream in catholicism, represented by the Spanish mystics of the sixteenth century such as Teresa de Avila and San Juan de la Cruz. They were in many respects kindred souls of the Spanish Reformers such as Juan de Valdés, Casiodoro de Reina, and Cipriano de Valera, who had to go into exile in that same century in order to escape from the Inquisition. They were the spiritual ancestors of Christians such as Luis de Usoz and Miquel de Unamuno in more recent times. As John A. Mackay (1932) argued, Protestant missionaries who came to Latin America found many Catholics eager to embrace an alternative form of Christianity. None of these persons was less Hispanic or less Portuguese because they embraced the Evangelical faith. Moreover, the Latin American identity includes African, Asian, and Indian elements besides Iberian Catholicism (cp. Escobar 1991a, 22-30). What we need at this point is a missiological evaluation of the use of the religious factor as an instrument to foster political uniformity in a nation.

In the third place comes the question of mutual recognition of the validity of the Catholic and the Protestant experiences. I think historical perspective helps me to understand the fact that for some Catholics, protestantism will always be some kind of religious anomaly. However, in the century of ecumenism and after Vatican II, one would hope that perspectives might have changed on both sides of the fence. In the pluralistic world in which we now live, the Latin American Protestant, Evangelical, or Pentecostal forms of religious experience should not be considered as types of anomalous sectarian behavior, in the same way in which Roman Catholic communities in the Scandinavian countries cannot be considered as anomalous sects. However, the approach taken by many scholars, journalists, and bishops toward Latin American protestantism, especially toward its popular forms, betrays the basic presupposition that they are anomalous forms of Christianity. Conciliar, Catholic, and Evangelical missiologists in North America have been more open to the ecumenical experience than scholars working in other fields of theological research. It is fascinating to see that among Roman Catholics in Latin America, foreign missionaries and missiologists are the ones who are pioneering a new approach to the presence of protestantism (cp. Escobar 1991).[5]

The need for mutual recognition and the possibility of working toward it was illustrated by the "Evangelical-Roman Catholic Dialogue on Mission" (ERC-DOM) and the excellent report that came from it. The report shows how much there is in common between Evangelicals and Roman Catholics in relation to the basic truths about the Christian mission.[6] However, after the report appeared in 1986, very little use has been made of it. As far as we know, in those regions of the world where it would be more important to consider it, such as Latin America, very little attention has been paid to it among Protestants and practically none among Roman Catholics. The possibility that things may change has been recently stated by Jesuit theologian Avery Dulles, in an article in which he gives account of the new papal calls for evangelization, and the fact that "There is increasing recognition that Catholics and conservative Evangelicals share many things in common" (Dulles 1992, 72).

LESSONS FROM HISTORY

The above caveats are indispensable in my opinion, because the past five hundred years of history of Christianity in Latin America constitute a privileged territory for the analysis of key differences or similarities between Roman Catholic and Protestant missionary approaches. Historians of Christian mission such as Latourette and Neill have offered in the past valuable comparative evaluations of these approaches.[7] Without abandoning their particular convictions, their own ecumenical spirit allowed them to make these comparisons without trying to prove that one methodology was necessarily more legitimate or correct than the other. The bulk of the historical research since these scholars wrote would seem to prove the validity of their global observations and evaluations. In the rest of this paper I shall discuss some areas about which there seems to be a good measure of consensus — areas in which clearly the past has a bearing on the conflicts and dilemmas of the present.

Anyone interested in Latin America has to be thankful for the flood of materials about the missionary work from Spain and Portugal that has appeared as part of the celebrations of five hundred years of Iberian presence in the New World. Even material that has an apologetic or controversial intention will help to clarify the vision of that important chapter in the history of missions. Roman Catholic bishops, in their assembly at Puebla (1979), came with a statement about Catholic mission in the sixteenth century that summarizes their own assessment of the situation: "It is true that in its work of evangelization the Church had to bear the weight of its lapses, its acts of complicity with the earthly powers, its incomplete pastoral vision, and the destructive force of sin. But we must also recognize that evangelization, which makes Latin America a 'continent of hope,' has been far more powerful than the dark shadows that unfortunately accompanied it in the historical context through which it had to live" (Eagleson and Scharper 1979, 125).

The Aim of Missionary Action

Let us take as a starting point the conclusions of a comparative study of Catholic and Protestant missionary work conducted by missiologist Norman A. Horner between 1956 and 1964. He finds that there is a key difference between the way in which each of these communities conceives of the aim of mission.

> Protestantism has traditionally laid great stress on individual conversion. There is much to commend this emphasis because Christian faith is indeed a relationship between each Christian and his Lord, and there can be no redeemed society apart from redeemed individuals. In Protestant missionary philosophy, these individuals are of equal importance not only in the sight of God but also as members of the Christian community. (Horner 1965, 26)

The sources for this concept of mission can be traced back to basic theological tenets of the sixteenth-century Reformation, but they were no doubt accentuated by the Pietist influence in the development of the Protestant missionary movement. Latourette is also explicit about this point: "Protestantism, particularly in the types which were most active in the spread of the faith, tended to stress the individual, the conversion of the individual, and the right and duty of each Christian to think for himself" (Latourette 1941, 45).

> In Roman Catholic thought, on the other hand — continues Horner — the impact of the church on the social environment is recognized as essential, and to Christianize institutions in human society is regarded as more immediately important than to win individuals. Individuals are not considered to be of equal importance in evangelistic procedure, but those who can most effectively bring Christian influence to bear on social institutions have top priority. . . . Individuals may be more or less easy to win, but Catholics feel that the process of founding a Christian community is not to be accomplished by indiscriminate multiplication of converted individuals. (Horner 1965, 27)

The sources of this approach can also be traced back to the sacramental and hierarchical dimensions of the concept of the church in traditional Catholic theology, which were probably refined and updated in the *ugglornamento* process of the Vatican II, but not radically changed.

Horner's description is proved by the classic work of Jesuit Robert Richard about the Roman Catholic evangelization of México in the sixteenth century. He writes in a very specific way about the application of missionary policies and methods because he considers that México and Perú were the countries "in which the colonizing and evangelizing effort was most efficacious and intelligent" (1982, 306). Writing in the 1940s, Richard said:

> I shall mention . . . an idea that is daily gaining greater acceptance among the theologians concerned with mission problems, the idea that the essential purpose of a mission among the pagans is not the conversion of individuals, but above all the establishment of a visible church, with all the functions and institutions that the expression 'visible Church' implies. (Ibid., 306)

Richard goes on to say that though at the time he is writing this missiological concept was new, it was consistent with the logic of Catholic ecclesiology, because:

> If divine grace is what converts a man (and I use the word 'converts' in its wide as well as in its narrow sense), and if the Church, by means of its sacraments, is the normal agent of spreading divine grace, since it is the intermediary between God and his creatures, it is logical to suppose that the principal task of the missionary consists in placing the normal means of conversion at the disposition of the pagans. (Ibid., 306-307)

Although the presence of the institutional church was a fact in Latin America, four centuries later it was not clear if it had accomplished its mission on that continent. Outside observers of the condition of Latin American catholicism in the first part of our century, like Maryknoll missionary William J. Coleman, pointed to its "dual nature." On the one hand it was undeniable that "Catholicism has struck deep roots in the culture of the continent," but on the other hand "the same observer finds an amazing superficiality that is even more obvious than the profundity of the catholic customs" (Coleman 1958, 4). Coleman gave some examples that reveal the deep contradiction:

> Together with a deepest Catholic piety and devotion to the Blessed Virgin, our sympathetic visitor witnesses no real regard for the mass and the sacraments. An almost fanatical concern for the Sacrament of Baptism, he finds is joined to a profoundly cynical view of the Sacrament of matrimony. A visitor's final conclusion is that whatever may be the tradition of this Catholicism, it reflects no real grasp of fundamental Catholic principles or suppositions. (Ibid., 26)

The justification of Protestant mission and presence referred to the same reality from a different angle. Thus, in the Jerusalem meeting of the International Missionary Council in 1928, John A. Mackay established the legitimacy of a Protestant missionary presence in Latin America on the basis of his own twelve years of experience among youth, intellectuals, and students on this continent. He dismissed the idea that Evangelical missionaries were "religious buccaneers devoting their lives to ecclesiastical piracy" and described the spiritual condition of the continent, "My work lay among the great unchurched masses of the South American continent. . . . The great majority of men in South America have repudiated all religion" (Mackay 1928, 121). Almost forty years later José Míguez Bonino, a well-known Argentinean theologian, offered this global evaluation of historical roots:

> Latin America was never 'Christian' in the sense that Europe or even North America can be said to be so. What took place here was a colossal transplantation — the basic ecclesiastical structures, disciplines, and ministries were brought wholesale from Spain and expected to function as a Christian order: a tremendous form without substance. (1964, 168)

This kind of mission field proved to be very fertile for Protestant missionary action, especially in recent decades. By 1916 there were 170,000 Protestants in Latin America and it is estimated that they are 48 million in 1990. A Catholic journalist says that "If current growth rates continue, Latin America will have an Evangelical majority in the early 21st century. Actually in terms of church participation 'practicing' Evangelicals may already outnumber 'observant' Catholics" (McCoy 1989, 2).

Theologians and missiologists who have embarked on self-evaluation and criticism of the existing forms of catholicism and protestantism in Latin America have been pointing to the need of revising basic concepts about the aim of mission. Within catholicism Juan Luis Segundo has been the most consistent critic of the concept of the church as an immense "machine to make Christians," and the pastoral approaches derived from it.[8] He thinks that the only way in which the church can face the colossal transitions brought to Latin America by urbanization, modernization, and secularization would be to change the pastoral approach in three directions. The church should move "from exerting pressure to nurturing freedom . . . , from protecting majorities to fashioning heroic minorities . . . , [and] from contracting alliances to relying on the power of the Gospel" (1978, 66,70,77). Segundo proposes a new pastoral approach that would include the revision of theological presuppositions related to the traditional concept of mission, a new ecclesiology more consistent with Vatican II, and a new commitment to evangelization.

On the Protestant side there was a development of significant proportions during our century. The missionary work of the old mainline denominations, which pioneered evangelization at the end of the nineteenth century and in the period prior to World War II, declined significantly after that war. It was substituted by the so-called "non-historic" independent mission boards and faith missions that grew rapidly during the post-war period. The individualism noted by Horner was characteristic of early Protestant mission work, but in spite of it a movement for cooperation and coordination of missionary organizations developed under the auspices of the Committee of Cooperation in Latin America. Continental gatherings of Protestants were held in Panamá (1916), Montevideo (1925), and Havana (1929), with increasing participation and leadership from Latin American leaders substituting the leading role of missionaries. These were years of an Evangelical ecumenism in which zeal for evangelism combined with contextual efforts and a strategic vision to penetrate all sectors of Latin American life with the Gospel.

After World War II, with the arrival of the non-historic faith missions and independent boards, a new stage began in which the individualistic thrust of Protestant missions took excessive proportions. Coupled with the ideology of the Cold War, this extreme individualism made impossible a cooperative Protestant missionary strategy, and delayed the development of a contextual social ethics to accompany church growth.[9] Pentecostal churches experienced phenomenal growth and added a new source of fragmentation. An early interpreter of these developments was missiologist Kenneth Strachan whose words, written in 1957, have a prophetic ring:

> For better or worse, the non-historical groups constitute a major factor in the determination of Latin America's Protestant future. The movement can spearhead the aggressive stepped-up program of evangelism that is so urgently needed to meet the challenge of an exploding population in the valley of revolutionary change. The movement can be used by God to infuse new life and vigor into older bodies that may have lost their vitality and momentum. But it can also be instrumental in sidetracking the Evangelical church down sterile bypaths of doctrinal extremes and religious oddities and tragically remove it from effective contact with the main stream of Latin American life. And it can so intensify and magnify its divisions as to make it hopelessly unable to resist and overcome the anti-Christian pressures that are building up in the world today. (Barbieri 1961, 71)

In spite of its significant numerical growth, protestantism finds itself today in a sad, polarized situation that thwarts its possibilities of providing the spiritual energy for alternative social and political ways at a time of crisis.

Mission and Empire

According to Latourette, as we look at mission history between 1800 and 1914, "one outstanding feature of the expansion of Christianity in this period was the comparative absence of active assistance by governments" (1941, 47). He reminds us that since the days of Emperor Constantine the spread of Christianity was a cooperative effort of monarchs and missionaries, and that "this had never been more marked than in the three centuries immediately preceding A.D. 1800, when the major part of the geographic extension of Christianity was accomplished under the direction of the Spanish, Portuguese, and Russian governments" (ibid., 47). The Latin American case illustrates well the principle here defined by Latourette. The Iberian missionary enterprise of the sixteenth century comes at the highest point of identification between mission and empire. We will explore briefly two aspects of this identification.

In the first place we see how the pace and style of the missionary work follows the pace and style of empire. There are two clearly marked stages in the process of establishment of the Spanish empire in Latin America. First, there was a decisive initial experience that goes from 1492 to 1550, in which a vast extension from California to Chile was submitted. The second was a "motionless" colonial period of establishment and decay that lasts until 1808, the year in which the independence movements start. There is a surprising speed in the conquest process. If we keep in mind that between 1492 and 1519 the Spanish were moving almost exclusively in the Caribbean Islands and briefly touching the coasts of the continents, the process of conquest of the great plateau empires of México and Perú took just thirty years. Pedro de Alvarado, who fought with Hernán Cortés in México in 1519, also took part in the conquest of Chile, at the southern tip of South America, twenty years later. This conquest followed the path of a search for gold and limited itself to the establishment of military garrisons and key cities, signs of occupation, spread over the vast territory of the continent. It was not a colonization effort like its Anglo-Saxon counterpart in North America a century later.

There is a growing consensus today about the fact that the task of evangelization within that frame of reference was never completed, and that Latin America was not properly evangelized. Ivan Vallier, one of the best analysts of the crisis in contemporary catholicism, has outlined the situation: "The Catholic religion was planted (perhaps 'scattered' is a better term) with great haste, throughout territories of vast proportions. Distances between religious centers were immense — a combined result of clergy shortages and the church's ambition to cover a whole continent" (1970, 24). Vallier also describes clearly the intense missionary activity of the initial stages of the conquest and the decline of it after a century:

> By the middle of the 17th century, most of the natives had been subdued. The fervor of colonization was depleted. Diocesan clergy, urban hierarchies, and the machinery of the Inquisition held the focal roles in ecclesiastical life. Although missionary work continued in frontier zones and among settled tribes the proselytizing posture of the church was broken. (Ibid., 47)

The coincidence between the mood and style of empire and mission marked decisively the sociopolitical life as well as the cultural and spiritual life of the Latin American societies. Venezuelan historian Mariano Picón Salas gives an eloquent picture of the situation:

> As the sixteenth century merged into the seventeenth, the Church likewise grew more sedentary and fond of luxury. It was more interested in dominating the Creole society of Spanish Americans then in harvesting Indian souls. . . . Immense wealth became unproductive as it flowed into the coffers of the religious orders and of the dioceses from the tithes and first fruits, from contributions of the crown and of feudal overlords. . . . The church-fortress, or evangelistic training center, of the early missionaries evolved into the elaborately ornate baroque structures of Spanish Creole architecture, and most of the intrigues in colonial cities emanated from the locutories of sumptuous convents. (Picón Salas 1962, 74-75)

A second effect of the coincidence between mission and empire relates to the institution called *real patronato* [royal patronage] and the way in which it fostered a missionary approach based on coercion and a confusion between civilization and mission. The colonial period could be divided in two parts: The time of the Habsburg dynasty up to 1700, and the time of the Bourbons after 1700. During the first part, the legal instrument of agreement between the crown and the church called *real patronato* was devised. Its effects were intensified to the detriment of the church during the second part. Lloyd Mecham, one of the specialists on this question, writes:

> Never before or since did a sovereign with the consent of the Pope so completely control the Catholic Church as did the Spanish kings in their American possessions. This union of altar and throne, known as the *real patronato de las Indias*, was unique and had no precedents in the history of church and state relations. . . . So rapidly did the crown develop a policy of control and administration over the patronage that by the end of the reign of Philip II the civil control over the church was thoroughly consolidated. Subsequent history added nothing to its essential nature, except perhaps to strengthen and expand even more the royal control. (Mecham 1963, 200, 202)

Mecham describes how the *patronato* gave colonial civil authorities power in the appointment of bishops (right of presentation), filling of ecclesiastical vacancies, removal and resignation of priests, monitoring communications between the Pope and the Church in Latin America, collecting the tithes and paying the clergy, founding and delimitation of ecclesiastical districts, control of church councils and synods, missionary initiatives, and maintenance of morals and dogma through the Inquisition.

One of the areas of research and publication fostered by the celebration of the five hundred years in Spain has been the publication of many primary sources and contemporary studies about the participation of missionaries and priests in the sixteenth-century debates about the legitimacy of the Iberian conquest. The Pontificia Universidad de Salamanca has been the center for this activity. It reminds us of the unique contribution to international laws that is represented by the effort to give juridical instruments to the conquest. However, the study of this process also shows how missionary methodology was influenced by the imperial philosophy. Spanish missiologist Leandro Tormo refers to the "military method" of mission that developed during the years of war against the Arab occupants of the Peninsula. It can be summarized in the phrase *primero vencer para después convencer* [first to defeat and then to convince] (Tormo 1962, 150-151). Charles Taber has reminded us recently that "The Iberian expansion presented a new feature in terms of the history of missions: for the first time on a major scale, missions are allied with secular power in a way that gave them the ability to coerce their audience and not only to persuade them" (Taber 1991, 23).

During the theological and juridical debates of the sixteenth and seventeenth centuries in Spain regarding the legitimacy of the conquest and its relationship with missionary activity, some missionaries argued against the use of coercion as a missionary method, and proposed methods closer to the New Testament model. Others, however (and they were the majority), argued that Christianity could only be understood and accepted by civilized human beings. The work of civilization was necessary as a step prior to christianization. Natural law as well as philosophical tradition could be invoked to prove that the Spanish crown was entitled to the use of force in the process of civilizing the natives of the Americas. Iberians were not alone in this kind of conviction. Max Warren has written about the ideas of English Puritan Richard Sibbes, who influenced the missionary concepts of Richard Baxter and John Eliot. He quotes from one of Sibbes's sermons about the conversion of Lydia (Acts 16: 14-15), in reference to the heathen world:

> Now God in preparation for the most part civiliseth people and then Christianiseth them, as I may say; for the Spirit of God would not be effectual in a rude, wild and barbarious soul; in men that are not men. Therefore, they must be brought to civility; and not only to civility, but there must be a work of the law, to cast them down; and then they are brought to Christianity thereupon. (Warren 1967, 87)

Reliance on political power and alliance with it at the missionary stage also brought the Catholic Church a situation of extreme dependence on civil authorities for her subsistence and continuity. This has marked the life of Latin American countries up to the present. Vallier's analysis calls our attention to the fact that "the relaxation of missionary activity interrupted the growth of a strong religiously based relationship between the clergy and the people." For him the missionary attitude implies actions of outreach and going to the people, making contact with them, teaching the faith, and attracting them to join a religious fellowship. In the absence of a religiously based relationship, the Church had to depend on the coercive power of the secular order.

> So long as the political situation remained viable and supportive of the formal Church, the territory was considered to be Christian. But in periods of crisis or conflict, the Church was unable to stand on its own as a general source of moral authority or as a carrier of basic values capable of encompassing, yet standing above parties in the dispute. (Vallier 1970, 48)

In my opinion, the contemporary inability of the Latin American hierarchies to deal in a pastoral way with the question of the Protestant expansion, and the resource to conspiracy theories to explain it or dismiss it, derives from this weakness analyzed so aptly by Vallier.

The main steps of Protestant missionary advance in Latin America are parallel to the crisis and decline of the Catholic Church. The pioneers of the Protestant movement came during the period of the war of independence from Spain (1810-1824). At that point Latourette's observation about the disengagement between empire and mission is especially significant. The period of Protestant penetration coincides with the period of liberation from the Spanish colonial yoke and the search for new economic alliances and new models of society. That explains the fact that some of the Protestant pioneers (i.e., the Scottish Baptist James Thomson) received an enthusiastic welcome from independentist leaders such as San Martin (Argentina), Bolivar (Gran Colombia), O'Higgins (Chile), and Dr. Mora (Central America). Liberal forces during the nineteenth century were at one and the same time hostile to catholicism and open to Protestant penetration. But only at the end of the century did Protestant missions see definite progress and the beginnings of national Protestant churches.

The relationship between mission and empire in the case of protestantism has been interpreted in different ways. Liberal historians and those who had a more positive attitude toward the process of modernization in Latin America have generally been sympathetic to Protestant advance, even if they were not converts to protestantism.[10] The educational and medical work, as well as the transformation of character and the consequent upward mobility, especially for the poor, were efforts of the missionary work from the historic or mainline missions before World War II. The significant growth of pentecostalism after the war, which became an indigenous force in its missionary style, was also interpreted from a positive perspective. Thus Emilio Willems's interpretation of Pentecostal protestantism in Brazil and Chile placed it in a historical continuum in which it emerges as a byproduct of changes affecting the social structures and values of Brazilian and Chilean societies. The value reorientation that can be described as "protestant ethics" helps the converts to function better in the new situation created by industrialization, urbanization, internal migration, and the opening of new frontiers (1967, 13). The fact that pentecostalism was attracting the popular classes in these societies would mean that the Pentecostal experience might be one of the ways open to masses that are in a state of latent or overt rebellion:

> Conversion to Protestantism, especially to its sectarian varieties, constitutes one of the many ways in which hostility and rebellion against a decaying social structure may be expressed. Correctly or incorrectly, the Catholic Church is often perceived by the masses as a symbol of the traditional order, or more specifically as an ally of its supreme exponent, the landed aristocracy. To the extent that the Church is perceived as a classbound institution it has become the target of such mass hostility. (Willems 1964, 103)

Willems's approach centered on institutional analysis of Pentecostal congregations and called attention to another factor that is important: the participative nature of Pentecostal liturgy and congregational life, which does not depend on literacy of education but on a disposition to be touched by the power of the Holy Spirit. In his analysis Willems referred especially to the significance of the *tomada de Espiritu* or "seizure" by the Spirit, which "puts a seal of divine approval on the individual who can now be elected or appointed to any office" (ibid., 106-107). The seizure becomes a form of legitimation within the Pentecostal congregations that has to be validated by energetic and successful proselytism. The seizure has an integrative effect, allowing thousands of persons from the lower social classes to become part of an organized group in which they could enter in community, contribute their participation, and receive affirmation, comfort, and a sense of belonging. This integrative factor was important for those persons who were part of a massive process of migration that had created forms of anomic life in the population that was crowding into the booming Latin American cities, at a time in which the Catholic church had no energies, resources, or vision to respond to that pastoral challenge.

With the predominance of the "dependence theory" in the social sciences since the late 1960s, came a new interpretation of the Protestant mission and presence. The leninist elements of the theory of imperialism were used to forge a new approach to the interpretation of Latin American history, in which special attention was paid to the economic factors underlying the political and cultural ones. For this view Latin America had been incorporated into the modern world as a dependent, not as a partner, in order to serve further development of new imperialist powers.[11] The colonial pact with Spain and Portugal was substituted by a new colonial pact and "the fundamental element in the new Latin American consciousness is the awareness that our political emancipation from Spain was — however justified and necessary — a step in the Anglo-Saxon colonial and neocolonial expansion" (Míguez Bonino 1975, 14).

Probably the most consistent and clear expression of this kind of analysis applied to Latin American protestantism has been provided by Argentinean theologian José Míguez Bonino. The subject of the Protestant identity in Latin America has been tackled with consistency in many of his writings, and the most systematic is probably his book *Toward a Christian Political Ethics* (1983). He thinks the conditions that facilitated the introduction of protestantism were the forging of a "neocolonial pact" that favored relationships with the Protestant countries, and the triumph of the modernizing elites over the traditional ones. Protestants served the purposes determined by the initiative and intention of the liberal elites. "What is clear in relation to Latin America, is that protestantism claimed and (within its limitations) assumed the role that the Latin American liberal elites had assigned it in the transition from a traditional society to the modern bourgeois world" (1983, 62). Awareness about this fact produces a "crisis of conscience," says Míguez Bonino and, though accepting the fact that protestantism played a significant role in breaking the power of the traditional colonial mentality, he feels obliged to ask, "Did we not in fact provide religious sanction to a new colonialism? Did we not in fact contribute to create the benevolent and idealized image of the colonial powers (mainly the United States) which has disguised the deadly character of their domination?" (1975, 18).

This interpretation demands a missiological evaluation that must separate what is a valuable contribution to understanding Protestant missionary work from what would be more a marxist framing of a missionary reality from the perspective of apolitical project. However, the longer history of the relationship between mission and empire in the case of catholicism should serve as a warning for Protestants today.

The Problems of Indigenization

One of the problems besetting the Roman Catholic Church in Latin America, especially significant for a church that celebrates five hundred years of existence, has been the lack of a native clergy. Juan Luis Segundo thinks that this is one of the marks that makes the Church look "exhausted and depleted." He sets the problem within the context of several related factors:

> In existence for four centuries now, it does not have enough priests of its own to carry out its functions; it must import them from abroad in such great numbers that they make up half of the priestly population. It lacks missionaries to send to its marginal inhabitants in rural regions and primitive wastes. It lacks pastoral agents of all sorts to do the work of fashioning truly liberative communities. It lacks the economic support it needs from its own faithful in order to satisfy its most urgent needs; here, once again, it must import financial aid from abroad. (Segundo 1978, 2)

Many missiologists who have dealt with this issue point to the sources of the problem in the practices of the colonial church. It is clear now from historical research that the Spanish church was reluctant to allow persons who were born in the colonies to become members of the hierarchy in the ten archdioceses and thirty-eight dioceses in Spanish America.[12] Thus, for instance:

> Friar Antonine Tibesar's calculations reveal that in México during the entire colonial period only 32 of the 171 bishops and archbishops were Mexican, and in South America only 64 of the 535 bishops and archbishops were American-born. In general, native-born and American-born priests had little prospect of rising to high positions in the diocesan clergy. This circumstance created a hiatus between the higher clergy and the priesthood and had grave consequences for the church. It is no surprise that the lower clergy supported the colonial struggles for independence, while the bishops, for the most part, remained staunchly royalist. (Greenleaf 1971, 6-7)

C. R. Boxer, who studied in depth the question of the training of an indigenous clergy, thought that though the development of an indigenous clergy was desirable in theory, in practice that process took a long time to develop outside Europe, and that in fact it never came to exist in some places. Boxer believes that "the formation of a responsible native clergy was opposed by those very missionaries who should have been in favor of it" and thinks that this applies both to Protestants as well as to Roman Catholics. He goes on to say that "whatever the theory may have been in practice, a colored indigenous clergy was apt to be kept in a strictly subordinate role to the white European priests, particularly where these latter were members of the religious orders — the regular clergy as opposed to the secular clergy" (Boxer 1978, 2).

Within the Roman Catholic Church the question of indigenization and mission had been tackled in a creative way, on the basis of missionary experience, by the *Propaganda Fide*, the Sacred Congregation for the Propagation of the Faith, which was created by Pope Gregory XV in 1622. Neill says that the *Propaganda* had "a prophetic quality of mind" (1986, 152-153). However, in relation to Latin America the *Propaganda Fide* could not have a direct influence because of the *Patronato* arrangement. The Council of Indies, a body created and directed by the Spanish crown, was the only organization through which the Pope could intervene to influence in the Americas. Coleman wrote that the special circumstances created by the *Patronato* did not allow "modern missionary principles" to influence Catholic missionary action in Latin America following the initial conquest stage:

> The modern mission principles were aimed at correcting one of the great defects in the Church in America; the lack of indigenization in the new country. By this is meant the failure to develop a native clergy and hierarchy capable of carrying on all the institutions of the Church. Without indigenization the Church always depends on outside help. . . . (Coleman 1958, 11)

In fact, the way Coleman deals with it, this is another example of the consequences of the alliance between empire and mission.

Within protestantism, this question is formulated in a different way. On the one hand, as Latourette points out, Protestant missions began during a period in which "[a] distinctive feature of the expansion of Christianity . . . was the extent to which Christian missions became an enterprise of the rank and file of the membership of the churches" (1941, 48). The missionary societies of Protestant origin were able to mobilize lay support and lay involvement in the missionary enterprise. On the other hand, in the Evangelical type of protestantism that fostered the missionary movement and nurtured it, there was an effective and consistent practice of the Protestant principle of the priesthood of all believers. The role of an ordained clergy, or a select group of people bound by special and very demanding vows, did not occupy in Protestant missions the key place it had in the Catholic case.

Indigenization was also facilitated by another key factor, which Neill describes eloquently: "The first principle of Protestant missions has been that Christians should have the Bible in their hands in their own language at the earliest possible date" (1986, 177). In Latin America, the distribution of Scripture in many cases preceded the presence of the missionary and prepared the way for it. The reading of Scripture as a requirement of entrance and continuity in the church (as well as the popular forms of Bible instruction developed as part of congregational life) gave to lay people the possibility of leadership in the local congregations and participation in mission. This was not possible at the same pace for catholicism, where the centrality of the eucharist in the life of the church always demanded the presence of clergy.

Evangelicals today consider that there is yet much to be done in relation to the training of leadership for their growing churches. Two missiologists who emphasize this need are William Taylor and Emilio Núñez, for whom the spectacular growth of pentecostalism has to be qualified:

> There are notable Pentecostal shortcomings, some of which the Pentecostals themselves acknowledge: a serious lack of trained leadership, the problem of r

growth without biblical teaching and discipleship, the tendency to center power in authoritarian leaders, artificial spirituality, lively but routine liturgy, and a spirit of legalism in the Christian life. (1989, 157)

On the other hand, Catholic observers themselves have come to acknowledge that an important reason for Evangelical and Pentecostal growth in Latin America today is their ability to mobilize the lay people for mission. Monsignor Roger Aubry, a Swiss Catholic missionary in Bolivia, observes the remarkable ability of Pentecostals to mobilize all members of their churches for the missionary task: "All converts are active members who have to promote the life of the sect and work for the conversion of people who are not converted yet" (1990, 111). Of course, he criticizes the fact that sometimes there is more a proselytistic than an evangelistic spirit. But with reference to Catholics he adds: "We must confess that among us, in spite of the serious efforts being carried on, there are few lay people actively involved in the pastoral life of their parish or their Church" (ibid., 112). It has been the genius of popular protestantism in the Third World to keep alive in their missionary practice the doctrine of the universal priesthood of the believers, which so many Christians affirm in theory.

I cannot resist the temptation to end this brief and incomplete review of history with two quotes from Ivan Illich, that forgotten iconoclast who so many times was quite right in his missiological pronouncements. By 1966 he had spent six years training hundreds of Catholic foreign missionaries assigned to Latin America, and he wrote an article that became a bomb for which he eventually was fired. Referring to the massive flow of missionaries and money that generous Catholics from the United States were sending to Latin America in the 1960s, he wrote words that today Evangelicals as well as Catholics should read carefully again:

This kind of foreign generosity has enticed the Latin American church into becoming a satellite to North Atlantic cultural phenomena and policy. . . . The Latin American Church flowers anew by returning to what the conquest stamped here: a colonial plant that blooms because of foreign cultivation. Instead of learning either how to get along with less money or close up shop, bishops are being trapped into needing more money now and bequeathing an institution impossible to run in the future.

This foreign transfusion — and the hope for more — gave ecclesiastical pusillanimity a new lease on life, another chance to make the archaic and colonial system work. If North America and Europe send enough priests to fill the vacant parishes, there is no need to consider laymen — unpaid for part-time work — to fulfill most evangelical tasks, no need to reexamine the structure of the parish, function of the priests, the Sunday obligation, and clerical sermon; no need exploring the use of the married diaconate, new forms of celebration of the and Eucharist, and intimate familial celebrations of conversion to the in the milieu of the home. The promise of more clergy is like a bewitch-
Quoted in Costello 1979, 284, 286.)

NOTES

1. I shall attempt to interpret historical processes globally, without much attention to detail (facts, names, and places). Wherever I do not indicate the sources where reference to them may be found, I am taking for granted that the data is well known. The best one-volume history of the Latin American Church is by Prien (1985).

2. "Here the term 'legend' is applied to the traditional literature that criticizes the people, history and national character of Spain, in part for cruelty in the conquest of native America, and in part for bigotry, pride, hypocrisy and other more or less undesirable attributes" (Gibson 1971, 4).

3. I have studied this briefly in *Los Evangélicos ¿Nueva leyenda negra en América Latina?* Mexico: CUPSA, 1991.

4. A good starting point can be a helpful anthology that is also a bibliographical guide about sources, H. McKennie Goodpasture (1989).

5. See also by S. Escobar, "The Significance of Popular Protestantism in Latin America: Conflict of Interpretations," in this book.

6. Meeking and Stott (1986). See also complete text in *IBMR* 10 (1), January 1986, pp. 2-21.

7. See for instance chapters 6-8 in Nell (1986). See also Latourette (1941), chs. 3 and 4.

8. Segundo has dealt with this theme in *De la sociedad a la teologia*; *Masas y minorias en la dialéctica divina de la liberación*; and *The Hidden Motives of Pastoral Action*.

9. Evangelical missiology from Latin America has been developing both a history as well as an interpretation of this development. See especially Steuernagel (1988; 1991).

10. An example of this is found in a collection of opinions from a representative sample of scholars, writers, and statesmen included in George P. Howard (1944).

11. A history written from this perspective, and limited at many points for its marxist approach, is by Jean Pierre Bastian (1990).

12. *Editor's Note:* The problem was even more critical in the Portuguese colonies. Brazil's first bishopric was created in 1551, half a century after its discovery; three additional sees were created over a century later, and three more ecclesiastical jurisdictions were added during the early part of the eighteenth century. They covered vast territories. Brazilian sees were often vacant or unattended by absentee prelates for lengthy periods. This continued until Brazil became an independent and anticlerical empire in 1821, after which the administrative apparatus of the church was strengthened. Through it all, the Catholic Church was very slow in appointing native and black men to the priesthood. Alfonso Gregory, *A Igreja no Brasil* (1965, 99-112); see also Gustavo Pérez, Alfonso Gregory, and Francois Lepargneur, *O Problema Sacerdotal no Brasil* (1964, 31-52).

PART TWO

THE DYNAMICS OF CHANGE

4

Protestant Mission and Evangelization in Latin America: An Interpretation

Guillermo Cook

"1992 may prove to be a watershed in the history of Christianity in Latin America, because virtually every segment of the Church had an opportunity to face up to the gigantic problems of the region and to clarify its understanding of mission." Guillermo Cook analyzes the theology, methodology, and tensions in the successive approaches to mission and evangelization in Latin America. This is an updated version of an article published in *Jahrbuch Mission 1992: Fokus Lateinamerika*, Evangelisches Missionswerk, Hamburg. Used with permission.

The Five Hundredth Anniversary of the beginning of Roman Catholic "evangelization" of the Americas — 1992 — was the occasion for five significant mission-related conclaves. In October, CELAM IV — the Latin American Conference of Bishops and the Pope — met in Santo Domingo to celebrate five centuries of Catholic evangelization and to promote (desperately, one supposes) a new missionary thrust called Lumen 2000. In September, base community and indigenous American Catholics and Protestants had met near Quito, Ecuador, in the "Assembly of the People of God" to ask penetrating questions about Roman Catholic praxis. Earlier, in July, a select group of grassroots Christians had met in Cochabamba, Bolivia, under the aegis of the Latin American Council of Churches (CLAI) to discuss some of the same issues.

In mid August, the Fourth Conference of Indigenous Evangelicals (CIEL IV) gathered in Otavalo, Ecuador. Immediately afterward, the Third Latin American Congress on Evangelization (CLADE III) met in Quito. Convened by the Latin American Theological Fraternity, it brought together more than one thousand Evangelical Protestants from every walk of life. The historical catalyst of all these conclaves was the five centuries of Iberian Catholic mission, and in the case of CLADE III, the two hundred years of Northern European and North American Protestant missions since William Carey (1792). Reflecting on the theme of "The Whole Gospel for All Peoples from Latin America," CLADE III challenged Evangelical protestantism in Latin America to practice *evangelización integral* [holistic evangelization].[1]

Thus virtually every segment of the Latin American Church had an opportunity to face up to the gigantic social, economic, cultural, and religious problems in Latin America and to clarify its understanding of mission theology and practice. With all that it represents, 1992 may prove to be a watershed in the history of Christianity in Latin America.

It is indeed unfortunate that Protestants are still divided on mission issues. There are perhaps five different understandings and practices of mission and evangelization within Latin American protestantism. The *traditional* evangelism of the pioneer missionaries overlaps today with *pentecostal* evangelism. Both feed into the new *crosscultural* missions approach, which is the new wave among Evangelicals. In radical discontinuity is *base community* evangelization. Each of these approaches sees itself as the faithful practitioner of the biblical witness, while in fact slighting important dimensions of the Gospel. A more *holistic* evangelization, one that is both biblically based and historically rooted in Latin America, is needed. One of the most significant aspects of CLADE III was that people representing each of these streams in Latin American protestantism were able to share their beliefs and be challenged by others without North American and Northern European intervention. Perhaps this was the reason for the virtual absence of controversy at CLADE III.

Although other chapters deal with Latin America, Protestant mission praxis today needs to be considered in the context of early Catholic mission practice. The Christendom into which protestantism thrust itself as an alien element, while monolithic and hostile, did prepare the way for latter-day evangelization.

EARLY CATHOLIC EVANGELIZATION

The evangelization that CELAM IV commemorated in Santo Domingo was not all negative nor oppressive, nor were Protestant missionaries the first to bring the Word of God to Latin America. At the very time of the "discovery" and conquest of the New World, the Spanish crown was making ecclesiastical reform an instrument of state policy. Cardinal Francisco Jiménez de Cisneros (1436-1517), Queen Isabella's confessor and later regent of Spain, also promoted the translation of the Scriptures into the vernacular (the *Poliglota Complutense*, 1520). The great Spanish mystics — Teresa de Avila, Juan de la Cruz, and Luís de León — flowered during the latter half of the sixteenth century. The friars who accompanied Columbus brought with them the vernacular Bible, along with their crusade ideology. It was not long before the Spanish Scriptures were printed in the New World. The Word of God was used in the defense of oppressed Indians (and less frequently of black slaves) by brave priests and bishops, such as Pedro de Córdoba and Antonio de Montesinos (Santo Domingo), Bartolomé de las Casas (Santo Domingo, Perú, and Guatemala), Antonio Valdivieso (Nicaragua), Pedro Claver (Colombia), Martinho de Nantes and Antônio Vieira (Brazil).

Spain was, nonetheless, fanatically intolerant. In the sixteenth century religion was an instrument of state policy, and so were the crusades against infidels and foreign ideas that threatened the hegemony of the recently forged Spanish state. This was the ideological legacy of the *Reconquista* — the centuries-long crusade against the Moors that ended in their total expulsion in 1492. That same year, Isabella and Ferdinand forced the choice of conversion, expulsion, or death upon all Spanish Jews. The flames of the Inquisition were fanned by the Reformation and Counter-Reformation. In the years following the Council of Trent (1545-1563), attempts at theological renewal and ecclesiastical reform only served to strengthen religious intolerance.[2] Protestant ideas, disseminated very early by marooned English and Dutch pirates and later by Northern European enclaves in South America and the Caribbean, threatened Spanish imperial hegemony and were ruthlessly suppressed.[3] Later, in the nineteenth century when the first Protestant missionaries arrived, Rome had only recently regained control of a Latin American Church that for over three centuries had been subservient to the monarchs of Spain and Portugal.[4] Rome was not disposed to be sympathetic to alien religious beliefs.

EARLY PROTESTANT SETTLEMENTS

The first Protestant settlers in Latin America were looking for wealth and religious freedom. At a time when Charles V ruled Spain and the Holy Roman Empire, Germans settled in a corner of Venezuela (1529-1546) and founded the port city of Maracaibo. The handful of Lutherans among them managed to convert the entire colony to their faith. French Huguenots, in search of religious freedom, established a colony briefly (1555-1567) near present-day Río de Janeiro. Both European settlements anteceded Jamestown in Virginia (1607). Dutch settlers wrested the northern reaches of Brazil from Portugal (1624-1654), where they were the first Protestants to evangelize the native inhabitants, even while they carried on a thriving African slave trade. In all three cases, the colonies were absorbed, destroyed, or pushed out by the Spanish and Portuguese. A fourth, a colony of Scots (New Caledonia) in the Panamanian jungles of Darien (1698-1700), was hounded to extinction by English pirates. Henceforth, Protestant colonizers were effectively barred from Latin America for almost two centuries.

In the nineteenth century, Protestant enclaves began to reappear with the permission of the newly independent nations, but with stringent restrictions on public manifestations of their religion. Virtually every country received them. Anglicans, Scottish Presbyterians, Welsh Baptists, and German Lutherans settled in Brazil and the Southern Cone of South America. While most ethnic enclaves were North European, a group of Waldensians came from Italy to establish a colony in Uruguay. After the Civil War (1866), disgruntled Southerners of several Protestant persuasions set up a slave-holding North American enclave (Americana) in the state of Sao Paulo, Brazil. Two decades earlier, a colony of southern U.S. blacks had been imported to the Dominican Republic by the Haitian ruler to work on the sugar plantations. With the exception of the forthrightly missionary Moravians (Caribbean coast of Nicaragua and Honduras, 1848 until today), there is little evidence that these enclaves undertook to evangelize the general populace, even after Protestants had gained a greater measure of religious freedom. The main contribution of the British and German ethnic colonies were the schools for their children, which the children of the ruling elite were also allowed to attend (Deiros 1992, 588-608, 617-638).

TRADITIONAL EVANGELISM

I have chosen to use "traditional" evangelism to describe the early missionary efforts of the "historical" or "mainline"[5] U.S., British, and other European Protestant denominations — Presbyterian, Methodist, Anglican, Congregationalist, and Baptist. The term "traditional" is not used pejoratively, but rather as an indication that their mission practice was rooted in church traditions of several centuries. Further, the core Christian doctrines that these churches shared became largely the tradition for mission in Latin America until today. Non-denominational mission boards that arrived later in Latin America owe much of their church polity, and certainly a considerable amount of their financial support, to the established churches.

The origins of traditional evangelism hark back to the eighteenth-century Evangelical Awakening in Britain and parts of the Continent. The Great Awakening in the nineteenth century propelled U.S. missionaries to Latin America.[6] They were fired by a zeal to convert Roman Catholics who were bound to a religious system that they deemed to be oppressive and idolatrous.

The early Protestant missionary effort involved several kinds of approaches by a variety of mission protagonists. A few of the missionaries maintained, initially, an open mind regarding the possibility of reforming the national Catholic churches from within. In several countries, the first Protestant evangelization focused upon the ruling elite with schools as the main tool. During the same period enterprising "colporteurs" distributed the Scriptures in key cities and rural areas throughout Latin America.[7] In this way, protestantism sowed the first seeds of grassroots democracy in the region. It was not long until Protestant missionaries were moving into the hinterlands and "planting" small congregations of believers.[8]

The arrival of protestantism in these lands was not generally opposed by the newly independent governments. In Guatemala and Brazil the first Protestant missionaries came at the invitation of chiefs of state. They hoped that protestantism might serve to weaken the power of the Roman Church in their lands, even as it brought to the ruling elite the intellectual and material benefits of Northern Europe and America.

Another kind of missionary thrust from the United States and Britain are the "faith" missions.[9] In early years, the personnel of these societies came from a segment of the historical churches that was dissatisfied with the waning of "missionary passion" in their denominational boards. More recent sources are independent churches in the United States. Initially, these societies were more active in Africa and Asia than in Latin America. But after World War II and the advent of nationalism and Communism in Asia, the energies of evicted mission societies turned to Latin America. They were characterized by a strong antipathy toward Roman Catholicism and fear of Communism, to which they attributed the anti-Americanism and the discontent of the masses of Latin America.[10] The anti-Communist crusade became the dominant characteristic of the most recent wave of North American Protestants, the so-called "sects," during the 1980s. We shall return to them when we consider Pentecostal evangelism.

The theology of traditional evangelism is, because of the different church traditions involved, difficult to place into a neat box. Nonetheless, the following elements do appear, with varying emphasis: (1) Obedience to the Great Commission (Mt. 28: 16-20). (2) Responsibility to rescue unbelievers from eternal hell. (3) Hastening the return of Christ; this concomitant of premillennial eschatology was often mentioned as *the* driving force of mission, particularly for many North American missionaries. (4) Undergirding these doctrinal concerns was the subliminal desire to spread the benefits of "enlightened" U.S. and North European societies among the unenlightened heathen of Roman Catholic America and, to some extent, to carry the flag of the country of origin.

The practice of traditional evangelism was usually characterized by personal witness, the free distribution of gospel pamphlets, and by public preaching, whether in the church sanctuary or on city street corners. The goal was "church planting," and thousands of local congregations were indeed established, principally in medium-sized cities and small towns throughout Latin America. In the 1950s, 1960s, and 1970s, specialized organizations from the United States introduced a variety of methods of personal evangelism and one-to-one discipling. During the same period, mass "evangelistic crusades" were very much in vogue. While the strategies, direction, and financing came from the North, the personnel was usually Latin American.

The crisis of traditional evangelism came to a head in the 1960s. Kenneth Strachan, of the evangelistically-oriented Latin American Mission, questioned the churches' reliance upon mass crusades. He proposed a methodology that would involve the totality of the churches' resources. It was expressed in the following "theorem:" "The expansion of any movement is in direct proportion to its success in mobilizing its total membership in continuous propagation of its beliefs" (Strachan 1968, 108). Under the leadership of Strachan's Latin American disciples, the Evangelism-in-Depth program spread year by year to a total of ten Latin American countries until its impetus died out in the mid 1970s (the methodology was also picked up in Africa, Japan, and a number of nations worldwide). North American mission agencies co-opted what had originally been a Latin American movement, dubbing the methodology "saturation evangelism" (Peters 1970). It was superseded by church "growth principles" and methodology, which came into vogue via the Institute of Church Growth, which is related to the School of World Mission, Fuller Theological Seminary, of Pasadena, CA. Mass evangelism experienced a resurgence on an even greater scale during the 1980s, with the help of new Latin American "evangelistic associations," which for the most part set up

Luis Palau

their administrative and financial base in the United States. Large evangelistic "crusades" are in decline in the 1990s, partly because of their low cost efficiency in terms of numerical church growth. In order to survive, evangelistic associations have found it necessary to diversify into radio ministries, publishing, family counseling, and evangelism of the leadership elite. A notable exception to this trend is Presbyterian evangelist Caio Fabio de Araujo, who also presides over an influential national association of Protestant churches and agencies. VINDE, his Brazil-based evangelistic association, is church oriented, even while it addresses social and political issues in his country.

PENTECOSTAL EVANGELISM

Origins of Pentecostal evangelism. Pentecostalism was born in Brazil, Chile, and Argentina very early in this century, almost at the same time as the Pentecostal awakenings in Europe and the United States. Despite the Swedish, Italian, and North American origins of the founders, these were very much Latin American awakenings (Hollenweger 1972, 63-66,75-110; Wagner 1973 15-27). Pentecostal evangelism was at first carried out at the local level by missionaries and national workers. During the decade of the 1940s, T.L. Osborne, a healing evangelist from the U.S., propelled the Pentecostals into the limelight in several Latin American countries. In 1952, evangelist Tommy Hicks went to Argentina (Wagner, 18-22). Home-grown evangelists such as Carlos Annacondia of Argentina made the headlines in the 1960s. During the next decade and until the present, Puerto Rican healing evangelist Gige Avila came to the fore. He was perhaps best known, at first, for his public smashing of jewelry and television sets and other symbols of sinful modernity. He went on to become a friend and confidant of Commander Daniel Ortega of Nicaragua. The voices of home-grown Pentecostal evangelists were, for a time, all but drowned out by the cacophony of the "electronic church," with its dubbed programs from North America. The decline of electronic religion after the notorious scandals brought Latin American Pentecostal preachers once more into the spotlight, men such as Caio Fabio in Brazil (see above) and Omar Cabrera in Argentina, whose movement "Vision del Futuro" claims a following of thousands.

The theology of Pentecostal evangelism is, of course, based upon the doctrine of the baptism of the Holy Spirit. The Third Person of the Trinity empowers the evangelist to heal and the everyday Christian to witness to the miracles that have occurred in his life and body. This theology is not without its contradictions. Curiously, Latin American Pentecostals favor the Schofield Bible with its dispensational and premillennialist notes, despite the fact that they relegate miraculous manifestations entirely to the early Church. Evangelistic practice aside, it is "the baptism" (usually with tongues and other physical manifestations), and not evangelistic witness as such, which is the primary evidence of Spirit filling. Pentecostal theology was at one time monolithically fundamentalistic and other-worldly, but this is beginning to change as it grows numerically and moves up socially.

Grassroots pentecostalism needs to be distinguished from the "health and wealth . . . name it and claim it" stream of the Charismatic or Neo-Pentecostal Renewal, which has appealed to a growing number of converts from the beleaguered middle class in Latin America. It is also distinct from "Kingdom Theology," the Neo-Pentecostal variety of Old Testament Reconstructionism. This neo-Calvinist heresy looks to Abraham Kuyper for political inspiration and to the Old Testament Law (Theonomy) for its theological rationale. Both ideologies, at times in tandem, exert considerable influence upon middle-class Neo-Pentecostals who worship in non-denominational megachurches.

Pentecostal practice. Pentecostalism has grown in large measure due to the spontaneous witness of its adepts among peoples from the lower strata of Latin American society. Traditional churches, while at first hostile to the movement, have gradually assimilated the liveliness of Pentecostal services. Whatever the official theology, a growing number of the active membership of traditional churches has assimilated Pentecostal beliefs. This has contributed to the growth of these churches as well. How much of this growth is the result of genuine evangelism and how much is the result of proselytism is difficult to ascertain because very few accurate records are kept. One suspects considerable superficiality as well.

The significant growth of Pentecostal protestantism and its causes, pro and con, have recently become the subject matter of much learned research. The focus of the critics is usually upon the invasion of sects during the latter half of the 1980s, as a result of wars and natural catastrophes. The importance of the sects should not, however, be exaggerated. By using self-serving or ideological (rather than theological) criteria, official Roman Catholic and leftist propaganda have both been guilty of irresponsible use of the term "sect." The tendency of the Vatican is to label as sect any group or movement that seeks to gain converts from Catholicism — self-admittedly in dire need of re-evangelization. But not all Evangelical missions and denominations are insensitively proselytistic, nor obsessively anti-Communist. Only a very few have been demonstrated to be tools of U.S. foreign policy. In the words of a respected researcher who has not been known for his sympathies to protestantism:

> Just as religion should not be reduced to a playing field for contending political forces, evangelical Protestantism should not be reduced to a political instrument for dominant interests. . . . Under the influence of Catholic and Marxist thinking, many observers have come to assume that evangelical religion has easily predictable political implications. [Protestantism is more probably] a generator of social change whose direction is not predestined. . . . Blaming evangelical growth on the United States suggests a deep distrust of the poor, an unwillingness to accept the possibility that they could turn an imported religion to their own purposes. (Stoll 1990, xvi)

The evolution of Pentecostal evangelism. Where pentecostalism was once accused of being otherworldly, it has begun to show surprising signs of social and political involvement. Middle-class and upwardly mobile Neo-Pentecostals have become involved in party politics, hoping to bring change to their nations. To a significant degree, pentecostalism and neo-pentecostalism have provided the impetus for numerous grassroots evangelism and mission-oriented organizations. They specialize in cross-cultural missions, as well as in witness to athletes, drug addicts, artists, street kids, homeless children, prostitutes, and many other people who are in need. People's needs have come to be seen not only as individual and spiritual, but also as social and political. This is particularly the case with indigenous (in contrast with foreign-dependent) Pentecostals who are closer to the grass roots. On a continent where systemic ills can no longer be ignored nor explained away — where even dedicated practitioners of the Protestant ethic are being impoverished — political awareness is on the rise. And social evangelism is gradually becoming a vital part of the Pentecostal arsenal.

Surprisingly, what liberation consciousness-raising could not bring about, the overlapping surges of pentecostalism and of poverty may be accomplishing. As Pentecostals and other impoverished believers attempt to understand their own plight, and as more fortunate and enlightened Christians stand beside them, their political awareness increases. The exposure of second- and third-generation Pentecostals to higher education, both religious and secular, is another influential factor. Some indigenous Pentecostals, aided by their own capable theologians and sociologists, are coming to grips with the causes of systemic evil. Meanwhile, more affluent Pentecostals and Neo-Pentecostals are the outstanding protagonists in cross-cultural missions.

CROSS-CULTURAL MISSIONS

During the decade of the 1980s, Protestant evangelization has added a new dimension: mission to the four corners of the world.

The origins of the movement. The ecumenical movement came to the definition of "world mission" in Mexico City in the 1960s. Inspired by the example of their parent churches, in the 1970s traditional Latin American churches here and there founded their own societies and sent missionaries to neighboring countries, as well as to expatriates in the "First World." Prior to 1967, however, "foreign missions" were virtually the exclusive preserve of the so-called First World — at least as far as Protestant Fundamentalists are concerned. The change is attributed to the Berlin Congress on Evangelization. This large gathering has been called "the beginning of a revival of a sense of urgency regarding evangelization among evangelicals worldwide," because it spotlighted the responsibility of the worldwide church. Too optimistically it was called "the end of Western missions and the beginning of Third World Missions."

The Lausanne Congress on World Evangelization (1974) gave a further impetus to cross-cultural missions. It "provided the incentive to deepen a sense of responsibility for worldwide evangelization" and to clarify its direction. The Lausanne Congress produced a Covenant that has been widely accepted by Evangelical Protestants as the theological foundation of the modern missionary movement, even while they ignore its appeal for social involvement. Fundamentalists are wary of the mission holism espoused by this Lausanne congress. They claim that because of it "traditional evangelism in the Western churches was not popular and almost died out, except in the then small separatist movements and churches" (Johnstone 1978, 12, 73, 175, 176). This is a historically inaccurate and highly ethnocentric view of recent mission history. It is also theologically inadequate.[11]

The absence of theological reflection often produces a univocal, dogmatic, arrogant, and impositional kind of witness to the grace of God in Jesus Christ. It is to this kind of mission practice that I am addressing myself at the moment. Alternative mission awareness will be dealt with in the closing section.

The theology of cross-cultural missions. The passion and the drive of those who today participate in cross-cultural evangelism are admirable. But the movement's greatest weakness is its lack of theological depth. The focus is largely methodological, seeking to extract patterns and strategies from the New Testament and church history. While instructive, patterns can also obscure the complexities of mission[12] and strategies can be simplistic and overly optimistic. The most popular mission textbooks reflect this same paucity of theological depth (cp. Pate 1987). Beginning from certain methodological givens, cross-cultural mission theoreticians make sweeping generalizations concerning church growth and expansion across cultural and geographical barriers (McGavran 1970, 13-63); a promising first step in a church growth theology of mission was taken by Alexander Tippett (Tippett 1970). The favored analytical tool is cultural anthropology with a functionalist approach. Little is made of the conflictive nature of social relationships, which has strong biblical support. Cross-cultural missions need to reflect more seriously on the great mission themes of Scripture — Creation, Salvation history, the Kingdom of God — in the light of the broad sweep of history.

The practice of cross-cultural mission can be studied from two directions. Starting from the top, mission is defined by the technocrats and theoreticians who train First-World missionary strategists, who with their Asian, African, or Latin American disciples pass on the vision and the urgency of the task to young people in the growing churches on these continents. It becomes their responsibility to try out the strategies and see if they in fact work. Large mission enterprises and training centers place a heavy emphasis upon strategies for world evangelization. The Missions Advanced Research Corporation (MARC), a division of World Vision International, offers the resources of its growing data bank on "unreached peoples" (Dayton and Fraser 1980, 537). Along with MARC, the Lausanne Congress on World Evangelization spotlighted several new technological resources for world evangelization. Church growth spokespersons from the Fuller School of World Mission made major presentations at Lausanne. Two later went on to spearhead movements that represent separate strands in the thinking of D.A. McGavran, the founder of the church growth movement.[13]

Peter Wagner has turned from an early interest in Latin America, where he taught for several years, to a concern for the growth of churches in the United States. Concerned that Evangelical mission interest is overlooking the millions of "unreached peoples," Ralph Winter in turn founded the California-based U.S. Center for World Missions. It is a conglomerate of semi-autonomous church-related and independent mission agencies, a missions think-tank, and a university training center. Winter's disciples can be found throughout Latin America. Missiology is becoming an accepted part of the curriculum of Bible institutes and theological seminaries, not to mention the specialized mission institutes that are springing up across Latin America.

Cross-cultural missions must also be seen from the level of local initiative. The result of the new emphasis on cross-cultural evangelism has produced a number of mission agencies with Latin American roots. In 1980, Lawrence Keyes of Overseas Crusades documented the activities of 462 Third World mission agencies — up 81 percent from a 1972 study (1983 55-62ff.). While this information is admittedly incomplete, Latin America has clearly lagged behind other regions of the Third World both in number of home-grown agencies and missionaries. This has been a cause for concern on the part of cross-cultural mission advocates. Many were shocked to learn that "only 7 percent of the non-Western missionary force is sent from the churches of Latin America. Even though one of every four non-Western Christians is Latin American, they send only one of every fourteen non-Western missionaries." In 1985, Keyes called for a new emphasis upon missions in Latin America. Accordingly, in late 1987, the first Congreso Misionero Ibero-Americano (COMIBAM) was convened in Sao Paulo, Brazil. "COMIBAM had the intention of being more of a process than an event, geared to heighten the awareness of the churches, the sharing of information, and the formation of missionary structures" (Phillips and Coote 1993, 131). Bringing together a large number of mission enthusiasts from all over Latin America, COMIBAM provided a significant impetus to cross-cultural missions in this part of the world. By then, several new mission agencies had appeared on the Latin American Protestant scene.[14]

> However, missiologist Samuel Escobar comments that "the meeting expressed a great amount of enthusiasm for the missionary task. Yet it failed to grapple with basic concepts in the understanding of mission including both the blatant reality of poverty that surrounded the very place where the delegates met, and the structures of mission at a time of crisis for traditional Latin American structures. Probably because of the North American model on which the conference was patterned, its observers missed a note of realism. (Ibid., pp. 130, 131)

All of this activity in the 1980s produced a fairly large number of young and enthusiastic Latin Americans who left their homes to take the gospel to distant lands — to proud Spain and Portuguese-speaking Africa, to Amazonian tribes, and even to the tribal peoples of Kenya. With five hundred years of Moorish influence prior to 1492 and their mixed Amerindian and African blood, Latin Americans, so the reasoning goes, may be better suited to evangelize Muslims and other dark-skinned peoples. With this in mind, dedicated young mission candidates work hard at learning Arabic and at studying Islamic religion and culture.

Crisis in cross-cultural missions? This missionary movement has relied perhaps too much on exogenous models that are out of touch with sociocultural realities and church practice. One example is illustrative. The "faith promise principle" is the financial mainstay of independent missionary societies in the United States. Independent congregations, along with a number of mainline churches, motivate their members to pledge specific sums, however small, to their yearly mission budgets. Funds can be designated "by faith" for individuals and for projects. On the basis of these promises, the churches will budget specific amounts for preselected missionaries and their societies, which usually are independent mission boards or specialized agencies. In North America, the Calvinist ethic ensures that the pledges will be fulfilled unless a crisis occurs, thus missionaries can count on steady support. This is not so in Latin America, where the enthusiasm can easily shift from one cause or person to another, to the detriment of the unfortunate cross-cultural missionary. As a result, large numbers of disillusioned Latin American missionaries began returning to their home bases.

The problem is compounded by inadequate theological and sociological training, which ill-prepares the missionary to meet the challenges of a new environment. The COMIBAM movement is presently having to reevaluate its missionary strategy. Belatedly, the leaders of the movement are beginning to realize the need for greater theological reflection, as well as social awareness. It may have been this awareness of need that made it possible for cross-cultural mission enthusiasts and social activists to listen to each other in the CLADE III Congress on Evangelization. One hopes that the commendable zeal for witness across frontiers that the COMIBAM movement demonstrated will not be lost while the leaders of the movement become more aware of the social and structural dimensions of the gospel.

COUNTERCULTURAL MISSION

We come now to an entirely different phenomenon in the Latin American protestantism: the mission of alternative ecclesial communities in resistance to the dominant culture. It is the response of a small but significant sector of Latin American protestantism to the social ecclesial crisis in the region. The movement does not have a well-defined institutional identity, but is spread throughout many of the Protestant denominations. In certain contexts of institutional and revolutionary violence, the movement draws its inspiration from the better-known Catholic Base Ecclesial Communities (BECs), while maintaining its own identity.

The origins of the movement are complex. Reacting against a hierarchical structure that centered upon the parish and diocese, small groups of grassroots Catholics began to meet together for prayer and Bible study. For the majority, the focus of their reflection was the poverty and institutionalized injustice in which 80 percent of Latin Americans are living. The movement spread until there were countless thousands of these groups throughout Latin America. Their text was Scripture and their context the oppressive and seemingly hopeless reality that engulfed them. This "new way" of understanding their environment led to a new perception of the Bible, to a new way of being the church, and to a radically new mission practice (Cook 1985, 89-107).

Meanwhile, as protestantism has increased numerically and the economic crisis has deepened in Latin America, a growing number of Protestants are becoming impoverished. Because of this, an indeterminate number of Protestant believers are looking for alternative forms of church life and witness. When this has taken the form of passive resistance, the groups have been forced to go into hiding. With noteworthy exceptions, their parent churches have not come to their defense. Elsewhere, small groups of socially aware and relatively affluent Protestants gather in "house churches" for worship, Bible study, mutual encouragement, and solidarity with the poor.

The theology of the countercultural communities does have, at some points, affinities with Catholic Liberation Theology. This is tempered with the doctrinal emphases that are peculiar to the various Protestant groups. Indeed, while the Catholic base communities have learned their methodology from the liberationists, they in turn seem to have drawn liberation theology closer to the Bible. And the BECs may have made discussion-oriented Protestant grassroots communities more ecclesial by pointing the way to a more vital liturgical experience. The mission emphasis of these communities is evidenced in two ways. It is *denunciation* of the bad news of social oppression. It is also *announcement* of the Good News through the Word prophetically proclaimed and the Holy Communion celebrated, as well as by the living witness of the community in an unjust world.

The practice of the countercultural churches is in response to concrete and specific issues that have to do with the totality of the lives of the larger community. In contexts such as Guatemala and El Salvador, grassroots community practice has required both overt actions in defense of human rights and clandestine resistance to the indignities of an unjust social order. Because they share their faith in a very low key, many alternative communities are accused by more conservative Protestants of a lack of evangelistic concern. Others combine oldfashioned evangelism with radical involvement in the defense of the rights of their fellow Christians.

The crisis of countercultural communities. On the Catholic side, there is evidence that the BECs have entered into a period of transition, if not crisis. The reasons are both ecclesiastical — conservative Vatican policies, which have weakened the position of the BECs — and geopolitical — the demise of socialist idealism. Recent evidence suggests that a significant number of BEC cadres are converting to grassroots pentecostalism (CEDI 1990). Protestant countercultural communities have also been discouraged by world events. For some, it is a time for turning back to their Evangelical roots, while others continue to search for viable sociopolitical alternatives.

HOLISM IN MISSION

What are we to make of the Protestant scene in Latin America? Do the disparate movements such as cross-cultural and countercultural mission have any chance of understanding each other? The organizers of the Third Latin American Congress on Evangelization (CLADE III), who represented every one of the movements we have described, hoped that meaningful and productive dialogue might come about. Faithfulness to our Lord and deep concern for the social crisis of Latin America demanded it.

The origins of holistic evangelism in Latin America can be found in the Lausanne Covenant to which, for the most part, conservative evangelicals pay lip service. The Latin American Theological Fraternity (FTL) and World Vision International have been foremost in promoting this document and publicizing it in Latin America.

The theology of holism has been developed in Latin America particularly by the FTL, which convened CLADE III.[15] A significant portion of the FTL's early theologizing came about in reaction to excesses in the movements reviewed in the first part of this article. Peruvian theologian Samuel Escobar commented that:

> The amazing reality of a massive Third World presence at Lausanne was a confirmation that, in spite of the profound changes of the past 50 years of world history, God has been calling unto himself a people with whom he is building his church in the remotest corners of this globe, even though it may be under persecution and thorough suffering. (Escobar 1976, 258)

Nonetheless, Escobar, a founder and former president of the FTL, critiques the theological underpinnings of this new focus on worldwide missions. He is critical of the cult of efficiency that measures evangelistic success solely in quantitative terms. He points out the error of the Dispensationalist doctrine that correlates the number of persons entering church with an acceleration of our Lord's return. Many British and European Evangelicals, he points out, provide ample proof of the fallacy of this position. Though not premillennial, they have tremendous missionary zeal. The criteria of efficiency is foreign to a biblical view of humankind and of history. Escobar continues:

> Although the N.T. church had a living hope and expectation of the Lord's return, we do not see any evidence that their missionary activity had as an aim the 'acceleration' of that return. Rather, their action grew out of their conviction of the truth and their resultant joy and faithfulness; it was activated by the Spirit working through his Word and his ministers. (Escobar 1976, 262-263)

Missiologist Orlando Costas quotes Emilio Castro of the WCC: "We have seen the end of one missionary era; we are beginning a new one in which the idea of world mission will be fundamental." Costas goes on to ask whether "An unevangelized world, caught up in a process of political, social, economic, and cultural awakening can be effectively evangelized by a church that is not indigenous?" (Costas 1974, 145, 162). René Padilla (until recently the FTL General Secretary) and Guillermo Cook have increasingly pointed to the grassroots movements within as possible models for Evangelical Mission.

Holistic evangelization. The term "holism" is either shunned by Evangelicals in Latin America as being akin to Liberation Theology, or adopted superficially by well-intentioned Christians who have not reflected sufficiently upon its implications. There are, however, churches that are practicing it, without necessarily using the term. In fact, not a few of the Protestant movements that are so lionized by theologically liberal churches in Europe and the United States are, in point of fact, thoroughly evangelical in doctrine, though perhaps not their evangelistic methodology. They are also risking life and limb in the defense of their fellow human beings in oppressive societies.[16]

The CLADE III Congress demonstrated that a holistic approach to mission and evangelization is on the rise in Latin America. Surprisingly, witness to the entire needs of persons and of society is being practiced and espoused by theologically conservative churches. Some of the most outspoken critics of structural injustice are Pentecostals. As we move into the next century, the question that is uppermost in the minds of many of us is whether the Protestant Churches will rise to the task and become prophets and missionaries in and from Latin America to the entire world.

NOTES

1. "Holistic evangelization" and "holism" (from the Greek *holos* = whole) in the briefest of terms refers to a full-orbed gospel based on the witness of Scripture. It implies the proclamation and practice of the Good News of salvation as both personal and corporate redemption and transformation because of the death, resurrection, and universal sovereignty of Jesus Christ. It demands individual repentance and faith as well as personal and ecclesial commitment to the mission of God in society and the whole of creation.

2. Two French reform movements attracted liberal Catholics in the eighteenth century. *Jansenism* (from Jansen, bishop of Ypres) was a radically Augustinian response to both the Reformation and the Counter-Reformation. *Gallicanism* tried, unsuccessfully, to make the French Church independent from Rome. These ideas proved more successful in the Portuguese-Brazilian empire where, for a decade (1760-1770), for reasons of state, the Church maintained its independence from Rome. In the nineteenth century, *Ultramontanist* clergy worked successfully in Europe and Latin America to return full ecclesiastical authority to the pope in Rome — beyond the Alps (*ultramontanus*).

3. The Inquisition did not have such an important role in the Portuguese colonies as it did in Spanish America, although heretics, Jews, and Protestants were persecuted and harassed.

4. At about the time that the Iberian colonies were becoming independent, Rome was able to impose a highly centralized and hierarchical church structure after centuries of *Regalism,* during which ecclesiastical authority was vested in the Spanish and Portuguese kings.

5. To call only these churches "historical" would be at least to question the historical validity of subsequent church-related mission efforts. "Mainline" is a term used mostly in North America and implies, pejoratively, a certain elitism.

6. The Wesleyan revival was at the heart of the Evangelical Awakening and carried over into the Great Awakening in North America. The Dutch pietist The-

odorus Frelinghuysen, the Presbyterian Charles Finney, and the frontier camp meetings were important catalysts in this movement.

7. James Thompson and Luke Mathews, from the British Bible Society, and Francisco Penzotti, and Daniel P. Kidder (Brazil), from the American Bible Society.

8. Presbyterians such as Ashbel G. Simonton (Brazil) and Edward Haymaker (Guatemala), Methodists such as William Taylor (Ecuador and Chile), an Anglican of the caliber of Alan Gardiner (Chile), and Baptists such as Frederick Crowe (Guatemala) grace the pages of early Protestant mission. There were also freelance pioneers such as Dr. Robert Reid Kalley, the first missionary to arrive in Brazil, from Scotland, after working in Madeira. He founded the first Portuguese-speaking Protestant congregation in Rio de Janeiro, which in time became part of the Congregationalist Church in Brazil. Latin Americans were also among the early Protestant pioneers. Persons such as Enrique Someillán, Aurelio Silveira, and Evaristo Collazo (Cuba), José Manoel da Conceição (Brazil), and Antonio Baudillo Hernández (Puerto Rico) either came from the United States or were the first converts of early missionaries. They risked their reputations and at times their lives to evangelize their fellow countrymen (Deiros *passim*).

9. The Central American Mission, the Bolivian Indian Mission, the Evangelical Union of South America, and the Latin America Mission were among the most active until the 1960s and 1970s.

10. Anti-communist attitudes actually appeared as early as the 1920s. But notable exceptions to this trend were Presbyterian missionary Edward Haymaker and Independent missionaries Susan and Harry Strachan (founders of the evangelistically-oriented Latin America Mission and of the Seminario Bíblico of Costa Rica). They argued against U.S. intervention in Nicaragua, and discounted the "Bolshevist" influence in Mexico, pointing instead to what we would call today North-South tensions (EMQ 1979, 170-174; Spykman et al. 1988, 217, 218).

11. See the comment by S. Escobar in the last section: "Holism in Mission."

12. See the "four phases of mission" (Keyes 1983, 3-9, 68-69) and the technical formulas in Douglas (1975, 225).

13. Cp. McGavran (1970).

14. E.g. the Asociación Misionera para la Evangelización Nacional (AMEN) in Perú, the Federation of Costa Rican Missions (FEDEMEC), and the Missao Antioquia of Sao Paulo, Brazil.

15. Born in the heat of debate over the meaning of evangelization during the First CLADE Conference (Bogotá, Colombia, October 1969), the FTL brings together a broad spectrum of Evangelicals. The writings of Samuel Escobar, René Padilla, Orlando Costas, and Guillermo Cook, among others, have become widely disseminated. Others have had their works published in Spanish and Portuguese. Other authors are Rubén (Tito) Paredes (an anthropologist and the new FTL General Secretary), Emilio A. Nuñez, José Miguel, Stella de Angulo (a Colombian medical doctor), and expatriate Estuardo McIntosh.

16. Such is the case with Lutheran Bishop Medardo Gómez of El Salvador. He is a living demonstration of holism in mission.

5

Five Waves of Protestant Evangelization

Mike Berg and Paul Pretiz

"The heart burden of the poor is poured out with tears and shouts." Two veterans of the Latin America Mission, an independent "faith" mission, tell the story of the five waves of Protestant missions and suggest a dozen reasons why Evangelical churches are growing. This is an authorized summary of several chapters from *The Gospel People* (Monrovia, CA: MARC/World Vision, Int., and Miami: Latin America Mission, 1992) by the same authors.

PROLOGUE

The casket wobbled and nearly slipped off the shoulders of the four brothers as they stumbled to the burial site. Women gasped and frantic hands reached out to steady their burden as it was lowered and slid into a niche. A mason sealed the opening with brick and mortar, the clinking of his trowel adding a final note. The pallbearers' aged father had finally come to rest.

Mario, the oldest of the brothers, was not drunk. A strong, rough-hewn man, he sweated out his livelihood swinging his *machete* to cut the lawns of the rich. Although he owned a tiny house on the edge of the fast-growing city, it was at the bottom of the hill, often flooded by the adjacent stream. Until recently, his drinking habit had worked against keeping food on the family table.

Painfully aware of his shortcomings as a husband and father, Mario had begun attending a gospel service in Antonio's house down the street. There, one night, he interrupted the preacher by standing up in the middle of the sermon to declare: "If anyone needs to accept Christ, it's me!"

Antonio was fortunate. He had a steady job. An Evangelical Christian, he had turned half of his scrap-lumber house into a meeting place by crowding his children's beds into the tiny living area. The "chapel" was furnished with backless benches and illuminated by a single bare light dangling from the ceiling.

Despite the humble meeting place, Antonio's guitar music and simple messages touched the lives of his neighbors who dropped in. A church was born.

56

The gospel also touched Mario's family. His wife, who added to the family income by working as a maid, also accepted Christ. And his son, Francisco, did, too. Barely literate, he followed his father's footsteps as a gardener. But another son spent half his years in a reformatory and one daughter became a teenage single mother.

But Ana María, another daughter, was a pretty teenager who committed her life to Christ in Antonio's house and stood firm in an environment where only God could keep her safe. She smilingly took charge of her younger siblings, taught in Sunday School, and was often first to speak when testimonies were called for.

"I want to serve God more than anything else," she told a missionary friend. But hopes failed when she had to drop out of school to become a maid. The job turned out to be a classic case of exploitation. At one crisis she called her spiritual mentor. The missionary had an idea.

"If you're quitting, here's your chance to go to Bible School," she suggested.

"But how could I possibly pay for that?"

"God has his ways. Look, if God wants you to quit, we can leave this afternoon and visit the school. We'll see if they accept you."

That afternoon they drove to the coast. The ocean, though only 85 miles away, opened up a new vista for Ana María. They watched the sun set as they crossed the bay on a rusty ferry. The next day they stopped to look at the school and a month later she checked in.

From out of the mire at the bottom of Latin America's society, God caused another flower to bloom.

The story does not end here. It concludes in the epilogue.

PROTESTANTS AND MODERNIZATION:
THE FIRST WAVE

In the early nineteenth century Latin American liberals began to see in northern Europe a model for Latin America. These Latin intellectuals would be the free-enterprise capitalists of today, hardly liberal by current definitions. But they advocated free trade, in contrast to the existing monopolistic economic patterns. And as "radical" liberals they pressed for secular government schools, instead of the church-controlled education of the colonial era. As the liberals came into power now and again, they encouraged immigration from the advanced countries of the North to modernize Latin America.

Welcoming these hardworking foreigners with their technology meant allowing them the right to practice their religion. The British established their Anglican churches and the Germans their Lutheran schools. Reluctantly, the door of religious freedom edged open. Though barely a ripple, these churches comprised the first wave of Protestant advance into Latin America.

An old "Cemetery for Foreigners" in many Latin American cities reminds us that even in death the Latin Americans held these Protestant immigrants at a distance. The sacred soil of the cemeteries blessed by the Catholic Church was not available to heretics; theirs was the Potter's Field.

In life, too, many immigrants kept apart from local society. Maps of many large Latin cities today still identify the locations of the Syrian Club, the British School, and the German Lutheran church where a shrill pipe organ plays Bach and the pastor (imported from Europe) attends to the German community. Today, Americans of the mainline denominations, rather than establishing separate English-speaking denominations, worship together with other expatriates in "Union Churches" or "Metropolitan Chapels" in every large city. In many cases these "chaplaincy" ministries to the foreign communities were the first permanent Protestant witness in a country.

PROTESTANT WORK ETHIC AND ENGLISH CLASSES:
THE SECOND WAVE

Meanwhile, the Latin Americans with liberal political and economic views, many of them Freemasons, went farther in their zeal for development. They suggested that even Protestant missionaries might be good for their countries. Such missionaries could introduce their schools, plus their Protestant values of hard work and a disciplined life. One suspects this might also have been a move to give the priests something to think about — at least a counterforce to check the power of the bishops. President Justo Rufino Barrios of Guatemala personally escorted the first Protestant missionary into the country in 1882, on his return by ship from a trip to the United States.

In the cities European-style Protestant chapels were often erected. These Gothic jewels contrasted with the surrounding architecture. Some have long since disappeared, like Panama's Malecón [Seawall] Methodist Church, built on a pier over the harbor. Some have been relocated. But in many cities these century-old monuments with their varnished pews and commemorative plaques bear testimony to the pioneer missionaries who constructed them, and who were the precursors of the second wave of Protestant advance — the coming of the historical denominations. Except for missionaries who entered Argentina, Brazil, and Uruguay earlier, this wave washed Latin America's shores in the second half of the nineteenth century.

An understanding among the denominations ("comity" agreements) assigned, for example, the Presbyterians to Colombia and the Baptists to El Salvador. Larger countries were partitioned to accommodate various denominations.

Liberal-minded Latin Americans wanted progressive schools, free from the catechisms and rigid educational methods of the Catholic-dominated institutions. They promised to send their children to such schools if missionaries established them. So, in addition to the missionaries' own concern for the educational needs of the countries, mission schools seemed to be an appropriate means to reach the people.

The reputation of the schools grew as they expanded, some of them in Cuba and Brazil becoming universities. Missionaries found themselves caught up in the educational and administrative process. Local teachers, often non-Evangelicals, had to be employed to meet government requirements — only local citizens could teach the country's history — and to fill the needs of an expanding curriculum. There just were not enough missionaries to go around.

A growing middle class was delighted to find a bilingual school or at least one with a good dose of English and with North American teachers. Evangelical parents balked at sending children to public schools where for religion classes attendance at mass was obligatory.

While mission schools helped meet the tremendous educational needs of Latin America, relatively few of the new believers in the churches entered as a result of the schools. Thousands of graduates, however, became *simpatizantes* [friendly toward the gospel].

But as some of the parent mainline denominations in the United States began to suffer the inroads of theological liberalism, parts of the work in Latin America began to slow down. In many a major city the old downtown "First" church lost its fire.

Sometimes the Latin American daughter churches of the mainline groups continued to be evangelistic while the North American parent denomination was becoming liberal. This caused some zealous Latin American daughter churches simply to fall out of step with the parent denomination, and the ties between the two were broken.

GOSPEL TRACTS AND STOREFRONT CHAPELS: THE THIRD WAVE

A new wave of men and women coming ashore in Latin America represented the "faith missions." With a loss of confidence by many in the theology of the mainline denominations and their respective missions, thousands of more conservative Christians found a vehicle for their missionary outreach in such interdenominational societies as CAM International (originally the Central America Mission, founded by C.I. Scofield of the dispensational Scofield Bible) or TEAM (The Evangelical Alliance Mission). The first CAM couple went to Central America in 1891. A greater number of "faith missionaries" arrived when the modernist–fundamentalist controversy peaked in the 1920s and the 1930s.

The missionaries of this wave tended to be graduates of the Bible Institute movement. The churches they planted started modestly in their own living rooms, in a new believer's home, or in a storefront. Tracts and simple literature were printed and a Bible school (with a curriculum adapted from the missionary's alma mater) was initiated in the back of the church. Radio was utilized when it became available.

When Tim, the missionary, found that young Felipe was an excellent prospect for further theological training, or that Mario needed a modest salary so that he could use his gifts to start new churches, or when Tim awoke to the need for funds to print a Bible study book, a problem arose. The faith mission structure leaned heavily on personal contact between the missionary and his North American donor friends. People in Mankato, Minnesota, were all too happy to buy Tim a jeep or contribute to his family's financial support. But their enthusiasm did not transfer easily to Felipe and Mario.

National believers often wondered why it was so hard to raise funds to print a book or get a scholarship. The denominations apparently had a freer hand to allocate funds and had more resources; everything was not so tightly linked to the missionary. Faith missions had money available for the Bible institute as long as the missionary was on the scene. It was therefore tempting to keep institutions under missionary control to assure their funding. Denominational institutions seemed less dependent on the missionary presence.

Despite these limitations, churches multiplied, radio stations installed larger transmitters, and Bible institutes graduated thousands of Latin American pastors and leaders.

Although Tim and his colleagues came from a variety of denominational backgrounds, there was surprisingly little argument about the kinds of churches to be produced on the field. Most practiced baptism by immersion and ended up with a congregational form of government. Although the mission boards were interdenominational, in each country the churches they created soon formed associations and became new local denominations.

CAMPAIGNS AND BIBLE STUDY GROUPS:
THE FOURTH WAVE

A huge, silvery blimp-like enclosure supported by the higher air pressure inside, the "Air Cathedral," was used for a while by Assemblies of God missionaries in Central America. The modern equivalent of the old tent meeting approach, this represented the campaign emphasis of the fourth wave of Evangelical advance, the newer denominations.

Traditional tents are still being used, too, for evangelistic campaigns. And the dry season in the tropics lends itself to open-air campaigns in large vacant lots. People still endure backless benches under strings of lights while they listen to a preacher present his message from a crude platform. The campaign may last three months, leaving the preacher hoarse and exhausted. Not many may respond on a given night. But if a total of five hundred respond over a three-month period and only 10 percent remain faithful, one still has a nucleus of fifty with which to begin a new church.

Not all missionaries of this fourth wave are Pentecostal; neither do all major in evangelistic campaigns. Conservatives of many of the old North American denominations despaired of regaining control of the organizations and the mission boards. Breaking away, new non-Pentecostal groups such as the Conservative Baptists or the more recently formed Presbyterian Church of America sent their missionaries south of the border with greater evangelistic fervor than the old denominations. Such groups were less inclined to have open-air campaigns than home Bible study groups.

Some of the older denominations, such as the Southern Baptists and the Mennonites, although already in Latin America, awoke to the needs in other countries and expanded their fields. The total number of missionaries of this wave and the previous one (faith missions) represented 90 percent of all North American missionary personnel overseas in 1989, and their proportion in Latin America was probably the same.

Already strong in countries such as Brazil and Chile, Pentecostals entered new areas and attracted new followers. They added prayer for the sick to the campaign approach and television to their media efforts. They replaced the piano and organ with electric guitars.

GRASSROOTS PROTESTANTISM: THE FIFTH WAVE

Enter a large Latin American Evangelical church and one thing you may note is an uneven floor. You can distinguish changes in the tile patterns in one or more places. The building has undergone numerous additions with the congregation's growth. Large paintings or murals grace the walls. In one of these, Christians are rising to meet Christ at his Second Coming. Another is that of an open Bible on a rock withstanding the boisterous waves of worldly forces.

The congregation sings the same chorus for ten or fifteen minutes. The song leader grasps the microphone in one hand and the other arm is stretched untiringly upward. The sermon is simple and invariably concludes with an altar call; streams of people move forward. Some may be responding to the gospel for the first time, others coming for reconciliation, for physical healing, or for the resolution of a spiritual burden. There is something reminiscent of traditional liturgies where there is always confession, reconciliation with God, and the granting of his peace.

There is no missionary in sight, and a visitor may feel that North America is left far behind. This is a church of the fifth wave, one with little or no history of organizational relationship with a foreign denomination or mission board. Sprouting from Latin American soil itself, these churches include such groups as the Brazil for Christ movement and the Rose of Sharon groups in Central America.

While a missionary is still trying to wean his church away from foreign subsidies and encourage his people to take more initiative, down the street the Christian butcher begins a preaching service in his home, singing to the accompaniment of guitars and maracas. There is no missionary to remind him that the service should be over at 9 o'clock or that the message should have three points. Cats and dogs wander underfoot and the children are noisy until they fall asleep. But the heart burden of the poor is poured out with tears and shouts.

The group becomes too large for the lay-pastor's living room, so it moves out to the patio under a covering of palm branches. And then, through incredible personal sacrifice — every peso goes for another bag of cement — a chapel is built. Before the cement is dry or the window frames installed, the group is concerned about a nearby squatters' village where there is no witness. That is considered a *campo blanco,* a "whitened field," where a branch preaching point must be established. When such preaching points become daughter congregations, the network becomes a new denomination.

Why do people elsewhere know so little about these fifth-wave churches? It is only natural that Baptist missionaries return home to report on Baptist work, and Alliance missionaries about the Alliance churches. It seems no one has any reason to report on what in some countries is the biggest wave yet.

What Makes Evangelical Churches Grow?

1. *A background of Christian knowledge already acquired in the Roman Catholic tradition.* Witnessing Christians in Latin America do not usually have to start at square one, explaining who Jesus is.

2. *A world view that still accepts the supernatural.* While this is often misdirected, a witnessing Christian can redirect a person's faith to Christ.

3. *Disenchantment with the Roman Catholic Church.* Among the reasons for a Catholic to leave are:

— Lack of priests and pastoral care;

— Contradictions discovered between the Church's teachings and the Bible;

— Moral failure of some clergy;

— Identification of the Church with the establishment (or sometimes the opposite: its identification with the revolutionaries).

4. *Religious liberty.* The Roman Catholic Church still exercises great political power in many countries. Protestants, in effect, are only tolerated. Missionary visas may be hard to obtain in many countries and there are subtle forms of social discrimination. Street services are illegal in Mexico (but in the shadow of the Benito Juárez monument in Alameda Central Park in Mexico City on Sunday afternoons there are large Evangelical street services). Problems, yes. But enough liberty for the gospel to take root in the hearts of people.

5. *Poverty and insecurity.* These are conditions that lead people not only to Christian communities where there is love and acceptance, but also to Christ, the ultimate source of strength in trouble.

6. *Evangelical use of mass media.* Rising literacy coincides with the wide distribution of easy-to-read versions of the Scripture. The fact that there are Evangelical radio stations in each Central American country is a partial explanation of the phenomenal Evangelical growth there. The electronic church, too, has brought the attention of millions to the gospel. But many culturally sensitive Latins are not impressed by the entertainment glitter of many U.S.-originated telecasts, not to speak of the scandals associated with some of these ministries.

7. *Evangelical church structure.* While some traditional denominations still limit preaching and presiding over the Lord's Supper to ordained seminary graduates, groups that are growing have actively encouraged the lay-pastor and given him authority. Or a layman starts preaching and establishes a church without asking anyone's permission. Communications theory supports the concepts that people are persuaded more often by others of their own kind. That lay-pastor who is a storekeeper may be more convincing in explaining the gospel to another merchant than someone more removed.

8. *Mobilization.* The Evangelism-in-Depth concept, according to which all Christians are encouraged to tell their friends about Christ, is operative in many

Evangelical communities. Typical mass evangelism attempts to multiply the audience for an evangelist. The mobilization concept attempts to multiply the evangelists.

9. *Faith in God's power.* The mobilization concept is an undeniable formula for growth. But if it is accepted cerebrally — no one can deny it is logical — it is not enough. People can be trained to witness and be exhorted to do so, but the ordinary person, Latin American or otherwise, is nervous and embarrassed, afraid he or she will say the wrong thing. Most churches will give lip-service to mobilization, but nothing happens.

The Pentecostal churches are often the ones in which mobilization really takes place. Theirs is a theology that empowers believers. People know that God will answer prayer about the person to whom they expect to witness, and they know that the Holy Spirit will give witnessing Christians the words to say and take away their timidity. Of course, the Pentecostals do not have a monopoly on these truths.

10. *Contextualization.* Just as the Apostle Paul was "Jew to the Jews, gentile to the gentiles," so the gospel expressed in Latin America must fit into its surroundings.

If *salsa* is the prevailing rhythm on the pop music radio show, it becomes the beat to which choruses are sung in church. Unison praying — each worshiper pleading to God regarding his or her personal needs — is more common than overly intellectual expositions. Worship forms and organization are spontaneous and personal rather than rigid and overly programmed.

11. *The critical mass.* When there are only a dozen Evangelicals in a city, as faithful as they may be in telling their friends about Christ and inviting them to church, growth will be slow in absolute terms. They only have so many friends and so many hours in a day. But if 10 percent of a city's people are actively witnessing — 10,000 believers in a city of 100,000 — hardly a person will not have some contact with that 10,000. The numbers grow like compound interest and, for the time being, the curves on the graphs get steeper. In many areas of Latin America this critical mass has been reached. We could not stop the movement even if we wanted to.

12. *A straightforward message.* Solo Cristo Salva [Only Christ Saves] is a common motto for campaigns, stickers, posters, and even graffiti. During the Evangelism-in-Depth movement in Bolivia, believers placed oil drums across the face of a barren mountainside in full view of La Paz, the capital. At night the drums were lit, spelling out the message in flames: Solo Cristo Salva. There is no compromise regarding salvation — it is only through Christ. Repentance and faith in him is the first step. The Bible is the book. This is simplistic to many, but for desperate people looking for straightforward answers, the Gospel People show they have no doubts about what to say.

The Flip Side of Success

1. *Authoritarianism.* North Americans are quick to note how strong (if not dictatorial) Latin American heads of government are, how top-down the man-

agement styles in Latin businesses are, or how macho and domineering the father of the family is. "How can we expect the churches and their pastors to be different?" we ask.

Some observers trace this authoritarianism to insecurity. The lay pastor who is a butcher without any theological training fears that his members will forsake him for a more attractive church. He may demand that no member attend any meeting other than those of his congregation.

2. *Legalism.* Many an Evangelical woman will never be seen in slacks or with makeup, nor will she shape her hair, leaving it straight and long. New, first-generation Christians may be forgiven for certain legalisms, but some churches never liberate their people from the "don'ts."

Some fifth-wave groups have adopted an almost Old Testament lifestyle under the law, like a group in Chile that, among other practices, celebrates the annual Feast of the Tabernacles, taking the congregation out of the city to camp in makeshift shelters in obedience to Jewish law.

 3. *Massification.* Dealing with people as a part of a great mass instead of attending to their individual needs is a temptation that often follows success. Many pastors deal with the crowd and not with the individual.

After the nationwide Evangelism-in-Depth movements of the 1960s, the Latin American Mission coordinators of these movements realized that something was missing. Thousands of new Christians were coming into the churches, but no one was personally taking the individual converts to help them with their problems. Therefore, the concept of believers taking responsibility to disciple new Christians has been the emphasis of the In-Depth Institute (International Institute of In-Depth Evangelization) for the past several years. People are starved for personal concern and love in many Latin American churches.

Roman Catholics who have learned something about spiritual sharing in the small Base Communities have said to Evangelicals who have been successfully capturing the crowds and erecting large buildings, "You seem to be going to where we have just come from."

4. *Reductionism.* "They preach from only five or six texts," critics say about some of the large churches in Chile. Reducing the gospel to only a few texts, or to certain topics such as healing, is another weakness in many churches. Some groups view all illness, psychological or physical, as demon possession and their major activity is exorcism.

Outside these churches systems are breaking down. The local factory is firing all its workers every thirteen weeks and rehiring them to avoid paying social security and other workers' benefits. Young people are joining the guerrillas. Deforestation is causing erosion that results in contaminated water. But in most Evangelical churches pastors say little that will enlighten the members about their responsibility in situations demanding justice, Christian discernment about political issues, or environmental concerns.

5. *Divisions.* For years, because missionaries of the mainline denominations in Latin America tended to come from the Evangelical wing of their denominations, and the churches they worked with were also Evangelical, the Gospel

teers, without money for Sunday School materials. It may be directed by a pastor with at best an evening Bible school education, himself a mechanic. Struggling against impossible odds, God's people meet, pray, sing, worship, hear God's Word, and win others.

EPILOGUE

After a year in Bible school, Ana María married Ernesto and soon they had two children. As a guard at the entrance of an office building, Ernesto filled in his empty hours studying to complete a high-school diploma in an extension program, and many more hours digging into the Scriptures. Together they helped start a small neighborhood house-church. But Ana María's dreams really came true when they were invited by a *Christ for the City* team to join them in founding a new church on the other side of town.

Acres of squatters' shacks had appeared there almost overnight. The government stepped in, laying out streets and building concrete shells of houses that the occupants themselves could finish while acquiring them on easy payments. The homes, all attached to each other in neat rows, represent an improvement, but the neighborhood is still more needy, more crime-ridden, and more violent than the *barrio* where Ana María spent her childhood.

The team's nurse gives classes in first aid and there is a program to tutor children after school. Ernesto and a teammate started dozens of home Bible studies. Soon the people transformed by Christ will become one more witnessing church.

In the most squalid *barrios* of tropical Latin America, God provides splashes of beauty and color — the flowers growing out of the used paint cans on the porches, or simply growing wild along the fences. Antonio, Ana María, Ernesto, and millions of other Gospel People are also God's splashes of color and hope for a drab and needy continent.

6

The Pentecostal Movement in Latin America

Juan Sepúlveda

"What are the causes of this spectacular growth? Is the Pentecostal movement homogeneous or extraordinarily diverse? Will the present level rate of growth continue? What kind of impact does this movement have and will it continue to have in Latin American Society?" After reviewing the sociological, psychosocial, and pastoral explanations, Pastor Sepúlveda offers some "Pentecostal reasons for Pentecostal growth." Juan Sepúlveda directs the Servicio Evangélico para el Desarrollo [Evangelical Service for Development] of the Misión Iglesia Pentecostal in Chile, of which he is a leader. He is widely known in ecumenical circles for his speaking and writing on Latin American Pentecostalism. The major portion of this chapter appeared in *Jahrbuch Mission 1992: Fokus Lateinamerika*, and is used with the permission of Evangelisches Missionswerk, Hamburg.

INTRODUCTION

Donald Dayton, a well-known student of Pentecostal roots, observed in a recent interview that "Pentecostalism was born in the United States, but is discovering its destiny in Latin America" (Dayton 1991b, 15–17). This statement well reflects the impact that Pentecostal growth in Latin America is having in academic, missionary, ecumenical, and even political circles. David Stoll has made some impressive projections based upon the Protestant growth index between 1969 and 1985 in several Latin American countries. He estimates that by the year 2010 Protestants will have surpassed 50 percent of the total population in countries such as Guatemala, Puerto Rico, El Salvador, Brazil, and Honduras (Stoll 1990, 8, 9). And the bulk of the Protestant strength is attributed basically to pentecostalism.

Questions of the credibility of these projections and the figures on which they are based aside, it is obvious that Pentecostal growth is producing a profound transformation in the religious field in Latin America. What are the causes of this spectacular growth? Is the Pentecostal movement homogeneous or extraordinarily diverse? Will the present level of growth rate continue? What kind of impact does this movement have and will it continue to have in Latin American society? These are some of the questions that I shall briefly attempt to answer in this chapter, with the help of some of the most serious students of the phenomenon.

IDENTITY AND DIVERSITY IN LATIN AMERICAN PENTECOSTALISM

The "Pentecostal experience" — characterized by a search for an intense experience of God through the Holy Spirit, by a quest for holiness, by a strong eschatological hope, and a great evangelistic zeal — is not new in the history of Christianity. In different periods of Christian history there have been movements that emphasized one or another of the above aspects. Nonetheless, the Pentecostal movement as we know it today began at the turn of this century. It was born from the various streams that flowed out of the Holiness movement that had been set in motion by John Wesley.

Pentecostalism bears the mark of the variety of its roots in the Holiness movement that sprang up in various churches in the United States and Europe. Beatriz Muniz de Souza quotes the statement of a Norwegian pastor:

> With respect to salvation through justification by faith we are Lutherans. We are Baptists because we practice baptism by immersion. In regards to holiness we are Methodists. Our aggressive evangelism makes us like the Salvation Army. But in relation to the baptism in the Holy Spirit we are Pentecostals. (Muniz de Souza 1969, 1964)

In the case of North American pentecostalism, Dayton often distinguishes between those churches that see themselves as heirs of the holiness movement, and thus value their Wesleyan heritage, and those that understand themselves totally as a new restoration movement of the church. According to Dayton, however, there is a four-point theological understanding that is common to both North American and European pentecostalism — salvation (justification–sanctification), healing, Spirit baptism, and the Second Coming of Christ (Dayton 1991, passim).

Pentecostal diversity is more complex in Latin America. One fundamental difference derives from its varied origins. There is on the one hand a virtually independent pentecostalism that was practically simultaneous with that of North America. This is the case, for example, with Chilean pentecostalism, which was born within local Methodism until the schism of 1910. The Brazilian case is similar, though not identical. These two cases represent the first expression of a "national protestantism," non-dependent upon foreign finances and organization. For these very reasons they were forced to generate their own style of pastoral leadership. Native pentecostalism developed organizationally and theologically with considerable autonomy from world pentecostalism. These factors made it easier for it to become rooted in the local cultures, giving to pentecostalism an authocthonous character, which it has retained until today.

On the other hand, there is a pentecostalism of missionary origin, usually from North America, but also from Europe (the Swedish pentecostals, for example), which came to Latin America when they were already fairly institutionalized and their doctrines well defined. This movement is financially and organizationally dependent, which accounts for their tenuous rootedness in the popular culture. Generally speaking, the pastoral ministry is closer to the traditional model — that is, pastors who are trained in various kinds of "Bible centers" or seminaries. However, many Pentecostal churches of European origin have achieved autonomy and now have a more authocthonous leadership style closer to that of the first type of Pentecostals mentioned above. In the majority of countries, and particularly in Central America, pentecostalism of missionary origin is predominant.

Another reason for diversification is the atomistic tendency that is evidenced by Latin American pentecostalism. In virtually every country, numerous schisms have fractured the Pentecostal movement. The causes of most of these divisions are to be found in the fragile nature of their ecclesial institutions, in internal power struggles, not to mention the divisions that have been engendered by doctrinal and ideological conflicts.

In synthesis, Latin American pentecostalism is extraordinarily diverse. Any generalizations must be carefully assessed. The same applies to the affirmations in this chapter.

EXPLANATIONS FOR PENTECOSTAL GROWTH IN LATIN AMERICA

Numerous studies have attempted to explain the growth of pentecostalism. The predominant theories fall into three general categories.

Sociological Explanations

The majority of the sociological explanations of Pentecostal growth have focused upon the structural changes in Latin American society in recent decades. All of these analyses start from the same socioanalytical paradigm: the transition from a fundamentally agrarian, traditional, and authoritarian (feudal) society to a society that is basically urban, industrial, modern, and democratic. Within the framework of this slow but irreversible process — which is leaving its mark upon the majority of our societies in this century — pentecostalism emerges as one expression or symptom of change.

The interpretations of the relationships between social change and the emergence of pentecostalism vary. Emilio Willems, for example, sees protestantism in general and pentecostalism in particular as a manifestation of modernity — "a reaction to the changes in the traditional way of living" (Willems 1967, 81; cp. Willems 1964). On the other hand, Christian Lalive, whose influence on subsequent studies is evident, sees pentecostalism as a form of symbolic survival of the traditional social structures. It helps resolve a situation of anomie affecting large sectors of the population due to the slowness and contradictions in the industrialization and urbanization process (cp. Lalive 1969).

However, both of these perspectives have in common the reduction of the Pentecostal movement to a kind of social adaptation mechanism, with little consideration for its religious specificity. In this view, the future of pentecostalism would seem to be conditioned more upon the vicissitudes of the social structures of Latin America than by its unique characteristics as a social movement.

Psychosocial Explanations

There is another kind of approach, complementary and not necessarily opposed to the previous perspective, which accents the massifying and depersonalizing characteristics of modern cities. Going beyond the question of the relative conclusiveness of the modernization process, this perspective stresses the massification of modern cities. In the large urban areas face-to-face relationships tend to disappear. In their place relationships are mediated by institutions and documents. From this it is only one step to the perception that modern societies have, virtually by definition, an anomic effect. In order to cope we search for community, we need togetherness as we look for clearer definitions of our roles and social fit, and we choose to depend upon or belong to a group that can protect us.

Although this approach has not been as fully developed as the sociological theory with respect to pentecostalism, Renato Poblete, a Chilean Jesuit, has applied it to the study of Puerto Rican Pentecostal communities in New York. This has been the frame of reference for Catholic studies of pentecostalism (Poblete 1969; cp. Poblete and Galilea 1984).

Pastoral Explanations

Another kind of explanation that one frequently finds among Catholic researchers relates the success of the Pentecostal implantation to the strong religious orientation in popular culture. Fr. Ignacio Vergara (1962) called it the people's "thirst for God." This approach is in effect a criticism of the Catholic Church. Because it is incapable of providing adequate answers to the religious needs of the people, the church leaves a vacuum that is filled by pentecostalism and other religious movements. One of the first to use this line of interpretation was the Chilean Fr. Alberto Hurtado (1941).

This interpretation concludes that pentecostalism grows by reaping in areas that have been neglected by the Catholic Church. There is a shortage of priestly vocations; the ratio of faithful per Catholic priest is extraordinarily greater than that of believers per evangelical pastors. Because the Catholic catechesis is weak, the people are lacking in religious culture. Pentecostalism also prospers because of the absence of community in the parish structure, due to the coldness and formality of the liturgy, and because of a scant missionary concern, taking for granted that everybody is Catholic. This kind of approach has caused Fr. Pierre Chaunu to observe that the success of Protestant proselytism represents an example of "substitute catholicism" (Meyer 1969, 291).

PENTECOSTAL REASONS FOR PENTECOSTAL GROWTH

Surveying the panorama of Pentecostal studies, Francisco Cartaxo Rolim, the Brazilian sociologist, wrote a number of years ago:

> Pentecostalism has been seen as a device for sociocultural adaptation by the poor classes in a society in transition. Thus, these authors are interested in explaining for us what Pentecostalism does, but they are not interested in showing what it is. To remain at the functional level is to characterize the Pentecostal religion socially and not because of its specifically religious dimensions. (Cartaxo Rolim 1979, 346)

In fact, the various approaches I have pointed out do speak more about the problems that pentecostalism addresses than of what pentecostalism is in and of itself. Thus we learn more about Latin American society as a whole than about pentecostalism as a social movement.

Cartaxo Rolim's contribution is an analysis of the "specifically religious structure of pentecostalism." More precisely, he studies the way in which pentecostalism produces its religious discourse and practices. He emphasizes one of the novelties and keys to why the popular sectors are drawn to pentecostalism: it breaks with the traditional differentiation between qualified producers of religious discourse and practice (the clergy) and mere consumers of these religious products. In pentecostalism every believer is a direct and legitimate producer of his or her religious world. They thus defy not only the traditional way of doing religion, but the very structure of a classist society. Of course, this challenge is symbolic and not political.

Although it is suggestive, Cartaxo Rolim's contribution remains on the sociological plane and does not tell us very much about the characteristics of the Pentecostal message and its offer of salvation. New studies have attempted to draw closer to the way in which Pentecostals understand themselves and their salvation message (cp. Canales 1991; see also Ossa 1991).

Taking this new research into account, and my own formulations from a more theological than sociological perspective, I shall point out some characteristics of Latin American pentecostalism that seem to me to be fundamental if we are to understand its success among the popular sectors.

Rather than a new doctrine, pentecostalism offers a new experience of God. It is a direct encounter with God without mediation. Theologically, the only mediator of this experience is the Holy Spirit who makes God present in a person's life. But with the removal of the priestly mediation, a cultural mediation —pentecostalism — becomes a popular mediation of the sacred.

The encounter with God is intense. Through his Spirit, God virtually invades a believer's life; he takes up residence there, filling life with new meaning. In fact, believers experience this encounter as a change of life — not in the objective conditions of life, but as a subjective change. What changes is the way in which we see ourselves, our families, and reality.[1] The ecstatic manifestations, such as speaking in tongues, dancing in the Spirit, and uncontrollable laughter or weeping, constitute something like the language of this unspeakable experience.

Thus, the Pentecostal experience provides a new identity to social sectors that have always been exposed to failure in everything they have attempted.

The Pentecostal experience does not happen alone. It takes place within an altogether accepting community. People who have been scarred by neglect, powerlessness, and loneliness find in Pentecostal communities full acceptance and togetherness without preconditions. But at the same time, the communities are missionary. From the moment in which they become part of a community, everyone feels called to develop a witnessing role in accord with his or her gifts — such as worship leaders, street preachers, visitors of the sick, etc.

The experience of God that pentecostalism proclaims is announced "in the language of the people." When the message communicators belong to the common people and have had the Pentecostal experience, they speak in a language that is simple and comprehensible to all their listeners. Their discourse is testimonial or narrative, and fits right in to the way in which the poor communicate and share their life experiences.

To summarize, we can say that although it is true that several structural factors in Latin American society do facilitate Pentecostal growth, the key causes of this growth must be found in pentecostalism itself and in the way of salvation it announces.

THE IMPACT OF PENTECOSTALISM
UPON MODERN SOCIETY

Traditionally the Pentecostal movement has understood that its impact on society is a function of its growth. In other words, the greater the number of those who are converted, the greater its influence in society. The goal, therefore, is expressed in such terms as "Chile for Christ," or, at a broader level, "Latin America for Christ." Behind these slogans is the implicit idea that when the majority of people in a given locality become Evangelical, and more precisely Pentecostal, then society will improve and become more just and good. This utopia cancels out any possibility of thinking of another kind of influence or impact upon society.

This understanding is beginning to change, curiously as a result of Pentecostal growth. On the one hand, their awareness of growth has produced in leaders a new perception of the role of pentecostalism in society. We now represent a significant sector of society whose views regarding public affairs have taken on added importance. So a new wave of a more politically aware pentecostalism has come about. Examples such as Guatemala — which has had two Evangelical (and Pentecostal) presidents, Brazil — where several members of congress are Evangelical, and Perú — which had an Evangelical vice president and several deputies, evidence our political strength and also have a demonstrative effect in other Latin American countries (cp. Martin 1991).[2]

On the other hand, it is clear that Pentecostal growth has not brought a commensurate and significant diminution in crucial social problems such as poverty, delinquency, alcoholism, drug addiction, etc. This evidence forces us to ask about the meaning of Pentecostal growth. Is it enough to evangelize and to grow in order to make a significant impact upon society? This question has also led to new kinds of linkages between Pentecostal congregations and their social milieu, particularly as acts of solidarity in the context of authoritarian regimes.

These changes, as yet in their initial stages, present pentecostalism with a number of challenges that have to do with the direction in which we need to move in society. At the same time, pentecostalism must face up to the institutionalization processes that all of this will require — better-trained pastors and laity, diversity in ministries, new relationships with other churches, etc.

Can we project the direction these changes will take? According to Donald Dayton, "it is possible to predict that in the next century pentecostalism will be very influential in Latin America. However, one cannot predict much about the direction that this influence will take, because Pentecostalism will also change when it moves into the center of society" (1991a, 17).[3]

NOTES

1. *Editor's note:* Sepúlveda develops this theme elsewhere: "This new meaning to life takes on added significance when one considers it against the background of the constant risk of failure that the urban and rural poor face. It is the risk of falling into drink, vice, delinquency, and moral degradation due to the problems of abject poverty and the lack of adequate role models" (1992a, 8).

2. See the chapters by Padilla and Miranda Sáenz in this book.

3. *Editor's note:* Sepúlveda notes that the public opinion polls in Chile show statistics on practicing Pentecostals concerning moral themes (divorce, abortion, premarital sex) that are more conservative than that of other Protestants and of the general public. But "the big surprise for us, undoubtedly, is how high the percentages really are, especially if we consider that we are dealing with the opinions of *practicing* Pentecostals. What could we expect, then from Pentecostal sympathizers?" (1992a, 13).

7

Religion and Poverty in Brazil:
A Comparison of Catholic
and Pentecostal Communities

Cecília Mariz

This article argues that the actual experiences of the members of Brazil's Pentecostal churches and of the Base Ecclesial Communities (BECs) are more alike than the sharply contrasting ideologies of these two movements might suggest. Both movements foster a sense of closeness to God, enhance self-esteem, provide support networks that are national in scope, develop leadership skills, promote literacy, and encourage a sober and ascetic style of life. The long-term consequences for the economic and political behavior of the members of these two movements may, therefore, be far less different from what most observers would predict. "To sum up, while a sober lifestyle seems to be an unintended consequence of the BEC members' experiences of the union of religion and life, a political orientation seems to be the unintended consequence of pentecostalism." The author lectures at the Universidade Federal de Pernambuco (Brazil). Her paper appeared in *Sociological Analysis*, Supplement No. 53.S, 1992, pp. 63–70. It is published with permission.

My aim in this chapter is to compare Brazilian base church communities (BECs) and Pentecostal Protestant churches in order to advance some hypotheses about the influences they exert on people's economic and political behavior.

Those who have studied these two movements tend to emphasize how different they are in their interpretation of the Bible, their perspective on society, and their conception of the Christian life (Ramalho 1977; Rolim, 1980). Most studies of Pentecostals, for example, focus on their pietism and their conservative values (Rolim 1985; Hofffnagel 1978; Bobsin 1984; Gomes 1985), whereas most studies of the BECs stress their potential for radical social transformation (Ireland 1986; Petrini 1984; Duarte 1963; Adriance 1986).[1] The prevailing view among scholars seems to be that over the long term the BECs will exert a leftward influence in Brazilian political life and that pentecostalism, by its encouragement of private piety and political docility, will indirectly support the forces of conservatism.

In this chapter I will question the hypothesis that these two religious movements will have different long-term economic and political effects. I will try to
show that there are limits on their abilities to put their official ideologies into
effect. Because they are organized in similar ways and their members have many
experiences in common, both groups in effect encourage behavior that is surprisingly similar. Consequently, the very process of attempting to live by the pre-
cepts of these movements generates behavior that does not entirely reflect the
values expressed in their official systems of discourse. I base this contention on
the field data I collected in Recife while doing research on my dissertation, and
on a critical reading of the work of other investigators.

A COMPARISON OF "IDEAL VALUES"

As previously noted, the literature has emphasized the difference between the
values espoused by the BECs and Pentecostals. According to many observers,
the politically conservative posture of Brazilian pentecostalism is the consequence of three distinct, but interrelated, value elements: (1) a sacramental and
individualistic interpretation of reality, (2) an unequivocal respect for established authority of all kinds, and (3) a belief that religion should not become
involved in politics. As Macedo (1986) and others have argued, these three
value elements of pentecostalism are diametrically opposed to the outlook of the
BECs, which emphasize: (a) a rationalistic and social structure approach to
reality, (b) a critical attitude toward constituted authority, and (c) the political
relevance of religion.

I do not deny that the ideal, verbalized values of pentecostalism and the BECs
differ in these ways, but I do criticize studies that focus primarily on the ideological elements of these movements and neglect the common experiences of their
members. In the following sections I will discuss these experiences and their
relation to the ideal values of each movement. I will then advance a general
hypothesis concerning the economic and political activities these experiences
encourage.

THE EXPERIENCE OF RENEWAL

The Pentecostal churches and the BECs are relatively new religious movements that became popular among the poor of Brazil during the 1960s. They
differ from more traditional religious expressions, such as folk Catholicism and
Afro-Spiritism, because their emphasis on the process of renewal takes place in
their adherents' lives. The experience or renewal means that a discontinuity
occurs in people's consciousness that involves a change in their ways of seeing
the world. Pentecostals, of course, stress an actual experience of conversion.
Although such an experience is less frequently reported by BEC members than
by Pentecostals, Duarte (1963) and Petrini (1984) observe that BEC members
refer to an experience of discovery and renewal that leads to a transformation of
their lives. Unlike Pentecostals, they do not change their religious affiliation, but

both BEC members and Pentecostals do undergo a profound change of worldview.

This experience of conversion, or "alternation," to use Berger and Luckmann's concept (1966), involves a questioning of the world as taken-for-granted. Both pentecostalism and the BECs require people to make choices to change the religious orientation they acquired by traditional means of socialization. Converts to either of these movements experience the limits of the conventional, common-sense view of life and become critical of it. The requirement of converting counteracts a fatalistic outlook on life by encouraging people to disagree with and rebel against reality as conventionally defined. It disposes people to believe that their lives can be changed. Even pentecostalism, with its otherworldliness and its respect for constituted authority, fosters a critical, nonfatalistic outlook on life that can work against the movement's official posture of avoiding involvement in "worldly" affairs.

THE EXPERIENCE OF RELIGIOUS REFLECTION

Since the religious choice Pentecostals and BEC members have made is not a traditional one, they must justify it in some way. In addition to invoking such "irrational" factors as miraculous healing or the effect of religious music, Pentecostals have had to elaborate a rationale to justify the superiority of their faith. The irrational elements only explain the *initial* attraction to the movement, whereas *continuing* participation is explained by other arguments that assert the universal truth of their religious beliefs. Both movements rely greatly on the Bible for these arguments, and both stress the importance of reading and knowing the Bible. Pentecostals have long been admired in Brazil for their religious knowledge, but the Catholic Church has not traditionally required the laity to be scripturally literate. BEC members have broken with its tradition, however, and they criticize lay Catholics' ignorance of the faith.

Both pentecostalism and BECs are highly verbal in their approach to religion, and words play an important role in their group life. In BEC meetings the use of posters containing slogans is common, and Bible verses are prominently displayed in Pentecostal churches. This emphasis on formal discourse and the written word stands in sharp contrast to traditional religions, which stress the expressive and aesthetic, rather than the cognitive aspects of religion. There are no slogans in Brazil's Afro-Spiritist centers or its folk Catholic processions. The Xangô religion of Recife emphasizes dancing, singing, and feeling, rather than thought and argumentation.

Pentecostals try to convert people by talking to them and reasoning with them. The attempt to convert by preaching assumes that people can choose their faith and lifestyle through rational processes. Therefore, in spite of pentecostalism's sacral approach to reality, it assumes, in effect, that religious choice is rational. This assumption underlies all missionary work. The importance of the written word and the theoretical elaboration of the faith has, as a consequence, encouraged people to become literate for the purpose of reading the Bible and to develop speaking skills for expounding scripture and discussing it with others (Novaes 1985; Rolim 1985). Petrini (1984) and Duarte (1983) have shown how BECs also enable people to express themselves better, and they point out that many BEC members report that participation in BECs taught them how to formulate ideas and opinions. The stimulus for reading, speaking, and forming opinions can be useful both for individual social mobility and for the organization of political movements.

THE UNION OF RELIGION WITH EVERYDAY LIFE

An attempt to link faith with everyday life is present in both pentecostalism and BECs. Unlike traditional religions, both movements require their members to change their everyday lives. As Max Weber (1958) observed, traditional religions enable people to interpret everyday events, but they do not ask people to make all their conduct conform to the norms of a religious worldview that devalues reality as currently constituted. They do not require a special orientation toward life, although they may require it of certain leaders.

Both pentecostalism and the BECs require their members to put their religious beliefs into practice, though they do so in different ways. Pentecostals stress a change of individual lifestyle and morality, and this regimen is supported by social sanctions within closed communities. Pentecostal ideology teaches that there is a sharp separation between spiritual life and material interests. Thus, when Pentecostals try to unify their lives through religion, they are ideally expected to separate themselves from worldly preoccupations. This means that in principle Pentecostals cannot participate in political disputes or strive for economic success. They are also expected to interpret the Bible literally and to apply it to their lives by reading sacral meaning into day-to-day events, interpreting them either as miracle or as the work of the devil (Bobsin 1984; Souza 1969).

BECs, on the other hand, encourage their members to unify their lives by using religious motivation and religious group action to solve day-to-day problems. Consequently, with them, the union of faith and life is manifested in political activities and other forms of collective social action. BEC members read secular meaning into the Bible, identifying miracles, angels, and devils with social disputes, leaders, and social injustices. The union of religion and life in the vision of the BECs implies secularization of faith by the use of ideas that come from the social sciences (Petrini 1984).

Nevertheless, despite their different assumptions and intentions, it seems that the attempt of the adherents of these two movements to unify their faith with their lives has strikingly similar results. When Pentecostals try to restrict their lives to spiritual matters and BEC members try to transform all spiritual questions into everyday problems, they experience the limits of the applicability of their ideal values and conceptions. As we shall see, Pentecostals are not able to live only a spiritual life, but find themselves involved in politics as well (Hoffnagel 1978; Stoll 1986; Kliewer 1982).

In the case of the BECs, the idea that spiritual needs can be satisfied mostly by the fight for social justice and equality, and through political activities, also faces limits. Betto's observation (1980) that some of the BECs prefer religious to political discourse is indicative of this limit. Betto attributes this preference to the difficulty middle-class priests and pastoral agents have in unifying political and religious discourse. In my opinion, however, this difficulty expresses the impossibility of completely merging spiritual life with politics, a project dear to many Catholic leftist intellectuals. Torres has shown that the secularization, or disenchantment, of the Bible is not as popular among BEC members as it is among their pastoral agents. There is an unavoidable tension within the BECs between the *políticos* and the *rezadores* [those who pray].

The convergence between the two movements at the level of everyday behavior can also be seen in the sphere of individual morality. Although BECs do not require the ascetic lifestyles that Pentecostals emphasize, their members do lead sober lives. Participation in BECs requires a dedication and commitment to the utilitarian issues of community life. BEC members do not have much leisure time and place little emphasis on personal pleasure. Consequently, BECs attract people who are already sober and serious-minded, and their experiences as members reinforce and support these dispositions. Insofar as an ascetic lifestyle is a useful instrument for coping with poverty, both movements may empower their members to do so.

THE EXPERIENCE OF COMMUNITY LIFE

Because of their organization in small groups, both movements offer an experience of community life. In itself, this is not an unusual feature of religions. Moreover, self-help behavior seems to be part of the lifestyle of many poor Brazilians (Campbell 1980). In this respect, Pentecostals and BECs offer only an *alternative* support network. But these alternative networks differ in important ways from traditional ones. For one thing, they are based on specifically sacred duties of helping one another (Novaes 1985; Fry and Howe 1975). When Pentecostals, for example, move to new communities they will find a group of like-minded people ready to receive them and offer them not only psychological and spiritual support, but they also share their limited material means. They may open their homes to someone who does not have a place to live, try to help others to find jobs, or offer childcare support.

In addition, the self-help networks of these two religious movements form a plausibility structure for the reinforcement of a religiously defined way of life. Petrini (1984) describes how the experiences in small groups lead to a development of friendship and community consciousness among BEC members that reinforces their emphasis on collective activities. Pentecostals, despite their individualistic interpretation of society, acknowledge that the maintenance of their faith and special lifestyle depends upon the support and control of their religious community, which they attempt to insulate from the effect of worldly influences.

Both movements offer psychological support in two different ways; first, by saying prayers in their meetings for people with problems; and second, by talking, listening, and advising. Both groups practice loud, spontaneous, common prayers, though Pentecostals tend to display more emotion than BEC members.

The BEC's supportive network does, however, function somewhat differently from that of the Pentecostals. BEC members help themselves by working together and finding collective solutions to shared problems, by building houses for each other, constructing bridges, organizing communal shopping, and the like. Pentecostals, on the other hand, tend to help one another individually. BEC members also help individuals, but unlike Pentecostals, they also extend help to people outside their group, especially to the poor. In addition, BEC members fight politically for the interests of poor people in general, whereas Pentecostals, owing partly to their self-imposed insulation, are primarily concerned with their own group and way of life.

But the experience of community itself necessarily adds a political dimension to the lives of Pentecostals. Their ideology does not encourage political participation, but when the personal, class, or religious interests of Pentecostals are at stake, many of them do become involved in politics. Pentecostals are very much opposed to communism, but their respect for a law-based, instead of a person-based, authority and their insistence that authority figures obey God's law has freed them from the traditional submissive-authoritarian elements of Brazilian popular culture and religion. Consequently, some Pentecostals have become involved in leftwing political movements, e.g., the workers' party, the *Partido dos Trabalhadores* (Conceiçao 1980; Rolim 1987).

To sum up, while a sober lifestyle seems to be an unintended consequence of the BEC members' experience of the union of religion and life, a political orientation seems to be the unintended consequence of pentecostalism.

REVELATION AND EMPOWERMENT

Both pentecostalism and the BECs have a prophetic orientation. Their members possess a revealed knowledge and enjoy a direct relation to God. As Lancaster (1987) shows, revealed knowledge and the possibility of communication with God without the mediation of priests and saints are elements not only of Pentecostal faith but also of the liberation theology that informs the BECs. Macedo (1986) observes that, despite their rationalized and secularized discourse, BECs are based on a prophetic knowledge that has been directly revealed by God. In this respect, both movements differ from traditional religious knowledge and are the medium of communication with God (Brandao 1980; Bobsin 1984).

The belief that all participants are inspired directly by God means that they are all competent to interpret the Bible and to preach. The experience of revealed knowledge and the assumption that any member can relate directly to God allow the development of a lay leadership. BECs and Pentecostal churches consist of relatively independent small groups that are mainly led by ordinary people who have ample opportunity to develop organizational skills, including the ability to mobilize themselves for collective action.

Because the members of both movements believe they possess a revealed knowledge, they have a feeling of superiority. Among Pentecostals this feeling is expressed and reinforced by their peculiar style of dress. Gomes (1985), Novaes (1985), and Bobsin (1984) report that, although many Pentecostals are poor in terms of worldly goods, they feel spiritually rich because of their special relationship to the Holy Spirit. Macedo (1986) and Petrini (1984) emphasize that members of the BECs are no longer ashamed of being poor because they believe that the poor are God's chosen people. Both movements change poor people's perceptions of themselves by offering dignity and self-esteem. The change in self-perception and the skills members acquire by participating in the activities of their religious communities may facilitate their social mobility and their political effectiveness.

On the basis of this comparative analysis of Brazilian pentecostalism and the BECs, I hypothesize that the long-term social and political consequences of these two movements will not be as different as their contrasting ideologies might lead observers to predict. Both movements foster a sense of self-esteem and superiority to others, provide support networks that are national in scope, develop leadership skills, promote literacy, and encourage a sober and ascetic lifestyle. In combination, these experiences, dispositions, and abilities can facilitate social mobility and can enable the members to promote or defend their interests in the political arena.

NOTES

1. Some authors, however, have argued that the BECs were not revolutionary groups (Fernandes 1985; Stoll 1986; Ireland 1986; Hewitt 1986). Other authors have also criticized the idea that Pentecostals were always conservative (Novaes 1985; Brandao 1980).

8

New Actors on the Political Scene in Latin America

C. René Padilla

"Our hypothesis is that today's 'politization' of Evangelicals is explained, in the first place, by the deep crisis that affects the Latin American countries and places their future under a big question mark, and, in the second place, by inherent qualities of the Latin American Evangelical movement." Dr. Padilla surveys the main aspects of the religious and political crisis and shows their connection with the political awakening of Evangelicals. The author, a noted New Testament scholar, is Publications Secretary of the Latin American Theological Fraternity and the editor of various magazines and books on missiological topics. This article first appeared as the introductory chapter in René Padilla, ed., *De la marginación al compromiso: Los evangélicos en la política en América Latina* (Buenos Aires, Latin American Theological Fraternity). It is reprinted with permission from *Transformation* (July/September 1992).

Never in the history of the Latin American nations have Evangelicals received as much attention from the media as they are receiving at present because of their involvement in national politics in various countries. This is a new phenomenon: people who until recently were regarded as an insignificant religious minority with no place in public life are now organizing themselves to elect their own candidates to high government positions.

There are several factors that explain the "apoliticism" that has generally characterized Latin American Evangelicals. This is not the place to analyze them, but at least three should be mentioned:

(1) The influence of missionaries whose teaching (perhaps more by what they did than by what they said) completely ignored the social and political responsibilities of Christians.

(2) The "minority complex" of Evangelicals, formed in an environment of religious hostility and even persecution, an environment in which survival itself

had pushed aside all questions regarding their possible contribution to the construction of a new society.

(3) The emphasis on a futuristic eschatology in Evangelical churches, in light of which the mission of the Church was reduced to saving souls, while social and political action was regarded as unrelated to Christian interests.

Although abstention from politics still persists in Evangelical circles, it is quite clear that it is now being replaced by a social engagement that could not have been imagined just a few years ago. The most significant illustrations of this change of great import for both Church and society are the following:

— the formation of an "Evangelical" political party (Organización Renovadora Auténtica) in Venezuela (1978);

— the emergence of an "Evangelical group" of thirty-three representatives in the National Assembly of Brazil (1986), and the formation of the "pro-Collor Evangelical movement" whose participation in the last presidential election was decisive for Fernando Collor's victory;

— the important participation of Evangelicals in the formation of Cambio 90 and in the election of Alberto Fujimori as President of Perú (1990);

— the election of two Evangelical leaders as members of the National Assembly of Colombia, probably the most "clerical" country in Latin America (1990);

— the election of Jorge Serrano Elias, a member of "El Shaddai" Pentecostal Church, as President of Guatemala (1991);

— the recent formation of an "Evangelical" political party (Movimiento Cristiano Independiente) in Argentina (1991).

Obviously, this is a real political awakening of Evangelicals throughout the continent. It is still too early to evaluate the long-range effects of this new phenomenon. For now we will limit ourselves to making a brief analysis of the factors that lie behind it and reflecting on the challenge that it poses to Evangelical Christians in Latin America.

POLITICIANS FOR TIMES OF CRISIS

If anything is especially noticeable in the image of Evangelicals projected by the mass media today, it is the heated controversy about their politics. In fact, the last few years have seen the resurgence of false anti-Evangelical accusations, according to which the phenomenal growth of Evangelical churches and the participation of Evangelicals in national politics are part of "a plan of ideological penetration" that reflects foreign (mainly U.S.) interests.[1]

The voices of the Roman Catholic hierarchy and the leftist liberationist fundamentalism are mixed in these virulent accusations. For the former, the advance of "the Protestant sects" endangers not only the Roman Catholic faith but also the cultural heritage of these countries because it undermines the "Catholic substratum" of Latin American culture.[2] For the latter, the advance of Evangelicals is an expression of an "imperialistic conspiracy" aimed at delaying the process of liberation of the poor.[3]

Such accusations are a smoke screen that hides the failure of projects that, however opposed to one another from an ideological point of view, have in common their failure to attract the great majorities living in poverty and oppression. In fact, neither the "new Christendom" project of traditional catholicism nor the pro-marxist liberationist project is today a focus of attraction for these large majorities. Instead, whether we like it or not, the poor are attracted to the Evangelical (predominantly Pentecostal) churches.

Our hypothesis is that today's "politization" of Evangelicals is explained, in the first place, by the deep crisis that affects the Latin American countries and places their future under a big question mark, and, in the second place, by inherent qualities of the Latin American Evangelical movement. In view of the limitations of space, we will have to restrict ourselves to surveying the main aspects of the crisis and showing their connection with the political awakening of Evangelicals.

The Socioeconomic Crisis

The worsening of the economic situation of the Latin American countries and the resulting impoverishment of the masses are clearly reflected in the figures provided by the 1990 Report of the Economic Council for Latin America (CEPAL). According to it, in 1980 there were 135 million poor in the region, in 1986 there were 170 million, and in 1989 there were 183 million, including 88 million indigent people (cp. Espoz 1990, 219-228). The problem that these figures pose is not only economic but also ethical, especially when they are compared with the figures related to world expenditure on armament.

In this context, it is doubtful that the "Protestant ethic" (with its emphasis on honesty, thrift, and the spirit of work) provides the way out of underdevelopment. Twenty years ago Christian Lalive d'Epinay cast doubts regarding the thesis — connected with the well-known Weberian idea of the relationship between protestantism and capitalism — according to which conversion to the Christian faith results in social upper mobility (1968, pp. 181-194). Although it is true that "the prohibitions that characterize Protestant life are the origin of some savings and of a more rational use of the modest family income," observed Lalive (ibid., 187), the ingenuous individualistic affirmation, "Change the person and all society will be changed," is shattered in Latin America as it crashes head-on into structural poverty.

Since Lalive wrote, with the striking deterioration of the economic situation of a high percentage of the Latin American population, the doubts have grown regarding the validity of individualistic solutions for the problems of underdevelopment. As a result, it is not surprising that a growing number of Evangelicals — generally members of poor churches — recognize today the need for structural changes and, consequently, the urgency of the political task. Such conviction, of course, is opposed not to commitment to evangelism, but to political passivity and to the idea that nothing at all can be done regarding the serious problems affecting the whole region today.

The Political Crisis

Sad to say, politics in Latin America has often been thought of as a means to individual success or personal enrichment. Embezzlements, bribes, fraud, and authoritarianism have been part and parcel of our political life. Hence, for the ordinary citizen to speak about politics is to speak about a "dirty business." This problem explains to a great extent why many honest people, exceptionally capable, have preferred to keep out of politics.

In the face of the moral and administrative corruption that affects our nations, the idea of creating "a political option led by Evangelicals," with its own ideology, has been taking shape, or at least the plan to attempt to elect believers to high government positions. This objective has received unexpected support on the part of many people who may not necessarily participate in an Evangelical church but share with Evangelical Christians their concern for a moral renewal of politics or feel frustrated with the corruption of political leaders. Clearly, in many cases Evangelicals have entered the political scene moved by the voters' desire to try new actors who are generally known because of their moral principles more than because of their religious convictions.

The Religious and Ecclesiastical Crisis

The second General Conference of the Latin American Episcopal Council (CELAM) held in Medellín, Colombia, in 1968, was a milestone in the history of the Roman Catholic Church. Leaving aside their traditional position, the bishops defined the Latin American situation as "a situation of sin," openly condemned the "institutionalized violence" fostered by capitalism and neo-capitalism, and declared themselves in favor of popular education and popular organizations, including the "base ecclesial communities." Medellín marked the beginning of a clear "preferential option for the poor," and that from an ecclesiastical hierarchy that traditionally had been identified with the powerful.

The Medellín Conclusions, signed by the one hundred and thirty bishops present, provided an ecclesial basis for the "Christian movement" emerging in the base ecclesial communities, especially beginning in the 1960s. The liberationist project and the theology of liberation that had taken shape within that movement made considerable progress and became a hope of renewal for the whole Roman Catholic Church. Little by little, there appeared the "popular Church," regarding which Pablo Richard wrote at the end of the 1970s: "If Medellín was the official and ecclesial expression of the 'prophetic minorities' before 1968, now this popular Church that is being born is the popular and massive expression of the Medellín texts" (1980, p. 56).

The third CELAM Conference held in Puebla, México, in 1979 reaffirmed the preferential option for the poor and acknowledged that the ecclesial communities are "a reason for joy and hope for the Church," "centers of evangelization," "motors for liberation and development," and "the source of ministries given to the laity" (Eagleson and Scharper 1979, pars. 96-97). There is, however, plenty of evidence to show that in the years that followed the tension between the popular Church and the institutional Church was resolved in favor of the Church of the new Christendom — the hierarchical Church which depends on government support to maintain her pastoral and ecclesiastical influence on society. At the end of the 1970s many had the hope that through the popular Church, "from the poor," the only and universal Church of Christ would be renewed as a Church "where the poor would not be the 'object' of evangelization or the 'object' of the Church's preferential love, but the evangelizing subject and the subject that builds up the Church" (ibid., p. 71). During the following decade this hope would be frustrated by a decisive turn toward the hierarchical-institutional Church, promoted by the Vatican — a turn in favor of the new Christendom, a confirmation of the hierarchical power of the Church, the continuation of the religious monopoly on Latin American society, and against the development of the base ecclesial communities.

If the shape that the religious world has taken during these last few years says anything, it proves that the self-preserving measures taken by the institutional Roman Catholic Church have been totally counterproductive. Thousands and thousands of Roman Catholics have left their Church and joined "the Protestant sects" (or other religious societies), looking for a more participatory environment where each person can be regarded as an "evangelizing subject and the subject that builds up the Church." The Evangelical churches flourish in the midst of a situation where the Roman Catholic "magisterium" represents in the religious sphere the same as the great concentrations of capital of the industrialized countries represent in the economic sphere: a system of oppression that imposes its norms of conduct on the large majorities. In the economic sphere common people resist the totalitarianism of the market by "building up networks of communication in the form of movements, organizations and ad hoc groups, both at the domestic and the international levels, through which to share with one another in a more personal way" (Santa Ana 1990, p. 230). In the religious sphere they resist the ecclesiastical totalitarianism by forming churches that are free from Roman control.

This reading of the situation is confirmed, up to a point, by the valuable socioreligious study of the expansion of protestantism in Latin America, *Tongues of Fire*, by David Martin (1990, pp. 19-23). He compares the social function of Latin American Pentecostalism today with that of Anglo-American Methodism (its most direct predecessor) in the past. Already in the seventeenth century, especially in England, Puritanism became an element of dissent in the face of the unity of Church and State, prepared the way for political and religious change, and opened social space for the flourishing of Methodism in a society in which the Anglican Church was part of the establishment. Later on, in the United States, Methodism became a decisive factor for the cultural shaping of the Puritan colonies, on which it definitely impressed its emphasis on voluntarism, individual freedom, and personal responsibility. With the emergence of Methodism, the separation of Church and State was consolidated and the link between Protestant religion and any form of totalitarianism disappeared. According to Martin, what we have today is a Latin American version of Anglo-American Methodism which, as its predecessor, may be interpreted as an anticipation of a freedom that is initially realized in the religious sphere but has the potential of spreading to the whole society.

The extent to which the institutional Roman Catholic Church has lost her power in the political sphere even among its own members is clearly illustrated by the result of the crusade led by Vargas Alzamora, Archbishop of Lima, Perú, against the Evangelical candidates associated with Alberto Fujimori. Neither the denunciation of their "political-religious proselytism," nor his warnings against their effort to break "the basis for Peruvian unity, the Catholic faith," nor his invitation for the Roman Catholic faithful to unite in order to stop the advance of "the sects" was sufficient to prevent that the popular electorate, mostly Roman Catholic, reject Vargas Llosa and elect Fujimori instead.

We are thus led to conclude that the entrance of Evangelicals into the national political scene points to the breaking up of the structures of the new Christendom characterized by authoritarianism and the marginalization of the large majorities of the population. The Roman Catholic hierarchy finds it exceedingly difficult to set aside the (several centuries old) premise that Latin American society is essentially Catholic; therefore they act with an integralist vision of Church and civil society, depending heavily on the support of the oligarchic State to maintain their position of power. The emergence of new actors shows that such a vision and such a dependence are quickly becoming obsolete, and that thousands and tens of thousands of Latin Americans, including many Roman Catholics, see in Evangelicals the promise of a new day for freedom and democracy.

POLITICIANS SHAPED BY AN EVANGELICAL COUNTERCULTURE

The Latin American crisis is fertile soil for the seed of political engagement by Evangelicals. There are also, however, internal factors, inherent to protestantism, which have made it possible for them to respond to that crisis with a political activism that has surprised observers and has become a matter of serious concern to many in the Roman Catholic hierarchy.

All these factors are related to a fact that David Martin emphasizes in his study of "the explosion of protestantism in Latin America": the high degree of social differentiation of Evangelical churches in relation to the surrounding world. As one can expect in view of the religious and cultural predominance of Roman Catholicism in these countries, an important aspect of this differentiation is the anti-Catholic attitude that characterizes the average member of an Evangelical church. In contrast with the "official" Church, which presupposes the integration of all citizens in a hegemonic socioreligious system, Protestant churches generally foster personal commitment, the participation of every member in the life and mission of the Church, individual responsibility, and voluntarism. The Evangelical movement thus offers — says Martin — an alternative society, "a protective social capsule" where many people receive a new identity and new models of initiative and voluntary organization. True, the cultural changes that it fosters have been up to now restricted to the members of the group, but it has the potential of becoming a true agent of social transformation: "The latent may be manifest and the limited free space devised by religion may be suddenly enlarged as it was in the Civil Rights Movement led by Martin Luther King" (ibid., p. 288). We suggest that this is exactly what is taking place at present. It is still too early to predict the impact of this new Evangelical presence on the political scene, but it is obvious that it will reflect the main characteristics of the Evangelical movement: mass mobilization, lay ministry, and spiritual motivation.

Mass Mobilization

The demographic explosion of protestantism in Latin America is a fact that does not need to be proved. In some countries more than in others, but in all these countries, without exception, the statistics give evidence of a phenomenal numerical growth in the last few years. It is estimated that in 1916, when the first Protestant congress was held in Panama, the Evangelical churches in this part of the world had about 300,000 members. It is estimated that Protestant membership now is more than forty million. David Martin does not exaggerate when he says that "It may even be the case that in parts of Latin America the number of Protestants regularly involved in worship and fellowship exceeds the number of Catholics" (ibid., 50). This is undoubtedly so especially in countries where there is a high percentage of Evangelicals, such as Brazil (20 percent), Chile (between 15 and 20 percent), Guatemala (30 percent) and Nicaragua (20 percent).

Critics of protestantism would like to explain this expansion as a foreign "invasion," but that does not reflect reality: one of the main reasons for growth is precisely the mass mobilization of members for evangelism in their own place. The discovery of this possibility of participating in the task that God has given his people produces amazing results among the poor with regard to their sense of dignity and personal value. Of every believer one may say what Gonzalo Baez Camargo says of the founder of Methodism: "Wesley's experience in Aldersgate was not only the conversion from a religion of self-justification to a religion of free grace alone. It was also the conversion from a rigid priesthood and a hierarchical order to a democratic faith and a popular system" (Baez Camargo 1981, p. 86).

The relationship between the numerical growth of protestantism and the entry of Evangelicals into the political scene is quite obvious. For the first time in history, protestantism has enough numerical weight to elect representatives to the highest positions in the national government. Furthermore, for that purpose it can display the same mobilizing capacity as the one it displays to accomplish its traditional purposes.

A very good illustration of this was what happened in the presidential election in Perú in 1990. That Alberto Fujimori, who spent the modest amount of twelve thousand dollars in his campaign, should defeat Mario Vargas Llosa, whose campaign cost one hundred and seventy million dollars, has only one explanation: all over the country, even in the most remote towns, Fujimori could count on a disciplined army of volunteer promoters, members of Evangelical churches. It was thus demonstrated that the mobilization of these humble communities of believers could be as effective in politics as it has been in the spreading of the gospel.

Lay Ministry

Both the mass mobilization and the lay ministry in Evangelical churches are derived from one of the fundamental tenets of the Protestant Reformation of the sixteenth century: the priesthood of all believers. There are those who claim, with good reason, that the early reformers were unable to break away from the clericalism of their day and were satisfied with a soteriological interpretation of this doctrine, failing to see its ecclesiological implications. In other words, they recovered the biblical teaching according to which all believers, being priests, have direct access to God through Jesus Christ, but failed to emphasize another (equally biblical) aspect of the same doctrine: that all believers, without exception, have a ministry through which they exercise their priesthood both inside and outside the Church. As a result, the old clericalism, so characteristic of Roman Catholicism, continued to affect the churches that emerged from the Reformation. The "ministers" (pastors and elders) would be perceived as a special priestly class, in contrast with lay persons.

It is probable that the influence of protestantism on the history of England and, later on, of the United States would have been considerably reduced had it not been for the rediscovery of the priesthood of all believers in Methodism in the eighteenth century. The famous Methodist "classes" (groups of not less than five and not more than ten members, created by John Wesley in order to foster the practice of Christian disciplines among believers in a methodic way) became real seedbeds of lay leaders. In time, hundreds of the "directors" of these "bands" — peasants, common workers, and professionals — would be commissioned to preach, many of them without ever leaving their regular jobs. As Baez Camargo has put it,

> with the role that Methodism gave to the lay Christian, there was the recovery of a forgotten and hidden aspect of primitive Christianity: that it had been primarily and above all a lay movement led by lay people; a movement with no hierarchical divisions, without clergy or a priestly cast, without church bureaucracies. (Ibid., p. 94)

The lay ministry is one of the characteristics that show that the protestantism which has taken root in Latin America is related to the revivalist protestantism of the eighteenth century. In sharp contrast with Roman Catholicism, which is clerical and hierarchical, the Evangelical movement in Latin America is truly participative. Regardless of their social position, their economic situation, or their academic preparation, people are given the opportunity to serve God and neighbor. By doing so, they are given a new sense of dignity and are encouraged to develop their personal capacities.

From this perspective, the presence of Evangelicals on the political scene is an expression of the changes that thousands upon thousands of people formerly

marginalized by society have been experiencing since conversion to protestantism. Evidently, many of the leaders of this lay movement believe that the time
has come for them to find a space to exercise in the political field the capacities
that they have discovered and developed in their own churches. It is not a
coincidence that many Evangelicals who now hold government positions in
various Latin American countries are also lay pastors with long experience as
leaders of churches or parachurch organizations.

Spiritual Motivation

No justice is done to the Evangelical movement in Latin America when the
attempt is made to understand it without taking into account its basic motivation:
the proclamation of the gospel of Jesus Christ. Of course, this does not deny
that, mixed with this purpose, there are other interests that are not as spiritual or
worthy of the Christian faith. In spite of this, the fact remains that no other factor
has so deeply marked evangelicalism as its missionary commitment, its real
concern for the spiritual needs of people. Also, in this respect the Evangelical
churches in Latin America prove to be, in general, heirs of the great Evangelical
revivals of the eighteenth and nineteenth centuries, with their emphasis on the
doctrine and experience of salvation by the grace of God, through faith in Jesus
Christ.

In this central evangelistic concern lie the roots of the traditional "anti-cathol-
icism" that has been (and continues to be even today) one of the most prevalent
marks of Latin American protestantism. However one may judge the polemical
attitude of most Evangelicals with respect to the Roman Catholic Church, he or
she will find it exceedingly difficult to suggest ways in which that attitude could
be avoided in a situation dominated by a Church that has always claimed to have
the spiritual monopoly of the continent. Under these circumstances, the preaching of the gospel according to the Reformed tradition has always been a subversive act, a "sectarian" religious action with a strong political connotation, since
it takes place in countries where for five centuries the existence of an integrated
Roman Catholic socioreligious system has simply been assumed. To prove it,
suffice it to remember the historical rivalry between Protestant/liberals and
Roman Catholic/conservatives in these countries.

With the numerical growth of protestantism, the relation between the Roman
Catholic Church and all the other churches has become even more complicated.
If in the past the Roman Catholic Church could count on government support to
maintain its religious hegemony, now it has to face politicians who question that
hegemony — and question it in the political forum — as Evangelical Christians
with a firm commitment to share their faith. Religious dissidence has always had
political connotations in Latin America — and now more than ever because
Evangelicals see the door open to affirm freedom of conscience for all (theirs
and that of others), and to affirm it from government positions in their respective
countries.

The struggle for religious freedom is part of the heritage of Evangelical
churches in this region. In various countries, this struggle was the only matter

that could awaken interest in politics among Evangelicals. It is not surprising that, now that they have ceased to be an insignificant minority, they should enter the political scene in order to create better conditions for the proclamation of the gospel. Nor should it be surprising that their entrance should be interpreted as a "threat" to the decaying socioreligious system.

THE CHALLENGES OF THE POLITICAL AWAKENING OF EVANGELICALS

In a chapter dedicated to the analysis of politics as "the sphere of the demonic," Jacques Ellul, one of the most outstanding Christian intellectuals of our time, states: "Politics is the contemporary image of absolute evil. It is satanic, diabolical, the very home of the demonic" (Padilla 1987, p. 4).[4] In the discussion of the topic, the distinguished former University of Bordeaux professor clarifies that his accusation is not against a particular kind of politics, rightist or leftist, but against politics as such, against concrete politics; not that of the definitions which emphasize "the common good" or "public interest," but that which is in fact practiced, that which has to do with the means to gain and maintain power over and against the enemies. According to him,

> All the rhetoric about politics as a means to establish justice, etc., is nothing more than a smoke screen that on the one hand hides the hard and vulgar reality and on the other justifies the universal passion for politics, the universal conviction that everything is political and that politics is the noblest activity, when in reality it is the most ignoble. In a strict sense, it is the source of all the evils of our time. (Ibid.)

What hope, then, is there for a Christian witness in the political field? Ellul's answer is decisive: "Christian leaders face a tragic dilemma: they either try to continue to be Christian and their politics is stupid (Jimmy Carter), or they are efficient politicians but cease to be Christian" (ibid.).

A great part of the problem lies in that being a Christian does not put a politician in control of the power games. As with any politician, whether Christian or not, he or she is often compelled to take positions and to make decisions that are far from desirable in the light of Christian principles. The conclusion seems to be inevitable: whoever puts faithfulness to the gospel above political efficacy would do well to abstain from participating in party politics.

If the presence of Evangelicals on the political scene proves anything, however, it is that, as we have seen, there are socioeconomic, political, and religious factors that at present force them to act on that scene. If in the past, when they were an insignificant religious minority, they could not avoid every kind of political involvement in a society whose life is strongly conditioned by institutional structures and relations, now, as a movement that is rapidly growing, they can avoid it even less. Under these circumstances, it is absolutely urgent that Evangelicals face the political challenge with true Christian integrity on both the practical and theoretical levels.

The Practical Challenge

To Evangelicals who are discovering the possibilities of political engagement, Ellul's qualification of politics as "satanic, diabolical, the very home of
the demonic" will sound extremely negative. It must be remembered, however,
that this qualification of politics does not come from a "fundamentalist" who has
cut himself off from the world, nor from a "spiritualist" who denies the need to
relate faith to public life, nor from a Christian who sees Satan's work behind
everything. It comes from a social and political scientist, a university professor,
and a prolific writer who has been active in politics in his own country. Its value
lies in that it emphasizes the dark side of politics and, by implication, the
dangers of temptation to power. The first lesson that Evangelicals have to learn
if they wish to serve God in the political sphere is that "power corrupts, and
absolute power corrupts absolutely" (Lord Acton).[5]

The acknowledgment of the demonic character of politics makes us aware of
the possibility that Evangelical politicians simply reproduce the same evils that
have greatly affected practical politics in the Latin American countries: personal
rivalry, administrative corruption, and opportunism. However brief, the history
of the participation of Evangelicals in politics in these countries provides enough
evidence to show that, sadly, Evangelical churches are not necessarily "the
moral reservoir of the nation" and that their members are not exempt from the
vices of politicizing. The use of Evangelical votes to promote personal ambi-
tions,[6] the manipulation to obtain public subsidies for the Evangelical cause as
special favors, the "sale" of votes to people of dubious conduct in Congress —
these are concrete examples of ways in which some Evangelical politicians have
misused power, posing a question regarding the possibility of a real healing of
Latin American politics through an Evangelical presence. All misuse of power
must be rejected in the name of the One who came, not to be served, but to serve
and to give his life as a means of liberation for many.

The recognition of the dark side of politics will also prevent Evangelicals
from assuming that they are qualified to exercise power "in God's name." History provides plenty of illustrations to show how foolish it is to tie God to a
particular party, ideology, or political program. Aside from the politics of Jesus
— the politics of the Kingdom of God — there is no Christian politics: there are
only *Christians serving God and society in the political field*.

This service, as any other (and perhaps more so because of the complexities
to be faced in this field), requires adequate preparation. Unfortunately, the large
majority of politicians in these countries are unprepared for their task, and
Evangelicals, in general, are no exception. The reason for this is simply that they
have had no time to prepare themselves because they have entered into politics
under the pressure of circumstances. Of course, it is highly doubtful that their
participation in politics will ever take place without this element of circumstanti-
ality. The fact remains, however, that Evangelicals who want to serve God in
politics have to prepare themselves for this task. The sudden change from a
negative attitude toward politics to an improvised participation is all too risky.

The best kind of preparation that Evangelical churches can offer to future politicians begins with the recognition of the urgent needs affecting the great majorities, and of the divine and human resources that local churches have to bring about concrete changes in society, at least on a small scale. There is no sense in struggling to have more Evangelicals participating in national politics if they are not fulfilling their vocation as salt and light and ferment on the lower and intermediate levels of civil society. This presupposes an ecclesiology that looks at the Church not in exclusively spiritual terms, as the proclaimer of the message of reconciliation to God, but in terms of a community with a holistic mission through which God wants to reveal his sovereignty over every aspect of life. Thus conceived, the local church pays serious attention to the preaching of the gospel and also to the task of educating and training, conscientizing and denouncing, informing and communicating, encouraging and organizing in its own neighborhood.[7]

All seems to indicate that the participation of Evangelicals in politics on the national level is just beginning in Latin America, and that it will grow even more in the coming years, predominantly as a means to facilitate the task of evangelizing the continent. One may ask, therefore, if what is beginning to take shape is a new Constantinianism in which the State and the Church (no longer the Roman Catholic but the Evangelical Church) join hands to "christianize" society. David Martin believes that there is no possibility for Evangelical Christianity to become "a substitute established church" (Martin 1990, p. 294). He may be right, but that does not deny that the Constantinian temptation hangs over Evangelicals, especially in countries where their numerical growth gives them a basis to think that their membership will soon include the majority of the population.

If one day a policy were imposed for the purpose of enabling the Evangelical churches to become the established Church of a Protestant Christendom — the Church that seeks to "evangelize" the whole society with the help of political power and of the institutions of civil society — once again it would be demonstrated that the Church fulfills her mission much more faithfully when it is in a position to denounce every form of abuse of power than when it shares the power of the system.

The Challenge on the Theoretical Level

Mark A. Noll (1991) has recently shown the great lack of political reflection among Evangelicals in the United States. According to him, for over two centuries North American evangelicalism has been characterized by moral activism, populism, intuition, and biblicism; consequently, its political activity has lacked theoretical support. If in the future, under the influence of these characteristics, says Noll, Evangelicals "repeat the imbalances of their history, Evangelical political action may be destructive and their political reflection non-existent" (ibid., 29).

What Noll says regarding North American evangelicalism may also be said about its Latin American counterpart: its theological deficit is such that the movement runs the risk of investing its energies in fruitless and even destructive political activism. Realizing this danger, the Latin American Theological Fraternity organized a consultation on "The Theology and Practice of Power" in the Dominican Republic, 24-29 May 1983. Out of that consultation emerged the *Jarabacoa Declaration*, a brief document whose wide distribution since it was issued shows: (1) that the need for Evangelical reflection on politics is a felt need, especially among the new actors on the political scene, and (2) that political theology in Latin America has a long way to go if it is to keep up with the great dynamism of Evangelical churches shown nowadays mainly in their fantastic numerical growth.

It would be naive to think that Evangelicals in one of these countries will be able to put together a "national political project" without forming interdisciplinary teams before to analyze the socioeconomic and political situation and to elaborate practical guidelines for action that would reflect Christian convictions. In no Latin American country that we know of does the Evangelical community have the human resources to accomplish such an ambitious objective. For this and other reasons, I do not believe that the best option for political action rooted in the Christian faith is the formation of Evangelical political parties, because, to speak of a political party is to speak of a national project to be applied by the government to the whole nation. From another perspective, David Martin reaches the same conclusion and proposes a more modest objective for Evangelical engagement in the political field in this continent when he states that

> the kind of voluntary organization represented by evangelical Christianity is contrasted with the Catholic Church precisely by its incapacity to promulgate the kind of norms which are tuned to *specific* conditions of the *whole* society. Its central priority is the recovery of moral densities and solidarities, and the regeneration of hope. (Martin 1990, p. 286)

A modest objective, to be sure, but one that may produce incalculable results in a continent in crisis where the political awakening of Evangelical Christians may point to the beginning of a new day.

NOTES

1. It must be clarified that the attack against Evangelicals with the accusation of favoring foreign interests is not new in Latin America. What Carlos Martínez has stated regarding México may also be said about the other Latin American countries: "Suspicion regarding their origin and aims, ways of life and reproduction; and accusation of receiving great quantities of money from abroad, especially from the United States, and of a sociopolitical conduct which undermines national sovereignty are arguments that have been repeated for over a century in order to disqualify those societies that dissent from the Roman Catholic majority" (1991, pp. 56-57). According to David Martin, Latin American Protestantism is not simply the result of cultural imperialism with headquarters in the United States, but "an indigenous enthusiastic Protestantism rooted in the hopes of millions of Latin American poor" (1990, p. 3). It is highly doubtful that the "Anglo-Saxon imperium" is characterized by "peaceable ideals" to be contrasted with the "militaristic ideals" of the "Hispanic imperium," as Martin has claimed. It is, however, evident that, in the history of Latin

America, Protestantism has served as a carrier of modern values (such as democracy) over against the values of the medieval world (such as authoritarianism).

2. The theme of the Roman Catholic nature of Latin American culture is often taken for granted in Roman Catholic official documents. See, for instance, the Puebla Document (Eagleson and Scharper, pars. 412-414). This premise is behind many of the arguments to characterize Evangelicals as defenders of foreign interests (cp. Boletín 1991, pp. 61-68).

3. These accusations coming from leftist fundamentalism do not exclude Evangelicals who have been under suspicion in their own communities because of their critical stance regarding the prevailing oppressive system. Thus, for instance, Jean Pierre Bastian accuses the members of the Latin American Theological Fraternity (who, according to him, have "no university education") of belonging to "the ideological vanguard which legitimizes the establishment" (1986/1990, pp. 230-231).

4. Only the Spanish text was available to the author.

5. This oft-quoted statement is attributed to Alexis de Tocqueville.

6. *Editor's Note:* "In May, Guatemalan President Jorge Serrano Elías pre-empted a congressional investigation into the misuse of public funds by staging his own coup d'état. He disbanded the congress and judiciary and assumed dictatorial control. On June 1, Mr. Serrano was ousted as his military benefactor bowed to international and local outrage over his actions" ("Public Intolerance for Graft is Toppling Latin Leaders," in *The Christian Science Monitor*, Wednesday, 16 June 1993, p. 4).

7. From this perspective, the following recommendation by the "Permanent Consultation on the Mission of the Evangelical Church," which took place in Colombia from June 1983 to October 1988, seems quite relevant: "To foster the wholistic gospel in the local churches, preparing people to work in different areas, to establish networks, to plan activities and to prepare the believers for the changes. To educate (by forming and informing) the Church to awaken it to Colombian realities. To create strategies for services, cooperatives, collaboration groups, collaboration networks, etc." (Final Report of the Consultation, Bogota, 1989, p. 24).

PART THREE

POPULAR RELIGION:
TRADITION AND CHANGE

9

The Gospel and the Andean Culture

Fernando Quicaña

"The invaders and those who followed them in their violation of the life of the Andean people are judged by Andean society for the aggravated crime of genocide; they, therefore, will be judged by God in the final judgment: (Mt 25:41). . . . Righteousness, truth, and industriousness are the basis of our Andean philosophy of thought and action. It is completely different from the behavior and attitude of Europeans. Andean social organization is actually closer to the communal way of life of the patriarchs of the Old Testament and the first Christians . . . in Acts." The author is a Peruvian pastor and a leader of an indigenous Evangelical organization called TAWA: Tawantin-suyuman Alli Wuillacui Apajcuna [those who take the gospel to the four cardinal points]. This paper was presented at the Third Latin American Congress on Evangelization (CLADE III), and has been translated with permission.

CULTURE

Culture may be defined as the collection of material and spiritual values, created and developed by human beings in their life experience throughout history. In the simplest terms, culture has to do with the customs created and applied in the life of a society (community, people, nation) and transmitted from generation to generation. A people's culture is not static or fixed, but changes gradually according to time and place. Examples are the type of dress, the design of houses, the type of transportation, etc.

When we refer to the existence of a culture, we come to realize that there is no such thing as a superior or inferior culture. Sociological and anthropological studies support and confirm this conclusion. In actuality, each society maintains and preserves its own cultural patterns or values. What occurs is that we confuse the fact that there are cultures in developed societies that dominate sociopolitically, economically, and theologically, while others are underdeveloped due to oppression and domination.

Dr. Tito Paredes, a Christian anthropologist, in a presentation on ethnocentrism and egocentrism says the following:

> There are individuals, peoples or nations who think and believe that their language, lifestyle, customs and way of thinking and behaving are better or superior to those of other individuals, peoples or nations. This superior attitude and conduct are completely erroneous. Each culture has its own values and customs and must therefore respect and appreciate other cultures, without discrimination, contempt, exploitation or violence toward the culture or toward human dignity.

THE ANDEAN CULTURE

The Andean culture is a collection of values, uses, and characteristic indigenous customs created by the people and applied by the Andean society (Quechuas, Aymaras) to the practical aspects of life. Culture, in this sense, may be appreciated in the social organization, beliefs, religion, music, housing, food, clothing, and medicine of the Andean people.

The Andean culture is as ancient as Western (European) cultures. History shows us that approximately three hundred years before Christ, our ancestors had already organized a social structure that ranged from small units, called *ayllus* [family relations] to larger political and geographical units, called *suyus* [large regions]. These large units were the Aymaras or Kollas, who inhabited the region south of Cusco and whose capital was Tiyawanaku; the Quechuas, who inhabited the region extending from the north of Cusco to Quito and Colombia, whose capital was Cusco; and the Ungas, who inhabited the coastal region and whose capital was Pachakamaq. These large *suyus* or regions later formed part of the powerful Tawantinsuyu, under the wise and prudent administration and government of the *Incas* [kings], founded by the Inca Manku Qapaq and his wife Mama Oqllu.

From history we know that the existence of navigable rivers, favorable climates, and productive lands favored the establishment and development of the great Old World civilizations. The Andean society, however, had no such advantages. The great Tawantinsuyu was born in rugged territory, far from the sea, with no navigable rivers; the land was uneven and the climate variable (burning sun, torrential rains, hailstorms, overnight freezes, and droughts). The historian Pedro Cieza de León accurately stated: "Great wisdom was needed to govern such diverse nations in such rugged land."

IDEOLOGICAL CONTRADICTIONS

In order for the gospel of the Kingdom of God to effectively penetrate the social life of the Andean people, we must point out the ideological contradictions between our Andean society and Western (European) society.

The Falsehood of the Europeans

Beginning in 1532, the Spanish invaders dedicated themselves to the illicit accumulation of wealth, the wealth of the great Tawantinsuyu. The theologians, lawyers, and philosophers of Europe discussed intensely the "Indian's right to freedom." At the debates held at the Junta de Burgos in Spain, Bartolomé de Las Casas was among the few who expressed themselves to be in favor of this right. The majority declared themselves to be against the "Indians."

These disparaging attitudes led the discussion to the issue of "whether or not the Indian had a soul" (Vatican document). In the meantime, Spanish invaders, supported by theologians and lawyers, sought to prove the "physical, moral, and intellectual impotence of the Indian," equating the Indians with "animals." In this way the invaders gathered support for the exploitation of our *ayllus*, carried out under the false pretense of "justice."

Juan Ginés de Sepúlveda, a theologian who supported Aristotle's theory that some men are born to command and others to obey, published a book in Rome in which he states the following concerning the condition and destiny of the Andean people (Indians): "The Indians are servants, barbarians, uncultured and inhuman by nature, and if they refuse to obey other more perfect men, it is just to subject them by force and by war."

The invaders took captive our Inca Atawalpa in Cajamarca, justifying their actions with Ginés de Sepúlveda's theory (ca. 1550); a theory that, while undermining the dignity of the Andean people, wholeheartedly supported the Spanish invaders. It is in no way consistent with the principles and doctrines of the Holy Scriptures. We therefore consider the unfortunately famous Sepúlveda as ignorant in his knowledge of the Holy Scriptures.

The Individualism of the Europeans

Individualism is a system that favors the individual, in order that he may act according to his own free will. He may, in other words, be free to fulfill his own desires, free of any conditions, ignoring or overlooking community and collective interests. The Spanish invaders, along with the Catholic Church, introduced individualism to Tawantinsuyu. Later on this individualism was strengthened in Peruvian society by the socioeconomic domination of England and later on of the United States. The resulting ideological structure of contemporary mestizo society is based on the individualism introduced by the aforementioned societies.

Individualism, therefore, is the ideological foundation of capitalism: the essence and aim of its laws, political relations, and morality. Individualism surfaces in the private ownership of the means of production, with its resulting disregard for social and community interests and complete opposition to collective systems.

The majority of Spanish and mestizo writers support an ideology of individualism. In this way they discredit the authentic history of Andean society, exaggerating negative aspects and making derogatory references to "lazy Indians" and "cheap half-breeds."

In conclusion, the invaders and those who followed them in their violation of the life of the Andean people are judged by Andean society for the aggravated crime of genocide; they, therefore, will be judged by God in the final judgment (Mt 25:41). Genocide is the methodical destruction of ethnic peoples that does away with their inhabitants and destroys their social organizations.

The Ideology of the Andean Peoples

Honest historians, as well as those of us who are descendants of the Andean people, recognize that the Andean culture was created and formed out of the ideological structure of the Andean people. Its organizational system and theocratic government (government in the name of the god Inti) are not copies or imitations of Old World European civilizations. During that time there was no communication between the two continents, nor did these two great societies know that the other existed.

The social organization and administrative system of Andean society are completely different from the ways and systems of the European Old World governments, and completely opposed to them. The life experience of the Andean peoples is essentially collective, communal, and participatory; it is functional and practical. On the other hand, as mentioned above, the life experience of the European is characterized by individualism and selfishness, it is theoretical and dominating.

Social organization. The social organization of the Andean people was theocratic; based on the *ayllu* and a family, community, and collective system, it was characterized by equality and an absence of social classes. The *ayllu* is the true democracy. Its primary activity is the *ayni* and the *minka*, cooperation between families and communities, where services are compensated for by the sharing of activities. For this reason our current political activity is not theoretical, but arises from concrete actions and experience, and is characterized by a lack of totalitarianism and verticalism. It is not, therefore, in any way similar to the theoretical model of Western society.

Andean society today is the heir of the high pre-Colombian culture, which is the reason we firmly and vigorously maintain our historic personality. Righteousness (*ama suwa*), truth (*ama llulla*), and industriousness (*ama qella*) are the basis of our philosophy of thought and action. It is completely different from the behavior and attitude of the European. Andean social organization is actually closer to the communal way of life of the patriarchs of the Old Testament and the first Christians, based on what we find in Acts (2:43-37; 4:32-37).

I want to specify that the *ayllu* cannot exist without the land; for this reason the Quechuas and Aymaras feel that we are a part of the land. In it we see the origins of the *Mama-pacha* or *Patsa* [Mother Earth], which year after year sustains the life of the Andean family. On many occasions, when the rich *caciques* or landowners and landed farmers have seized their mother earth, the Quechuas and Aymaras have sacrificed their lives.

The understanding of the Andean people is consistent with the teaching of the Holy Scriptures: "By the sweat of your brow you will eat your food until you return to the ground, since from it you were taken. For dust you are and to dust you will return" (Gn 3:19; 2:7).

Communitarianism. This term is derived from the word "community." The community or *ayllu* is a human grouping that inhabits a specified territory, participates in common experiences and traditions, has its own customs, and maintains an awareness of its unity and solidarity within its *ayllu*.

Andean communitarianism is a movement that is deeper and more spontaneous than a family nucleus or social class. Those who participate actively in community property struggle together to maintain the existence of the community through a philosophy of work called *el ayni, la minka,* and *la mita* [task], based on the moral code.

The collective is a group of persons joined together by a common interest that discourages and in fact suppresses individual ownership of property. Its principles for social life and joint participation are based on the practice of equality, natural justice, and respect for the moral authority of the elders, called *kuraq.* As mentioned previously, the Andean people have developed their own philosophical, political, and theological understanding, and do not need to copy or imitate ideologies from the Old World. At that time there was no relationship between these continents, especially during the period of the great Tawantinsuyu. The Andean society, therefore,

(a) *Was not capitalist.* There was no such thing as private ownership of the means of production (based on individualism), for the enrichment of a minority, through monopolies and the exploitation of man by man.

(b) *Was not communist.* Class struggle did not exist. Slavery was unknown, and the economic interests of the *ayllus* and *suyus* were community based and governed by the "trialogue." As a result, there were no needy inhabitants in all of Tawantinsuyu.

(c) *Was theocratic.* Social life and the philosophic and political principles of Andean society were based on the cosmic religion *Tayta Inti* and *Mama Pacha* or *Patsa.* Those who governed the great Tawantinsuyu were considered children of the god Tayta Inti, since both civil and religious laws were of divine origin. They were defined in this way to assure the Andean society of a high level of morality and an irreproachable ethic, subject to the trialogue.

The moral code. In an organized society, such as the great Tawantinsuyu, efficient administration was necessary. The development of a penal and civil code was important for the interrelationship of culture and law. In this way the administrators and the people were provided with a guide for positive conduct and behavior that sought mutual respect within the society. Our ancestors, the administrators of the Andean society, established laws, commandments, and ordinances that were summarized in a trialogue.

The trialogue (kimsan kamachicuy). The trialogue — *Ama Suwa, Ama Qella, Amallulla* (Quechua) or *Jan Juntata, Jan Jaira, Jan K''ari* (Aymara) — was a wise idea developed by our ancestors and put into practice efficiently in the Tawantinsuyu. The Quechua and Aymara peoples cherish the trialogue in our consciences and practice it in our daily lives.

Ama Suwa or *Jan Luntata.* Honesty and faithfulness to your neighbor is one of the important qualities that a person should have. Trust between neighbors leads to honor and not to treason.

Ama Llulla or *Jan Jaira.* Truthfulness is the other important characteristic of a person. To lie is to destroy the morale of your neighbor and, therefore, of society.

Ama Quella or *Jan K''ari*. A person must not deny his neighbor his strength, since the prosperity of the society depends on the joint strength of all its members.

The trialogue of Tawantinsuyu thus coincides with the decalogue of Moses that we find in the Holy Scriptures.

Faithful obedience to the trialogue. The laws summarized in the trialogue were faithfully followed by everyone, from the *Inca* down to the last man of the Tawantinsuyu. The trialogue was the basic norm and the foundation for society in the Tawantinsuyu. The *Inca*s who governed the Tawantinsuyu could not act arbitrarily, despotically, or according to their own interests. All political, economic, and socioreligious decisions were governed and regulated strictly by the trialogue.

Whoever transgressed the trialogue was severely punished, beginning with the *Inca* and on down to the last man of the *ayllu*. Andean political philosophy states that *the government is for the well-being of the governed*. The trialogue is present in the conscience of the Andean people (Quechua and Aymara). We know the good that we must do and the bad that we must not do, what is permitted and what is forbidden.

With pride we say and affirm that our *ayllu* ancestors were a cultured people, with a high moral standard and an irreproachable ethic. Thieves were unknown in Andean society; there were no lazy people and no liars.

Marriage, as the basis of Andean society, was considered to be very sacred, so much so that divorce did not exist. Still today there is deep respect between spouses in Quechua and Aymara communities. If adultery should occur, it is severely punished, in order to avoid a bad testimony for the society. Our ancestors did not know the Holy Bible; however, there are many similarities between their laws and the teachings of the Bible.

Theological Understanding

Our ancestors had concrete ideas about the existence of the true God. They knew him by the name of *Pachakamaq*, which means "Creator of the universe," but they also worshipped other gods such as the sun, the moon, and the *Mama Pacha* or *Patsa*. Garcilaso de la Vega (a descendant of *Inca*s) states the following:

> The Incas and their subjects greatly venerated Pachakamaq. Asked who Pachakamaq was, they responded that it was he who gave life to the universe and sustained it, but that they did not know him because they had not seen him. For this reason they did not build him temples or offer him sacrifices, but they worshipped him in their heart, that is in their mind, and they referred to him as the unknown god.

Agustín de Zárate, in referring to the story of the priest Valverde says:

> Valverde told the king Atawalpa that Christ our Lord had created the world; the Inca responded that he knew nothing of this, and that he believed nothing but that there was a god, and the earth their mother and that Pachakamaq had created everything there was.

The Spanish invaders, in order to justify the presence of their genocidal religion, have tried to discredit the theological understanding of the Andean people by saying that "the Indians are idolatrous." To this end they established the macabre institution called "exterminators of idolatry." Through this institution they have destroyed the temples, observatories, and the religiosity of our forefathers. The priests Hernando de Avendaño and José de Arriaga, named by the archbishop of Lima in 1617, were among the most fervent in carrying out this task. The Spaniards considered Pachakamaq to be a "demon." However, Garcilaso clarifies:

> The Indians never gave the name Pachakamaq to the devil; they called him *supay*, and when speaking his name they spit first as a sign of a curse and a demonstration of their rejection of him.
>
> But if I, who am a Catholic Christian Indian by the infinite grace, were asked today what the name for God is in my tongue, I would say "Pachakamaq," because in the language of Peru there is no other name for God but this one. The Incas established laws and demanded obedience so that the entire empire would know that they were to worship none other than Pachakamaq, the supreme God and Lord, and the sun for the good he did for everyone. Everything that the historians say is improper. (Royal Commentaries I, ch. 2)

Space and time, or world view. Our theologian ancestors (*amawtas*) divided the universe into three regions:

Hanaq Pacha [heaven] is the dwelling place of the obedient and good who are rewarded for having faithfully fulfilled the trialogue — Ama Suwa, Ama Llulla, Ama Qella. They said: "Way up in heaven life is peaceful, full of happiness, free from toil and sorrow."

Kay Pacha [this life, earth] is the dwelling place of people and animals. In the *Mama Pacha* or *Patsa* grow the plants and earthly spirits that move in the springs of water (*pagarina*), among the cliffs (*wamanis*) and in the caverns (*wari*). The *Inca*s, being children of the sun, governed the *Kay Pach* benevolently.

Uku Pacha or *Supay Wasi* [hell] is the dwelling place of the wicked, those who disobey the three commandments. It is the place of pain and suffering. There is no way to escape from the *Uku Pacha* [hell] to the *Hanaq Pacha* [glory].

Kawsarimuy [resurrection]. Our ancestors believed in the immortality of the soul and the resurrection of the body for a future life. As evidence or proof of this belief, they tried to preserve the bodies of the dead as well as possible. When the Spaniards opened the tombs and scattered the bones of the dead in their search for treasure, the Quechuas begged them not to, since the bones needed to be together for the resurrection.

There was a custom among the Quechuas and Aymaras that has survived until today. Each year, on the second of November, those who are not Christians prepare the favorite meal of a loved one who has passed away. They place the meal in a special room with the idea that during the night the spirit of the dead one will come and savor this favorite dish. The Quechuas and Aymaras did not have a written language, but this tradition has been preserved in their practice with the firm belief that the souls of their loved ones are immortal, that they are alive and will one day be resurrected bodily and will all be together again.

THE GOSPEL IN THE ANDEAN COMMUNITIES

Around the year 1949, through the efforts of Quechua and Aymara believers, the good news of the Kingdom of God came to the Andean communities. Later our foreign missionary and mestizo pastor brothers organized the churches. It is important to reflect on the fact that our brothers, both missionaries and mestizo leaders, by virtue of their cultural and ideological upbringing are socially dominant, autocratic, and individualistic. In keeping with these characteristics, they established churches of their own denominations in the Andean communities. In doing this they ignored our ideological, philosophical, and theological principles: community and collective life, social organization, religiosity, beliefs, music, medicine, clothing, and worldview. We are endowed with these cultural values just as other peoples are in their own cultures.

From the time these foreign missionaries and mestizo leaders began to organize churches in the Aymara and Quechua communities, they taught about the difference between "that which is spiritual and that which is worldly." This concept was difficult for the Andean people to understand, since our religiosity is objective and holistic. Our brothers, believing that they were "acculturating" the Indians, incorporated their individualistic cultural ideologies along with the teaching of the gospel. As a result, new believers, in obedience to their pastors or missionaries, no longer wanted to participate in community activities such as communal work projects, assemblies, the *minka* and the *ayni*; they were considered to be "worldly." In response, community leaders demanded even more vigorously that Christians fulfill their duties and obligations as members of the community. In many instances this lack of understanding resulted in persecution of the Christians, not so much because of their faith in Christ, but because of this cultural conflict.

Faced with this apparent persecution, new Christians would move to other locations, leaving the communities where the were born and raised to congregate in urban or mestizo churches. Yet according to the teaching of the Bible, Protestant believers must propagate profound social, economic, religious, and political changes in their communities, because the gospel is the "power of God" that transforms persons through the Holy Spirit so that they may practice justice, righteousness, and honesty, being the "light of the world and salt of the earth." The gospel is not merely a religion to divide and create enmity among Christians. On the contrary, Jesus Christ has interceded with the Father that all Christians may be one (Jn 17:20-24), because they are created in Christ for good works (Ef 2:10).

Another of the negative aspects of the introduction of the gospel into the social life of the Andean people were the denominations. In many cases many different denominations were established in the same community, thus breaking the bonds of unity that existed in the *ayllu*. The communities divided into rival religious groups. As a result, the Quechua or Aymara non-believer interprets the gospel as something negative and harmful to the community and to their religiosity. This leads them to hate and persecute the gospel. In some ways, our mestizo and missionary brothers, while they were protecting the interests of their denominations, have adversely affected the significance of the gospel and the unity of the Christians, such as we see it expressed in John 17:20-22.

Communication Breakdowns

When a mestizo preacher is trying to communicate God's message to the Andean people, in a culture that is unknown to him and in a language he does not fully command, the message is transmitted vertically (*sayanpa*); it is therefore impossible for it to penetrate the ears of the Andean people. But if we communicate this same message in parallel form (*waqtampa*), the message of God becomes understandable. It is comprehensible to the ear of the Andean people because it is communicated from their own cultural experience and in their language.

All written communication has a content and form; the Holy Scripture has content and form. Content is the original meaning of the Scripture, what God wants to say to humanity. Content is like the soul that does not change and remains forever. Form is the literary style of the writer, how God speaks to humanity. Form is the body, it changes and is modified depending on time and place.

The content of God's message cannot change, it is immovable, it remains the same for ever and ever. However, it is possible to change the form of the message depending on the time, the cultural context, and the life experience of those receiving it. For example, in Matthew 26:39, the King James version says, "Let this cup pass from me." A more popular version says, "Free me from this bitter cup." The Quechua version says, "Free me from this suffering." The content of the message has not changed in the least, it remains the same. What has changed is the form or style, the way the message is communicated.

Seminaries and Bible Institutes

Bible institutes or seminaries were founded in the ancient Tawantinsuyu (Perú) by foreign missionaries. In these institutions the students received instruction in theology, homiletics (the art of preaching), hermeneutics (the art of interpretation), etc., which are based on European or North American cultural concepts. There is no such thing as a course for teaching and learning about evangelization in the context of Andean society — in spite of the fact that there are more than eighteen million Quechuas and Aymaras in Bolivia, Perú, and Ecuador. The Quechua or Aymara young person who studies in these seminaries must necessarily submit to the cultural impositions of the professors and the contempt of the mestizo students. The Quechua or Aymara student is forced to adapt to the mestizo way of life and become individualistic, selfish, and domineering.

As a result of this psychological and moral impact, the Quechua or Aymara young people begin to feel contempt for their own cultural experience, their idiosyncrasies, their mother tongue; they end up rejecting or denying the culture of their birth and are left without a cultural identity.

Graduates of seminaries and Bible institutes who return to their Quechua and Aymara communities preach what they learned in their "alma mater": incorporating the formal style, the legalism and authoritarianism, the inflexible time frame for worship services, etc., of the European culture. They impose, autocratically, customs that begin to destroy the cultural values of the Quechuas and Aymaras.

This type of preaching contains "purely human criteria" (of the flesh), characterized by arrogance and pride, and is not guided by the Holy Spirit. Thus the Quechuas and Aymaras are denied a deeper knowledge of the Holy Scriptures. We hear in the prophetic voices of the mestizo preachers discourses on love, justice, and equality that we do not see in their practice.

The majority of seminary professors do not have experience in Andean pastoral ministry. Consequently, their teaching is theoretical and academic, geared to the urban areas, and not practical and dynamic for the Andean people. Graduates, upon returning to their Quechua or Aymara communities, preach in Spanish to demonstrate their superiority, their great knowledge of theology, apologetics, homiletics, hermeneutics, etc. They use examples and comparisons from other countries and Greek words, all of which are completely strange and foreign to the Andean people.

These cultural and theological impositions are an offense to an Andean society that has an ancient culture and, as such, is part of the heritage of Perú. These people are guilty, therefore, of cultural "ethnocide."

The Attitude of Christ and of the Apostles

Our Lord Jesus Christ, in proclaiming the message of the Kingdom of God to his people, never acted arrogantly or with pride. His attitude was one of humility; he spoke Aramaic, his mother tongue, and the *koine* Greek, which was spoken by the common people, instead of using the classical Greek (Phil 2:3-7). When the Apostle Paul gave himself to Christ he was transformed by the Holy Spirit. From that time on he rid himself of his professional pride and cultural privileges. He said: "I consider everything a loss compared to the surpassing greatness of knowing Christ Jesus my Lord, for whose sake I have lost all things. I consider them rubbish that I may gain Christ" (Phil.3 :4-9). "I do all this for the sake of the gospel, that I may share in its blessings" (1 Cor. 9:23). In the same way, the other apostles used the term "servant" to manifest their humility.

The Apostle Paul, in speaking about the use of language in the church, says: "Undoubtedly there are all sorts of languages in the world. . . . But if I do not grasp the meaning of what someone is saying, I am a foreigner to the speaker and he is a foreigner to me. . . . I would rather speak five intelligent words to instruct others than ten thousand words in a [strange] tongue" (1 Cor. 14:10, 11, 19).

THE EXPERIENCE OF THE ANDEAN CHURCH

The Quechua and Aymara churches are changing. After a decade of clarification and reflection we now have a certain amount of freedom to serve our Lord Jesus Christ from our own cultural experience, to praise our God with our own music and to enjoy an abundant life in Christ (Jn 10:10). Our mestizo and foreign missionary brothers are slowly recognizing their mistakes and are coming to appreciate our cultural values. Together we can evangelize more effectively, jointly proclaiming the Kingdom of God through the power of the Holy Spirit, among the Andean people.

The year 1978 marks a historic turning point in the Christian life of the Quechuas. In July of that year a meeting was held in Huancayo of the leaders of five denominations under the guidance of the anthropologist Dr. Tito Paredes. After three days of prayer and reflection on the Word of God, we felt the power of the Holy Spirit. Each one of the leaders recognized his mistakes. Instead of edifying the church of Christ, we have been destroying it with "purely human criteria, envy, discord, and division," with the sole purpose of defending our own denominations (I Co 3:3-9)

As a spontaneous result of this meeting and under the direction of the Holy Spirit, a fraternal organization was formed called the "Evangelical Quechua Committee of Perú" (now TAWA), whose only objective is to promote the evangelization, edification, and growth of the Quechua churches. This committee established certain guidelines:

1. To seek peace in the conflict that exists among denominations and to work for brotherly unity, respecting the organization, doctrine, liturgical customs, and style of worship of each (Jn 17:20-22).

2. To carry out an evangelistic and pastoral ministry that takes into account the cultural values of the Andean people, without copying the ideologies of the Old World, which have caused so much confusion for the Quechuas and Aymaras.

3. To organize seminaries and workshops for training leaders in theology and Bible, based on the Holy Scriptures, and from the ideological perspective of the Andean people.

4. To promote the organization of Protestant Andean music festivals, using our autochthonous melodies from the different geographic locations and dialects we belong to, in order to affirm our culture in the process of evangelization.

5. To motivate the church to serve the community through farming, literacy, health, and communication projects. To make known to autochthonous peoples their universal and constitutional rights.

Agreements Reached in Congresses

I will quote the agreements reached in international and national congresses in favor of the Andean society.

The Declaration of Ayacucho. The evangelical Quechuas-Quichuas of Ecuador, Bolivia, and Perú met in the first congress, held in Ayacucho, Perú, in

August of 1979. Declaration number two states the following: "We recognize that our culture has many positive aspects that in the past were rejected and denied in the communication of the gospel, but that the church is now discovering and using these for the glory of God; for example: music, community work, crafts and textile art."

The fourth declaration adds: "We commit ourselves to uniting our spiritual and cultural efforts in order to fulfill the Great Commission given to us by our Lord Jesus, among our people and through the world."

CLADE II. In Huampaní, near Lima (Perú), in November of 1979, the Second Latin American Congress on Evangelism (CLADE II), brought together 266 Latin American Evangelical leaders from 30 denominations and 22 countries. The fourth agenda for the evangelization of autochthonous peoples states as follows: "Spanish speakers must demonstrate a human attitude of respect and love among autochthonous groups, showing that we truly believe in equality. Avoid the transplanting of inadequate systems that can result in cultural demoralization and disintegration."

The Second National Congress of Peruvian Quechua Leaders was held in Yungay-Ancash in September of 1980, with the participation of six denominations and eight Quechua-speaking provinces. The third resolution reads: "We recognize and are aware of the fact that sin has affected the Quechua culture as it has all cultures, but we also know that the gospel transforms the human being and his culture and gives new perspectives through redemption in Christ."

CONCLUSION

Freedom in Christ from spiritual oppression and theological and liturgical impositions has as its only purpose to glorify our God without cultural barriers — from our Andean context — and without the humiliation that prohibits us from fulfilling our purpose of serving and worshiping our triune God. When someone unjustly or without cause censures our cultural experience, we feel oppressed, discriminated against, and deprived of our freedom and, therefore, cannot enjoy abundant life in Christ (Jn 10:10).

In his word God says: "Let my people go so that they may worship me. If you refuse to let them go I will plague you. . ." (Ex 8:1-2). Our mestizo brothers must reflect seriously on the teachings of the Holy Scriptures in order to avoid the crimes of "ethnocide and genocide."

Jesus Christ has empowered his church to guide the destiny of the redeemed in the midst of society without confusions or errors. There must therefore be cooperation and moral and spiritual support among the churches without ideological and theological impositions.

The Quechua and Aymara church, as a part of the Kingdom of God and as members of the church of Christ, has been given the necessary gifts to carry out the process of spiritual development without theological and liturgical supervision. We recognize that our culture has many aspects that favor the communication of the gospel among the Andean people. Our foundation is the Scripture, because it is our only authority and rule of faith, the guide for our conduct and behavior as children of God; and it allows us to value our cultural way of life.

In national and international congresses we do not seek to create rebellion or negative attitudes that would offend the dignity of our mestizo brothers. What we seek is true freedom in Christ, in order to better evangelize our Quechua and Aymara brothers, and to worship and praise our God according to our context and cultural reality. The Word of God tells us: "So if the Son sets you free, you will be free indeed" (Jn 8:36).

To conclude, the Word of God declares that all persons are God's creation and that their purpose is to glorify God.

Translated by Elisabeth Cook

10

Conflict of Interpretations of Popular Protestantism

J. Samuel Escobar

The author examines the "missiological lessons" derived from the explosive growth of "a popular form of Protestantism" in traditionally homogeneous Roman Catholic societies. "This phenomenal change of religious affiliation takes place in one of the most critical periods of social transition for Latin America, in which the condition of the poor urban and rural masses continues to deteriorate, reaching levels of bare subsistence." This chapter brings together an article published in *Missiology* (April 1992) with material prepared for presentation in the 1991 American Academy of Religion conference (November 1991). It is used with permission of the author.

The rapid growth and massive presence of popular protestantism in Latin America during the last three decades has become one of the most puzzling and challenging missiological realities of our time. Some Catholic observers go as far as predicting that popular protestantism might become the predominant religious force in Latin America at the eve of the Third Millennium, "If current growth rates continue Latin America will have an evangelical majority in the early 21st century" (McCoy 1989, 2). It could well be the movement that carries the seeds for the reformation and completion of Christian mission in Latin America and from Latin America to other parts of the world. It could also be the religious source for new forms of social and political participation of the emerging classes and subcultures that are changing the sociological and political maps of the region. On the other hand, the Protestant upsurge and the Catholic reaction could be sparks that ignite a religious war of catastrophic proportions.

In this study we will consider in a special way the most recent wave of numerical growth of popular protestantism in Latin America, within the framework of the religious history of the continent. We will focus especially on the different approaches that have been used to interpret it. Because this numerical growth of protestantism has influenced political events in several countries, it has prompted analysts and interpreters to consider the social and political significance of this growing religious minority. At the same time, the Catholic hierarchies, as leaders of the predominant religious force in the region, are especially interested in the religious or missiological significance of this phenomenon. We must examine critically the merits and insufficiencies of sociological approaches based on modernization and dependence theories, as well as their interaction with current theological trends. The global interpretations of Latin American protestantism offered by sociologist of religion David Martin and anthropologist David Stoll came to prominence in 1990 and must be evaluated, considering especially the contribution of Martin and his use of historical and theological insights absent from previous efforts of interpretation. Finally, reference will be made to Catholic missiological interpretations.

The basic thesis and intention of our own analysis is missiological. From the perspective of the fulfillment of the mission of the church, the recent explosive growth of a popular form of protestantism in Latin America is filled with missiological lessons. On the one hand this is because Latin American societies traditionally have been considered as homogeneously Roman Catholic. They constitute the region of the world where the largest proportion of Roman Catholics (42 percent) live now, but their church has to face the fact that currently "every hour in Latin America an average of four hundred Catholics move to membership in Protestant sects" (Damen 1987, 45). On the other hand this is because the frame and background for this phenomenal change of religious affiliation is one of the most critical periods of social transition for Latin America, in which the condition of the poor urban and rural masses has continued to deteriorate, reaching levels of bare subsistence. Religious leaders as well as political analysts pose constantly the question about the role of churches in the efforts to transform Latin American societies into more viable forms of human coexistence.

Although research and writing of the history of protestantism in Latin America is still in its initial stages, Protestant growth has become a privileged field of observation for historians and social scientists. In the theological discourse of recent decades much use has been made of that kind of research. One of the main tenets of the Latin American theologies of liberation is precisely the new reading of the history of the church that they propose (Escobar 1982). This new perspective comes from a way of understanding historical processes that is shaped by the social sciences, and especially by Marxist class analysis. The outcome of this interdisciplinary approach has been that the mission of the Church and her self-understanding have come to be formulated in categories that owe more to sociological analysis, ideological choice, and political preference than to the traditional theological and biblical categories. From a missiological viewpoint it is imperative to understand and evaluate the scope of the determinative role played by the social sciences in contemporary theology and missiology. This understanding and evaluation will allow us to perceive with more clarity if this interdisciplinary work has contributed to a better understanding or to a misunderstanding of Latin American protestantism and its mission in the world today.

The need for clarification of methodology in the writing and interpretation of the history of religious communities does not apply only to protestantism. In an important book about the history of the Roman Catholic Church in Brazil and her role in the political life of that country, Scott Mainwaring (1986) outlines critically the main approaches currently used in the writing of church history in Latin America, and in the interpretation of the life of the Church. He describes them as "institutional analysis" as practiced mainly by North American scholars, "a neo-Marxian approach" preferred by Latin Americans, and "the classical line of analysis" of the fathers of sociology of religion: Weber, Troeltsch, and H. Richard Niebuhr (ibid., 1). Mainwaring's approach is eclectic and draws from the three others. We find this eclectic approach more congenial with our own understanding and analysis of Protestant history in Latin America (Escobar 1975, 1978, 1989), and thus we will be using our own modified version of Mainwaring's approach. However, our analysis must be preceded by a brief historical outline of the Protestant presence in Latin America.

THE NATURE OF POPULAR PROTESTANTISM

In order to understand the growing churches and denominations that we are calling "popular protestantism," we need to draw up a basic typology of protestantism in general. The classic typology adopted by Costas[1] and others groups Latin American Protestants into three broad types: Mainline Protestantism, Evangelical Protestantism, and Pentecostal Protestantism, using as a criteria their history, theological stance, and global relationships.

The social and political significance of each one of these types has been interpreted in different ways, as we will see later. However, in the contemporary situation and from the missiological perspective the matter could be approached in a different way, taking a lead from the observations of contemporary Catholic missiology. From an examination of Catholic missiological literature in Latin America it is evident that for the Catholic Bishops and missiologists, not all Protestant churches but the popular forms of protestantism are a matter of concern and even anxiety. Thus the well-known missiologist Mgr. Roger Aubry says that the Catholic Church has no problems with "traditional Protestant churches with whom we have ecumenical relations, sharing the same longings for evangelization, justice, and peace" (Aubry 1990, 105). The case is different, he says, "with sects of a Pentecostal type or those that have affinities with Pentecostals in their form of worship and in their doctrinal structure" (ibid., 105). Among those he mentions as problematic because of their rapid growth are Assemblies of God, Church of the Nazarene, Church of Christ, Church of God, and Holiness Churches. Quoting *Pro Mundi Vita* Aubry points out that these "sects" are the ones that grow more vigorously, and that "they constitute almost 80 percent of the non-Catholic confessions, for instance, in Nicaragua 73 percent, in Costa Rica 83 percent, in Guatemala 84 percent, in Chile 14 percent of the population" (ibid., 105). The official directory of the Bishops for ecumenism includes Baptists and other growing communities among the "sects" (CELAM Doc. No. 52, 121). The Documents of the Bishops in Medellín (1968) and Puebla (1979) also keep the distinction traced by Aubry between these two basic types of protestantism.

The functional typology of protestantism implicit in the descriptions and distinctions offered by Aubry corresponds to the one I have proposed elsewhere (Escobar 1987, 52-60) as a way of understanding the contemporary situation of protestantism in Latin America. There is on the one hand an Ecumenical Protestantism linked to the conciliar movement of the Geneva-based World Council of Churches (WCC), which carries on an active dialogue and joint programs of action with the Roman Catholic Church. Its most visible corporate expression of unity is the Latin American Council of Churches (CLAI). Several Mainline Protestant churches and a handful of Evangelical and Pentecostal churches are members of CLAI and of the WCC. On the other hand, there is also an Evangelical Protestantism in which we can place Evangelical and Pentecostal churches, by far the largest section of the Protestant presence in Latin America. Some of the largest Pentecostal churches, as well as several of the denominations that Mgr. Aubry mentions in his book, are linked to a loosely connected fellowship called the Confraternity of Evangelical Churches (CONELA), which is associated with the World Evangelical Fellowship. Some members of CONELA would prefer to call themselves "fundamentalists," and in fact their stance corresponds to that of North American churches which use that name for themselves. However, the majority prefer the name *Evangélico*, which in the way they have come now to use it corresponds to the English term "Evangelical." There are also a good number of *Evangélicos* who have remained outside of both CLAI and CONELA.

The fracture between these two forms of protestantism in Latin America is clear and it has widened in recent years due to a variety of reasons, including their different concepts about mission and diverging attitudes toward the Catholic Church. Anyone familiar with Latin America knows that there is no exaggeration in a statement from René Padilla, based upon his missionary experience in Argentina. He has observed that the words of Dutch missiologist Johannes Verkuyl can well be applied here: "At a time when the Vatican is moving more and more in the direction of a new 'counter-reformation,' it is ironic that many mainline Protestant churches cooperate more closely with the Vatican than with Protestant Evangelicals" (Padilla 1991, 32).

Within the *Evangélico* movement popular Pentecostal churches form a distinctive group, also the largest in size, indigenous in its nature and inspired by a contagious apostolic and evangelistic spirit. They have some of the marks of the early Pentecostal movement in North America that Hollenweger also associates with indigenous non-white churches in other parts of the world, namely: orality of liturgy, narrativity of theology and witness, maximum participation at the levels of prayer reflection and decision-making, inclusion of dreams and visions in worship, and a unique understanding of the body/mind relationship applied in the ministry of healing by prayer (Hollenweger 1986, 6). Several missiologists and sociologists prefer to isolate pentecostalism as a separate movement, for the sake of precision, as a third type of protestantism different from the Ecumenical and the Evangelical. Thus, for instance, Donald Dayton has argued, on the basis of sociological and theological criteria, that Pentecostals constitute a unique ecclesiastical reality, and that in order to understand and evaluate it traditional categories are not adequate. Dayton argues specifically about the need to distinguish Pentecostals from the conservative protestantism that is known as "Evangelicalism" (Dayton 1988, 401-402). However, the Latin American experience thus far demonstrates that many Pentecostal churches and denominations have kept their links with Evangelical Protestantism and have associated with it for cooperative ventures in mission.

Until the 1960s there were Latin American Protestants in ecumenical circles who described Pentecostals as "sects" (Obermüller 1957, 19). After the WCC Assembly in New Delhi, where two Pentecostal denominations from Chile became members of the WCC, the use of that label was modified. The WCC is presently trying to intensify contacts with Pentecostals, as well as with independent African churches (Van Elderen 1990, 109), and, according to Juan Sepúlveda, there are ecumenicals who have been considering a way that would make possible "a massive incorporation of pentecostalism in the ecumenical movement" (Sepúlveda 1989, 80). However, Sepúlveda, a Pentecostal pastor from Chile, writes from his own experience:

> In the ecumenical movement one can perceive attitudes such as a radical criticism that sees in pentecostalism an intrinsically alienating religiosity centered in the proclamation of an ultramundane salvation, or the respectful appraisal that discovers in Pentecostals a defiant challenge. (Ibid., 80)

Of course, lines of demarcation between different forms of Latin American protestantism are not mathematically precise, and, as we have already said, the complexities of ecumenism and cooperation have kept many Protestants out of organizations such as CLAI and CONELA. In the search for cooperative forms of missionary action and reflection, boundaries are crossed in all directions. Thus, for instance, there are several kinds of Pentecostals, Nazarenes, Baptists, and members of Holiness Churches and of the Christian and Missionary Alliance, among those persons involved in the missiological action and reflection of the Lausanne movement, the Latin American Theological Fraternity, and the International Fellowship of Evangelical Mission Theologians. But in the ranks of these movements there are also Lutherans, Reformed, Presbyterians, and Anglicans. They have chosen the Lausanne Covenant as an expression of a basic doctrinal consensus and a clear commitment to a holistic pattern of mission. The Latin American Theological Fraternity, one of the widest platforms of debate and expression for Evangelical Protestantism in Latin America, will be sponsoring the CLADE III Third Latin American Congress of Evangelism (24 August - 4 September 1992 in Quito, Ecuador) with the motto "The whole Gospel, from Latin America, for the whole world."

THE CONSPIRACY THEORY:
A PERSISTENT LINE OF INTERPRETATION

The first global interpretation of protestantism in Latin America that has persisted in varied forms may be described as "the conspiracy theory." The term has been applied for this purpose by some contemporary Catholic publications. In an article describing the current reaction of some Catholic sectors in view of the growth of popular protestantism, John McCoy says:

> So far, the typical reaction of the Catholic hierarchy to losing its flock has been to advance the "conspiracy theory." According to its most extreme version Protestant sects bankrolled by the CIA are sent to Latin America to destroy liberation theology and further U.S. imperialism. (McCoy 1989, 2)

This contemporary version emphasizes the reference to the alleged foreign connections of the Protestant movement, linking it to the imperial designs within the Pax Americana. McCoy quotes Honduran bishop Luis Santos, who complains about the "aggression toward our right to be a sovereign and independent republic, because—consciously or unconsciously—sects speak for conquest, ideology, and Yankee neocolonialism" (ibid., 2). This theory presents clearly not only a way of looking at protestantism and interpreting it, but also a certain self-understanding of catholicism. Catholic self-understanding has changed because of Vatican II, and the process of self-criticism involved in the updating (*aggiornamento*) that it proposed. But it has also changed due to the social and political experiences of Catholics after the 1960s, which were the ground from which Liberation theologies emerged. However, the conspiracy theory has remained as a form of interpretation of the Protestant presence. If in the first stage Protestant missionary action and presence were interpreted as part of a liberal-masonic-communist conspiracy, in its contemporary version the theory sees protestantism as part of a North American imperialist conspiracy.

Thirty years ago, within the frame of the Cold War, the conspiracy theory linked Protestant penetration with Communism. During the Congress of Evangelical Communications in Cali, Colombia in 1959, Father Luis Enrique Benoit, a parish priest, made a radio broadcast lamenting the foreign penetration in Colombia:

> We are no longer Catholics, we are no longer democratic people, because Protestantism and communism have won us over. . . . We are already dominated. Poor Colombia . . . has been invaded by two foreign powers who have made us lose our nationality and our Catholic faith: communism and Protestantism. . . . We must understand that Protestantism is a corrupting force and the promoter of the most vile immorality. (Barbieri 1961, 75)

Numerous texts from Catholic bishops, priests, and laymen who followed this approach were collected by Juan José Arévalo, former President of Guatemala. In them protestantism was presented as allied to communism. Thus Sergio Mirofanda Carrington said that:

Responsible North American circles, who encourage and perhaps finance the so-called 'Protestant pastors' who are arriving by thousands on these shores, thereby aid Communism. These peoples will remain Catholics or after a brief sojourn with protestantism will fall into atheism. *From Protestantism to Communism* is for us only a short step. (Arévalo 1963, 148-149)

Historian Hans Jürgen Prien, who also offers a representative sample of reactions from the Catholic hierarchies of Latin America against protestantism in the late 1940s (Prien 1985, 800-801), illustrates well the logic of the conspiracy theory. For Prien these reactions on the part of the Catholic Church show "the stubborn adherence to the colonial model of Latin American christendom as catholic unity, which does not look for the causes of the ruin of that model in its own failures, but in the masons, liberals, and also in the protestants engaged in proselytism" (ibid., 801-802). The basic assumption that there is a foreign conspiracy that uses Protestant missionaries as agents of economic and political penetration has persisted not only in sermons or pastoral letters from the clergy. It has been also the working hypothesis of many pieces of research in contemporary scholarship.

In the 1940s and 1950s, Protestant interpreters themselves acknowledged the fact that the Protestant movement that was growing at that point had come through the work of foreign missionaries because, as a Mexican Methodist said, "missions are always an importation. The Christian faith was strictly indigenous only to Palestine" (Baez Camargo 1959, 126). However, they also accumulated evidence to show that "The Evangelical faith has become 'naturalized.' It has taken firm roots in Latin American soil. In most countries a strong indigenous leadership has developed. There are many and substantial independent movements, self-supporting and self-propagating" (ibid., 128). Alberto Rembao, another Mexican, said it even more eloquently, stating that the Evangelical community in Latin America "is not the feeble congregation of outcasts hanging around the philanthropic skirts of foreign missionaries, but rather a most powerful ferment with sufficient energy of radiation to alter for good the social atmosphere and the spiritual climate of a whole continent" (Rembao 1948, 57).

For these interpreters protestantism had been accepted enthusiastically by Latin Americans who, being deeply religious, were, however, dissatisfied with catholicism.

No movement can possibly take root with such force, neither can it grow at such an amazing rate, unless it has found a soil that contains congenial elements for its germination and nurture. There must be a secret frame into which somehow it dovetails a golden thread to be strung to some deeply seated but frustrated aspirations to which it gives satisfaction. (Baez Camargo 1959, 128)

The conspiracy theory has persisted even at the highest level of the Catholic hierarchies, but the most articulate criticism of the theory has come from the ranks of modern Catholic missiologists, and among them the Belgian Franz Damen who works in Bolivia has offered a straightforward argument. He quotes an article by Mgr. Antonio Quarracino, former president of the Latin American Conference of Bishops (CELAM), in which he refers to "the avalanche of the sects." The article has as a background and a basic presupposition the main themes of the conspiracy theory. Before we refer to Damen's comments on Mgr. Quarracino's article, we must acknowledge that there is evidence that sectors of the New Right in the United States (which became prominent in the Reagan era) were interested in the use of churches and theologies in Latin America for political purposes. It is also well known that some televangelists-politicians such as Pat Robertson had connections with conservative Central American regimes linked to some Charismatic groups. The facts have been documented by Catholics such as Penny Lernoux (1989), Protestants such as Gordon (Spykman et al. 1988), and religiously non-committed researchers such as David Stoll (1990). However, missiologist Damen offers some clarification on the basis of field research and comparative studies in several Latin American countries. The popular Protestant groups that grow faster are either indigenous to the continent or, if they originated in North America, they have quickly become Latino-Americanized in both leadership and finance (Damen 1987, 54). He concludes that "it is yet impossible to prove that a strategic connection exists between the expansionist North American policy toward Latin America and the proliferation of religious sects in the continent" (52).

Damen says that the use of the term "avalanche" is indicative of a state of mind in the hierarchies of a church that for centuries "widely enjoyed the benefits that in more recent years some governments give to the sects" (ibid., 58) and was "accustomed since the Conquest to the exercise of a hegemony in the religious field" (63). The idea of an avalanche "suggests the horrible experience of a gigantic mass that in a sudden, violent, and uncontrollable way throws itself upon an innocent and unarmed population, which desperately tries to defend itself against such disgrace" (47). The truth of the matter is the opposite, says Damen, because the sects "rely rather on a relatively good reception on the part of the people" (55). Damen concurs with Mgr. Kloppenburg that the migration of great masses of population from catholicism toward sectarian movements in Latin America today is quantitatively larger than the movement from catholicism to protestantism in Europe during the sixteenth century. "We live today at a crucial moment in the history of Christianity in Latin America," concludes Damen, and because of that he suggests that the image of the avalanche and the conspiracy theory should be abandoned and a more realistic approach adopted (63).

PROTESTANTISM AS A FORCE FOR MODERNIZATION AND DEMOCRATIZATION

The study of the fast-paced changes that Latin America experienced in the 1950s and 1960s was carried on by several social scientists within the general frame of "modernization." The title of one of the most extensive and careful analyses of what was happening to the Roman Catholic Church during that period, *Catholicism, Social Control and Modernization in Latin America* (Vallier 1970), is eloquent in itself. Vallier set his understanding of the transformation of the Catholic church within a summary of historical developments and a description of the social processes that were taking place on the continent. But the core of his work, and the approach in which he pioneered a field, was the institutional analysis of catholicism in Latin America (Mainwaring 1986, 3). In this aspect some of the studies about protestantism that were done during that period emphasized also an analysis of the internal life of the Protestant congregations in order to formulate what was their social and political significance.

In the creed and self-understanding of the early Protestant communities, Mainline and Evangelical Protestantism, there was a clear conscience of their modernizing potential, which was understood especially in a polemical contrast with Roman Catholicism. Míguez Bonino notes that:

> All the Protestant congresses from Panamá (1916) to Buenos Aires (1949) sound this note. Catholicism is considered the ideology and religious structure of a total system, that of the outworn seigniorial Hispanic order that was forced on Latin America and must now disappear in order to make way for a new democratic order of freedom. Protestantism, which has historically inspired such order, offers itself as a religious alternative for the new world. (1983, 62)

However, it is important to keep in mind that the first type of protestantism that was subject to social analysis, based on a systematic collection of empirical data, was the popular Pentecostal movement in those countries where its growth was more significant: Chile and Brazil. The key work about both countries in this area is Emilio Willems's *Followers of the New Faith* (1967). The general frame of reference for this approach has been provided by the modernization theories that were influential in the 1950s and 1960s, especially in the North American social sciences. Protestantism was seen as one of the forces contributing to the process of modernization and democratization of Latin America. Another important interpretation of pentecostalism was provided by Christian Lalive d'Epinay in his massive study *Haven of the Masses* (1969), which focused on Pentecostals in Chile. However, Lalive's approach in his working hypothesis and his interpretation went beyond the limitation of modernization theories.

Willems's interpretation of Pentecostal Protestantism places it in a historical continuum in which it emerges as a byproduct of changes affecting the social structures and values of Brazilian and Chilean societies, such as foreign immigration and secularization. Once established, protestantism becomes itself a factor contributing to social change, because the value orientation that can be described as "Protestant ethics" helps the converts to function better in the new situation created by industrialization, urbanization, internal migration, and the opening of new frontiers (Willems 1967, 13). The fact that pentecostalism was attracting the popular classes in these societies would mean that the pentecostal experience might be one of the ways open to masses that are in a state of latent or overt rebellion. Willems says:

[C]onversion to Protestantism, especially to its sectarian varieties, constitutes one of the many ways in which hostility and rebellion against a decaying social structure may be expressed. Correctly or incorrectly, the Catholic Church is often perceived by the masses as a symbol of the traditional order, or more specifically as an ally of its supreme exponent, the landed aristocracy. To the extent that the Church is perceived as a classbound institution it has become the target of such mass hostility. (Willems 1964, 103)

Willems's approach majored on institutional analysis of Pentecostal congregations and called attention to another important factor: the participative nature of Pentecostal liturgy and congregational life, which did not depend on literacy or education but on a disposition to be touched by the power of the Holy Spirit. In his analysis Willems referred especially to the significance of the *tomada de Espíritu* or "seizure" by the Spirit, which "puts a seal of divine approval on the individual who can now be elected or appointed to any office" (1964, 106-107). The seizure becomes a form of legitimation within the Pentecostal congregations, which had to be validated by energetic and successful proselytism. The seizure had an integrative effect, allowing thousands of persons from the lower social classes to become part of an organized group in which they could enter in community, contribute their participation, and receive affirmation, comfort, and a sense of belonging. This integrative factor was important for those persons who were part of a massive process of migration that had created forms of anomic life in the population crowding into the booming Latin American cities. The research of Lalive in Chile offered abundant data to illustrate and trace the lines of this integrative factor, referring it especially to the role Pentecostal pastors played in the creation of a substitute community to replace the agrarian hacienda or *fundo* from which the rural migration came.

The seizure experience had also an egalitarian effect, because participation in the community and even the possibility of contributing to its life did not require status symbols such as money or education, which were predominant as forms of legitimation in the surrounding society. Participation in the liturgical life of the communities included the gift of prophecy by which simple, illiterate people could give a message that was heard and accepted by the entire community. This was in contrast with the Catholic experience where the teaching function was entirely in the hands of the ordained clergy or even mainline Protestant communities where the lay people who exerted leadership were selected by factors such as education and verbal articulateness. In some cases what started at the level of liturgical participation could be extended to the level of decision-making processes in the community. Willems concludes that "The principle of unrestricted social mobility embodied by the Pentecostal sects, is obviously at variance with the limited opportunities for upward mobility within the general society" (1964, p. 107). That in itself was an excellent training ground for participation in the secular society where a democratization process was taking place.

Conversion to pentecostalism included also an emphasis on some marks of character as indication of "the change of life" on which the Pentecostal message about the redeeming power of Christ placed especial emphasis. As in the case of

Evangelical Protestantism, pentecostalism presented the convert with specific prohibitions against the use of alcohol and tobacco. But what was especially significant in the Pentecostal credo was that the prohibitions were accompanied by the strong emphasis on an emotional experience of conversion, a seizure from God's power, which in some cases was the key point of breaking away from the old habits so common in the popular classes of the urban world. In the Pentecostal experience the ascetic lifestyle included in conversion was also accompanied by a celebrative form of worship and communal life that was a great help for endurance among those who had gone through the experience of conversion. Pentecostalism offered a joyful and celebrative asceticism. From a social and economic perspective this new lifestyle also contributed to improving the daily life of believers. This new lifestyle generated savings, encouraged entrepreneurship, and could in time bring upward mobility. "The economic significance of Protestant asceticism lies in the fact that it frees part of one's income for the acquisition of things that symbolize a higher level of living" (Willems 1964, 251).

The positive evaluation of the Protestant experience in this approach came from a tacit or explicit acceptance of the modernizing trends in Latin America following Western patterns of the capitalist societies. In this interpretation the modernization process was frequently set in contrast to the feudal order of the colonial days, which had remained in spite of a century and a half of independence from Spain. This interpretation did not question the validity and applicability of those patterns of modernization and democratization, generally taken from the Anglo-Saxon and European models, for Latin America. In fact, it took the assumptions of the liberal project that had been the ideological frame of reference for political and economic developments until World War II. This analysis centered on an understanding of micro processes within the Protestant communities, with the assumption that the general direction of the historical development — the macro process of society as a whole — would follow almost naturally the pattern of development of the West.

PROTESTANTISM AS AN INSTRUMENT OF A NEW COLONIAL PACT

Already by 1928 the Peruvian Marxist José Carlos Mariátegui had offered an interpretation of protestantism within the frame of Lenin's theory of imperialism. That year another Peruvian, anthropologist Luis E. Valcárcel, published a book about the rise of the "new Indian" in Peru with the significative title of *Storm in the Andes*. Valcárcel announced that in the highlands of his country the native races were emerging as a dynamic social force that was bound to provoke deep and radical social transformations. One chapter of Valcárcel's book pointed to the positive transforming and uplifting effect of the work of Seventh Day Adventists on the life of the Aymara communities around Lake Titicaca. The narratives and the analysis offered by Valcárcel about the rural life of the Aymaras stressed the key role of the Adventist educational system, but also some of the same factors that Willems considered later on in the analysis mentioned above: redemption from alcoholism, egalitarian community life, and a renewed sense of dignity coming from integration in a new community. In the preface to this book Mariátegui made it clear that he did not share the enthusiasm of Valcárcel about the Adventists, because these were the avant garde of imperialist interests from North America (Valcárcel 1972, 12).

What characterizes this form of interpretation of protestantism is the fact that it places the religious phenomenon within the global historical process of imperialism in a critical way. The Leninist elements of the theory of imperialism were used to forge a new approach to the interpretation of Latin American history, in which special attention was paid to the economic factors underlying the political and cultural ones, and in that form:

> dependence theory came to be formulated. For this view of Latin America had been incorporated into the modern world as a dependent, not as a partner, in order to serve further development of the imperialist powers. The colonial pact with Spain and Portugal has been substituted by a new colonial pact. . . . The fundamental element in the new Latin American consciousness is the awareness that our political emancipation from Spain was—however justified and necessary—a step in the Anglo-Saxon colonial and neocolonial expansion. (Míguez Bonino 1975, 14)

This new reading of history places economic initiative in the centers of financial, political, and technological power, especially in North America, for which Latin America constitutes a periphery.

> Latin American underdevelopment is the dark side of Northern development; Northern development is built on third-world underdevelopment. The basic categories for understanding our history are not development and underdevelopment but domination and dependence. That is the crux of the matter. (Ibid., 16)

The imperial advance from the center to the periphery, in order to establish a domination that will allow exploitation, is not only the export of capital and technology but also the export of ideologies, and religion is understood within the category of ideology. Religion would be the cover-up of imperial advance and would fulfill two functions: to explain the rationale behind imperialist presence and advance and to foster an attitude of submission in the minds of citizens of the peripheral dominated nations.

When this analysis is applied to the understanding of a religious phenomenon such as catholicism or protestantism, the three elements mentioned above play an important role. First, the global setting of the analysis emphasizes the role that religion plays within the larger frame of imperial advance. Second, the analysis of religion in itself pays special attention to economic and political factors and frequently places the intentionality of the religious act in relation to those factors. Third, the analysis always involves a valuative criteria that has ethical value judgments, judging the religious movement by the relation it has with the "historical project" that the analyst has embraced.

Probably the most consistent and clear expression of this kind of analysis applied to Latin American protestantism has been provided by the Argentinean theologian José Míguez Bonino. The subject of the Protestant identity in Latin America has been tackled with consistency in many of his writings, and the most systematic one is probably his book *Toward a Christian Political Ethics* (1983). Míguez Bonino evaluates the role of Mainline and Evangelical Protestantism within his critical appraisal of the liberal project. In a clear and eloquent way he formulates his interpretation in some global statements about protestantism in Latin America. According to his reading of history, the conditions that facilitated the introduction of protestantism were the forging of a neocolonial pact that favored relationships with the Protestant countries, and the triumph of the modernizing elites over the traditional ones. As the analysis develops, protestantism is placed as a movement that, rather than having a dynamism of its own, serves the purposes determined by the initiative and intention of the liberal elites. "What is clear in relation to Latin America, is that protestantism claimed and (within its limitations) assumed the role that the Latin American liberal elites had assigned it in the transition from a traditional society to the modern bourgeois world" (1983, 62). Awareness about this fact produces a "crisis of conscience," says Míguez Bonino, and though accepting the fact that protestantism played a significant role in breaking the power of the traditional colonial mentality, he feels obliged to ask, "Did we not in fact provide religious sanction to a new colonialism? Did we not in fact contribute to create the benevolent and idealized image of the colonial powers (mainly the United States) which has disguised the deadly character of their domination?" (Míguez Bonino 1975, 18).

With varying degrees and in different parts of their work, other interpreters of protestantism have taken this critical and even condemnatory approach. This is for instance the key that Swiss historian Jean Pierre Bastian has used in his brief history of protestantism in Latin America (Bastian 1990), which in its periodification and in the general presentation of the material follows closely this approach, especially in his treatment of the third epoch (1959-1983). On the other hand, Bastian's detailed research about protestantism in Mexico, with a careful consideration of primary sources and a more detailed institutional analysis, has provided for the study of Mainline and Evangelical Protestantism in Mexico during the late nineteenth and early twentieth centuries, the kind of factual and empirical basis for interpretation that Willems provided for pentecostalism in Brazil and Chile (Bastian 1983, 1989). Another critical approach that places the dynamics for Protestant advance in the imperial design of North American sources is the work of Rosa del Carmen Bruno-Joffré about Methodist educational work in Perú (Bruno-Joffré 1988).

It is important to realize that this reading of history not only includes an explanation of historical phenomena but also definite evaluative judgements on the basis of ethical reasons related to the political option assumed. It also includes the proposal for an alternative historical route that would correspond to the general movement of history: the end of capitalism and the coming of a socialist society in which all the injustices and alienations of the capitalist and imperialist world will be replaced by an egalitarian, truly democratic form of life that will eliminate misery and inequalities and allow for the fulfillment of human potentialities. The dependence theory analysis or "Latin American neo-Marxian analysis" as Mainwaring calls it (1986, 12-13) has two elements that are equally important. It is analytical and uses economic and social data for a description of the dynamics of societies, but it is also projective. Its analysis of the present is always done in light of a proposal about the future. Otto Maduro has expressed it with much clarity:

> We presuppose the *possibility* of a Latin America without oppression—with neither oppressors nor oppressed. From the perspective of this datum and this possibility, our sociological examination will prefer an orientation toward those socio-religious processes that appear to have contributed to the generation and reinforcement of the situation of oppression, as also, complementarily toward those other socio-religious processes that seem to debilitate relationships of oppression and contribute to the development of the popular classes as autonomous and combative classes. (Maduro 1982, 34-35)

In an article about popular piety in Latin America, Míguez Bonino applies this kind of analysis, coming to the conclusion that the popular piety (both Catholic and Protestant) which exists on this continent "can only be regarded as profoundly alienated and alienating, a manifestation of a slave consciousness and an instrument for the continuation and consolidation of oppression" (Míguez Bonino 1974).

This approach to the significance of protestantism in Latin America has also been applied to study the role and significance of protestantism in Europe. Míguez Bonino and another Methodist, Mortimer Arias, have applied this interpretative method to what they propose as a new reading of the significance of Methodism in English-speaking countries, which for Latin American Methodists comes to be a rereading of their ecclesiastical heritage (Kirkpatrick 1988). The conclusions of Míguez Bonino are summarized in this global statement: "Historically, Methodism seems to have been useful for the incorporation of significant sectors of the rising British proletariat to the liberal bourgeois ideology that undergirded the consolidation of the capitalist system and reinforced its imperialist expansion" (Duque 1983, 72). An important part of the analysis that Míguez Bonino and Arias offer is the way in which it clarifies the social and political connotations and significance of some basic doctrines of the Wesleyan heritage. This is a most helpful exercise because usually doctrines are understood only in terms of their intellectual significance in relation to other doctrines and the ideologies of a particular historical moment. From a pastoral and missiological perspective this type of analysis can contribute to the formulation of practices that will take the context of the life of the church more seriously.

On the other hand the analysis runs the risk of reductionism when it establishes too easily connections with the imperial enterprises of a particular moment, especially when it places the initiative for religious life and behavior only or mainly on the economic and political motivations of the imperial forces at work. One of the excesses of the "Black Legend" about the missionary work of

Spain and Portugal in Latin America during the sixteenth and seventeenth centuries is precisely that it does not take adequate account of missionary actions that were motivated away from imperial interests or even against them. This approach tends to ignore some facts and the analysis is marred by the selectivity of the data. It is precisely what happens today when the reductionist approach is used in the formulation of a new "Black Legend" in Latin America, this time about popular protestantism. Bastian has offered a more systematic critique of the reductionism of some contemporary approaches, such as those of Domínguez and Huntington (1984), which have reduced explanations of protestantism to a modern conspiracy theory (Bastian 1985, 61).

A NEW APPROACH TO THE INTERPRETATION
OF POPULAR PROTESTANTISM

The publication of the recent global studies by Stoll (1990) and Martin (1990) shows that the phenomenal growth of Evangelical and Pentecostal forms of protestantism throughout Latin America has been under the scrutiny of historians and social scientists in the most recent decades, and that a respectable body of research about this subject has accumulated, to the point that new global interpretations of the phenomenon can be attempted. This coincides with the development of new and more ecclectical approaches in the study of Roman Catholicism in Latin America, like the one developed by Mainwaring (1986), quoted above. He is aware of the limitations of a functionalist institutional analysis approach, but he also tries to use the best it provides in as much as it clarifies issues that otherwise would remain hidden. At the same time, though critical of the "neo-Marxian approach" coming from dependence theory and Liberation theology, he takes some insights from it, as well as from classical Weberian sources. There is also a convergence at this point with the new approaches coming from some Catholic missiologists who are taking a different kind of look at popular protestantism, as we will see later in this article.

About the study of this subject, David Martin warns his readers that "the whole field is fraught with propaganda and the investigator is bound to be caught in a cross fire whatever position he takes up" (1990, 292). In the Introduction of his book he offers a clarification that can be taken as an important methodological proviso, especially significant in this moment of Latin American life:

> I would add that I also want to avoid "framing" these worlds lived in by the Latin American poor in language of covert political hostility, or encasing them in grand notions of the right or main path of social evolution. It is a strange perversion of our intellectual culture that we so often want to have people and movements framed in this way in order to tell us if they are politically all right. We demand a secular version of the "last judgement" here and now. That I will not and cannot give. (Ibid., 1)

The interpretations we have briefly considered thus far illustrate some ways in which scholars have framed Latin American protestantism, encasing it within the projective or utopian visions of an ideological choice or in language of covert religious and/or political hostility. Recent events in Eastern Europe put a big question mark beside the assumptions about the general march of history that were the frame for dependence theory, liberation theologies, and the kind of social analysis advocated by Maduro above. The basic conditions of oppression and injustice have not changed in Latin America, and the mission of the Church cannot avoid the questions they pose. There is also a long Christian tradition of identification with the poor or the victims in social conflict. However, the vision of a desirable society that may embody the values of the Kingdom of God in the Latin American context will be reformulated, paying more attention to biblical truth and Christian doctrine and the lessons from the practice of believers rather than to historical materialism.

On the other hand, showing the possibility that even a Marxist analysis may provide valuable insights, Martin has demonstrated how some salient features of the object of study can help the scholar break away from the practice of an ideological reductionist "framing" of such object. He refers to the study of Blanca Muratorio (1981) about Quichua-speaking peasants in Colta. The specifically Marxist direction of the research is "in the way capitalistic forms relate to pre-capitalistic forms and how the latter may even expand as capitalism advances" (Martin 1990, 103). In the process of study Muratorio discovers some unique characteristics of the Quichua Evangelical communities in this area and the way in which their alternative forms of solidarity and networking, as well as the power of language as they used the Bible in their own tongue, were contributing to create a new sense of personhood and ethnic dignity and self-assertiveness. Martin finally comments:

> This Marxist analysis is interesting in that its empirical observations closely coincide with those of non-Marxist anthropologists. Its focus is, of course, on the way in which an oppositional consciousness may be formed which is not however a class consciousness equipped with a sophisticated theory of change. The analysis lacks any anthropological lament for the fabric of older relationships, even "idyllic" paternalism, since it assumes a process of development. What all the studies indicate is the self-creation of new identities and the invention or adaptation of new forms of mutual exchange and solidarity. (Ibid.,105)

David Martin sets his presentation of Latin American protestantism and explains why he has chosen as a broad frame to interpret it "the four hundred year clash between the Hispanic imperium and the Anglo-Saxon imperium" (9), and "the dramatically different ways in which Catholic cultures and Protestant cultures have entered into what we call modernity" (26). As a global frame of reference this one does more justice to the nature of the object that is being studied than the reductionist approach of class analysis within the neo-Marxian approach of dependence theory. The fact is also that, as Mainwaring says, neo-Marxian analysts "tend to understate the autonomy of religion and the Church vis-à-vis class. Religion can be a powerful force in determining political orientation, frequently even more powerful than class" (Martin 1990, 12). Martin also provides a sociological interpretation of the evolution of protestantism in Europe, and especially in the English-speaking world, to show the logical basis for his use of Methodism as a model that he will apply to understand pentecostalism in the Latin American case.

Both Martin and Stoll are specifically interested in the social and political effect of the Evangelical presence and message. Pentecostalism is explained by Martin as a way in which "millions of people are absorbed within a protective social capsule where they acquire new concepts of self and new models of initiative and voluntary organization" (284). In this he coincides with the analysis of Willems above. Martin thinks that, like Methodism at the beginning of the Industrial Revolution in Britain, pentecostalism flourishes today in Latin America as a "temporary efflorescence of voluntary religiosity which accompanies a stage in industrialization and/or urbanization" (294). However he is cautious to point out that the European experience may not necessarily provide a universal paradigm. On the other hand Stoll believes that "the history of social movements is replete with shifts from a redemptive (saving one's soul) to a transformative (changing the world) emphasis, or vice-versa, often after the first generation" (1990, 329). As he speculates about the future social effect of Evangelicals and Pentecostals in Latin America, he envisages three possible scenarios: a confrontation with the state that would make them a redemptive force, social mobility that would create a dynamic rising middle sector to change society by negotiation and leadership ability, or thirdly a failure to become a major force for social change because of sectarianism and a refusal to assume political responsibilities. Though he thinks that the third "is the most defensible scenario at present," he also believes that "evangelical Protestants are giving Latin Americans a new form of social organization and a new way to express their hopes" (331), thus acting as "survival vehicles" in a time of serious social crisis. Stoll concludes that: "Where traditional social organization is breaking up, evangelical churches constitute new, more flexible groups in which participation is voluntary, where leadership is charismatic, and which are therefore more adaptable to rapidly changing conditions" (ibid.). The observations of Stoll can be compared with the Pentecostal experience and the theological reflection about it offered by Juan Sepúlveda, who has tried to interpret the theological evolution of Pentecostals and the possibility of a Pentecostal evolution away from the social conservatism that the movement adopted at a given point in their recent history (Sepúlveda 1988).

On the basis of the data assembled and in coming to their conclusions about the social role of Evangelicals and Pentecostals, both Stoll and Martin also develop a fascinating critique of Liberation theologies. Martin reminds us that "Liberation theology is a major rival to Pentecostalism," a reason that explains why the more cautious members of the Catholic hierarchy have accepted it in spite of its critical attitude to traditional catholicism. He then goes on to point out that Liberation theology has not been a successful competitor to the Pentecostal advance. "The reason [says Martin] is that however much it represents 'an option for the poor' taken up by hundreds of thousands of the poor themselves, that option is most eloquently formulated by radical intellectuals . . . not usually 'of the people.' Liberation theology has a decidedly middle-class and radical intellectual accent alien to the localized needs of 'the poor'" (Martin 1990, 290). Stoll coincides with Martin: "The central exercise in liberation theology, consciousness-raising, raises a tangle of issues. To begin with there is the risk of failing to speak to the actual needs of the poor as opposed to idealized versions of those needs" (Stoll 1990, 312). He comments that the kinds of defiance of the established order that Liberation theologians encourage among the poor "have been suicidal in many times and places," and his criticism becomes acid when he points out that "Given this fact of life out in the hard places where liberation theology must prove itself, the frequent assumption of the need for revolutionary upheaval indicates that more or less safely situated intellectuals have had an outsized role in its production" (ibid., 313).

MISSIOLOGICAL LESSONS

My thesis is that *popular protestantism in Latin America is one of the most surprising manifestations of* what theologian Gustavo Gutiérrez has called *"the irruption of the poor"* (Gutiérrez 1982, 108), and what missiologist Walbert Buhlman has called "the coming of the Third Church" (Bühlman 1986, 6). It has to be understood within the frame of a new age in the history of Christianity, in which as Andrew Walls says "its main base will be in the Southern continents, and where its dominant expression will be filtered through the culture of those continents" (Walls 1985, 221). Of course it is important to point out that most of the militants of popular protestantism have not embarked on the kind of liberation movements proposed by some Liberation theologians. However it is undeniable that in its style and social composition the movement is an irruption of the poor. Of course this popular protestantism is a form of Third Church that is located at a certain theological distance from Rome, but it has enough Christian content, indigeneity, and contextual relevance to the Third World to be considered as a vigorous form of that Third Church which Bühlman sees emerging from the grass roots.

My thesis and conclusions come from a life lived in close contact with popular protestantism, but they have been suggested also by the more recent observations of three Catholic missiologists, Franz Damen,[2] Roger Aubry,[3] and José Luis Idígoras.[4] Due to the controversial nature of the issue I have preferred to use the perspectives of these Catholic missiologists rather than the self-interpretations of Protestants themselves.[5] This is possible to the degree to which as Catholics they are open to accept the realities of religious pluralism. These missiologists represent good examples of how it is possible to move from a "police" approach to protestantism, which views it as an anomaly that should be eliminated or corrected, to a "pastoral" approach, which uses the data provided by serious scholarship and tries to learn the missiological lessons that religious minorities can teach to the institutionalized forms of a religious majority.[6]

None of the Catholic missiologists I am quoting would abandon their Roman ecclesiological convictions. When they use the term "sect," they put sociological and theological content in it to mean something less that fully Christian. I do not read at any point in their material that they would go as far as looking at popular protestantism as one of the many movements that the Spirit of God has raised for the renewal of the church in the twenty centuries of Christian history. But their evaluation of the movement is prompted by a deep missiological concern, and that opens their eyes to the missionary dynamism of popular protestantism. They are deeply concerned by the fact that after five centuries of Catholic presence, in the region where 42 percent of the Catholics of the world are now living, a large foreign missionary force is still necessary to keep the church alive. The opposite should be the case: a Catholic missionary force should be going from Latin America to the unevangelized regions of the world. However, an official report from the Fourth Missionary Congress held in Lima (February, 1991) laments the fact that "the proportion of Latin American missionaries does not even reach 2 percent of the total missionary force in the world" (COMLA IV, 267). What lessons can be drawn from the impressive growth of popular protestantism in Latin America?

It is a religious movement. Even taking into account political connections and connotations, the key to understanding popular protestantism is to acknowledge that it has "its own religious dynamism and logic," says Damen (1987, 53). "They respond in their own way to the religious demand of the popular masses," says Aubry, pointing to the tremendous vacuum of the millions of poor people going through social transitions, unattended by the Catholic church (Aubry 1990, 106-107). Idígoras observes that through reading of the biblical text and the explanations of pastors, "the members of the sects search above all for the religious experience of God. An emotional experience that will communicate his spiritual riches to them" (Idígoras 1991, 242).

Idígoras goes even further, contrasting mainline protestantism with the popular one. He says that secularism has diluted and weakened the faith of many mainline liberal protestants and that "liberal faith has no energies to throw itself into the missionary task" (1991, 237). He then criticizes the elitist theological education of Catholic priests who have an initial philosophical formation "in an environment which is obsessed by rationality."

> That is why we should not be surprised that among the priests in our countries so many have emerged who are enemies of popular religiosity or proposers of secularized systems such as the integration of dialectical materialism and theology. And the people themselves have realized that, differently from the protestant pastors, many priests are more concerned with the worldly problems than with the religious ones. (Idígoras 1991, 245)

Idígoras's analysis is not simplistic and Evangelical Protestant missiologists can benefit from it. In another chapter of his book, which deals with the popular aspects of the sixteenth-century Reformation, he questions Peter Berger's assumption that protestantism was a secularizing movement. He points to the spiritual thrust of Luther's reforming intention. "Luther the humanist and Bible scholar was also a religious man and a man of the people. And . . . the modern protestant sects have learned how to develop that popular streak that was present in their founders" (Berger 1966, 197-198). It is along this line that I value the work of the Brazilian missiologist Neuza Itioka, a member of the Free Methodist church. Coming from her experience within popular protestantism in a country that confronts spiritism and African religions, she believes strongly that one of the most important issues for worldwide mission in the 1990s is the confrontation with destructive supernatural evil forces that oppose the missionary enterprise.

> The rational intellectual approach we have used for so long brings only new infor-
> mation, a new way of thinking. What we need to reach people who coexist daily
> with the supernatural is the powerful presence of the risen Christ. He is the mission-
> ary and evangelist par excellence. Without his intimate involvement, we have no
> mission and there will not be transformation in the lives of people. (Itioka 1991, 36)

It is a popular movement. Aubry observes that popular protestantism grows among the most destitute and marginal sectors of the population, the popular masses who are disarticulated socially and culturally (Aubrey 1990, 106). Idígoras stresses the more popular character of North American protestantism, in contrast with the European one, and also observes the rise of authentically popular protestant movements in several Latin American countries: "they are popular Christians, with a rudimentary theology, endowed with heavenly visions and itinerant preachers who move through streets and squares" (Idígoras 1991, 238). Idígoras says also that he has noticed that what some priests find more offensive in the sects is precisely that they are both religious and popular. For him these priests show how they have distanced themselves from the real peo-ple.

Both authors concur in the opinion that one of the secrets of the protestant growth in popular sectors is the ability of their leadership to remain close to the people, speak their language, and develop patterns of ministry that avoid elitism. Though both catholic priests and popular protestant pastors come from the same popular sectors, the latter "live closer to the people and their training is usually less philosophical and more theological" (ibid., 245). Their preference for sim-ple Bible reading and commentary without resource to exegetical methods al-lows them to remain closer to the popular mind with a preaching style that is closer to the religious feeling of the people. "Because of that there are not many theologians among the pastors of the sects, but there are charismatic preachers and speakers of theatrical television programs" (246).

A characteristic note of the popular theology would be the concentration on the religious element and the lack of concern for the social problems, fueled sometimes by a simplistic eschatology. From it comes the condemnation of Marxism and liberation theologies. Idígoras rejects the idea that these attitudes are due to injunctions coming from imperialist authorities (ibid., 247). A mark of popular religiosity, both Catholic and protestant, he says, is this retreat into the private and internal realm in which the sacred has the primacy above the ethical. Ritual and sacral elements are considered morally superior "because the first table of the decalogue is more important than the second and some way or other the former contains the latter" (248).

It is a movement that mobilizes people for mission. Observers of popular protestantism agree that it has a remarkable ability to mobilize all members of their churches for the missionary task. "All converts are active members who have to promote the life of the sect and work for the conversion of peop'e who are not converted yet," says Aubry (1990, 111). He criticizes the fact that sometimes there is more a proselytistic than an evangelistic spirit, and that some methods do not show respect for the freedom that is necessary in evangelization. And with reference to Catholics he adds, "we must confess that among us, in spite of the serious efforts that are being carried on, there are few lay people actively involved in the pastoral life of their parish or their Church" (ibid., 111-112).

Damen observes that among pentecostals "the task of evangelization is not assigned to a specialized personnel, because it is the *mission* of each member of the community" (Damen 1987, 60-61). With the smallest missionary force Pentecostals have relatively the biggest rate of numerical growth. Idígoras analyzes carefully the missionary methodology of popular protestantism with massive meetings in the open air, "where faith is proclaimed and the multitudinous emotion is transmitted like fire" (Idígoras 1991, 243). He stresses the fact that the evangelistic activity is not limited to the church building, but that groups invade streets and squares, "and audaciously they even go house by house and speak *opportune et importune*" (244), and he adds that "A Catholic priest, because of his training, would feel out of place in such situations" (144). On the other hand, quoting the results of a religious survey, Damen observes that "public and formal proselitism is not the means through which the sects communicate most effectively with the outsiders and that instead the family relations, friendship, and confidence are far more important" (Damen 1987, 61-62).

Aubry refers also to the fact that in popular protestantism pastors and leaders are accredited by active participation in the evangelistic task "among the people, sharing the same life, speaking the same language, suffering the same scarcities." Advance and progress in the level of leadership are the fruit of the exercise of the evangelistic charism "more than the result of academic formation that usually is very limited. Biblical studies are complementary" (Aubry 1990, 114). Idígoras feels very strongly that this identification of the leaders with the people at the level of ministry, liturgy, pastoral work, and teaching methods is very successful precisely at the points where Catholic priests are failing because of their elitist formation (Idígoras 1991, 246-248). Finally Damen calls our attention to the fact that some groups which have experienced tremendous growth in recent years have been working systematically and insistently in evangelization for many decades, in spite of the hardships and the discouraging lack of immediate results (Damen 1987, 49). He feels that part of the reason for "conspiracy" and "avalanche" theories is that those who have suddenly taken notice of the protestant presence conveniently ignored it before.

It is a movement that creates community. Our three missiologists do not spare criticism of these popular churches. They criticize their escapist eschatology (Idígoras 1991, 247), which makes them insensitive to social problems, their dualistic theology, which condemns the world as "completely lost" (Aubry 1990, 110), and their ostentatious display of healing and prophetic gifts (Idígoras 1991, 243). However, these missiologists do not deny the positive social effect of popular protestantism. Aubry points out the value of community life in these churches, in face of the uprooted experience of persons who have lost their points of reference:

> The atmosphere of a community of converted people, who praise the Lord and find religious and human warmth in the midst of a faceless society and of almost anonymous parishes, is something essential for human life. Only within a community can the new convert persevere, experience the riches of faith and its implications for life. (Aubry 1990, 112)

Idígoras analyzes carefully not only the popular nature of this protestantism but also some characteristics that would place it as an elitist antipopular movement. He refers for instance to the adoption of a more ascetic lifestyle, abandoning alcoholism, and a more literate spirituality based on the reading of the Bible. These new attitudes and habits, adopted consciously and in tension with their previous Catholic lifestyle, would be according to Idígoras the source of a certain arrogance through which a minority distances itself from the masses, and finds a new identity and a source to put up with social ostracism. To this could be added the self-affirmation of the lay people in contrast with a more hierarchical Catholic church life centered on the person of the priest. Idígoras observes that during the sixteenth-century Reformation certain enlightened and progressive minorities adopted the same attitudes against the Catholic church. What is new in the case of Latin America is that "the elitism of the enlightened ones has been passed on to simple and ignorant people" (Idígoras 1991, 241).

We have not dealt in depth with the theological presuppositions that provide the framework for the missiological observations we have considered thus far.[7] It is interesting to read what the sociologist David Martin, who does not necessarily share those presuppositions, has to say at this point, in the conclusion of his massive study of popular protestantism in Latin America:

> By far the largest conduit for evangelical Protestantism is provided by the massive movement of people from countryside or hacienda to the megacity. The new society now emerging in Latin America has to do with movement, and evangelicals constitute a *movement*. Evangelical Christianity is a dramatic migration of the spirit matching and accompanying a dramatic migration of bodies. (Martin 1990, 284)

Martin analyzes a vast amount of data from the accumulated research of the last two decades about Latin American protestantism. Much of that research has studied the life of popular protestant communities in most Latin American countries at a micro level. When it comes to the effects of the process of conversion Martin arrives at this conclusion:

> In undertaking the migration, people become "independent" not at all by building up modest securities but by the reverse: by the loss of all the ties that bind, whether

these be familial, communal or ecclesial. Pentecostalism in particular renews these ties in an atmosphere of hope and anticipation rather than of despair. It provides a new cell taken over from scarred and broken tissue. Above all it renews the innermost cell of the family and protects the woman from the ravages of male desertion and violence. A new faith is able to implant new disciplines, re-order priorities, counter corruption and destructive machismo, and reverse the indifferent and injurious hierarchies of the outside world. Within the enclosed haven of faith a fraternity can be instituted under firm leadership, which provides for release, for mutuality and warmth, and for the practice of new roles. (Ibid., 284)

Catholics and Protestants in Latin America are asking themselves about their participation in the mission of the church *Ad Gentes*. I believe that the missiological lessons of popular protestantism offer some clues to formulate and visualize the nature of mission from the Latin American periphery to the rest of the world in the coming century.

NOTES

1. Costas's discussion of the different typologies used in the last decades by Míguez Bonino, Lalive d'Epinay, and Rubem Alves is a helpful summary of the question (Costas 1976, 30-50).

2. Franz Damen is a Passionist priest, a Belgian missionary who has specialized in the study of sects and serves as Executive Secretary of the Department of Ecumenism of the Conference of Bishops in Bolivia.

3. Mgr. Roger Aubry, a Swiss Redemptorist priest, was president of the Department of Missions of CELAM from 1974 to 1979, and has been a missionary in the jungle of Bolivia since 1970.

4. José Luis Idígoras, a Jesuit theologian who has taught in several Catholic theological schools in Peru is presently president and professor of a seminary in the jungle of Peru.

5. See also the chapter by Fr. José Comblin in this book.

6. Regarding recent Catholic missiological interpretations of popular Protestantism see my article "Mission in Latin America," in *Missiology*, April 1992.

7. Though popular protestantism does not have an elaborate theological articulation, I think interesting clues to understanding some of these points and their missiological lessons may be found in the final report of the *Evangelical-Roman Catholic Dialogue on Mission* (ERCDOM), Grand Rapids: Eerdmans, 1986.

11

Popular Spirituality as an Oppressive Reality

Stanley Slade

"Certain aspects of the spirituality of the people will reflect a genuine commitment to God and the forces of life. Other aspects express something else. They reflect the wounds of a people repeatedly injured — the introjection of the values and ideologies of their oppressors. A new popular spirituality that has been coming into being in recent decades is rising from the ashes of an old, disintegrating, popular spirituality." The author was a theological educator in El Salvador, and is the Director of Planning of International Ministries, American Baptist Churches. This chapter is reprinted from the *American Baptist Quarterly* with permission of The American Baptist Historical Society, Valley Forge, PA.

INTRODUCTION

Both the sources and the expressions of spirituality among Latin Americans are numerous and varied. In fact, to speak of "*the* popular spirituality"[1] is to use a false singular. In any given country in Latin America one can find not a monolithic spirituality, but several spiritual modalities present among the people. How much greater the variety, then, if one seeks to speak of all of Latin America!

Every specific local expression of spiritual life will contain both positive and negative elements. Certain aspects of the spirituality of the people will reflect a genuine commitment to God and the forces of life. They are expressions of a faith that refuses to give up, in spite of all of the forces — both past and present — that seek to crush or eliminate people. But, on the other hand, certain aspects of popular spirituality express something else. They reflect the wounds of a people repeatedly injured. They reflect the introjection within the people of the values and ideologies of their oppressors.

There is another factor that makes it both interesting and difficult to speak of popular spirituality in the present moment. We live in the overlapping of two ages. There is a new popular spirituality that has been coming into being in Latin America during the past two decades. But this new spirituality is like the phoenix, rising from its own ashes. It is rising from the ashes of an old popular spirituality that is in process of disintegration.

These three factors — variety, ambivalence, and the tension between old and new — make it extraordinarily difficult to carry out an accurate analysis of popular spirituality in Latin America. Rather than pretend such an achievement, right at the outset we wish to acknowledge openly two further factors that condition the following article. First, the author does not have personal experience in all of Latin America, but only in Mexico and Central America. And, within these geographical limits, his real base of experience is much smaller: his work has been with the baptists of El Salvador. Second, the following article will not seek to be balanced in identifying both positive and negative aspects of popular spirituality.

To be totally clear, the following paper will attempt merely to present several negative aspects of traditional popular spirituality, aspects which still predominate in the vast majority of protestant churches in El Salvador. In all likelihood, there will be multiple connections between these aspects of Salvadoran experience and the forms of popular spirituality that can be found in other places. It would be truly surprising if there were no similarity between the Salvadoran situation and other contexts that have received the impact of the same great historical forces. Nonetheless, the following does not pretend to be a final word, but rather an invitation to analyze the specific contexts of each participant in the Consultation. Our hope is that the following observations and comments will be useful for those who seek to carry out investigations of popular spirituality in their own contexts.

The negative aspects of popular spirituality in El Salvador appear to spring from two old and powerful sources, together with a third source that is smaller and more recent. One of the ancient sources is medieval catholicism — the form of Christianity that came to El Salvador during the Conquest and remained more or less intact until the seventh decade of this century. The second ancient source is political and economic oppression — the structure of internal and international relations that has characterized Salvadoran life (not without superficial changes) from the Conquest to the present. In addition to these two major sources, among protestants one finds a third important source of popular spirituality: foreign missionaries — especially those from North America.[2]

The three sources just mentioned have by no means been isolated or independent forces. On the contrary, they have been intimately intertwined in the history of El Salvador. The first two cooperated for several centuries in the establishment of a world full of negative consequences for the vast majority of the people. And, when the third source made its appearance, it was incorporated into the established world as a kind of escape valve: its critique of the established way of life functioned, paradoxically, to consolidate it. The protestant rejection of the status quo has offered the people an individualistic and other-worldly alternative. This has enabled suffering people to submit and endure — rather than work for the transformation of their common life in history.[3]

Although the sources we have mentioned cannot be isolated, it is useful to distinguish between them and separate them for the purpose of analysis. Therefore, we will organize the following remarks under three headings, headings that reflect the present consequences of each source. In these consequences, we see three "absences" of God: the absence of a loving God, the absence of a just God, and the absence of an incarnate God. This is not to make spirituality a matter of doctrine. Each of these "absences" of God does in fact have a doctrinal aspect. But, first and foremost, these are "absences" that shape the life of faith in its daily activities. In other words, the three headings refer to three truncations of daily spirituality.

Before turning to this three-part analysis, it will be helpful to have some sense of the whole. For this reason, we will begin with a brief description of popular religious experience among Salvadoran baptists.

A GLIMPSE OF SALVADORAN EXPERIENCE

The average Salvadoran baptist lives in a very difficult world. It is a world of obligation and submission. We must resign ourselves to poverty and injustice. We must do our duty in life and also in the church. Life is hard, but our sinfulness really deserves even worse. So, even though things are tough, God is good.

The poverty and suffering one endures is, in fact, just a divinely ordained test, one that prepares us for an eternal reward. Poverty is hard, but it prepares our souls for their heavenly journey. In heaven there will be happiness and rejoicing, but here on earth we have to pay the price of the ticket. So, we must keep ourselves out of the sinful activities of the people around us: drinking, dancing, smoking, card playing, going to movies — even playing soccer is sinful. And, instead of getting involved in those sins, we need to go to church. God does not ask us to be creative or to take initiative, He only asks us to be obedient and submissive. We are nothing. We cannot expect to achieve anything in this world. God is everything, and only God can accomplish things in the world. The only thing that we are called to do is to go to church. So, day after day, week after week, we go to the worship services at church.

It's not that we expect to be transformed by going to church. Nor do we attend worship to find a boost toward a different way of life. We don't arrive at church expecting to reflect on our lives and to learn. Faith is not something you think about, it's something you feel. Actually, we're not really interested even in serious Bible study. Not that anyone would come right out and say such a thing, but lots of folks repeat the old saying, "the letter kills, while the Spirit gives life." And, when folks say this, they're really talking about Bible study: trying to use our human intelligence to understand the Bible is worse than a waste of time, it's actually very dangerous. When you get right down to it, the only thing we go to church for is to satisfy the strict and distant God who demands that we worship Him. God may be good, but He's definitely going to punish any lack of loyalty to the activities of the church.

Now, it's true that in church things are said about the love of God. And, someday we're going to experience that great salvation that He has prepared for us. But, in the meantime, we know that God only responds to those who pay their dues: He only takes care of those who make the sacrifice to attend all the worship services, the vigils and the fasts. You've got to make a lot of sacrifices . . . that is, unless you can find a prophetess or an evangelist with the gift of divine healing. Those kinds of folks, because they have "pull" with God, can get you a blessing, even though you're not worthy. Even if you're not even worthy of taking the Lord's Supper in church, they can usually help you out. At least, that's what everybody says. Unfortunately, there are times when even they can't get you a blessing.

In the community, there are people who say that things could be different. They say that the poor can get organized and make a better life. They try to get folks to work together. It sounds nice, because we really need some big changes around here. But it's a lie. All those people are doing is getting involved in politics. They're just stirring up trouble, and it'll come to no good: God said we should submit to the ruling powers. All this noise about social justice is really nothing more than rebellion against God. This world of ours will never change. But the Lord is good. He knows our limits. Some day he's going to come rescue us from all this suffering.

The foregoing sketch may seem like a caricature. In a way, it is. Any attempt to describe such a complex reality in a few lines has to emphasize only a few points, and leave out a lot of the rich texture of life. So, the few points mentioned may appear in exaggerated form. However, the points are not false, only exaggerated. In fact, traditional protestant spirituality (which, at bottom, has a lot in common with traditional catholic spirituality), is a spirituality of resignation and sacrifice. It is not directed toward changes on the plane of history, but seeks solutions for its tremendous needs by means of two ahistorical paths. One is emotional: the hope of a heavenly reward helps us to "hang in there" and endure the present. The other is magical: the protestant equivalent of playing the lottery is to go to the prophetesses and to those who claim to have the gift of healing. God is confessed as good, but *experienced* as distant, severe and — though nobody dares to say it — unjust. So, just as one needs to seek out people with "pull" in order to get along in daily life, so too with God. The average human being is seen as a guilty and helpless sinner.

THE ABSENCE OF A LOVING GOD

During the Middle Ages, the Christian church underwent important changes, both in its understanding and its practice of the gospel. This history has been studied and explained innumerable times in the last five hundred years. Nonetheless, due to its great importance for the kind of popular spirituality that exists in El Salvador, a few points need to be mentioned very briefly here.

In its unavoidable process of institutionalization, the church committed the avoidable error of copying the contemporary top-down organizational model of hierarchy. Despite the clear rejection of this model by Jesus (Mark 10:35-45), the church became a power structure. The direct access to God by every believer was replaced by a system of mediation. A class of priests was established, with authority and access to God far beyond the ability of the common people. Educating only priests, and celebrating the liturgy only in Latin, were two mechanisms at work at the practical level to reinforce strongly the message that only priests had access to God.

At the same time, the very act of worship underwent a radical change in meaning. The eucharist lost its fundamental character of thanksgiving (*eucharisteo*) for the finished work of Jesus Christ. It became, instead, an act of sacrifice which, in spite of its magical efficacy, needed to be repeated frequently. No longer a moment of thanksgiving and intimate encounter with a loving Father, worship became a formal and mysterious moment, in which one used sacrifice to protect oneself from a distant, angry, and vengeful deity.

The magical efficacy of rites and masses became ever more important as the church emphasized a pessimistic view of history. The fall of Rome during the formative years of Christianity helped lead the church to a pessimistic view of humanity and history. The church did not teach the faithful to expect real progress in history. Rather, earthly life came to be seen only as a test, during which one either gained or lost eternal blessedness. Life would not be advancing, but only marking time.

There is obviously a great deal more that could be said about the characteristics of faith in the Middle Ages. But the few points mentioned above are sufficient to recall the general situation. All of us know that this sick model of Christianity entered into a profound crisis that, after several failed attempts, led to the protestant Reformation. But, in the very moment in which the Reformation came to birth, the Christendom model that the Reformers rejected came to America with the Conquest. In this way, one expression of the Christendom model managed to escape from the crisis. For us, the important thing is to realize that the European crisis of Christendom came to America via surface mail, on the slow boat. And, as happens even today with Latin American mail service, the slow boat was incredibly slow. It took some four hundred and fifty years to arrive. The signs of its arrival included things like the birth of catholic base ecclesial communities, the Medellín (Colombia) bishops' conference, and the appearance of Latin American theology of liberation — to say nothing of the explosive growth of protestant churches.

Today, Latin American churches are going through a time of tremendous ferment. A lot of energy and creativity is at work, among both protestants and catholics. However, equally present are the consequences of nearly five hundred years of medieval catholic spiritual formation. These consequences are visible not only within the catholic communities, but also among protestants.

For example, listening to the prayers of Salvadoran baptists, one hears the powerful echo of medieval spirituality. The brothers and sisters do not converse with a loving God who is present at every moment. They talk to a severe and distant God, one who is angry and vengeful. But, in fact, they do not "talk" with him. They cry out to him from far away, pleading and begging for his mercy. They are not at all confident that the Lord hears them — much less that the Lord loves them. Just the opposite: it is necessary to win his favor. One must merit, must "become worthy" or, at least, "buy" his blessing. Frequently, believers enter into a kind of barter, offering to pay God in kind for services rendered.

In addition to such ways of praying, one finds that people look for someone to serve as a mediator between themselves and God. As protestants, they do not pray either to Mary or to the saints. Instead, they seek the intercession of a pastor, or better, an evangelist — or better yet, a missionary. As one of many possible examples, I recall a visit we made to a small rural congregation several years ago. A baptist who suffered from a large assortment of health problems was waiting for me in the sanctuary. When he heard that the missionary was going to arrive, he walked several kilometers in order to take advantage of the presence of such an important mediator. He wanted the missionary to pray for him because, "surely the Lord will hear your prayer, brother."[4]

We may note in passing that this God who listens more attentively to the anointed is also seen as physically removed from the people. There is some awareness that God is present in every moment of life. But, much stronger among the people is the idea that God is distant from everyday life. God has to be searched out in the sacred space of the church building. And, in many protestant churches, when people want to draw near to God during the time of intercessory prayer, what they do is physically approach the pulpit (just as generations of catholics have drawn close to the altar). The pulpit of a protestant church functions in ways strikingly similar to the "holy of holies" in the ancient Jewish Temple.[5] In fact, the entire sanctuary tends to have the character ancient peoples ascribed to their temples: it is seen as the sacred navel of the world, the point of connection between the distant divine world and our own profane world. The presence of God fills the sanctuary, but no more. It does not spill out into the larger world, so as not to become polluted by human sinfulness. For this reason, one goes to the sanctuary not to meet with other believers, but to establish genuine contact with God (a contact made possible also by the efforts of the mediator one encounters there). It should also be noted that this sacred character of the church building means that it cannot be profaned by non-religious activities.

Another example of the presence of medieval piety within current popular spirituality is the custom of holding vigils. This practice is especially prevalent among pentecostal and neo-pentecostal groups. And, due to pressure from such groups, it is spreading through other protestant churches. These vigils are a monthly, and sometimes a weekly practice. The participants speak clearly and openly in terms of "sacrifice." One "sacrifices oneself" for God in the vigil. And, implicitly but clearly, one expects to be repaid by a God who has been satisfied by such sacrifices. Very much in the style of traditional catholic processions, and of self-flagellating penitents, the believers attend the vigils and mistreat their bodies in an effort to satisfy the severe God who demands sacrifice.

If the idea of sacrifice is clearly present in the case of church vigils, something very similar seems to inform believers' attitudes toward normal worship services. Attendance amounts to paying one's dues to God. Church members — especially in the peasant congregations — demand that their pastors celebrate many, and lengthy, worship services. They demand all these worship services, but they do not come to them with any sense of expectancy. One does not detect a strong desire for fellowship with other believers and to celebrate the blessings of God. There is no expectation that one will be transformed by means of the worship service. With impressive dedication, the believers attend worship in order to get time-cards punched. At bottom, they are paying for their (future) salvation on the installment plan.[6]

This last point about the real function of attendance at worship finds support in the tastes of church members as consumers of sermons. If a preacher spends too much time talking about grace and the love of God, people complain. Many brothers and sisters prefer to listen to sermons about hell, the wrath of God, and the coming judgment. Frequently, they want the pastor to use the pulpit to bawl them out. What is behind such preferences? Among other things, there are at least three items worthy of mention. First, the more the pastor emphasizes the faults of the believers, the more sense it makes to do precisely what they are doing: it makes sense for vile sinners to spend so many hours at worship, because their debt with God is so enormous that there is no other way to pay it off. Second, there is something that has a great deal to do with factors we will discuss in the next section. From the *conquistadores* to the farm foremen, those in authority have almost always abused and chewed out the people. This has become the standard way for people to be treated by those with power and authority. So, people are accustomed to such treatment. It may be that, at bottom, they are not all that thrilled about it, but it is certainly known and understood. Third, there is one factor that points somewhat in another direction. Not everything here is masochism. Many people want to hear sermons about hellfire and damnation not in order to apply them to themselves, but in order to carry out an exercise of vengeful imagination. While the preacher is speaking, they do not see themselves in the flames of hell. They see others: their enemies, the people against whom they cannot avenge themselves in the real world. This and the preceding point have a lot to do with the psychological consequences of oppression. Resentment and the desire for revenge are products and expressions of the experience of powerlessness.

The analysis of popular religious expression has thus led us to the problem of people's socioeconomic experience. The distant, angry, and punishing God who appears in popular spirituality takes us by the hand and leads us to the farm, to government offices, to the barracks, and to the classroom, places where the poor have spent centuries suffering at the hands of distant, angry, and punishing authority figures. For this reason, although there are many other specifically religious expressions that could be discussed, we will now move to the second aspect of popular spirituality: the absence of a God of justice.

THE ABSENCE OF A JUST GOD

There is no need to romanticize the pre-Columbian past in order to appreciate the cruelty and the profundity of the social changes introduced by the Spanish Conquest of the sixteenth century. The Mayas, Incas, and Aztecs ruled vast empires, complete with imperial injustice and oppression. Nonetheless, injustice took a quantum leap with the arrival of the Europeans.

We need not reproduce here the data that are described and explained in detail in other places.[7] It will suffice to mention briefly just a few aspects of the feudal colonial system and its contemporary consequences.

The social system exported to Latin America by the Europeans was a kind of feudalism.[8] This system included a powerful classism, which translated also into racism upon arrival in the Americas. The entire system functioned to benefit and sustain its apex. In those days, there was no need even to disguise the facts. It was unnecessary to create façades of "democracy." Nor was there any need to devise theories of "trickle-down" economics. Social inequality was clearly and "naturally" legitimated by the hierarchical theology of the medieval church.

The social system — and, in fact, the entire created order — was seen in terms of the "great chain of being." At the top of the chain was God. At the bottom was inanimate matter. Human beings appeared in between, but in a highly stratified manner. The vast majority of the population appeared in the lowest positions assigned to human beings. "Naturally," then, it was reasonable that they should spend their lives serving those above them in the chain of being. Those others were, after all, their "superiors," both in terms of social position and in terms of proximity to God.

The duty of the great majority, then, was to stay in their place. Pride was not understood in terms of the arrogance of the high and mighty, but in terms of any attempt to rise on the part of the lowly.

In El Salvador today — if not in all of Latin America — the feudal system has entered into crisis, but continues to dominate the social situation. There is a great deal of class consciousness, but not the revolutionary variety espoused by marxists. It is not a consciousness of struggle, but of submission.[9] People of the lower classes understand very clearly how they are supposed to relate to their "superiors," and almost always do exactly that. To cite one example out of many, the following conversation occurred when an angry landowner returned to the capital after a visit to one of his farms, about four years ago. When asked why he was so angry, he replied:

— "Those blasted guerrillas have been fouling things up at the farm."

— "What have they done? Have they stolen or destroyed anything?"

— "Worse! I was talking with Tony, the foreman. That shameless turkey actually had the nerve to look me in the eye!"

In the presence of his employer, the peasant has no business raising even his eyes, let alone his voice. He has no rights. For the powerful classes of El Salvador, the current social conflict is not only (or even primarily) a question of economics. It is a matter of having their entire world of meaning threatened. For them — and for the poor — beyond material wealth is the belief that the rich are a different kind of being. So, the poor can never cross the gulf that separates them from the rich.

This style of interaction (domination/submission) has become a general pattern in Salvadoran society. It characterizes not only the relations between landowner and laborer, but also serves as the backdrop for all relations between people of unequal position or power. From the farm foreman to the schoolteacher, the most common model for the exercise of authority is abusive. Instead of speaking to the subordinate as an equal, and seeking to motivate him or her through positive incentives, superiors tend to treat subordinates as inferiors, motivating them solely through applications of a verbal cat-o'-nine-tails. For example, to "encourage" students to do better on their assignments, it is common practice in Salvadoran schools for teachers to chastise and mock the less successful students in front of their classmates.[10]

Among the many current aspects of Salvadoran life that are consequences of this social formation, at least three deserve to be mentioned here. First, as we noted in the previous section, the abusive model of authority is so common that church members expect to find it both in God and in their pastors.[11] Abusive sermons are preferred to messages of consolation. And, if God is confessed as good, his goodness tends to be seen along the lines of the "good landowner," and not at all in terms of a loving father. Second, this social formation continues to reinforce the notion that different classes of persons belong to different levels in the great chain of being. So, naturally, God listens more attentively to pastors, evangelists, and foreign missionaries. Third, the disparaging attitude of the "superiors" has been introjected by the poor majority. For this reason, passivity and resignation are far more prevalent than creativity and initiative, and one hears this refrain among the people: "We ain't nuthin'."

In passing, we may note another aspect of Salvadoran popular spirituality that, in a certain sense, arises as a consequence of what has been mentioned so far. In El Salvador, when something important is at stake, forgiveness is all but impossible. Obviously, forgiveness is a problem in the entire world, not merely in Latin America or El Salvador. However, the elements thus far discussed combine to make it exceedingly difficult to forgive in El Salvador. Why? On the one hand, the theological heritage has not emphasized the forgiving nature of God, but exactly the opposite. So, if even God is vengeful, why shouldn't we be? On the other hand, the psychological defense of the powerless is resentment. If one is unable to even things out in the outside world, it can at least be done in the inside world. One seeks revenge in the world of the imagination (and finds much help in sermons about hellfire and damnation). One gets used to nurturing one's bitterness and resentment, because there is no other way to satisfy the internal drive for "justice." So, religious and socioeconomic factors combine to make forgiveness all but impossible. Clearly, this radically limits the possibility of achieving true community in the church (to say nothing of the larger society).

In El Salvador, then (and perhaps in the rest of Latin America), traditional popular spirituality reflects the experience of the absence of a God of justice. It reflects the experience of the presence of a god who shows partiality, a god who legitimates a situation of oppression of the vast majority at the hand of a tiny minority. Such an experience produces passivity instead of creativity, revenge instead of forgiveness, resignation instead of initiative, and the vicious cycle of relations of domination and submission.

THE ABSENCE OF AN INCARNATE GOD

What has been the influence of protestantism in the face of the aforementioned factors? Due to the kind of protestantism that came to Latin America,[12] the impact has not been what one might have expected. The protestant Reformation developed as part of the broad cultural move to reaffirm the world that has come to be called the Renaissance. People like Max Weber (in *The Protestant Ethic and the Spirit of Capitalism*) have explained how the Reformation helped people to give religious significance to their work in the construction of the world of history. So, one might think that the protestants would have helped Latin American spirituality to abandon medieval otherworldliness and plant itself firmly in the world of history.

In fact, the majority of protestants in Latin America have moved in a different direction. The theology of the missionaries has generally been full of social and historical pessimism. It has been a message of rescue for individual souls. In addition to their theology, the missionaries had a very practical reason to be otherworldly. Although some became naturalized citizens of the countries in which they worked, the immense majority have spent their careers as guests in those countries. They have not been citizens, but visitors. So, even if they had wanted to become involved in questions of public life and the common good, their status ruled out such involvement. So, both in word and in deed, the churches learned from the missionaries that they were not to function as public agents within their societies.

In addition to such factors "internal" to the protestant missionary movement, there is another, external factor that contributed to the formation of protestant popular spirituality. The strong — and at times violent — reaction of the catholic church fomented a "siege mentality" among the protestants. In the face of a hostile world, the brothers and sisters did not seriously contemplate the transformation of the world, but only how to protect themselves and rescue others from it.

The experience of being a persecuted minority has left a deep imprint on the protestant communities. Today, it is rare to encounter persecution of protestants by the catholic church. However, many protestant congregations — especially in rural areas — continue to live on the defensive. This shows up in the common practice of negative preaching: investing large amounts of energy criticizing other faith communities (both protestant and catholic). Frequently, one finds congregations — and even entire denominations — that do not have their own positive identity. Their identity is based on little more than their rejection of all other groups.[13]

Missionary theology and practice, in combination with catholic hostility, led to an anti- or other-worldly spirituality. The important world is not this one, but the other, beyond history. History is going to hell. Salvation is something one arranges individually, outside the realm of history. Social and political life is, at best, a distraction — and, at worst, a curse. So, the good protestant does not get involved in historical movements or political activities. Rather, he or she concentrates on nurturing his or her soul in the worship services in the churches.

This does not mean that protestants have in fact managed to live outside the world, nor that they have been truly "apolitical." The rejection of "political involvement" has been anything but consistent. On the contrary, it has generally been closely related to the North American fundamentalist reading of Romans 13. The "apolitical" stance of protestants has been, almost always, a right-wing stance of nearly blind support for the governing powers. So, to no one's surprise, protestant evangelists have encountered eager support from the most authoritarian governments of Latin America.[14]

However, the official posture of the protestant churches has been apolitical. And, in the same way, although protestants have not managed to live without their bodies, their spirituality has been decidedly anti-material. The incarnation of God in Jesus Christ has not been an important theme. It has been much more important to emphasize, on the one hand, Jesus's divinity and, on the other, the sinfulness of the human body. (The body has definitely not been viewed as an instrument able to be used both for good and for evil, but as something evil in itself.)

So, in contrast to its impact in sixteenth-century Europe, in twentieth-century Latin America, protestantism has served to reinforce the historical pessimism and anti-materialism of medieval theology. Instead of motivating the faithful to seek historical solutions to their problems, protestantism has simply helped them to endure.

In El Salvador, then (and perhaps in all of Latin America), traditional protestant popular spirituality reflects the experience of the absence of an incarnate God. It reflects the experience of a god who does not affirm, but rejects the importance of the body and material life. The previously mentioned "sacrifices" demanded by this god almost always include a strong dose of mistreatment of the body. Instead of the Creator of a good material world — terribly disfigured, of course, by human sin — the church has presented a god of souls. This god has cared nothing for the redemption of the whole creation, but only for the rescue of individual souls.[15]

CONCLUSION

Before a phenomenon as complicated and diverse as popular spirituality in Latin America, it would be a delusion to pretend to arrive at "conclusions" after so little work. We have hardly begun to scratch the surface. Nevertheless, this essay must come to a close. It remains to be shown by more scientific and detailed studies whether our suggestions are in fact true or false. But this article will have achieved its purpose if it has motivated its readers to improve upon the work begun here.

What we have tried to do is describe oppressive or dominating elements within popular spirituality, and identify their sources in different aspects of the historical processes that have shaped Latin American peoples. Our hypothesis is that oppressive factors from the past have managed to establish themselves within popular spirituality, converting the same into an instrument of domination. Of course, this is not the whole truth. There are also good and liberating elements within popular spirituality.[16]

It should be clear that the author is in favor of the transformation of traditional popular spirituality that is currently under way. All over Latin America there is an earnest search for a new spirituality. The negative elements we have mentioned are distortions of the biblical message, the message of a God who is committed to liberating human beings from death and sin in all its forms. For this reason, from our perspective, we can look forward to the development of a spirituality that is, simultaneously, more faithful to the biblical sources of our faith, and more useful for the integral salvation of Latin American peoples.

NOTES

1. The phrase "popular spirituality," as it has come to be used in Latin American theological circles, denotes a complex reality (or constellation of cultural traits). The word *popular* in Spanish is used to refer especially to the poor. Because the poor typically constitute the vast majority of the population in Latin American countries, "popular" also carries the idea of large numbers of people (as it does in English). So, those who speak of "popular spirituality" typically have in mind the religious sentiments and practice of the large numbers of poor people at the bottom of Latin American societies.

The word *popular* also has a political *sitz im leben*: though used occasionally by those of other persuasions, it is most often found on the lips of those with a leftist or revolutionary orientation toward the status quo. For this reason, "popular spirituality" is also, in fact, used to denote *not* the religious attitudes and practices of all of the poor, but rather of those among the poor who are in some way committed to the transformation of society. However, it is not always recognized that this progressive group is not truly representative of the attitudes, values, and practices of the majority. However beneficial its agenda might be for the poor, it does not truly reflect the reality of the larger group.

It is the contention of this article that the poor tend to be guided by a spirituality that is not in fact liberating, but oppressive. In this way, the article seeks to correct an overly-romantic view of the poor, and the tendency of some progressive writers to confuse this romantic construct with reality.

This combination of factors just mentioned makes it difficult to find an English equivalent for the Spanish word *popular*. Perhaps our word "grassroots" comes the closest — though it doesn't carry the same socioeconomic or political freight. We will stick with the literal translation, "popular," hoping that the strangeness of its usage here will help the reader to be aware of the factors just mentioned.

2. Anyone even vaguely familiar with the history of Latin America will also want to look at a fourth important source. The pre-Columbian peoples of Latin America were not a blank slate, waiting to be written upon by the Europeans. Nor did they totally submit to the new cultural forms brought by the conquerors. Even today, in many parts of Latin America, it is possible to find religious activities that use Christian façades to express very different meanings. Therefore, a complete discussion of popular spirituality in Latin America would have to include an analysis of the pre-Columbian heritage operative in each country or region. However, every investigation has to have some limits. Here in El Salvador, the variety of pre-Columbian backgrounds, together with the attempt to exterminate indigenous peoples in

1932, make it tremendously difficult to investigate the indigenous sources of popular spirituality. For this reason, the present article will not even attempt to discuss the contribution of indigenous cultures to Salvadoran popular spirituality.

3. We should note in passing that this consolidating function is precisely what has made Protestantism so attractive to Latin American governments in recent years, as they have felt threatened by the changes within Catholicism. It is well known that the most repressive governments of Latin America have enthusiastically opened their doors to Protestant evangelists. Despite the fact that the Protestant message carries within itself the seed of the destruction of such governments, the rulers have clearly seen that most current expressions of Protestantism function to produce "model citizens": people who freely and fervently submit to the governing powers, and do not get involved in social or political issues.

4. In the case of foreign missionaries, a simple historical fact contributes to this attitude among the people. The Catholic Church in Latin America has never managed to become self-sustaining at the level of church leadership. It has always depended on a vast infusion of foreign priests and religions. Unintentionally, this fact in itself has taught people that you need a different category of human beings in order to gain access to God.

One may suppose that there is also another socio-theological factor at work here. Missionaries and evangelists have more "pull" with God than the local pastor because they are usually wealthier. We arrive at church in a vehicle. We make trips abroad. In comparison with the poor members of local congregations, we are wealthy. And, whatever may be said explicitly, the churches continue to be full of the idea that God shows partiality: he favors the rich and punishes the poor. Material wealth is seen as proof of the intimacy between God and the rich.

5. This is clearly visible also in the specific ways in which women are marginalized in many Protestant congregations. It is permissible for a woman to speak to the congregation — as long as she doesn't do so from the pulpit. Especially among rural churches, women are typically not allowed to enter that holy place.

6. This, of course, has everything to do with the absence of any expectation of real transformation in history — whether of individuals or of the world. Salvation is seen as a magical transaction, something that takes place outside of this world and its history. Salvation is guaranteed, then, by frequent visits to the sacred space. Naturally, one seeks to reduce the contradictions between what is done in the sacred space and what one does in the profane world. However, no matter how much the preacher may harp on the need for such change, people know that what will really matter on Judgment Day will not be their daily lives, but the number of hours they invested in church activities.

At the same time, especially in the rural churches, another factor enters into play. Both their poverty and their religious mores keep the believers removed from common means of entertainment (movies, TV, parks, playing soccer, etc.). So, the church also functions as just about the only acceptable source of entertainment.

7. The bibliography is vast. For those who are unfamiliar with this field, a beginning can be made with the famous work of Eduardo Galeano, *The Open Veins of Latin America*, or with the more scholarly tomes produced by CEHILA (Comission of the Latin American Church).

8. In other words, more or less the same thing happened in the religious and socioeconomic fields. A model or historical formation that had entered into crisis in Europe encountered new life upon escaping to Latin America. These models managed to save themselves from the crisis and live on — largely intact — in the New World. It will, of course, be no accident that both the religious and the socioeco-

nomic structures have entered into simultaneous crises in Latin America during the last thirty years.

9 Obviously, there are those who would vigorously dispute this affirmation. For them, the struggle in El Salvador during the last twenty years — ten years of political struggle, and ten of politico-military struggle — demonstrates precisely the existence of revolutionary class consciousness. The author recognizes that Protestant church people (for reasons we will discuss in the next section) may be seriously out of step with the rest of the population. On the other hand, the inability of the revolutionary forces to mount a genuine general insurrection during the last ten years of armed conflict may suggest that our observation has a significant element of truth.

10. Speaking of education, it has clearly been an important tool for keeping the dominated poor in their place. Even today, few Latin American countries are serious about educating all of their people. Illiteracy is endemic. Despite the limited resources of these countries, the lack of adequate education is not a problem of scarce resources, it is a problem of scarce political will. The apex of society has not wanted to share the power of knowledge with those at the bottom.

In the church, sometimes this necessity is presented as a virtue. Those who, in any case, have no chance to become educated, often repeat the saying, "the letter kills, but the Spirit gives life." In other words, popular spirituality includes a strong dose of anti-intellectualism. People take pride in their ignorance, as if it were a guaranteed path to God. Without justifying such an attitude, one can certainly appreciate it as an act of protest against the use of education as an instrument of domination.

11. In fact, it is possible to speak of a "vicious circle" of domination. The model of domination/submission is so deeply rooted that, if an oppressed person manages to attain some quota of power, he or she is most likely to use it to oppress others. That is, instead of taking into account his or her own disagreeable experience of having been dominated, he or she becomes a dominator. Instead of breaking the cycle of domination, he or she perpetuates it. So, when the oppressed have a chance to wield power, they tend to reproduce the circle of domination.

Every congregation, however small, presents opportunities to wield power. That is why Salvadoran faith communities are, almost always, religious boxing rings. Occasionally in an explicit way, though typically in a more disguised form, the churches are full of power struggles.

12. Although missionaries of various countries and church traditions have worked in Latin America, the primary influence has come from North Americans. And, their arrival in Latin America generally occurred after what Timothy Smith, Donald Dayton and others have called "the great reversal." Churches that carried out holistic evangelism (social and personal, "spiritual," and "material") during the first half of the nineteenth century, entered the twentieth century having repented of their social action. As part of the broad process that led to the controversy between fundamentalism and modernism, the churches lost the integration that had guided their efforts decades before. For this reason, many (probably the vast majority) of the missionaries that came to work in Latin America brought with them a truncated theology: theirs was a gospel not for communities and bodies, but for individual souls.

13. Of course, living on the defensive also has current causes. The proselyting competition among the churches is often very strong. As a consequence, congregations tend to become even more closed toward the outside. They also tend to enter into a competition of legalisms and "sacrifices": each congregation claims to be the best — or even the only true church — on the basis of its legalistic practices. If

church "X" demands that women use veils, our church must demand the same — or even more.

14. In a radically polarized context, like that of El Salvador, sometimes the government itself gets involved in "evangelism." A couple of years ago, a Catholic catechist in a small Salvadoran town received a visit from the army. The lieutenant explained to the catechist that, if he wanted to stay alive in that town, it behooved him to leave the Catholic parish and join the Pentecostal church down the road. The lieutenant saw the local priest as subversive, but recognized that the Pentecostals were good people and faithful citizens.

15. Precisely here we encounter an interesting contradiction in the Pentecostal movement. On the one hand, both in doctrine and practice, the Pentecostals seek to be at least as anti-material as the other churches. However, their enthusiasm for the Holy Spirit has actually moved them in the opposite direction: the practice of divine healing. Clearly, it makes no sense to heal that which has no value. But this contradiction stops no one. The tremendous physical needs of the people have moved divine healing into the center of the Pentecostal movement. In fact, one may well suspect that precisely this rupture with the anti-material framework of Protestantism has been one of the vital factors in the explosive growth of the Pentecostal movement.

16. Perhaps it would be useful to give an example that, at the same time, reveals our vision of the dialectical nature of things. We have severely criticized the "culture of sacrifice" in the churches. It is blasphemous, for it converts the God of the Bible into a Moloch, who demands human sacrifice in order to placate his wrath. It is blasphemous, because the God of the Bible, instead of demanding human sacrifice, offers himself in loving service to human beings. Nevertheless, precisely at this point appears the value of the culture of sacrifice within the churches. At least, there is an awareness that a genuine disciple of Jesus Christ has to deny himself or herself in some fashion. If the true purpose of such "sacrifice" can be understood, and if more important forms can be found for its exercise, then the blasphemy can easily be turned into *imitatio Dei*. In this sense, Salvadoran believers are much closer to the heart of God than, for example, the U.S. believers who have swallowed the "gospel of prosperity," with its blatant egotism. In the same way, we see important and recoverable values also present in all of the negative aspects of popular spirituality criticized in this paper.

12

The Genesis and Practice of Protestant Base Communities in Latin America

Guillermo Cook

"What God is doing amidst his people really escapes our theological comprehension . . . especially among the base of the Christian Community. This eagerness for liberty, this enthusiasm for building a new society, this revolution, is evangelizing the church." Dr. Cook reveals a little-known aspect of Evangelical growth in Central America. This is an updated version of an article published in *Evangelisches Theologie*, Nº 6-91, Evangelisches-Theologiches Universität Tübingen. Used with permission.

During the 1980s, the Base Ecclesial Communities (BECs) in the Latin American Catholic Church attracted worldwide attention. Very little notice was paid to a similar phenomenon in the Protestant churches. There are several reasons for this. To begin with, Protestant BEC-type groups were far less numerous than their Catholic counterparts; and for reasons of security they have maintained an extremely low profile. Furthermore, grassroots communities in a more freewheeling Protestant milieu would not seem to be as unusual as are the Catholic BECs within a very hierarchical church. Protestantism took root in Latin America as a series of small group movements that posed an implicit challenge to the religious status quo. In this they were following in the footsteps of their Protestant forefathers.[1] In addition, three distinctive practices of Base Communities — Biblical reflection, a more Christ-centered worship, and lay leadership — were more or less taken for granted in Reformational churches.[2] However, at one crucial point, given their otherworldliness and lack of social involvement, Protestant congregations were compared unfavorably with the Catholic BECs by students of religious phenomenology, and largely discounted as historically relevant.

Then, in the 1980s, a kind of Protestant base community began to appear here and there in Latin America — particularly in situations of popular insurrection and violent governmental repression. They first appeared in Guatemala, El Salvador, and Nicaragua. The Protestant *comunidades* are sustained by their faith in God and the Bible, and by the example of their own and Catholic martyrs. In a part of the world where Catholics and Protestants have been hostile to each other for generations, Archbishop Oscar Arnulfo Romero has become an inspiration, if not a saint, to some grassroots Protestants.

FACTORS OF CHANGE

Three factors are at work to change the Protestant awareness of their social environment and their responses to it: the socioeconomic and political crisis in the region, with its attendant violence, and their surprising numerical growth.

Social and Economic Factors

The Protestant work ethic is undermined because of the magnitude of the crisis. Although Protestants continue to appeal to the mystique of divinely ordained upward mobility, in actual fact, working-class and peasant Protestants are finding it increasingly more difficult to subsist, let alone to prosper. In fact, an increasing number of lower-middle class Protestants are also becoming impoverished. The trend is noticeable, even in a country such as Costa Rica, which not too long ago was considered to be fairly prosperous. Protestants are joining the ranks of the unemployed and the dispossessed. Increasingly one finds dirt-poor Protestants facing the same problems as their far more numerous Catholics neighbors. They are being forced out of their rented houses in the working-class suburbs, or being pushed off of their small plots of land into the growing *barrios marginales* that fester around the major cities of the region. The problem would be much more acute if it were not for such safety nets as the strong Latin American family loyalty, a certain amount of spontaneous Evangelical solidarity, and Protestant aid programs.

Violence becomes endemic. It is both cause and effect of the social crisis in Latin America. The ravages of war in every Central American country except Costa Rica, in Colombia, and in Perú, have not left Protestants untouched. In the Guatemalan highlands, during the regime of Protestant president General Efraín Ríos-Montt, entire villages of native Americans, some of them almost a hundred percent Protestant, were virtually wiped out or forced into exile (Spykman et al. 1988, 38-40). Protestant lay leaders, even those belonging to native American fundamentalist churches, were sought out, tortured, and in some cases brutally dismembered. In 1982 a Christian Reformed missionary working with the Presbyterian Church of Guatemala narrowly escaped abduction by the military after he helped a Kek'kchí pastor who had been tortured reach freedom. Other native leaders were not so fortunate. Protestants who managed to survive remarked upon the theological sophistication of the interrogators. Catholics and Protestants alike fled to refugee camps in Mexico, Honduras, and Costa Rica, where Protestant congregations mushroomed among them.

In Nicaragua and El Salvador innocent civilians, some Evangelicals among them, were blown up or maimed by land mines, or bombed out of their homes by either insurgent militia or government forces. Protestants, along with Catholics, were forcibly conscripted, tortured, exiled, or jailed, their women raped and their children savaged, on the merest suspicion of collaboration with the insurgents. Noel Vargas was a young Pentecostal pastor and recent seminary graduate. In October of 1983, he was working as a schoolteacher on a farm cooperative in a Nicaraguan village near the Honduran border. Noel was murdered by a band of contras along with the co-op director and the health worker, both of whom were members of the Church of the Nazarene (Spykman et al. 1988, 143-145). In Perú, lay Quechua Presbyterians were dragged out of their rural chapel and executed by a military patrol, on suspicion of being Shining Pathway cadres. This atrocity produced a sharply-worded protest by the conservative Evangelical Confederation of Perú (CONEP) and galvanized Protestant involvement in defense of the native American population. Socioeconomic and military violence radicalized peasant Protestants along with their Catholic relatives and neighbors. One result of this process has been base church communities.

Protestant growth. Protestants are personally becoming more aware of the violence in their societies simply because there are more of them. In a country like Guatemala where an estimated three out of every ten inhabitants is said to be Protestant,[3] and where at least 5 percent of the population has been killed, few rural Protestant families have been left unscathed. Protestant growth in a context of socioeconomic crisis has increased the possibilities for awareness of the need for social change. The growing number of very poor Protestants is increasingly open to change. Not surprisingly, the dwindling middle class — Protestants included — has usually been more inclined to preserve the status quo.

THE GENESIS OF THE PROTESTANT BASE COMMUNITIES

It is virtually impossible to document a clandestine movement. All that I can do is to sketch some facts that I was able to discover or personally witnessed and experienced. There were similarities and differences in the emergence of the Catholic and Protestant BECs. They shared the same environment and were similarly aware of being a different kind of church community, though in different ways. Both Protestant and Catholic base communities were born out of a dynamic and creative interaction between grassroots initiatives and pastoral concerns in a context of death. But at this point we find significant differences.

Not many Protestant churchmen dared to openly defend the cause of the poor,[4] while in the Catholic Church the concerns of the poor had the cautious support of a bishop here and there. Most of the Protestant leadership, when faced with human rights abuses against their own grassroots colleagues, chose to look the other way. It was less compromising to dismiss activist pastors as "radical" and "Marxist" than to demonstrate pastoral concern at whatever cost.

Encouragement for base community initiatives came primarily from several sources. (1) An occasional pastor or North American missionary from a theologically conservative church who had had his or her consciousness raised while defending the civil rights of their national colleagues. (2) "Parachurch ministries" (there were several hundred at the time), which specialized in solidarity work, holistic development, pastoral accompaniment, and leadership training (both theological and practical) without denominational distinctions. (3) Ecumenical Bible reflection and prayer groups wherever the situation had become particularly oppressive or challenging.

Vestiges of colonial Christendom remain, despite the separation of church and state in most of Latin America. Roman Catholicism maintains considerable authority. It provides, at least theoretically, a legal and religious rationale for the Catholic BECs. This was not the case with the Protestant *comunidades*, which are largely unprotected. In their search for ecclesial models, they either copy the Catholic model (usually unsuccessfully) or strive to find their own identity, all the while resisting the very Protestant tendency toward sectarianism. This is probably why I found more ecumenical BECs than outright Protestant *comunidades*.

EARLY PROTESTANT COMMUNITIES IN LATIN AMERICA

The first Protestant missionaries to come to Central America brought with them a U.S. frontier kind of church that strongly emphasized the local congregation. This model in some ways resembles a base community, except for the rugged individualism of its leaders, which stands in stark contrast to the community orientation of the BECs. A fundamental component of the church identity of the early Protestant congregations was their Bible-based preaching. The Lord's Supper or holy communion, though important, was secondary — perhaps in reaction to Catholic sacramentalism. One of the reasons for the rapid growth of Protestantism are the many preaching points that sprang up around established churches, and with the advent of Pentecostalism, more spontaneity. In their early stages these preaching points or prayer groups were a kind of base community. Growing Protestant churches also found it necessary to subdivide into small groups for nurturing and mutual support. Although a prayer or Bible study group might in time become another "local church," in the interim they had no ecclesial identity of their own. They were usually very much under the supervision of their pastor. As a general rule, they did not celebrate the communion without his presence or explicit permission. This is, of course, somewhat different from the Catholic BEC practice.

The early history of the small-group movement in Latin American Protestantism probably accounts for the relative lack of ecclesial identity that I observed among the Protestant *comunidades*. They have tended to see themselves less as expressions of the church in their own right than as small groups that meet (often clandestinely) to reflect on the Bible in their own context. In Guatemala in the late 1980s informed sources reported some several hundred of these communities. They tended to be meetings of lay workers from a wide spectrum of Christian communions who, without abandoning their respective churches, met with a certain regularity to reflect upon their own situation, with the Bible in their hands. The leaders of these *comunidades* were chosen by their peers for their

gifts, irrespective of their denominational ties. Lacking the institutional protection that the Roman Church can provide its own BECs, the ecumenical communities must either go underground or find a suitable umbrella. One *comunidad*
that I visited gathers the leaders of every religious body in the isolated mountain
village, including groups that are affiliated with fundamentalist denominations.
This base community is recognized as a local church by the leadership of a
widely respected conservative denomination. Most of the denominational hierarchy, however, seemed unaware of the ecumenical nature of that congregation!

Small but significant pockets of Protestant *comunidades* can still be found
throughout Central America. A large and respected Baptist church in El Salvador has worked for several years with *grupos de solidaridad* — non-denominational rural cooperatives that also serve as Biblical reflection centers. In the
same country, the Lutheran Church, at great risk, fosters ecumenical base communities. Both groups have suffered physical harm at the hands of government
death squads. Despite the peace accord between government and guerrillas, the
lives of local church leaders continue to be threatened. During the heyday of
Nicaraguan Sandinismo, Baptist congregations were encouraging the growth of
comunidades. Over the years, Mennonites have been promoting grassroots initiatives in Honduras. A handful of Baptists, Nazarenes, Church of God, and
Independents struggle to maintain base community ideals in Costa Rica. Each of
these expressions of the base community church has managed to hold on to its
own distinctive liturgy, church discipline, and doctrine, alongside varying approaches to social involvement.

THE WITNESS OF THE PROTESTANT BECs

Something new has been happening in Central America. A Protestant lay
pastor summed it up in the following words:

> What God is doing amidst his people really escapes our theological comprehension
> . . . especially among the base of the Christian Community. . . . This eagerness for
> liberty, this enthusiasm for building a new society, this revolution, is evangelizing
> the church. This may seem like heresy, but today it is the truth. Never before have
> we seen how evangelical Christians and Catholics can meet together in a village of
> the highlands to celebrate their faith, because there are no longer ministers nor
> priests in this zone. (Fried and Gettlemen 1983, 230-231)

The anguish of violence is not the only factor that draws together the peasant
peoples of Guatemala, El Salvador, Honduras, and Nicaragua into Protestant and
Catholic base communities, in such numbers that it exceeded "the limits and
technical capabilities" of the support groups. It is also hope that brings them
together. A hope so great, the same layman testified, "that for the first time we
can feel it profoundly. This people which . . . had been silent and bent over . . .
[have] overcome this situation to rise up proudly amidst the pain, with hope."
This is a situation that, "for those of us who have worked in the service of the
Lord as Protestants . . . is a miracle . . . of God" (ibid., 231).

NOTES

1. Grassroots church communities are not, of course, new to Protestantism. In fact, they go back to the New Testament concept of *ekklesia* — originally a technical term for the town meetings in Greece. When Christianity became the official religion of the Roman empire, numerous grassroots ecclesial movements (so-called heretical sects) nipped at the church's heels for a millennium, right up to the Protestant Reformation. During the Reformation period, and in crisis periods from the sixteenth to the eighteenth centuries, base communities of different sorts appeared on the fringes of Protestantism. Most of them, like the Anabaptists, early Quakers, Congregationalists, Radical Pietists, and Methodist classes, were eventually swallowed up by mainstream values and institutions. Protestantism came to Latin America by way of North America, fueled by pietism and invigorated by Methodist frontier revivalism. Small groups were peculiarly suited to evangelism and nurturing in a hostile religious environment (Cook 1985, 173-199).

2. One sees in the Catholic BECs a renewed emphasis upon Reformation values such as the priesthood of the believer and the fourfold Reformation doctrines: *solo Christo, sola gratia, sola fides*, and *sola Scriptura*.

3. The PROLADES church growth institute in Costa Rica estimated the Central American Protestant membership, in 1987, as follows: Guatemala, 29.6 percent; Nicaragua, 17.2; Costa Rica, 17; Honduras, 11; and El Salvador, 9.7. These are adjusted estimates based upon 1985 data. By way of contrast, a 1989 study by a Gallup-related center in Costa Rica reduces the local percentage to 8.9, suggesting that Protestants are losing membership, including to the Catholic church (cp. Kessler 1990).

4. El Salvador is a unique exception. Lutheran Bishop Medardo Gómez has taken over the public prophetic role that was once filled by Archbishop Oscar Romero. The leaders of the Baptist Association, and in particular the Emmanuel Baptist Church, have also risked life and limb to protect the integrity of their base community congregations.

13

Popular Religion and the Church: Hopes and Challenges at the Dawn of the Fifth Centenary

Maria Clara Luchetti Bingemer

"Neither Jesus nor the apostles had the arrogance to suppose that the people to whom they announced the Gospel were lacking in culture, faith, or identity." The author reviews some of the effects of the Conquest on the culture and religion of our native peoples. Popular religiosity, she argues, came out of the ensuing cultural and religious conflict and can yet have a positive role in evangelization. The author is professor of systematic theology at the Catholic University of Brazil. Taken from *SEDOS Bulletin*, no. 24, 1992, with permission.

INTRODUCTION

On the eve of the fifth centenary of the discovery and evangelization of Latin America, the Church has turned with hope to the Fourth Latin American Bishops' Conference at Santo Domingo. The Conference met in October (1992) to discuss the theme "New Evangelization, Human Promotion, and Christian Culture." Much has been thought, spoken, and written about this conference and the expectation which it arouses. Among the prominent themes to be explored is "Religiosity" or "Popular Religion." It is a theme that can be traced to the very origins of the conquest and the colonization of the Americas. It is a theme that causes us to reflect on the cultural diversity of our peoples and on the growing consciousness of the enormous aggression committed against them.

In these reflections, I will attempt: (1) to review some of the effects which the conquest had on the culture and religion of our native peoples; (2) to examine how the ensuing cultural and religious conflict brought the popular religiosity of our peoples; (3) to pinpoint the place that this form of religiosity has in the recent history of the Latin American Church.

EFFECT OF THE CONQUEST ON NATIVE AMERICAN RELIGIOSITY

A "Conquered" Religion

The conquest was not only a political and military event, arising from the voyages of discovery; it was also a religious event. The Europeans brought their religion along with their culture and civilization. They considered this religion to be the only true religion, which had to be given as a very precious gift to the native population.

The voyage of Columbus had as a central objective, the glory of Christianity, its expansion, and the Christianization of the newly discovered continent. The deep religiosity of the Genovese navigator and the Spanish and Portuguese conquerors who followed him furthered this colonial project. The goal of christianizing the continent shaped the conquerors' treatment of the new lands and their inhabitants; it also influenced future evangelization.

Cristóbal [carrier of Christ] understood himself to be at one and the same time, a colonizer and an evangelizer. Las Casas saw the Genovese navigator as "the first to open the doors of our Mother ocean in order to let our Savior Jesus Christ pass through to those faraway lands and kingdoms until then unknown." Columbus's worldview led him to ignore and even despise the values and the culture of the inhabitants. He ignored the diversity of their languages and wanted to bring some of them before the King of Spain, so that according to him, they could "learn to speak." Not only are their languages and their ways of communicating inferior and unworthy of consideration, worse still, they simply do not exist as such. He had the same attitude to their religion.

Columbus's religiosity permeated his way of thinking, his actions, and his attitudes toward the newly discovered land and the people he found there. Like a new Adam he gave Christian names to the land, totally disregarding the Indian names. By so doing, the conqueror acted as if the land, and the world of the people he *discovered* were his own.

Columbus and those who followed him did not respect the religious rituals and symbols that belonged to the very depths of the lives of the people. They considered the native religion as magic, demonic, superstitious, or barbaric. They identified the physical nakedness of the indigenous people with a holistic, cultural, religious nakedness that needed to be covered by their superior religion.

Conquerors or Evangelizers?

There is another side to the coin. The conquerors came to bring civilization as well as Christianity to the natives, but they also wanted to take something away — the gold and the riches they found on the continent. Thus arose conflicting interpretations about whether they were conquerors or evangelizers. If the Indians were human beings, they were capable of receiving the Gospel message and they must at least be considered deserving of receiving it and they must be evangelized. On the other hand, if the objective is to take the Indians' gold and they resist, then they must be dominated. As inferior beings, they had to be subjugated by the superior conquerors. Very soon, these two understandings were superimposed, one on the other. Without judging the intentionality of the conquerors, the transmission of the new religion was irretrievably confused with domination, subjugation, and cruelty. This perverse confusion between the colonizing project and evangelizing aims put its seal on how the evangelization of the Latin American continent took place and how it was interpreted.

I do not want to generalize, but the fifth centenary should be an occasion for us to recognize what happened, and acknowledge how much it influenced the evangelization of Latin America. The pastoral problems that we experience today and their consequences can be traced back to the moment of Columbus's arrival on the continent.

The Good News

Neither Jesus nor the apostles who followed him had the arrogance to suppose that the people to whom they announced the Gospel were lacking in culture, faith, or identity. Even though the Gospel as Good News offers a radical vision of God, Jesus did not reject the traditions of the people of Israel. Permeating the entire Gospel message, there is a very fertile and rich tension between tradition and the Good News.

The God that Jesus calls his Father, the *Abba* whom he presents to men and women as the God of life and the God of the poor, had much to do with the God of Israel. The *Abba* of Jesus is the God of Abraham, Isaac, and Jacob. He is not the God whom the Pharisees have kidnapped and taken from the people by transforming religion into a heavy burden. The *Abba* of Jesus is a liberating God who has freed, and still frees people from captivity. He is the God that Jesus talks about, whom he sees as his Father, whom he presents as the God who prefers prostitutes and publicans to the Pharisees. It is not that the God of Jesus has nothing to do with the God of Israel. Jesus announces a deeper, and more profound truth about God. He also recognizes that the people had searched for that God, dialogued, and walked with him, learned how to praise and adore him, and tried to keep their covenant with him.

The same is true of the apostles. The genius of Paul was that he opened the doors of the Church to the pagan world and to the gentiles while recognizing the truth of their past. He did not oblige them to conform to the pattern of the synagogue and the Jewish religion. Recall his speech before the Council of the Areopagus.

> Men of Athens, I have seen for myself how extremely scrupulous you are in religious matters. I noticed as I strolled around admiring your sacred monuments, that you had an altar inscribed: To an Unknown God. Well, the God whom I proclaim is in fact the one whom you already worship without knowing it.

He does not treat the Athenians as people without beliefs, or assume that they are only waiting for him to arrive to announce some sensational news.

This age-old challenge continues to face us today. How do we respect the culture and religion of the other? How can we communicate what we believe is true about faith without doing violence to the cultural values and the religious beliefs that are already present? How can we recognize the seeds of truth in other religions? How can we be open to the Good News, when that Good News does not fit into our institutionalized patterns of religious experience?

LATIN AMERICAN CATHOLICISM BETWEEN TRADITION AND MODERNITY

In Latin America, the conquerors refused to recognize the identity of the native population. Because of this historical fact, I think that we can see a number of conflicting attitudes toward Christianity.

The first attitude is simply a refusal by some or part of the population to become Christian.

A second attitude, very common to later generations, is that of seeming to accept Christianity but in fact not doing so. Blacks who arrived in Brazil as slaves were strongly constrained to become Christians. They responded by giving the names of Christian saints to their divinities while continuing to worship them as divinities. Later this became what we call Afro Brazilian, syncretic religion. During their religious services there are elements of Catholic ritual, the Eucharistic celebration, and the use of the names of Jesus, Our Lady, and the saints.

The third attitude is to accept, assimilate, and create a different synthesis. I think that this expresses the profound originality of what we call popular religiosity. The Catholic religion is lived according to the identity and the experience of the people in a particular time and set of historical circumstances. There are similarities with institutionalized forms of religion, but there are also significant differences. In popular religiosity, celebration belongs to the cultural universe of the people; it is inseparable from their living faith. This is found more commonly in rural areas than in urban settings. But, even when rural people migrate to areas surrounding large cities, they retain a very traditional ritual for celebrating the sacraments and religious feasts.

People retain the custom of pilgrimage to sanctuaries of the Virgin. Needs that are connected with the everyday life of people are celebrated in the context of their Christian faith and in ways that are distinct from those of the official Church, but it also represents a rich potential for evangelization. It challenges the church to recall and rediscover the message of the Gospel today for people who are being influenced by the processes of modernity and secularization. There is a flame of faith to be protected, a hidden treasure that must be sought out even if the challenge surfaces questions and ambiguities.

In some Latin American countries a very strong element of secularization followed on Vatican II. *Gaudium et Spes* was at times misinterpreted with serious pastoral consequences. Some examples: in spite of the people's great devotion to the Virgin from the churches, traditional practices were judged to be superstitious. Such actions provoked strong feelings of resistance among the people.

Medellín stressed the richness that is hidden in the experience of our people. The bishops spoke about the positive value of popular religiosity, while calling attention to elements that called for evangelization. Puebla goes further. It speaks not only of popular religiosity, but also of popular religion. The label "religiosity" is a subtle form of discrimination that marginalized popular religious experience. Puebla reminds the Church to be attentive to the concrete expressions of popular religion in Christianity. It calls attention to the fact that if the Church is not able to respond to the people's thirst for God, to their real experience of God as present in those religious expressions — the resultant vacuum will be filled by something else.

New Religiosity in Latin America: Challenge to a New Evangelization

In Latin America, we no longer live in a homogeneous or even predominantly Christian world. The historical Catholic and Protestant churches see a growing exodus to sects. New religious movements are now a significant presence in Latin America and Christians have to live their faith in a pluralistic religious world. The process of modernity has touched a large part of the continent. The younger generations live their lives in the midst of modernity. They experience a crisis brought about by belonging to two worlds — one, permeated by the values of tradition and the other, which is in constant flux.

Three years ago, I had a conversation with a well-known Chilean theologian, a remarkable man who has lived for more than twenty years in a poor *barrio* in Santiago. He told me that he could communicate well with adults but not with young people. They are shaped by the mass media, influenced by a global culture, and constrained by oppressive patterns of behavior.They no longer have the clear sense of identity that their parents and grandparents had. The process of evangelization must take this into account. There must be a different pastoral approach to the young. This is a major challenge as we move into the next five hundred years of Christian presence in Latin America.

Sects

In Brazil, sects and religious movements are growing in an amazing way. Because of a tradition of syncretism, Brazil provides fertile soil for this kind of phenomenon. New Japanese sects are growing along with the Pentecostal branches of the Protestant churches. We could argue that because of their extremely oppressive situation, the poor are more susceptible to these sects and find in them a more affective and flexible form of religious experience. But, what we are witnessing today is that middle class, intellectuals, ex-socialist militants, ex-atheistic thinkers are also joining the sects and the new religious movements.

In Brazil one religious movement began in the middle of the Amazonian rain forest. It has an ecological orientation combined with Christian elements. The fact is that more and more university students, artists, and intellectuals are joining this religion. At the center of its ritual is a liquid taken from an Amazonian plant. Drinking the liquid causes vomiting, which is seen as part of a purification process and is followed by visions and mystical experiences. The National Council for Drugs examined the contents of the liquid to see if they were addictive. They declared it safe.

In some aspects this is a very rigid religion. Adherents make a vow of chastity. The concept of authority is vertical. People from Rio and Sao Paulo are leaving the city to live in the middle of the forest. It is an amazing phenomenon and has been one of the main subjects of discussion at recent meetings of the Bishops' Conference. We need to examine this phenomenon with great attention and respect. What is God calling us to as a Church through these movements?

The Experience of God — First Condition of All Evangelization

Two years ago I wrote an article for one of the Brazilian newspapers. My position in that article, one which I continue to maintain, is that we live in a historical moment in which our people suffer massive identity loss. We, as Church, are not responding to them. Our liturgies are cold, our structures rigid. We have an impersonal understanding of the community of faith. Our people do not feel welcomed as persons or received by name when they go to Church. The new movements and sects are more flexible and more affective. They are also manipulative. At times their leaders grow wealthy from the donations of the very poor.

It is necessary to acknowledge that these new religious movements know how to reach people. They respond to a need for affective involvement. Perhaps we Catholics are too rational. Rationality affects our way of thinking, writing, and praying. We want to organize experience. Reason has a place in life, but we are living in a historical moment in which experience must come first. Karl Rahner, one of the greatest theologians of this century, reminds us that Christians of the future will be mystics or they will not be Christian. I think this recognition of the immediacy of religious experience explains the success of these new movements. People are contacted at an experiential, not rational level.

One of the problems with liberation theology and even some Basic Communities is that efficiency, action, and the transformation of history may be taking first place. Our desire for liberation, theirs for justice and for transforming the world must be rooted in our experience of God, the God of life, and not in social analysis. Social analysis is necessary but it cannot be an absolute, because, when models fail, everything falls apart.

Signs of Our Times

What are we to do? Where is the pattern that we are waiting for? In thriving Christian communities, celebration, liturgy, and spirituality are central; these communities refine their hope and continue to struggle to realize an option for the poor. Their struggle is rooted in the God of life. Until recently, theologians in Latin America were usually called on as resource persons to make an analysis of a situation. It is symptomatic that more and more we are now being called to preach retreats, to lead days of prayer, to combine analysis and spirituality. The Bible is more and more central. Something is happening and the religious life and even the most engaged and militant Christian is going through a deep change. As we look beyond Santo Domingo, the Church in Latin America is living through a special and rich moment in its history.

The Church must rethink its role. This demands a deep spiritual formation in the experience of God and an appreciation of mystery as reflected in the religious life of the people, the pastoral agents, the so-called Marxists, the militants, the marginalized, the poor.

So what must the Church do? I do not pretend to have the answer. We need to reflect together to discover new directions. When the Spirit breathes and people are open, anything can happen. It is perhaps too soon after Santo Domingo to give answers. However, perhaps it is the moment to draw attention to popular religion, the people's experience of God, the way they have resisted religious oppression during centuries and kept alive the flame of a living faith.

CONCLUSION

This moment is rich in its call to refound and to rediscover the ways in which the people of Latin America seek for an experience of God. It calls us to celebrate with our people, and to rediscover the very profound gift that is their faith. It calls us to work with this gift, not at the margin of it, not in spite of it, not against it, not by ignoring it, not with suspicion of it, but to work in dialogue with it. We are living out what Las Casas spoke of in the sixteenth century, when he said that even though the Indians did not adore the true God, the God of the Christians, it was necessary to recognize that their God was true for them.

It would help us as Christians and as missionaries to rediscover how our God is true for us. The way we communicate this and the way we help others to experience God will lead to some common ground — a common ground found in the experience of life. Where there are signs of life, then there is a genuine experience of God. Even if the signs of life do not come from our institutions or from our ecclesiastical structures, if they are real signs of life, God is there. I think that this is the great challenge which our complex religious world holds out to us today.

PART FOUR

AREA STUDIES

14

Guatemala:
Mission in Situations of Violence

Judith M. Noone

"The Gospel of Jesus Christ offers a solution to situations of ethnic violence: 'That all may be one . . . see how they love one another.' But as long as Christians live without recognizing the repercussions of what we do, violence will escalate. Things will not change while we manipulate Christian love, diluting it into charity that we dole out for political interests." The author insists on the complicity of foreign missionaries of all stripes in helping to plant the seeds of ethnic conflict in the Guatemalan highlands. This chapter was originally presented at a meeting of the Eastern Fellowship of Missiologists, 13-14 November 1992. It is used with the author's permission.

In the process of wrestling with this question of the "relevance of mission" to the phenomenon of ethnicity, cultural identity, separatism, and pluralism, I have come ever more clearly and unavoidably to see that in that part of the world where I have most recently been in mission, in the highlands of Guatemala, we missioners have helped not only to plant the seeds of ethnic conflict but also to actually create those ethnic groups which today are at violent odds with each other.

Who we are as missioners and what we do is never simply and purely preaching the Word of God. It never has been and most likely will never be so. Whether deliberately or unconsciously, we are always also preachers of cultural values and political ideologies. We live the Word of God contextualized. We are bearers and beacons of cultural values, occasionally manipulated for ultimately political purposes. Ethnic identities are not a package of givens received at birth but rather work themselves out in social situations over time. Boundaries between ethnic groups are not impenetrable walls but rather permeable membranes through which we threaten or enhance each other's values, customs, and beliefs. However clear this may be to us today, we must realize that this is an astounding and recent insight that is only now informing the social sciences. The word "ethnicity" was not even in our dictionaries until 1973.

The extent to which ethnic groups are created through social interaction with outside groups, as well as internal adaptations negotiated by the members, is something we are only recently exploring with any clarity. The extent to which our presence and efforts as Christian missioners has had a formative ethnic influence on groups with whom we have been in mission is a vast frontier that has yet to be explored, with understanding and reconciling sensitivity. The extent to which we too have been formed by our interaction with people of other ethnic groups is something else to consider. I suspect, though, that such an investigation would reveal that our crusty Western Christian arrogance has kept us so busy converting the rest of the world that we have been prevented from being enriched as much as we might have been, and as we still may be.

MAYAS AND LADINOS IN A GUATEMALAN VILLAGE

I would like to take you with me to a beautiful little spot where ethnic conflict between the indigenous Mayan people and the *ladinos*, or mestizo people, is chronic. It is a little town where Mary Duffy and I lived from 1985 until 1991, and I would like to show you what we found there. Then I would like to back up in time to see how the present situation came to be, and finally, to take a look at how different Christian groups are responding there today. All we knew prior to our arrival in San Andrés Sajcabaj, El Quiché, Guatemala in 1985 was that the people were barely beginning to emerge from the climax of a thirty-year-long civil war, from large-scale massacres waged by the military government in the early 1980s in the name of fighting communist subversion. All of the pastoral agents of the Catholic Church, except one native-born *ladino* priest, had left the diocese in June of 1980 following the deaths of hundreds of catechists and three Spanish priests. The pastoral agents believed that their dramatic exodus would draw international attention to the atrocities being perpetrated by the army. Instead, the repression accelerated to hellish proportions.

The Catholic catechists had been targeted because they had become organized and active in improving the lives of their communities. And the Catholic pastoral agents were targeted because they were the catalysts enabling the largely Indian people to crawl out of their centuries-long misery. Objective and conservative sources estimate that more than a million of the 9 million people in Guatemala were displaced or forced to seek refuge in neighboring countries in the early 1980s, and more than 400 villages had been completely destroyed. An estimated 100,000 have been killed in the past 30 years and there are roughly 20,000 people presently living in the mountains for more than ten years in *pueblos de resistencia*, or pueblos in resistance.

When we actually found ourselves in San Andrés, an isolated town of two thousand people with another 12,000 living in some thirty villages scattered out into the plains and up into the surrounding mountains, the chasm between Indians and *ladinos* became immediately apparent. We heard whispered stories of violence about *ladinos* leading soldiers out into the villages to slaughter Indians. We were aware too of the terror felt by some *ladinos* in towns when the soldiers who apparently protected them were absent for several days.

I vividly remember an early incident that clearly dramatized the lines of social and ethnic distinction. The bishop had sent us a bale of used clothing. Against our better judgment we did as he requested: we distributed the clothes. Two prominent Indian leaders suggested that we do it one Sunday morning after the celebration. Without actually publicizing the project, word spread and every relatively well-dressed *ladino* in town came to church for the first time. Actually they stayed outside chatting loudly during the celebration and then came in for the distribution of the clothing. What was to have been an orderly procedure turned into bedlam as the *ladinos* climbed over each other and the retiring Indians in order to grab what they could. The Indians did not protest nor compete but rather, after the stampede had passed them by, picked up their babies and baskets and left to go home to their villages. Later that afternoon I was puzzled by a well-to-do *ladina* woman and embarrassed for her. The owner of a well-stocked store, she came to our house to say that she had been unable to come to church that morning but wondered if we still had some clothing we could give to her sons. She was not a Catholic and we had never seen her close to the church before.

The brash and shameless ways of the *ladinos* continued to baffle me until I began to realize how they came to be. Neither did I understand the humble, affectionate, and honest manner of the Indians, though it was not problematic for me personally, until I reflected upon the origins of their conduct. Neither of the ethnic groups — not the *ladinos* nor the Indians as we know them today — existed five hundred years ago. They were created by the Siamese twins of conquest and evangelization. However well meaning and/or blinded by prejudice born of arrogance, it was foreign missionaries who helped to plant the seeds of today's ethnic conflict.

For fifteen years after the initial conquest of what is known today as Guatemala, the conquerors at first raped and later cohabited with Indian women until the arrival of the first Spanish women in 1539. With the establishment of pure Spanish households, the generation of mestizo offspring was banned from the Spanish homes and inheritance because they were not pure-blooded and were condemned as dissolute, untrustworthy, unruly and wicked. An indication of the racial prejudice suffered by the mestizo outcasts is found in the very name *"ladino."* A Spanish word meaning "sly, shrewd, crafty," it was applied to the Jews and Moors in Spain at this same point in history when the Inquisition and the conquest coincided in 1492. In addition, the *ladinos* were prohibited from living in Indian towns where the missionaries "protected," "pacified," and "evangelized" the Indians. It was feared that the Indians would be corrupted by the *ladinos*. By the end of the eighteenth century Archbishop Cortés y Larraz, journeying to the farthest corners of the diocese, which stretched from modern day southern Mexico to Costa Rica, sent a secret "moral geographic description" to the liberal King Charles III. In it he expressed his surprise and horror at finding throughout Guatemala, on the fringes of the white and Indian towns alike, an extensive world, "licentious, miserable, and violent, of the rural *ladinos*." He wrote that the *ladino nucleos* seemed to be "fortresses for the devil from which he laughs at all natural, divine, ecclesiastical and royal laws." After estimating that *ladinos* comprised between a third to a half of the total population of the colony, he concluded, "that's a lot of people to be abandoned" (Martínez Peláez 1970, 283).

Ladinos, then, were left — by colonial and ecclesial powers alike — to fend for themselves. They learned how to survive in a world in which they were outcasts on two fronts. They lived in a world where their identity was defined in negative terms: they were and still are neither Indian nor Spanish. More often than not, they are quite passive in relation to the Church perhaps because the Catholic missionaries have been, since colonial times, quite passive in relation to them. The missioners were overburdened, it would seem, with attending to the Indians in the countryside and the Spanish aristocracy in the cities.

While the *ladinos* acquired character traits that enabled them to survive in their hostile world, many of the Indians accommodated themselves to the process of evangelization and colonization by accepting the veneer of catholicism and half-secretly keeping alive their Mayan heart and soul. Leonardo Boff points out that all early missionaries began with the supremely arrogant though unquestioned presupposition that Christianity was the only true religion: the Indians' religions were only false, they were the work of Satan. Method alone was open to discussion: whether to use violence and force, or, in the words of Las Casas, "a delicate, soft, and sweet method." Either method was calculated to achieve the same effect, which was conversion (Boff 1990, 17).

Throughout Latin America today, 1992 is not so much the year of the Five Hundredth Anniversary of the Conquest as it is the celebration of five hundred years of resistance. It is true that the indigenous peoples of Guatemala, to a surprising degree, have largely retained their Mayan communities, customs, dress, and languages through five hundred long, cruel years of conquest. Yet it is also true that the stereotypically submissive, long-suffering, humble Indian character is as it were a camouflage created to protect the Mayan heart from the otherwise natural predators, the conquerors and evangelizers alike. Their stance and indeed their character, as we know them today, did not exist before the conquest and the beginnings of evangelization.

And so we arrive at today. To what extent are we bolstering or liberating the characteristics of those ethnic groups which our predecessors helped to forge? Who are we in this present ethnic conflict?

DO CHRISTIAN MISSIONS CONTRIBUTE TO VIOLENCE?

The first Catholic missionaries to Latin America, of course, arrived with the conquerors. More recently, in the late nineteenth century, Protestant missionaries entered Latin America at the invitation of liberal national aristocracies in the service of the neocolonial project of modernization over and against Catholic rigidity and cultural control. Catholic and Protestant missionaries were pitted against each other for political purposes. Missioners have more often than not been emissaries of the elites: the national aristocracies that have invited them, and the foreign elites that have selected them and trained them and given them the wherewithal to be in mission.

More recently, in this century, many of Guatemala's foreign Catholic missionaries were invited by the wealthier classes to educate their children. Later, after the Cuban Revolution, when 70 percent of the clergy fled the island, Latin American bishops realized that the extremes of poverty and wealth in their countries lay as potential fertile grounds for the cultivation of communism. In the early 1960s Rome issued a worldwide appeal for aid to shore up the Latin American Church and to stem the tide of communism. Following Vatican II the trend to move out of institutions into *barrios* and villages brought missionaries and national religious work into contact with the appalling conditions in which the masses live. Here within a relatively short period of time and on a large scale we see the Church being converted.

In Guatemala, church-aided programs directed toward enabling the largely indigenous people to improve their lives had such an impact on grassroots peasant organizations that by the late 1970s the threatened Guatemalan military defined any type of organizing as tantamount to subversion. In 1982 it was said, "We [the army] make no distinction between the Catholic Church and communist subversion" (Simon 1987, 44). In fact no distinction was made between communists and people of any faith who were preaching and helping people to build the Kingdom of God.

While socially conscious Protestants and Catholics alike were suffering persecution and death, other Christians were actually helping to fund the violence. General Rios Montt, the president by coup, was a born-again Christian and member of the Church of the Word based in Eureka, California. Deprived of U.S. military aid because of Guatemala's long record of human rights violations, he immediately became friendly with televangelist Pat Robertson. The first interview with Rios Montt after the coup was aired on Robertson's "700 Club," during which he made frequent appeals for prayers and financial support. Washington applauded such charity. Part of the scheme was to improve Guatemala's image in the United States by portraying the general as a deeply religious man struggling to save his country from communism. Robertson was especially helpful, telling his television audience that "the general is putting down wrongdoers and punishing those who are evildoers . . . let it be an example of what God can do when His people are in charge" (Lernoux 1989, 158). In fact, under the born-again Christian general and with the help of televangelical political propaganda and funds from the United States, the repression soared to hellish proportions. Our topic here is Christian mission responding to situations of ethnic violence. It could more accurately be called in this case "Christian mission creating ethnic violence."

MULTIPLE ROLES — CONFLICTING EXPECTATIONS AND PERCEPTIONS

Walking a tightrope. Closer to the present day, then, Mary Duffy and I arrived in San Andrés in 1985 in response to a request from the Guatemalan bishop that we "accompany the widows and orphans of the violence." We came as Catholic, North American women and as such we would be interacting with the distinct groups in the village with a fluid emphasis on one, two, or all three of these identities. To complicate the situation, who we understood ourselves to be did not necessarily coincide with what others wanted or expected us to be. Our concern as missioners in San Andrés was to do whatever we could to help narrow the chasms between groups as survivors crawled out of the violence. We lived the constant unrelenting tension of walking a tightrope between the various groups — always balancing alliances, trying not to appear to favor one group over the others. At the same time, because recent propaganda had clearly branded Catholic missionaries as subversives, we were very careful not to inflict our potentially compromising friendship on anyone.

As Catholics we were perceived by some to be communists, friends to the Indians, and enemies of the army. Our hope when we decided to live in San Andrés was to find a little adobe house on the edge of town so as to be able to live as normally as possible as neighbors. Instead, it became obvious that we had no choice but to live in the parish house or *convento*, which was beside the colonial church. It had been taken over by the army for a couple of years during the violence and used by them as barracks and interrogation center, the house into which hundreds of people were dragged and from which none emerged. Though it was left totally gutted by the army, without window glass or plumbing or electricity, with blood-stained walls a reminder of the horrors lived and died there, it was the highest, best-built, and potentially most comfortable structure in town. Not only the bishop but the people in town wanted us to live in that house as a dramatic symbol that the Catholic Church was back in business again, the lights on, the bells ringing. Only in the process of preparing these reflections have I come to see the convent as a potent symbol for many of the often conflictive aspects of life in San Andrés.

The convent was originally home to the foreign priests who had sown seeds of hope for a better life, which was interpreted by some as communism. It was also center of worship, the sacred shrine of the patron saint and his entourage, which had been built on top of the ruins of a Mayan temple in the mid-1500s. Literally overnight the convent became the army barracks, a place of torture and "disappearance" and burial ground for no one knows how many people. Not many years after the disappearance of their husbands, widows would come to grow vegetables in our backyard and would discover bones. Simply by living in that house we seemed to be associated in various ways with all that it symbolized.

Our being Catholic meant being related to the other Catholics who had previously lived in the house: the Spanish priests who were paternalistic, providers, promoters of the Catholic Action movement that was hostile toward Mayan religionists, and clerically very much in charge of the church. I have mentioned that we did not know exactly what we would be asked to do or able to accomplish in San Andrés. However, the very day of our arrival, we realized that the Catholic Action people expected us to fill the slot left by *padrecito*, both in a clerical and a material sense. This required from us a constant balancing act, as energy-consuming as that of balancing alliances. To do what we could to help people in need while not encouraging them to wallow in that need — without allowing them to force us into being maternalistic or allowing them to depend overly upon us. This was very evident on the material level, as will become clear later on in this story.

Culture of fear. Far more subtle was the social passivity of the people, an attitude that can only be understood within what has been called a "culture of fear." It is an all-pervasive atmosphere of deep trauma, mistrust, confusion, and mourning throughout the country. Most of the male leaders had been killed or had fled. We were constantly careful to respect the healthy fears of the survivors. We knew they could read the political climate far more accurately than we would ever be able to do; yet we did not want that situation to force us into leadership positions that could establish dependencies. An illustration of this kind of tension — from a distance it is actually humorous though at the time it was more than trying — was a situation that became apparent shortly after we arrived. On Sundays previous to the violence people had been accustomed to gather for Mass. Just prior to our arrival they had begun again to meet to pray the rosary. As soon as we moved in they expected us to ring the bell, light the candles, sweep the church, read the Gospel, distribute communion, give a homily, baptize the babies, and probably take up a collection.

It is true that we were far less vulnerable than they in this violent atmosphere. We were less apt to "be disappeared." Our dilemma was how to be sensitive to a situation that was potentially dangerous for the people who emerged as leaders, even while we tried to avoid the other danger of encouraging their passivity. Nor did we know to what extent their willingness for us to lead was rooted in the recent violence or in the past five hundred years of conquest and submission. Wherever the roots of passivity were nourished we hoped our years with them would empower them and not prolong the conquest.

Aid and dependence. Another constant — I would say daily — tension stemmed from the expectation that the people had of us — as Catholics, foreigners, and missioners — to be a source of material aid. The diocese was enormous in geographical extension but small in terms of personnel. When Mary and I arrived in June of 1985 to the Quiché diocese of 9,000 square kilometers, 500,000 people and 21 towns and 500 villages, we raised the number of pastoral agents from a total of nine people to eleven. For the first couple of years the bulk of our time and energy as a diocese — and indeed the energies of the church on a national level — were focused on relief-related concerns: food, school supplies, medicines. Our concern was not where to get relief, because supplies were arriving unsolicited from compassionate and politically conscious people all over the world. Rather, we were concerned with the problems of distribution — how, to whom, and where.

The two of us had had experience in Bolivia and Mexico with "hand-out" kinds of situations and dreaded the inevitable difficulties and divisions. We spent long hours over a period of several months talking with representatives from all of the villages about the pros and cons of accepting the aid. They clearly saw how receiving the food could create dependencies but pointed out that too many people were in dire and immediate need to refuse it. Clearly the aid could not be turned down. But how to receive and distribute it in ways that would not be divisive nor cause dependence? How could we instead bring people together and help them to pick themselves back up, together with their communities? This was another of our constant concerns: how to deal with immediate crisis situations while laying the foundations for long-term social change to counteract the cause of the crises.

Developing solidarity. Not only was the help needed, it was crucial to provide a legitimate rationale for people to get together. The ever vigilant army assumed that any gathering of people was for "subversive" purposes. There were innumerable incidents of people who had been turned into the army just for meeting to pray the rosary. Especially in those first few years, we were constantly aware of the people's need to get together, and we looked for safe opportunities. After months of meetings in the villages, and at the parish level with village representatives, it was decided to form committees to make lists of the neediest families. We constantly stressed the importance of including equal numbers of Protestants, followers of the Mayan religion, and Catholics. Though the *indigenes* predominated in most of the villages, we encouraged them to involve their *ladino* neighbors. Unfortunately, some of the neediest persons were warned by their Pentecostal sects not to accept help from the Catholic communist church, thus widening divisions in a time of universal need. Those on the list would receive the food each month on the condition that they agree to plant and tend a vegetable garden. Committees of women met once a month for classes in nutrition and vegetable gardening in order to be able to replicate the same class in their villages. The actual amounts of rice, flour, corn, and oil that each family received were so small as to be sufficient for only a couple of days out of the month. But the real contribution of the program was the organizing and the broad-based leadership the distribution required, and the vegetable gardens, which continued to provide sustenance when the food program was suspended — at the request of the people — three years later.

Women leading the church. We were the first women in the history of our town to be in such a position as to be regarded as official agents of the Catholic Church. At first, while we were still strangers, we were apparently the objects of wonder or of amused curiosity — especially when we dared to drive on the rain-ravaged road while the experienced truck drivers were waiting for it to dry. In a society where women routinely ask permission of their husbands before leaving the house even to go to market, we began to see, however, that at a deeper level women do, in fact, have potentially more political space than men. Ironically, in a macho and militaristic society where women are not taken seriously, women can do more than men; they can get away with more because they are not watched with as much suspicion. We concluded that this situation was born of the violence. Indian men, those who survived, are hesitant to show too much activism and allow the women to do so instead. In fact, throughout Latin America, this has happened precisely in those countries which have suffered unspeakable violence. Women have initiated movements similar to the famous Argentinean Plaza de Mayo mothers who demanded information about their disappeared, and contributed to the downfall of the generals. CONAVIGUA and

GAM are two such women's movements that are growing with great strength in Guatemala today.

Ladino individualism and Indian community. To keep the social seesaw as level as possible, we took every opportunity to form friendships and become involved with the *ladinos* in town. It was one of our biggest challenges. After we were approached several times by individual poor Ladina women who were looking for handouts, we invited them to meet as a group to see if there might be a mutually beneficial project that they could undertake together. They seemed excited about raising vegetables on a little plot of land that we could loan them in the Church's backyard, using seeds that we would help them to get inexpensively. But when they realized that we were not offering them a salary but rather the chance to work together to make some money by selling vegetables, they immediately disbanded. In contrast to the Indians who had survived the past five hundred years in community, the *ladinos* had survived by competing with each other in exploiting the Indians. It is a stance so entrenched that cooperative endeavors among *ladinos* are rarely seen.

The numbers of *ladino* strangers who presented themselves to be godparents for Indian baptisms during the fiesta gave us the idea to offer an annual three-night course for *ladino* and Indian godparents, as well as parents from the village. It was a chance to provide the opportunity for the *ladinos* to get together with each other and with the Indians in a more or less socially equitable setting. Eventually a core group of *ladinos* and Indians (mostly women) began to meet regularly to pray the rosary and to study the Bible. One *ladino* couple, Felipe and Marta, to whom I will return in just a moment, were outstanding in their commitment and participation.

PASTORAL SOLIDARITY AND
PROPHETIC DENOUNCEMENT

I briefly mentioned the tension that we faced between attending to daily crises and working for long-term changes. In October of 1989 the army launched its "Final Offensive." As a result, 20,000 people were bombed out of the mountains where they had been living in scattered, makeshift, and isolated settlements called "communities in resistance" ever since they had fled the army in 1981 and 1982. When the offensive began, the Guatemalan bishops happened to be holding a routine meeting in the capital. And we, the pastoral agents of the Quiché diocese, were in our routine diocesan meeting learning from firsthand reports of the slaughter that was actually underway.

A group of us was commissioned by the diocesan agents to go to the bishops in the city to tell them what we had heard and to urge them to act immediately to protest the massacres. We were told that the bishops were responding to the situation with a pastoral letter that would be published in a few months' time. Meanwhile bombs were falling on innocent people. We had to do something. The immediate something we did was another cause for tension, an ambiguous and profoundly uncomfortable situation. The National Bishops' Conference asked our diocese to take turns distributing foodstuffs in the concentration camps where the bombed-out, traumatized, and sick people were being herded. Our presence assured a just distribution of the food and security for the innocent civilians; but we feared that it also gave the appearance that we were working with the army. While the soldiers bombed people out of the mountains, the Church seemed to be there to welcome them into concentration camps!

However, while we were responding to the immediate situation, the bishops were indeed working on a prophetic document with the potential for long-term deeper change. *Clamor Por La Tierra* [Cry of/for the Land] calls for a revolution in the centuries' long structure of land ownership. This is the most electrifyingly "subversive" topic in Guatemala today, because the problem of land is universally recognized to be the source of the present massive misery and oppression.

RESPONSES OF THE VARIOUS RELIGIOUS GROUPS

Catholic "sects." Within the Catholic Church itself there are various groups which are not always friendly toward each other. There are the active, progressive, and persecuted "Catholic Action" folk. And a new phenomenon since the violence is the Charismatic Movement, which, with its otherworldly non-political focus, is a safe harbor for many survivors of the violence. It would be fascinating to ferret out the political agenda at the core of the fact that it was the conservative Opus Dei bishop of the neighboring diocese who encouraged the Charismatic Movement and its exportation to other dioceses.

Another numerous and prominent group within the Catholic Church are the *costumbristas*, those baptized Catholics who in an increasingly public manner practice the Mayan religion. The natives who follow the *costumbres*, or religious "customs" of their ancestors, have for centuries been "in the closet" because of the fierce opposition of the Catholic clergy. However, as 1992 approached they coalesced and emerged as a strong indigenous political and religious presence, which is at least tolerated and at best appreciated by many of the established Christian Churches. In fact, on 12 October 1990, we attended an ecumenical meeting in Guatemala City with Presbyterian, Lutheran, and Methodist friends. Once convened, we unanimously voted to postpone our meeting in favor of participating in a national indigenous Mayan ceremony at a sacred site that was an hour's drive away.

Where the Spirit might eventually lead us in relation to the people of the Mayan religion is not yet clear. What is certain, however, is that the traditional hostile stance of the Christian churches toward the Mayan religionists must be readjusted to a stance of respectful mutual dialogue. To continue our five-hundred-year-old history of hostilities will not only further the ethnic violence. It will also continue to deprive Western Christianity and the Mayan world of the deep wisdom and richness that is to be found in both traditions. We must at least speak with one another in an attitude of wanting to learn from each other's experience and knowledge of God at the heart of our common humanity.

Protestant groups. Other Christian groups in our town were the Mennonites,

Methodists, Wycliffe Bible Translators (SIL), and a group that calls itself "The Project." I shall describe each of them briefly.

There are roughly ten Ladino Mennonite families in San Andrés who, true to their peaceable and separatist philosophy, do not proselytize. We came to know and to be friends with the Mennonites through the town clinic where four of them are caring and competent nurses and technicians. The two town pharmacies are owned by Mennonite families. On several occasions, when confronted by life-and-death medical situations, one of the pharmacists would radio the Mennonite center in Guatemala City to ask that their small plane be sent to transport someone to a hospital. They always did this without concern for the religious affiliation of those they helped; nor did they insist on remuneration.

The Primitive Methodists are another largely *ladino* group that is made up, for the most part, of one large extended family. Soon after our arrival in San Andrés, some of the Methodist women befriended us and invited us to their Bible study group. I always enjoyed those gatherings and appreciated their persistent and lavish prayers for my conversion. Eventually, though, I explained to them that I should stop meeting with them — at least for a while — because some of the Catholic women were asking me how I could meet with the Methodists when they had always been told not to go to the Protestant Churches. I had only been there a short time and didn't have an answer.

I firmly believe, though, that we, ecumenically-minded Christians, have to come up with a way of being and working and living our faith together, most especially in the more volatile parts of the world. We seem to be able to do it in peaceful places such as Westchester County. But where cooperation and respect and understanding and reconciliation are most sorely needed are in places such as San Andrés. In places of ethnic violence religious distinctions almost inevitably create unbridgeable chasms. Or perhaps more accurately, the apparently unbridgeable racial and class chasms play themselves out in religious alliances.

Just two weeks after our arrival in San Andrés, we received the visit of a young North American couple. They were members of the Wycliff Translators, or the Summer Institute of Linguistics, who had been assigned to our town. A French sociologist friend of ours, who was familiar with the many allegations of Wycliff's CIA connections in Latin America, was convinced that they had been sent by the CIA to keep an eye on us. "Isn't it suspicious," he pointed out, "that they should appear out of the blue immediately after your arrival?" We paid no attention to his assessment and regularly enjoyed the couple's company for supper or a cup of tea, a birthday party or as their children were born. Through our contacts with them, however, we came to see how any one of us, unwittingly, can be used by people with powerful political agendas.

The couple had been assigned to see to what extent the Quiché language was being used by the churches in the village in order to assess the need for a New Testament in the Quiché dialect of San Andrés. This, we somehow did not realize, involved copying down from our bulletin board notices in Quiché about church meetings, our visits and courses. Several months after their arrival the wife told us how impressed their superiors were with what we were doing in San

Andrés. In reply to my puzzlement, and subsequent horror, she explained that their annual report — which included information about the content, location, and participants in indigenous activities of the church — had been filed in the central computer of the University in Guatemala City, to which virtually anyone in the world, including the Guatemalan military, had access.

To this day I am not certain whether they were extremely naive or we were extremely paranoid. But when we reminded them that thousands of indigenous people and entire communities had been annihilated for being active Catholics; when we pointed out that here they were providing detailed information about specific individuals and communities that were picking themselves back up, our friends saw our point and shuddered with us.

The point here is not to tell tales about our friends, a committed and good-hearted couple. The point rather is that however clear our Christian agendas might be, other cultural and political agendas are being served and have always been served. People's identities and, at times, very lives hang in the balance.

The last group in our town I will mention is "The Orphans' Project." It is connected to a church in Guatemala City — though we were never able to ascertain exactly which one — with financial backing from California. The person responsible in San Andrés is a *ladino* who, after the obligatory two hours of anti-Catholic and anti-Methodist Bible study, offers a free lunch to all his neighbors' children who attend regularly. Because of infighting among the local staff, the project divided, spawning a program for widows. This program lures desperate mothers to live in a cinder-block ghetto where they and their children are fed and instructed, it seems to us, in total disregard for the indigenous community-centered tradition.

This is one illustration of a growing phenomenon that the bishops strongly address in their recent pastoral letter:

> The presence of the sects is a cultural challenge. . . . The culture of Guatemala is being transformed and the social fabric is being torn apart by groups who fight among themselves. The Guatemalan character is becoming impregnated with fanaticism, intolerance, individualism, and rampant aggressivity. What is more, the sectarian preaching on the salvation of one's soul leads to a loss of historical sensitivity, of social commitment and human solidarity.

In August of 1992 we received word that our *ladino* friend Felipe, whom I mentioned above, had been stoned to death by the brother of the director of the "Project." We may never know why. Distinct rival Christian affiliations no doubt fueled the fire of animosity, which resulted in murder.

CONCLUSION

Only last week I received a copy of the routine newsletter of our friends from the Summer Institute of Linguistics. They ask for funds to help the project buy a jeep and mention the dangerous "Mayan philosophy" whose influence is becoming more and more visible. Some Christians, then, in reaction to the revitalized

Mayan religious tradition, will no doubt grow more militant in their opposition to it. The more established churches, on the other hand, as was mentioned above, are at least showing signs of moving toward dialogue. This tension is already amply illustrated in the reaction by Rome, and no doubt other Christian groups, to the Latin American Bishops' working document for their Santo Domingo Conference. In it the bishops stress the importance of the indigenous and African-American cultures and the need for profound inculturation of the Christian message over and against Rome's commitment to retaining European cultural forms.

The Gospel of Jesus Christ does indeed offer a solution to situations of ethnic violence: "That all may be one . . . see how they love one another." But as long as Christians live without recognizing the repercussions of what we do, violence will escalate. Things will not change while we manipulate Christian love, diluting it into charity that we dole out for political interests. Until we recognize how demeaning and debilitating well-meant charity can be, we will continue to be agents of division and sowers of ethnic violence. Our task as Christians is to recognize the full implications and far-reaching multifaceted repercussions of our mission work and the ethnic consequences, for they are surely there. Most importantly, we have to find ways to stand together.

A parable. I saw this parable on the television show *Twilight Zone* years ago and it often came to mind while I was working on these reflections:

It is the day after the national elections in which the democratic candidate won over the socialist candidate. To celebrate, the democratic winner invited some friends to go on a hunting trip with him. He took them, in a time machine, back to the age of the dinosaurs. To protect the ecological balance they were instructed to do two things: to stay on the wooden walkway through the pristine countryside, and only to shoot those animals which had a red mark on them. The mark indicated that the animal would soon die a natural death in any case, and so shooting it would not alter the ecological balance. The party spent a successful day shooting dinosaurs and was returning to the time machine when one of the men slipped off the sidewalk and stepped on a butterfly that was sitting on some dinosaur dung. They thought nothing of it and walked on. However, when they returned to the present day, they saw the headlines announcing that the socialists had won the election.

We cannot know what effects our lives will have in a thousand years. But we can and we must walk with care and reverence, mindful of where we step. And for God's sake, and for the sake of God's people, let us walk together and keep each other from slipping along the way.

15

El Salvador:
Liberation and Resurrection

Kim Erno

"Whenever I have been in El Salvador I have always been keenly aware of my own complicity in the sinfulness of this world. While this complicity is exposed I have not become mired in despair because of how the Salvadoran people have chosen to respond to my presence. Having every right to turn me away, they extend their hospitality." The author is pastor of St. Stephen Lutheran Church in Silver Spring, Maryland. He is co-chair of the Central American Task force for Washington, D.C., and serves on the Board of the National Debate for Peace in El Salvador. His unpublished paper is used with permission.

On the morning of Sunday, 11 February 1990, at approximately 7:45 a.m. the Salvadoran Air Force launched an attack on the village of Corral de Piedra with three helicopter gunships and two A-37 planes. For a period of two hours they bombed, strafed, and fired rockets into the village. Five residents were killed — four children and one adult: José, 28; José's daughter Blanca, 2 (whose body was found enfolded in the arms of her father); José, 10; Estelia, 9; and Ana, 1. Sixteen others, again mostly children, sustained injuries. Corral de Piedra is a village of approximately four hundred inhabitants in Northern El Salvador. It is an agricultural cooperative populated by former refugees from the Mesa Grande refugee camp in Honduras. In honor of the six Jesuits and two women who were murdered by the Salvadoran military on 16 November 1989 the people of Corral de Piedra have renamed their village: Comunidad Ignacio Ellacuría. Ignacio Ellacuría, S.J., was the rector of the University of Central America in San Salvador.

The father sat perfectly still in his chair. Ten days before he had raced with his child for cover during the attack by the Salvadoran Air Force. They had sought refuge in the one brick building in the community, thinking that this would afford them the greatest protection. They were wrong. Rockets fired from helicopter gunships ripped through the house and through the flesh of those inside the house. Among the dead was the child of the father who now sat perfectly still. During the attack the father had tried to protect the child by cradling it in his arms. There were scars across the father's face, arms, and legs indicating where he, too, had been wounded offering his own body as a protection for his child, but none of those wounds compared to the internal wound, the grief that he bore as he stared vacantly off into the distance with his arms outstretched to embrace a child who was no longer there. I know now that when I looked into the grief-stricken face of that father I was looking into the face of God, the face of one who has lost an innocent child because there are those who are so overcome with a greed for wealth and power that they are willing to crucify the innocent. There are those who want to gain the world so much that they are willing to lose their own souls in the process.

At first the Salvadoran military denied the attack. Then the military said, "There was just one helicopter and one rocket fired. It was just a mistake. Sorry." This was no mistake. The tin roofs of several dwellings were riddled by machine-gun fire. Rockets struck not only the dwelling where the casualties occurred but in at least fourteen other sites. So low were the helicopters flying that a Catholic sister in the village at the time of the attack could look into the face of the gunners. This was no mistake. As a self-sustaining agricultural cooperative, Corral de Piedra provides an alternative economic model to the coffee, cotton, and sugar export economy that keeps the oligarchy rich. The attack on Corral de Piedra fits a pattern of attacks on cooperatives carried out by the henchmen of the oligarchy, the Salvadoran military.

Just a mistake. Sorry. How do you say you are sorry to a father who was holding his child in his arms one minute and the child was gone the next? The explosive force of the rocket was so great that the remains of the child could not be retrieved. I held a piece of that rocket in my hand. It was "MADE IN THE U.S.A." What was burned into my conscience that day was this:

> *The people of Corral de Piedra do not need our apologies.*
> *The people of Corral de Piedra do not need our rockets!*
> *What they do need is our repentance.*
> *What they do need is for us to take the rockets back.*
> *What they do need is our commitment to walk with them toward the Reign of*
> *God to stop the reign of terror that rains rockets on their children.*

With the signing of the peace accords on 16 January 1992 the hope is that the reign of terror is over. While there is great cause to celebrate, there is also much that remains to be done to resurrect a land and a people that have been crucified for so long. My greatest source of hope that peace and justice will reign in El Salvador comes from the people of El Salvador who are so passionately engaged in a daily struggle for life. In the following reflections I hope to offer back in a small way what these Salvadorans so freely bestowed upon me, namely, an experience of God's abundant grace. Whenever I have been in El Salvador I have always been keenly aware of my own complicity in the sinfulness of this world. Holding a U.S. rocket fragment will do that. While this complicity has been exposed I have not become mired in despair because of how the

Salvadoran people have chosen to respond to my presence. Those who have suffered under a war bankrolled by the United States would have every right to turn me away — to say "Gringo, go home, you have only brought us death!" Instead they extend their hospitality — a hammock to sleep in, a tortilla to share, a story to tell. Without ever saying so, their embracing of this foreigner who comes from the same land as the rockets and the bullets becomes an act of grace. The power of that grace has transformed my life.

CHILDREN OF THE EXODUS

"Who are these children dressed in red?
They must be the ones that Moses led . . ."
Walter Robinson

"Que queremos? What do we want? *La Misa!* The Mass! *Donde?* Where? *Corral de Piedra!"* That was the chant on a mountain road leading to Corral de Piedra. I was part of a religious delegation from across the United States that had been invited to Corral de Piedra to celebrate a memorial mass with that community and to investigate and report on the atrocity that had occurred ten days earlier. Needless to say the Salvadoran military did *not* want us to reach Corral de Piedra. We had left the capitol of San Salvador and negotiated our way through military check points late into the night, finally arriving at the city of Chalatenango at 1:00 a.m. After a brief sleep at the convent we started up the dirt road that led to Corral de Piedra. Just outside the city of Chalatenango we were stopped at the last military checkpoint before Corral de Piedra. We waited and waited in the hot, brilliant sun. We were at a standoff with the military. We had also heard that if we were not in Corral de Piedra by a certain time that the community would send a delegation to join us at the checkpoint. In the afternoon a truck filled with women and children and a few older men arrived from Corral de Piedra. The people poured over the sides of the truck. I went to help the children climb down, thinking how beautiful, how precious they were, like our own children here . . . thinking of all that the children of Corral de Piedra had been through. Before that day was over I would also find out how courageous and faithful they were.

There we were. Salvadorans and North Americans together, in the hot sun on this mountain road. We sang songs and we prayed prayers together. The military said that the Salvadorans could not advance any further toward Chalatenango and that the North Americans could not advance any further toward Corral de Piedra. We negotiated with higher and higher levels of authority, first the Salvadoran soldiers at the checkpoint. Then a Salvadoran Army captain was sent. Then the local commander, the colonel himself, came. Finally, the U.S. military advisers arrived. We kept saying, "All we want to do is to be able to go and celebrate the memorial mass."

During the course of the negotiations a leader of our delegation asked the Salvadoran captain. "If we walk down the road will you shoot us?" The captain smiled, "Do we look like assassins?" he replied. This was not the most reassuring answer!

Then it happened. I saw some movement up by the Salvadoran soldiers who had formed a line across the road. A Salvadoran woman took one of the members of our delegation by the arm and said, "Come with me." We started moving forward toward the line of soldiers armed with machine guns. The captain motioned for more soldiers to join the line. He tried to turn us back. He tried to intimidate the people shouting in an enraged voice, but every time he opened his mouth the people chanted, *"QUE QUEREMOS?* WHAT DO WE WANT? *LA MISA!* THE MASS! *DONDE?* WHERE? *CORRAL DE PIEDRA!"* The voice of the captain was drowned out by the voice of the people. We continued to move forward. A Salvadoran soldier put his hand on my chest to stop me but a young Salvadoran woman took me by the arm and led me through. This was the same for all the others who passed through. Children surrounded the North Americans so that the soldiers could not physically reach them, took the North Americans by the arms, and led them through the armed soldiers. Children, who a few days earlier had witnessed the deaths of their brothers and sisters at the hands of this same military, led us through. The children who had died were resurrected in the faith and courage of these children. It was an exodus experience. Soldiers armed with machine guns were washed away by a wave of unarmed children, women, and men. I could not believe that we had made it through and were on our way to Corral de Piedra. The people were determined that we be witnesses. It was an exodus with the children leading the way.

BROKEN BREAD . . . BROKEN BODIES

"This is my body. . . ."

There are times when the offering of our prayers and fasts and tears and letters on behalf of those who suffer injustice no longer feel adequate. Such a time came for me on 2 December 1989, the ninth anniversary of the martyrdom of Jean Donovan, Ita Ford, Maura Clarke, and Dorothy Kazel, four North American churchwomen killed by Salvadoran National Guardsmen. Just a few weeks prior to this anniversary the list of martyrs had been expanded to include six Jesuits and a mother and her daughter (Ignacio Ellacuría, Amando López Quintana, Ignacio Martín Baró, Juan Ramón Moreno Pardo, Segundo Montes Mozo, Joaquín López y López, Elba Julia Ramos, and Celina Maricet Ramos), murdered at the Central America University by members of the U.S.-trained Atlacatl Batallion.

I participated in a rally and an act of civil disobedience in front of the White House protesting U.S. policy in El Salvador. In that year our government poured over one million dollars a day into that tiny land to support its government and war machinery. After we have done all we can to stop this madness, we offer the only thing we have left — our physical presence, our bodies in an act of conscience. We are handcuffed, carried away in a police van, charged, and released. In a very, very small way this becomes an act of solidarity with those who daily offer their bodies for the sake of a just world. Oddly enough, the act of participating in civil disobedience, being arrested, can be a liberating experience. At the moment my hands were handcuffed behind my back I became keenly aware that my life is out of my hands and in the hands of God and that this is true not only for that moment but for all the moments of my life. Part of my preparation for this moment of liberation came from sharing in a meal of liberation.

After we had knelt and prayed on the sidewalk in front of the White House and as we continued to pray and sing, a woman in the midst of our gathering reached into a pouch and took out a broken piece of bread. She broke off a piece and then passed it to the person next to her. Slowly, little by little, the bread was passed, broken, and shared with the crowd on the sidewalk. By the time it came to me, there was just this little bit of bread. I broke a piece off. I heard a priest across from me whisper, "Such a tiny piece." I placed it in my mouth and passed the rest of it on. I had little to eat that day and the taste of that small morsel of bread filled my mouth unlike any bread I had ever tasted before. It was satisfying. It was enough. There is not a time when I share in the eucharist when I do no envision that morsel of bread and hear the words of that priest.

Little did I know that this same priest who had whispered, "Such a tiny piece of bread," would be the one I would see a few weeks later hold in his hand a tiny piece of bone from the skull of a child killed in Corral de Piedra. With great dignity he held the fragment of bone alongside the fragment of rocket with U.S. markings. A tiny bone from a tiny skull. I had held the piece of rocket but I could not bring myself to hold that little piece of bone. The piece of rocket, so cold and hard, turned out by the machinery of war alongside this little bone, so precious . . . so fragile . . . created by God.

This is my body. Both the bread in my hand in front of the White House and the bone in his hand at Corral de Piedra were the body of Christ. I am absolutely convinced of that. If Jesus is not present with those who offer their bodies for a just world and with the broken bodies of the victims of an unjust world, then I do not know where the body of Jesus is.

In September 1989 the Salvadoran government and the Farabundo Martí National Liberation Front (FMLN) entered into negotiations to end the civil war and to resolve the root causes of the war. These negotiations broke down with the escalation of human rights violations and the collapse of any political space for those in opposition to the government, which was most dramatically illustrated with the bombing of the National Federation of Salvadoran Workers Headquarters by the National Police on 31 October that left 81 people dead, including Febe Elizabeth Velásquez, the leader of the organization and an outspoken critic of the government. In November the FMLN launched its most major offensive since the start of the war. The fighting was intense in the capitol of San Salvador and in other major cities and in the countryside. The counteroffensive by the Armed Forces began with the aerial bombardment and strafing of the poor and working-class neighborhoods. The claim was that this was to dislodge the rebel forces. Yet when those same forces entered the wealthy neighborhoods like Escalón, the bombing ceased. The civilian casualties were enormous. One of the neighborhoods that was especially hard hit was Mejicanos on the northern edge of San Salvador.

ON THE WAY TO THE CROSS

"They stripped him . . . ."

The parish hall of San Francisco in the neighborhood of Mejicanos was converted into a medical clinic. Ten youths formed themselves into a stretcher brigade and braved the streets to bring in the wounded. They had been well prepared for this sacrifice. Ten years before, the priest from this parish, Father Octavio Ortíz Luna, had brought the youths on a retreat. He had given them two questions to reflect on during the night: "What does it mean to be a light to the blind?" and "What does it mean to liberate the oppressed?" Suddenly there was a knock at the door. Father Luna answered the door and was killed on the spot by a death squad. He provided the answer to his own questions through the giving of his life. His body is buried beneath the altar. These youths provided the answer to his questions by risking their lives to rescue the wounded. Three hundred wounded were brought to the parish. There was nothing to bind their wounds so the altar cloth was removed from the altar and ripped into strips to serve as bandages. Some might interpret this as a sacrilegious act. Imagine shredding and soiling an altar cloth! On the contrary, I find this to be a profound expression of the sanctity of the altar cloth. Each Maundy Thursday we Lutherans strip the altar, removing the cloth as a reenactment of Jesus being stripped of his clothes on his way to the cross — a cross that he bore in order to heal the violence and injustice of this world. Any church that is not prepared to strip its altar in order to bind up wounds is bound to be irrelevant in a world where people bleed to death because of violence and injustice.

A PROJECT OF LIFE

"Let the dead bury the dead . . ."

Ricardo is the sexton for the parish of San Francisco. He does the things that church sextons do. He sweeps. He dusts. He takes out the trash. He cleans the bathrooms. His work is necessary for the life of the community. Ricardo carried out these basic tasks in a very faithful and dignified way until there came the day, in fact several days, when it became impossible for Ricardo to fulfill his duties. It became impossible for Ricardo to keep the church clean. He could no longer sweep the floors nor dust the pews because the wounded were everywhere, lying on the floor and on the pews. Not all of the wounded survived. A mother and her child were dead before they arrived, killed instantly by aerial fire. The top of the mother's head was shot off. Ricardo was called upon to do something that was not part of his daily duties. He took on the task of burying the mother and her child. He decided to bury them on church grounds because the aerial bombardment prevented access to the cemetery. When the ground forces of the Salvadoran Army arrived and saw the grave, they accused the parish of burying arms and insisted that Ricardo dig up the grave of the mother and child. Seven times the army squads came. Seven times they made this same accusation. Seven times they made Ricardo dig up the bodies of the mother and child. Seven times Ricardo reburied the bodies.

For the first time I understood the words of Jesus, "Let the dead bury the dead," in an entirely new way. What had once sounded like such harsh words from the mouth of Jesus now had a ring of compassion. Those on a mission of death have a morbid fascination in verifying the results of that mission again and again and again. The mission of Jesus is a project of life. The dead deserve their rest so that they too can be incorporated into this mission and resurrected to life.

On 16 January 1992 after 12 years of civil war that took over 75,000 (mostly civilian) lives, the FMLN And the Salvadoran government signed the peace accords. The provisions of the accords include: a cease-fire effective February 1st; the total demobilization of FMLN combatants in 20 percent increments by October 31st; the reduction of the Salvadoran armed forces by 50 percent within two years to include the dismantling of U.S.-trained "elite" battalions notorious for human rights violations; the disbanding of the National Guard and the Treasury Police, two paramilitary organizations involved in death-squad activity, by March 1st; the formation of a Truth Commission to review and purge the Armed Forces of the most flagrant human rights violations; the creation of a civilian national police force to replace the one currently under military control and that would include some former combatants from both the FMLN and the Armed Forces, although the majority of new recruits are not to be former combatants; land is to be distributed to former combatants of both the FMLN and the Armed Forces; land holdings in conflictive zones are to be legalized or the tenants are to be resettled and granted title to nearby government land; the 1983 constitutional provisions that set a limit on large land holdings are to be enforced thereby providing land for redistribution; and the formation of a Committee on Peace (COPAZ) to oversee the implementation of these accords. Already there have been obstacles to the accords. The National Guard and the Treasury Police simply changed names and never disbanded until intense international pressure was applied. A campaign to forcibly evict peasant families and cooperatives from the land was carried out in some sectors. There is much that remains to be done to turn a piece of paper into a lasting peace. Salvadorans understand that the accords are only a beginning but a beginning worth celebrating.

THE GREAT FIESTA

"A man once gave a great banquet, and invited many; and at the time for the banquet sent his servant to say to those who had been invited, 'Come; for all is now ready.' But they all alike began to make excuses. The first said to him, 'I have bought a field, and I must go out and see it.'. . . And another said, 'I have bought five yoke of oxen, and I must go to examine them.'. . . Then the householder in anger said to his servant, 'Go out quickly to the streets and lanes of the city, and bring in the poor and maimed and blind and lame. . . . Go out to the highways and hedges and compel people to come in, that my house may be filled. For I tell you none of those who were invited shall taste my banquet!'"
(LK 14:16-24)

1 February 1992 — San Salvador

Today is the first day of the cease-fire of the twelve-year civil war that has taken over 75,000 lives. All day people have been pouring into *La Plaza de los Mártires*, The Plaza of the Martyrs, for the great fiesta celebrating this historic moment. Those who have come from the countryside were up before dawn to make the long journey to the capitol to celebrate this new day. The highways and streets and lanes leading to the plaza are bursting with people. The press of the crowd is so great that the street vendors struggle to keep their wares and tables from toppling over. Jesus tells the story of someone who once threw a great banquet and was rebuffed by all those who were first invited. From the host's perspective they each had a very lame excuse. The first had become a great landowner and had to oversee his fields. Another had acquired a number of livestock and had to tend to them. Still another had just been married. In El Salvador this too is a luxury. Many of the poor do not have an official church wedding because they cannot afford to do so. After hearing all these lame excuses, the outraged host sends word out into the streets to invite the poor and the blind, the maimed and the lame. When the banquet is still not full, the host sends word out of the city into the countryside, *el campo*, so that the poor *campesinos* might also join the celebration. Today that is what happened in El Salvador. Someone said earlier that when Oscar Romero was assassinated the people mourned, but in Escalón (the wealthy neighborhood of San Salvador) they threw a great party. Now the reverse is true. Those with expansive fields and the cattle to graze on those fields and the money to throw expensive parties are not celebrating. This is a celebration of the poor, the marginalized, the *campesinos*, and those who have cast their lot with them. The people sing and dance into the night. They are more than 75,000 strong. The Plaza of the Martyrs is full. The ranks of those who are singing and dancing are swelled by the martyrs. The poor, the blind, the maimed, and lame, those who have been robbed of their land, their sight, and their limbs, are joined by those who have been robbed of their lives. They also are present this night. You can feel the movement of their spirit in the plaza that bears their name. Their presence is symbolized by a huge banner of the beloved martyr, Monsignor Romero, hanging from the cathedral with this proclamation: *"MONSEÑOR RESUCITASTE EN TU PUEBLO!"* — "MONSIGNOR, YOU ARE RESURRECTED IN YOUR PEOPLE!"

HOPE IN THE LAND OF EL SALVADOR

"... suffering produces endurance, and endurance produces character, and character produces hope. ..."

(Rom. 5)

The first time I met Esperanza, "Hope," was in the middle of the night two years ago when we were on our way to Corral de Piedra. I recall at the time being amazed at this woman who had come through a conflictive zone in the dark of night to the convent where we were staying to coordinate medical treatment for the wounded from that village.

Once again I had the privilege of encountering Esperanza, this time as a guest in her home just four miles from the Honduran border, a region that has suffered immensely under intense military attack for the past twelve years. Once again we met in the dark of the night. In the candlelight — there is no electricity — she told us stories of *esperanza*, stories of hope. Her children and husband joined us so that they too could hear the stories they have heard so many times before. As she spoke, the light from the candle illuminated a picture of her eldest son who had been slain on Christmas of 1990. The picture rested behind the candle on a bench that for all intents and purposes had become an altar. In a few days her son would have celebrated his nineteenth birthday. In a few days Esperanza will give birth to another child. In spite of all the suffering and death she has experienced, this is a woman who is determined to bring forth life with all of her being. Hope is pregnant with life!

When the Salvadoran military first began to attack villages in this region, a bomb exploded on the roof of Esperanza's house and her youngest son was wounded in the head. He is now six but was only an infant at the time. After this the people fled from the Salvadoran Army, hiding in the mountains, in ravines, in caves, wherever they could find shelter. Her infant son cried so much they were afraid the soldiers would discover them, so Esperanza brought him to a cousin of hers who was about to give birth and therefore would be able to nurse him. Esperanza also sought refuge with the cousin, who advised her to turn herself into the army. Esperanza protested, "Why should I turn myself in? I've done nothing wrong!" When the Salvadoran Army began a house-to-house search in the area looking for "guerrillas," Esperanza implored her cousin to protect her by claiming her as a daughter. Her cousin, a member of a fundamentalist church, refused, saying that she had to obey God's laws and therefore could not tell a lie. Esperanza countered, "You are lying for a greater good!" Still the cousin refused. When the soldiers arrived they did not ask if anyone else were there. They only asked if there were any more rooms, which there were, the kitchen where Esperanza with her son had gone to hide. With no time to waste Esperanza built a huge fire in the oven so intense that the room was soon full of smoke. When the soldier stood in the doorway the smoke filled his eyes. He could not see anyone and left. When all the smoke had cleared, Esperanza and her son were still alive. All because of quick wits *esperanza* — "hope" — was kept alive!

We asked Esperanza for her impression of the peace accords. "It is only a piece of paper," she replied, "we hope and we will see." Among those who have endured great suffering there are those whose strength of character is such that they still dare to hope, a hope that is conveyed in the stories they tell of their own survival, like the story of Esperanza that continues to give hope to her family and her people. No wonder that a Salvadoran military report on strategies to undermine the community formation that has taken place in this region recommends introducing electricity and television. The report concludes that the images of consumerism portrayed on television will fragment the community, especially among the youth, regardless of whether or not they will be able to obtain these material goods. But for now the stories of Esperanza continue to be told by candlelight and ingrained in her people. Speaking of her youngest son she said, "He has heard these stories so many times that he thinks he lived through all of them. He will say, 'Remember mama when we ate nuts in the mountains when we were hiding from the soldiers in 1982?' And I will say, 'Yes, I remember when we ate nuts but you don't because that was three years before you were born!'"

Esperanza is about to give birth any time now. May this be a time when *esperanza*, hope, is born anew in her land, in her people, and in those of us who have heard a little of her story!

A LESSON FROM EL SALVADOR

"For if we have been united with him in a death like his,
we shall certainly be united with him in a resurrection like his."
(Rom. 6:5)

How do those whose lives have been drained by twelve years of civil war find room in their hearts to welcome strangers who come from the land that has financed the war? How do children who have seen the broken bodies of their playmates find the courage to stare down the very same forces of death? How do teenagers who often can be so absorbed in their own lives become those who risk life in order to bring the wounded to safety? How do those who have known so much suffering and death keep hope alive? These acts are only possible through the power of God's Living Word. In El Salvador God's Word of liberation for the oppressed and resurrection for the crucified is not bound and gagged in some ancient manuscript. The Word is let loose because God's Word in the biblical narrative gives expression to their own words.

The telling and the retelling of the Exodus story is intertwined with the telling and the retelling of their own exodus escapes from a brutal military power. Thus God's power to liberate the oppressed is confirmed within their own reality. Upon hearing the Exodus story, those in the refugee camps who had fled would declare: "That's our story! We gathered our children and fled from the Salvadoran Army. We crossed the river while the army pursued and attacked us. We have been in the wilderness, eking out an existence, learning the power of living as a convenantal community and now we are ready to claim our promised land!" These are the people who repatriated to places like Corral de Piedra. By placing themselves in the story and the story within themselves, the people, and perhaps especially the children who are so enthralled with stories, are empowered to reenact the Exodus, to pass through a line of armed soldiers because in their hearts and minds they know how the story goes and their expectation is that the same God who led the Israelite children leads the children of Corral de Piedra.

Likewise the story of the passion and resurrection of Jesus is not bound to first-century Palestine. When people hear the story of the betrayal, nighttime arrest, torture, and slow, excruciatingly painful execution of one who had cast his lot with the poor and the landless and the widow and the orphan, they cannot help but give a familiar nod, for this too is a story that they know all too well. It is the story of José and María and Rutilio and Julia and Joaquín and Celina. It is the story of those whose names were sold for a price or blurted out under pain of torture. It is the story of those who were snatched off the street or from their beds in the dark of night or captured in daylight by those who sped away in jeeps with darkened glass. It is the story of those who were beaten with a bag over their heads and ridiculed by their assailants. It is the story of those who were stripped of their clothes and their dignity. It is the story of those whose bound and mutilated bodies were tossed on a garbage heap as a visible warning to all others that this is what happens to those who side with the poor. After all, the purpose of the crucifixion was not simply to eliminate Jesus as the leader of God's movement but to so terrorize his followers that the movement itself would be paralyzed and defeated. The same is true in El Salvador. Torture and executions are done in a very systematic, deliberate fashion. The passion of Jesus becomes the passion of those who have chosen to follow the way of Jesus in the pursuit of God's reign of justice and peace.

We know, of course, that the gospel narratives do not end with the crucifixion of Jesus. Jesus was raised from the dead. The encounter with the Risen Jesus who was crucified leads to a dramatic conversion of his followers. Those who had once cowered behind closed doors now take to the streets in a public demonstration of their undying support for God's reign. There is no guarantee of security. Their bodies could still end up hanging from a cross. With the resurrection comes a willingness to run that risk, because through this encounter with a power that is greater even than the power of the world's death squads comes the ability to begin to live life beyond death. Threats of death and the actual infliction of death itself no longer wield absolute power over their lives. A Salvadoran union worker, Pedro Cruz, was captured and taken to the Treasury Police notorious for their brutal treatment of prisoners and death-squad activity. During his interrogation and torture Pedro was told that he was to be killed and have his body stuffed into a garbage dumpster. Pedro replied, "If all you can do is kill me, go ahead!" Somehow, somewhere, Pedro had crossed a boundary, knowing that he could not and would not be bound by death. Already he had begun to live a resurrected life.

The proclamation of the resurrection within the reality of the Salvadoran experience is expressed through the word *Presente!* It is a word of courage, a word of hope, a word of perseverance, a word of celebration, a word of triumph in the face of death. The Salvadoran custom is for one person to call out the name of a martyr. The entire assembly will then reply, *"Presente!"* I have experienced this within the context of worship, at rallies, and during marches on the streets of Washington. Like the good news of the Risen Jesus this is a word that cannot be confined. As the roll call of martyrs continues the response intensifies. *"Presente, Presente, Presente"* not only rings in the ears but also fills the hearts and souls of those who are so bold as to respond on behalf of the dead, "No I am not dead! I am alive, present here in this Body!" Those who are living give voice to those who are dead, or could it be that those who are dead give voice to the living? Furthermore those who remain are committing themselves to pick up the crosses that were borne so faithfully by those who were slain. By incorporating the martyrs, who now live with death as a past event, into their own lives the death-dealing forces of oppression no longer have any power over them. Archbishop Romero once said, "If they kill me, I will rise again in the Salvadoran people. . . . May my death, if it is accepted by God, be for the liberation of my people, and as a witness of hope in what is to come. . . . A bishop will die but the church of God which is the people will never die." Indeed this was confirmed by the banner that hung in the plaza: "Monsignor, You Are Resurrected in Your People!" Those who have known the passion of Jesus become even more bold in their pursuit of God's reign because they have also come to know his resurrection.

As El Salvador lives up to its name by emerging from the cold tomb of twelve years of civil war, it offers a lesson to a world emerging from a Cold War proclaiming a "new world order." There will be nothing new about a world order that is based on the enslavement and crucifixion of the world's poor. What is more, the gospel or good news from El Salvador is that an order built on such a foundation is bound to fail. In El Salvador we are witnesses to a power that is greater than horses and chariots, helicopters and tanks; a power that is greater than torture chambers and death squads; a power that is greater than the cross. When an enslaved and crucified people bind their destiny to God's Living Word, which promises the liberation of slaves and the resurrection of the slain, then they are bound for victory. To be embraced by such a people is to be touched by God's grace and called to join in the long procession that leads to that victory.

16

Nicaragua:
Political Metamorphosis of Evangelicals

Adolfo Miranda Sáenz

Before 1972, to defend the rights of the poor and the oppressed was to be labeled "communist." Then the earthquake changed Nicaraguan and Evangelical history as disenchantment with the Somoza regime increased, even among Evangelicals. Meanwhile, the popularity of the Frente Sandinista continued to grow, especially among young people. Evangelicals were not outside of this current, though most never did accept them. The polarization has not totally disappeared, although it is less clear-cut under the strongly pro-Catholic Chamorro administration. The author, a Baptist, a lawyer, and a journalist, cooperates as a volunteer with the Antonio Valdivieso Ecumenical Center in Managua. His article was first presented as a paper at the Latin American Theological Fraternity sponsored Consultation of Evangelical Politicians, in Buenos Aires, Argentina (October 1991). It is reprinted with permission from *Transformation* (July/September, 1992).

Just a few minutes after midnight, when 23 December was only beginning, the capital of Nicaragua was destroyed by a violent earthquake. Most of the buildings in the downtown area of the city instantly collapsed and a huge fire did away with whatever the tremor had left standing. The Christmas celebration two days later was the saddest in the history of this country. A history full of sad pages, stained by blood and pain. A history of earthquakes, hurricanes, wars, foreign interventions, misery, and exploitation.

CEPAD AND THE AWAKENING
OF THE EVANGELICAL SOCIAL CONSCIENCE

A small group of Evangelical leaders headed by the Baptist physician and pastor, Gustavo Parajón, met days later in the destroyed patio of Managua's Baptist School, under the shade of a leafy tree, to establish the Comité Evangélico Pro-Ayuda a los Damnificados (CEPAD: Evangelical Committee for

Aid to Disaster Victims). Gradually many Protestant denominations and institutions joined CEPAD. Hundreds of Evangelicals offered their help as volunteers. Thousands of food rations were served daily, clothes were distributed, medical attention was provided for anyone who could be attended, with no religious sectarianism of any kind.

Nicaragua's dictator, Anastasio Somoza, formed a National Emergency Committee presided by himself. Everyone in Nicaragua knew that the generous international aid sent from the five continents was monopolized by the dictator's army and managed by his son (and namesake). Only a part of that aid reached hungry, roofless, and naked people. Most of it was commercialized by the governing class.

But CEPAD directly channeled international aid from churches and religious groups the world over. This institution refused to form part of Anastasio Somoza's National Emergency Committee's "common fund." Nicaraguan Evangelicals organized around CEPAD defied the tyrant and fed the hungry, clothed the naked, and lovingly housed the homeless. It was the first political action of the Evangelical church in the history of Nicaragua. CEPAD went on to stand for Evangelical Committee for Development Aid.

As a church, Evangelicals in Nicaragua had always stood outside of politics. Its complex of a minority persecuted by a Catholic majority caused it to withdraw to its internal affairs and not participate in civil society. Its only contact with "the world" was for proselytizing purposes. So the life of the church unfolded independently from the country's social evolution. The Evangelical tradition in Nicaragua made it stay away from politics as a church. A result of North American conservative missionary discourse was the conception of "not contaminating oneself" with the things of the world. The Lord's words, "my kingdom is not of this world," were applied literally in the worst fundamentalist sense; "give to Caesar what is Caesar's and to God what is God's" was followed as a direct and decisive command to maintain a church totally separate from anything having a political character.

THE NINETEENTH CENTURY

The political history of Nicaragua contains many pages on the struggle between Conservatives and Liberals. Conservatives were known, among other things, for being clerical. Conservative administrations made a compatible marriage with the Roman Catholic Church and they persecuted and discriminated against Evangelicals. Then, toward the end of the nineteenth century, the liberal revolution of José Santos Zelaya triumphed. Like all liberals of his age, Zelaya was anti-clerical and favored freedom of religion and conscience. Since then Evangelicals have felt more comfortable with liberal governments than with conservative ones. This contributed to Evangelicals generally voting for liberal candidates and to the participation of some, on a personal basis, as activists in the Liberal Party. However, even during liberal governments conservatively-minded Catholics harassed Evangelicals.

Political liberalism developed valuable principles in this country. The most prominent national heroes to stand in defense of the country's sovereignty, Augusto Cesar Sandino and Benjamín Zeledón, were brought up in the stream of liberal thought. Unfortunately, the founder of the Somoza dynasty, Anastasio Somoza García, also took cover under the liberal banner — or rather, he usurped the banner of liberalism. So it was that in Nicaragua liberalism and *somocismo* came to be confused; and Evangelicals who saw conservatives as their persecutors supported *somocismo* for decades under its guise of liberalism.

Three Somozas ruled Nicaragua: Anastasio Somoza García, his eldest son, Luis Somoza Debayle, and the youngest, Anastasio Somoza Debayle. During the Somoza regime, some "puppets" pretended to occupy the presidential seat, acting as "bridges" between one Somoza term and another, so as to keep up appearances with regard to the prohibition of reelection. One of these presidents, Dr. René Schick, maintained a certain dignity and independence and so gained public appreciation; but he died before finishing his term of a supposed heart attack under circumstances that for many were dubious.

During the entire Somoza era Evangelicals as a church had no community participation in politics, but the average Protestant was usually a Somoza liberal. The Somoza era was also a period of extreme anti-communism, especially after the triumph of the Cuban revolution. The United States launched an anti-communist propaganda offensive of considerable magnitude. The Cold War between the two great superpowers, the United States and the U.S.S.R, had reached its highest levels. All this made an impact on the mentality and the attitude of Nicaraguan Evangelicals.

THE COLD WAR

We now know that part of the anti-communist propaganda was based on reality and part on exaggeration. *Perestroika* has uncovered the abuses of the socialist regimes and history has also revealed the exaggerations of North American propaganda. In any case, for the Evangelicals of Nicaragua, as for the majority of the people, the world was divided into "good" (headed by the United States) and "bad" (headed by Russia). Russia meant atheism, religious persecution, the denial of society's most treasured values — family, freedom, and the church. Russia was the standard-bearer of communism, a doctrine that was generally viewed as the "Antichrist" and the incarnation of Satan himself.

There was no debating of ideas, no scientific and rational discussion on the subject. Communism was condemned a priori, without debate. A Christian should not only simply reject communism but also become a crusader in the battle against communism: that is to say, be an anti-communist. At the same time, capitalism, and in particular the capitalism of the United States, was considered the kingdom of righteousness. Being a Christian meant not only being anti-communist, but also pro-capitalist.

North American missionaries who controlled national Evangelical churches greatly contributed to these manichean postures; missionaries who were bred in the United States with those same naive and fanatical concepts; missionaries who were viewed with veneration and reverence by Nicaraguan Protestants. There was a mystique that surrounded missionaries. In a certain way they were considered, subconsciously of course, as angels come from paradise (i.e., the United States).

Needless to say, these circumstances, product of an age and of environmental influences, in no way take away from the excellent evangelistic work, and the dedicated and meritorious actions of these missionaries. Their example must be imitated by new generations of Evangelicals, but without making idols of them and hiding their weaknesses. They certainly had received a poor political education, which they passed on to the Evangelical people of Nicaragua.

Concurrently, the Somozas were the main anti-communist banner bearers. This added another dimension to their image, that of defenders of "Western and Christian values," so prized by Evangelicals.

Everything opposed to these so-called "Western and Christian values" was considered "communist." Following this line of reasoning, Somoza went to the extreme of accusing his conservative opponents and those of the Social-Christian persuasion (whom Luis Somoza called "little red fish swimming in holy water") of being communists. Of course, any social movement that defended the rights of the poor and the oppressed was classified as "clearly communist." Because of their mindset and education, Evangelicals followed the same line of reasoning.

THE ROMAN CATHOLIC CHURCH

While in the Roman Catholic church a theology of liberation began to develop and Catholic youths gained awareness through the more progressive priests, Evangelical churches did not even talk of social issues. Among Catholics, youth movements with a new social mindset flourished rapidly. Among Evangelicals the process was slower and more difficult.

It is known that the Roman Catholic Church lacks the communal cohesion in its parishes characteristic of our Evangelical churches. In an Evangelical church most members know each other fairly intimately and there is a strong relationship between its members. This commendable characteristic, good and quite Christian, was paradoxically what slowed down the development of a more open social consciousness in newer generations, in young people, since the influence of older people, their leaders, was repressive with the exception of a few cases.

On the other hand, Catholics did not have the influence of North American missionaries with the characteristics described. Keeping in mind all the aspects pointed out, the almost natural rejection of any progressive social movement by Evangelical churches should come as no surprise, and, all the more so, in the case of the Frente Sandinista de Liberación Nacional [Sandinista National Liberation Front], then an outlawed group.

At the same time, while Catholic priests preached frequently against social injustice and against the Somoza dictatorship, the preaching of Nicaraguan Evangelical churches followed the pattern set down by international preachers who transmitted their image through television and massive campaigns, giving a spiritualist and individualist message, emphasizing "personal" sins and ignoring "social" ones (as well as their causes and consequences).

This was the situation when the 1972 earthquake took place, which changed Nicaraguan history and the history of Nicaraguan Evangelicals. One of the things crushed in the aftermath of the earthquake was the mask covering the true face of the Somoza dictatorship. Up until the time of the earthquake, Anastasio Somoza Debayle carefully guarded appearances. The earthquake awakened his ambition more fully and made him shed his mask. Evangelicals who had trusted him in all good faith began to be disillusioned. As mentioned earlier, CEPAD was the first ecumenical joint venture put into motion by Evangelical churches in the social arena and opposed to the interests of Somoza. From that moment on, Evangelical churches continued to advance, though slowly, toward more progressive postures and a more aggressive role in national politics.

EVANGELICALS AND THE SANDINISTA REVOLUTION

Starting in December of 1972, there was a rise in the degree of government corruption and cruelty that made it lose progressively more of its social base among the population that had supported it, including Evangelicals. Notwithstanding, several Evangelical leaders were faithful to *somocismo* until the end. Sadly, some of them were even ardent defenders of Somoza before the U.S. Congress when the Carter administration censured his violation of human rights and when the rejection of world leaders was almost unanimous.

Somocismo's degree of decomposition progressively rose, in an accelerated rhythm, especially in the period beginning in 1972, after the earthquake, and continuing to the triumph of the Sandinista Revolution in 1979. Concurrently, the degree of political awareness in the people and the subsequent repudiation of *somocismo* continued to grow. From the ranks of the Somoza party, including some of his ex-government officials, deserters crowded to an opposition growing in strength.

Traditional political parties who opposed Somoza were not able to capitalize on the people's discontent since they had themselves been discredited by internal divisions. The main party among them, the Conservative Party, in addition to being internally divided, had come to a political agreement with Somoza before the earthquake; and this caused resentment among the people. Thanks to that agreement, Conservatives obtained offices in the Somoza administration (the so-called "minority offices") — some townships and 40 percent of Congress as previously agreed.

In contrast, the popularity of the Frente Sandinista de Liberación Nacional continued to grow, especially among young people. Evangelicals were not outside of this current. Slowly more young people from Evangelical churches, and some older, more progressive leaders began to sympathize with the Sandinistas. The Sandinista Front represented the hope that a new generation of people who had not given in to corruption would liberate the country from Somoza and take power. Their leaders were young people admired for the idealism, courage, and integrity that allowed them to undergo the cruelest and most infamous tortures, clandestinity, and exile for their ideals.

It was not easy for Evangelicals to accept the Sandinistas. Many never did accept them. The Sandinistas were considered "communists" and therefore enemies of the church. They did not deny their marxist-leninist education and it was no secret that Fidel Castro supported them. But there was in the people, and in an ever growing number of Evangelicals (though always a minority in churches), the feeling that "despite their being communists," the Sandinistas were good. The people, disappointed by Somoza and traditional politicians, needed to believe in something or someone, and here were these courageous, noble, and idealist youngsters who had defied the tyrant by kidnapping the entire National Congress of the Republic (taking over the National Palace in order to do so), including his brother-in-law and ambassador to Washington, Guillermo Sevilla Sacaza. In return, the Sandinistas managed to get their people out of Somoza's prisons, thousands of dollars in payment, a great amount of national and international publicity, and the massive sympathy of the people. Then the Sandinistas took over some cities for hours. They went on to control them for days. The population's enthusiasm grew. Then came the final offensive . . . and finally the triumph of 19 July 1979. Thousands of Evangelicals were at the "Plaza de la Revolución" (formerly, "de la República") cheering for the Sandinista leaders on the day of the victory. Thousands of others, maybe even more than in the former group, stayed at home fearful of the destiny of the country now that it was governed by "communists." Hundreds of Evangelicals, mainly the richest ones, and above all those who had dealings with Somoza or one of his group, and some military men form the Guardia Nacional, emigrated to exile, mostly to Miami. Some were taken prisoners.

In the final stage of the Somoza regime, a strong process of polarization began among Evangelical churches. Churches that had traditionally been strong were divided in two groups who emphatically rejected each other. Some were accused of "communism" and others of being "accomplices to the crimes of the Somoza dictatorship." That polarization lasted throughout the time that the Sandinistas governed; and today, many traces of that division have still not disappeared. Of course there were corrupt people within Evangelical churches: *somocistas* in the worst sense of the word. But many honest and good people, excellent Christians, rejected the Sandinistas for ideological reasons, due to their political upbringing, to ignorance, or to confusion. The Sandinistas were really not too popular among the Evangelical fold, and in spite of the process of the Sandinistas' effort to come closer to Evangelicals, to which I will refer further on, the majority of Evangelicals were never pro-Sandinista.

AFTER THE REVOLUTION

Once the revolution had triumphed, a considerable number of middle echelon members of the Sandinista Front evidenced classical or orthodox communist stances: a militant atheism, a rejection of anything having to do with religion, an a priori disqualification of any private ownership of the means of production, and some anti-Evangelical postures (for instance, one that held that Protestants were C.I.A. agents). Assuming that the Sandinista leadership was anti-Evangelical, some hotheads, opportunists, and others desirous of gaining the new government's favor, participated in the takeover of Evangelical temples. That attitude has still not been forgotten by many Evangelicals.

However, the Sandinista National Leadership never assumed an anti-Evangelical or even anti-religious posture. If the Sandinistas were "communists," they were very unique communists, since there were Catholic priests in their government cabinet and they sought to come closer to Evangelicals from the very beginning.

From the very outset, the Sandinistas acted as the forerunners of *perestroika*: self-avowed marxists-leninists, highly nationalist, with a militancy of believers among its majority, and proponents of a mixed economy, non-alignment, and political pluralism.

Within the ranks of believers, Catholic and Evangelical alike, the debate revolved around whether it was possible to be a marxist and a Christian at the same time. Those who rejected Sandinismo did so thinking that being a Sandinista was something incompatible with their faith. Others, who felt closer to Sandinismo (sympathizers and militants) repeated the slogan popularized by the Sandinista Front, which maintained that "between Christianity and revolution there is no contradiction."

The so-called "popular church," inspired by liberation theology and at odds with the hierarchy, emerged within the Catholic church. Among the Evangelical community opposing factions arose that threatened to divide several denominations. Because of the prudence of some leaders, divisions were avoided that would have signified a permanent and very painful rupture.

As time went by and the revolution matured, Evangelicals began to lose their fear of the Sandinistas. The situation evolved in such a way that those Evangelicals who now reject Sandinismo do so on purely political grounds, due to their ideology and not because of religious reasons.

At the time of the revolution's success there was an Evangelical movement that had fully supported the Sandinistas even during the insurrection stage and that lost its belligerence as the years went by — the Eje Ecuménico de Nicaragua [Ecumenical Axis of Nicaragua] led by José Miguel Torres, a Baptist pastor. He was cofounder, along with the Franciscan priest and liberation theologian Uriel Molina Oliú, of the Centro Ecuménico Fray Antonio de Valdivieso. Father Uriel Molina, proponent and director of the Center, became the main figure of the "popular church." Once the revolutionary government settled in Nicaragua, the State Council was created (an organism that co-legislated with the Junta de Gobierno de Reconstrucción Nacional, or Government Board for National Reconstruction) and in it the Ecumenical Axis had a seat occupied by the Baptist pastor José María Ruiz, one of the most beloved and prestigious Baptist pastors, widely respected by all Nicaraguan Evangelicals. This venerable pastor, ninety-eight years old at the time of this writing, was the first Evangelical pastor to occupy the office of congressman in this country.

The most important aspect of Reverend Ruiz's position is that he occupied his seat in direct and specific representation of an Evangelical organism and due to his position as an Evangelical pastor.

Later on, during the 1984 national elections for President, Vice President, and representatives for the National Assembly, José María Ruiz's name and that of the layman Sixto Ulloa (also a Baptist) appeared on the list of candidates nominated by the Sandinista Front. Both were elected. Both had been nominated precisely as representatives of the Evangelical people and both were worthy representatives during all of their term in the National Assembly.

Sixto Ulloa was obliged to renounce his post as Director of Public Relations for CEPAD in order to accept his candidacy. Though he did not represent CEPAD with his assembly seat, no one could separate him from his commission. Sixto Ulloa was a result of CEPAD where he learned the Christian spirit of service, the Evangelical *diakonia* that characterized his term as congressman.

UNITY IN CHRIST IN THE MIDST OF DIVISION

CEPAD was not only the first Evangelical expression of social concern in the country, it also acquired such a large profile in the life of the churches and within the Evangelical community that it spontaneously became the Council of Evangelical Churches of Nicaragua.

In order to answer to its new role CEPAD changed its structures and consequently adopted a new name with the same initials: Consejo de Iglesias Evangélicas Pro-Alianza Denominacional [Council of Evangelical Churches Pro-Denominational Alliance]. During the convulsive period while the revolutionary process unfolded — with divisions, polarizations, and war — CEPAD, as the Council of Churches, kept the Evangelical community united.

I cannot explain CEPAD to myself as anything other than a miracle of God. How else to explain the existence, survival, and strengthening of an organization like CEPAD in a place as complicated as Nicaragua? Within this organization, the most conservative churches stood alongside the progressive ones. In CEPAD Evangelical leaders opposed to the Sandinista government sat alongside Evangelical leaders who supported it. Everyone was there. There everyone got along. God was using men like Dr. Gustavo Parajón, CEPAD's founder and president, to maintain a balance and the unity of His people.

The Sandinista government quickly realized that the natural place to go in order to dialogue with the Evangelical community was CEPAD, and so they drew closer. The relationship between both groups was cordial. The government respected the institution and the Evangelical churches it represented, and trusted its main representative, Dr. Parajón. This made it possible for CEPAD to mediate with the government so that essential pastors and Evangelical leaders would be exempted from military service in order to prevent a void in denominational leadership. CEPAD was also able to free many Evangelicals who had been incarcerated unjustly — people who had been falsely accused or whose rights had been abused by lower-echelon party members who did so much damage to the Sandinista Front. In difficult situations CEPAD negotiated for pardons, prison chaplaincies, and the defense and promotion of human rights.

During the Sandinista period, the National Assembly, thanks to the mediation of CEPAD and of congressman Sixto Ulloa, the number of Evangelical denominations and institutions that were recognized as legal entities multiplied five times over that of any time in Nicaraguan history. The Political Constitution of Nicaragua, which was approved by the National Assembly with a majority Sandinista vote, established the broadest freedom of religion and conscience. Included in the text verbatim were articles drafted by CEPAD's Committee on Legal and Human Rights Affairs. The Assembly heeded all of the recommendations of CEPAD, except for the matter of conscientious objection to military service.

The Evangelical community was participating fully in national politics. Not in the partisan politics, but in Politics (capitalized); in the formation of a new society; in contributing the values of the Gospel to the construction of a civil society; in small and big things, including the process of creating the country's Magna Carta. The political metamorphosis of Evangelicals in Nicaragua was completed in a wonderful and glorious way. The people of God had become aware of their reason for existing in this world. No longer would their light be hidden under the table or their salt lose its saltiness. And civil society came to view the Evangelical people with well-deserved respect.

Other Evangelical organizations emerged; some as a support for the revolution — like the Evangelical Committee for the Promotion of Evangelical Responsibility (*Comisión Evangélica de Promoción de la Responsabilidad Social,* CEPRES); others for research and theological and social studies — like the Center for Interecclesiastical Social and Theological Studies (*Centro Intereclesial de Estudios Teológicos y Sociales,* CIETS). There was an Evangelical upsurge, an Evangelical flourishing within the Nicaraguan revolutionary process.

OPPOSITION

However, there were also reactionary and counterrevolutionary leaders and persons, but not for religious reasons; rather it was their political option. Some people slandered CEPAD, accusing it of being an organization in the service of the Sandinista Front. The United States was the source of an attack promoted by the Institute for Religion and Democracy (IRD) based on slander and responding to the position of ultraconservative sectors of the Evangelical right. This position was echoed by some Nicaraguan Evangelicals.

Vain attempts have been made, and are still being made, to create organizations parallel to CEPAD. These have been orchestrated by foreign entities (like the one headed by Pat Robertson) that aspire to become representatives of the Evangelical community and to return to an "apolitical" past. To this end they appeal to phrases such as "Christ-centered" or "Bible-centered." But the Evangelical people have matured enough not to look back and become pillars of salt.

Recently, the Assemblies of God withdrew from CEPAD, accusing it of being "political" (which to them is bad) and Sandinista. Nevertheless, their pastors are still members of the Pastors' Assemblies of CEPAD; some are even leaders of these groups and refuse to obey orders to sever ties to this committee.

POLITICAL AWARENESS

There is now a healthy political awareness in the Evangelical people as well as a clear political ideological stance among the Evangelical leadership. Each leader knows if he belongs to the right or to the left, he knows what he stands for, and he participates in the political debate in which the church, like any living organism existing in society, participates. No longer do people act in response to traditions or unknown influences; rather each person has taken a totally conscious political option.

I had the pleasant experience of commenting, for the benefit of the Evangelical community, on the new Political Constitution of Nicaragua via an Evangelical interdenominational radio station ("Ondas de luz"), article by article and for more than a year. For several years, on this fifteen-minute daily radio program, I answered questions posed by Evangelicals on the laws of the country. Unfortunately, the station was later run by a group of very conservative executives and the program was canceled. The positive aspect of the experience was that the Evangelical community showed an interest in the development of civil society, in Politics (capitalized).

The contribution of the Evangelical people to Nicaraguan society has been most valuable in the struggle for peace and national reconciliation. As of the Esquipulas Accords, and as a resolution of the five Central American presidents, a National Committee for Reconciliation was formed in each country. This committee was to be composed of a Roman Catholic bishop, a government delegate, an opposition delegate, and a member considered to be an outstanding citizen in society. In Nicaragua, the president of CEPAD, Dr. Gustavo Parajón, was designated as the outstanding civilian member of the Committee. It was a new and important opportunity to serve God and men; a chance to contribute to the establishment of peace and national reconciliation. Dr. Parajón had the support of the General Assembly of CEPAD and of the Evangelical people of Nicaragua, including pro-Sandinistas and non-Sandinistas.

Also, in war-racked areas, the local pastors formed peace committees that performed an outstanding task. In remote mountain villages, pastors were sometimes the only ones trusted by soldiers, Sandinista authorities, and contras. During the Violeta Barrios de Chamorro administration, the disarming of the contras in the southern region (Nueva Guinea, Region V) was possible thanks to the mediation of these peace committees; they were encouraged and supported by Dr. Parajón and CEPAD.

In the 1990 summons to elections, the Sandinista Front listed among their candidates for municipal council members in districts across the country dozens of Evangelical pastors. These were viewed as the community's natural leaders, open to the community and no longer subject to the sectarianism of the past. The

Sandinista Front did not win the presidential election and it achieved less than an absolute majority in parliament; yet it still occupies a strong position as a relative majority since the winning coalition is divided into fourteen parties of different ideological positions. In addition, the Sandinistas also won in several municipalities where Evangelical pastors are now part of the municipal councils. Even in municipalities where the Sandinista Front did not win, some Evangelical pastors were able to remain among the minority council members.

The National Opposition Union, UNO, listed Dr. Rodolfo Mejía Ubilla among its candidates for congressmen. He obtained a seat in the National Assembly and he now presides over the Commission on Justice for the Nicaraguan parliament. Dr. Mejía, a lawyer and member of the Liberal Constitutionalist Party, holds conservative ideas and has been schooled in the old reactionary ideology, but everyone recognizes in him an upright and respectable person. He belongs to the Baptist laity, as does Sixto Ulloa whom he replaced, though with an opposite political approach. Both are Evangelicals and are appreciated by the Evangelical people.

Curiously, Rev. José María Ruiz, Sixto Ulloa, and Dr. Rodolfo Mejía Ubilla are members of the same church: the First Baptist Church of Managua. Coincidentally, I also belong to the same church. We all love each other as brethren. Our pastor is Dr. Gustavo Parajón.

The inference should not be drawn that all or even most Evangelicals adopted the position held by CEPAD, nor that Dr. Parajón's charisma was sufficient to maintain unity in spite of the diversity of opinions. It is true that Dr. Parajón played an important role as leader of CEPAD, avoiding the political atomization of Evangelicals or the polarization into two strong opposing camps. But anti-Sandinista currents, which were also anti-CEPAD, were actively antagonistic.

The National Council of Evangelical Pastors of Nicaragua (*Consejo Nacional de Pastores Evangélicos de Nicaragua*, CNPEN) was the most important expression of this current. It did not develop to any extent due mainly to the repression exercised by the Sandinistas during the state of national emergency the war obliged them to enforce.

MRS. CHAMORRO

Following the victory of Mrs. Violeta Barrios de Chamorro, these groups have grown in strength. Although CEPAD maintains the leadership with the support of the majority of Evangelicals, there is a strong Evangelical anti-CEPAD movement. It is significant that the strongest denomination, the Assemblies of God, is no longer a part of CEPAD. Although its withdrawal took place before the electoral victory of the UNO, the importance of its separation is felt more strongly now that there is greater freedom of expression.

The victory of Mrs. Violeta Chamorro, for whom many Evangelicals voted, should not, however, be considered a victory of Evangelicals on the right. The president's clear identification with the Roman Catholic hierarchy has irritated Evangelical groups of all positions, because there has been clear discrimination of customs duties for the Catholic church and (unconstitutional) taxing of Evangelical churches. Some Christians, including those on the right, desire a return to Sandinista treatment of Evangelicals.

It should be made clear that Mrs. Chamorro's victory was not due to pro-Chamorro votes, but rather to pro-peace votes. That is, the majority of voters sympathized with the Sandinista Front, but were convinced that a Sandinista electoral victory would only lead to the continuation of a war that had already cost them far too high a price. To vote for Mrs. Chamorro meant to vote for the end of the war, by removing every pretext on the basis of which the government of the United States could continue to finance the Contras.

Perhaps if the UNO candidate had been some other person this phenomenon would not have taken place. The fact that Mrs. Chamorro is the mother of two important Sandinista leaders — one the director of *Barricada*, the official Sandinista journal, and the other the wife of one of the leading Sandinista congressmen — influenced many committed Sandinistas to vote for her in order to obtain the peace they so earnestly desired. After all, the mother of two Sandinistas could not be too bad an option for the Sandinistas.

Christians from around the world should join with courageous Nicaraguan Christians in intense prayer and active solidarity on behalf of my country and the churches that have suffered so much. We are filled with hope and trust in the God of history.

17

Brazil:
Base Communities in the Northeast

José Comblin

"The BECs are looking for their own way between two poles. Some tend to be parish substitutes or function as virtual parishes. Others tend to focus on being popular movements." For reasons of social process and ecclesiastical inertia, the BECs in northeastern Brazil are in crisis. The author, a Belgian priest who has worked in Brazil for many years, suggests that the base communities borrow a page from the Pentecostal churches. This is an abridged translation of "Algumas Questoes da Prática das Comunidades Eclesiais de Base no Nordeste," *Revista Eclesiástica Brasileira*, vol. 50, N⁰ 198 (June 1990). It is used with permission.

Northeastern Brazil has its peculiarities, and these carry over also to the Church. My own experience is circumscribed to the northeast so that I cannot extrapolate my observations to other regions of Brazil. Conceivably, in other regions the situation is different, and so my reflections would not apply. In any case, it may be that my comments will elicit reflections and comparisons that could be useful elsewhere.

In numerous places in northeastern Brazil one hears talk of "weariness," "routine," and "crisis" in the Base Ecclesial Communities (BECs). Ten years ago, in a number of localities, there were many groups and lots of enthusiasm. Now, even in those places where notorious social confrontations once took place, the *comunidades* are now mired in apathy. What does this all mean? Some priests, pastoral theologians, and sociologists believe that the day of the BECs is past. And the local bishops are even more perplexed.

As for me, I believe that here in Northeastern Brazil the BECs are facing the challenge of having to move from the prophetic phase — spontaneous and im-provising — to an institutional phase. Every inspired idea goes through a similar evolution, whether it is in society or in the Church. It happened to the religious orders, to theological schools, pious and devotional movements, and to lay religious organizations. A prophetic movement that is incapable of becoming a stable institution will die or disappear. It may leave behind memories, stamp its mark upon history, and build an occasional monument to its passage through time, but it will disappear nonetheless.

Institution as such is not in opposition to the Spirit, but there is not a necessary connection between them. There are aged institutions that have long since lost their initial inspiration. They are so preoccupied with their own subsistence or continuity that they no longer provide any real service to the world. And there are institutions that inspire and point the way; they provide the organization people's movements need to move ahead and create history. Because it is only institutions that make history. Without them prophets have no lasting links nor do they leave their stamp upon history.

However, a word of caution is in order here. Institutions are not created by decree. An institution is not simply a legal entity. A decree can give legal recognition to an existing institution, but it cannot grant existence to what does not already exist. Communities become institutionalized in fact and not on paper. They take on the features of permanent social realities and are endowed with whatever structures they need for their continued existence. Whether or not they are officially recognized is of little import. Normally, institutions are officially recognized after a long formation process. For example, the parish began to take shape in the eleventh century but only acquired full juridical recognition at the Council of Trent.

THE IDENTITY OF THE BASE ECCLESIAL COMMUNITIES

There are many questions, discussions, and concerns. The Brazilian Conference of Bishops is uneasy. It seems that the identity of the BECs is not clear. With so much that has been written about them, how is it that we still have not reached an understanding of their identity?

But the matter of identity brings up a prior question. Who is qualified to define the identity of the Base Ecclesial Communities? At first glance it would seem that it is the prerogative of the episcopacy to define the Base Ecclesial Communities, to establish their goals, their means and movement. But, in fact, this is not the case. It is up to the bishops to define the "ecclesiality" of the communities, but not their content, because this can only become manifest after a long historical process. If authorities attempt to enclose an institution within a predefined scheme, they will hinder its normal evolution and create unnecessary conflicts. This is, in fact, what happened to Catholic Action.

I shall not attempt to offer conclusions as to the nature of the Base Ecclesial Communities. I will rather suggest some points that could clarify the debate and contribute to a solution. Let us look first at those concerns about the BECs that the magisterium has put on hold — questions it cannot and probably will not be able to resolve for many years. Secondly, we can consider the factual evidence. What is taking place at this moment with the existing *comunidades* in the northeast? Finally, we shall attempt to draw some basic data from all of this that may serve as a possible new starting point.

Puebla Did Not Define the BECs

The Puebla Document includes a ten-page section (paragraphs 617-657, on Base Communities, parishes, and particular churches) that speaks at length about the BECs. It also describes them in some detail in paragraphs 640-643. Let us refresh our minds with a look at the central portion, which contains a long list of characteristics:

> As community the BECs bring together families, adults, and young people, in an intimate interpersonal relationship grounded in the faith. As an ecclesial reality, it is a community of faith, hope, and charity. It celebrates the Word of God and takes its nourishment from the Eucharist, the culmination of all the sacraments. It fleshes out the Word of God in life through solidarity and commitment to the new commandment of the Lord; and through the service of approved coordinators, it makes present and operative the mission of the Church and its visible communion with the legitimate pastors. It is a base-level community because it is composed of relatively few members as a permanent body, like a cell of the larger community (par. 641).[1]

Please note that this text does not provide any insights as to what a Base Ecclesial Community *is*. It merely informs us concerning what a BEC must *have* in order to be ecclesial. But the foregoing description is also applicable to many groups: the Home and Family Movement, Marriage Encounter, groups of the Focolari, Schönstatt, and Charismatic Renewal movements, etc. The description does not say anything that is unique and specific to the BECs. It leaves a fundamental question hanging in the air. What is the relationship of a Base Ecclesial Community to the parish and thus, what is the place of the BECs in the Church?

On the one hand, Puebla's exposition on the BECs is placed at the beginning of a three-part series: BEC — parish — diocese. This gives the impression of a homogeneous continuity; i.e. in the same way that all Catholics belong to dioceses and parishes, they also belong to Base Ecclesial Communities. The position and the structure of a BEC would seem to be analogous to the position and structure of a parish and a diocese.

However, this impression is contradicted by other texts. Puebla says that "the parish carries out a function that is, in a way, an integral ecclesial function" (par. 644). But a Base Community is not integral. It only fulfills a partial function. It does not involve Christians totally but only in certain aspects of their lives. This is confirmed by the total silence about Christian initiation when the BECs are described. The foundations of the Christian faith are provided, not in the BECs but in the parishes — in baptism, confirmation, catechism, and first communion. Finally, the parish is called "a center of coordination and guidance for communities, groups, and movements" (par. 644). We might suppose that the same people are members of communities, groups, and movements. However, this is probably not the case, because in fact Catholics choose from a range of available options. The BECS bring together only one sector of the parish and carry out only partial functions. They do not involve every Christian. Not only for non-

BEC Catholics, but also for BEC members, the parish continues to be the fundamental place of belonging that opens the door to the *corpus* of the Church.

Because Catholics can chose neither their diocese nor their parish, if there were in fact a homogeneous continuity between them and the BECs, membership in the *comunidades* would be obligatory, instead of voluntary and free. Except in the case of religious orders, the military, and prelatures, Catholics are attached to a particular parish and diocese by virtue of residence. We can conclude then that Puebla probably did not mean to convey that membership in a BEC was obligatory. In any case, no one was yet even thinking along these lines. At the most some were perhaps conjecturing that a day would come when this might be the case.[2] But so far this has not happened. A Base Community is a voluntary and free group, according to the Puebla document.

Meanwhile, the fact that the BECs are singled out in this way — as being in continuity with parish and diocese — implies a desire to give them a more prominent place than the other groups. But what place? The term "*cell* of the larger community" (in the Puebla Document) does not make matters any clearer because the text does not explain what it means by "cell." If it is a *Base* Community merely because it "is composed of relatively few members," it shares this characteristic with countless other groups in the Church that might also merit being called "cells."

In brief, the Puebla text leaves everything very much up in the air. We could say the same thing about the other magisterial documents. The bishops could say no more and they did very well to not do so. They left the door open for something different, without that something having to follow a path that has already been abstractly defined. They left a space open for those things which are called Base Ecclesial Communities. Yet, what the bishops did do, because it was their mission to do so, was to define the conditions by which BECs can be considered ecclesial.

If the bishops were to try to further define the BECs they probably would not agree. A few might suggest that the entire diocesan and parish structures should be defined on the basis of the BECs, but very few bishops would agree to this. The great majority is willing to allow freedom of movement for the *comunidades*, but without trying to fit the entire pastoral ministry of the diocese within the BEC scheme. As it turns out, a BEC-based pastoral ministry is only viable in dioceses that have virtually homogeneous and almost totally marginalized populations. In dioceses that have more complex populations the bishops have to attend do a multiplicity of groups, tasks, and organizations.

So, our lack of definition remains. BECs belong to parish and diocesan structures but we still do not know how they relate to parish and diocese. It is not clear whether they are obligatory or voluntary. More concretely, nothing is said regarding their role in Christian initiation (baptism, chrism, first communion).

A New Way of Being Church?

This oft-repeated formula has, unfortunately, many ambiguities. The article "a" is ambiguous, as is the word "new." When we say "a new way of being church" we can mean "the new way of being church" or "one of the new ways of being church." We can, on the one hand, imagine several new ways of being church, for example, the way of the Charismatic Renewal, the Focolari, the Cursillos, etc. And among these new ways there is one that is called "Base Ecclesial Community." Or rather we can mean that *one* — only one — new way of being church has appeared, which is the BEC.

When we say "new" what do we mean? New can have a quantitative or a qualitative sense. "A new way" can signify "another one," as when we say that "a new star (another star alongside of all the others) has appeared in the heavens." In this sense a new way of being church would stand beside other ways. "New" can also mean "different," that is, a qualitative newness. The BECs then, would be a different mode of being church (*the* different form, or one of several different forms). But different from what? Do they differ from the parish or the diocese? Are they different from Catholic Action? Different from the traditional associations?

As we can see, the formula does not explain a thing, while it maintains all of the ambiguities for the interlocutors of the Base Communities.

The Real Situation of the BECs

In the first place, the Base Ecclesial Communities exist in the midst of the poor and are virtually nonexistent among the middle classes. Given this situation, one should not expect them to involve the totality of Catholics. We shall return to this conclusion later.

Secondly, the BECs are looking for their own way between two "poles" that constantly require their services. Some tend to be parish substitutes or function as virtual parishes. Others tend to focus on being popular movements. The orientation of the communities depends to a large measure upon how the communities began and on the challenges that they have faced along the way. Frequently the *comunidades* in the countryside and villages tend to be quasi-parishes and the communities on the periphery of the cities tend to identify with the popular movements.

The "virtual parish" communities. The groups that meet regularly in rural chapels to organize religious activities are usually called *comunidades*. These groups can be compared to parishes because they offer some of the religious services that are administered in the city churches — the Sunday celebration, the catechism and novenas, the preparation for baptism and, on occasion, for marriage. They are also in charge of the first communions, they visit the sick, and pray for the dead. They amount to a partial decentralization of the parish. Their social style is also similar to that of a parish, because all of their activities are strictly dependent on the authority of the vicar. The *comunidades* leaders (or animators) are invested by the vicar either explicitly, or more frequently implicitly (and are no less effective because of this). As virtual parishes, the BECs are obligatory mediations because they monopolize the religious services. Whoever needs the parish services must either pass through the Base Community or find other alternatives, such as an accommodating priest in a neighboring town who does not work with *comunidades*.

In these communities the model is paternalistic, the same as in a parish. Such

BECs practice a benevolent authoritarianism, like that in most parishes. There is neither debate, discussion, nor participation. The animators who are appointed by the *padre* exercise absolute authority, which is at times less tempered by love than by the authority of the priest. In the Brazilian Northeast the great majority of the so-called "communities" in the rural areas lean in that direction.

The "social movement" communities. A different kind of BEC evolved in urban areas. They are the result of concerted social action that is centered on problems of land, housing, water supply, transportation, electricity, schools, health, as well as community and alternative projects by Caritas and other non-governmental organizations (NGOs). Similar *comunidades* can also be found in rural settings where land struggles were once uppermost. These communities often specialize. They tend to gather around the causes that first got them going or in which they continue to be engaged. They are select and elitist groups of active militants — voluntarist and committed — and therefore quite different from the mass of the people. Nonetheless, they do manage at times to mobilize large numbers of people for specific causes.

Normally there should be more participation within this type of community — more dialogue, more horizontal or collegial communication. However, in the situation in northeastern Brazil, it is very difficult for a group to manage to maintain itself in the struggle without the support of a pastoral agent, particularly a priest. Without realizing it, the agent becomes the de facto leader by virtue of his prestige and of his infinitely superior cultural formation, which allows him to move more self-assuredly within the wider society. And the leaders who benefit from the confidence of the pastoral agent are automatically invested with unquestioned authority.

Communities such as these gradually begin to look like social action groups, and the tendency is for them to move more and more in that direction. In certain cases these communities are gradually reduced (in a process that is as inexorable as it is unconscious) to becoming much like labor-union locals, or a group of PT (Workers' Party) militants. In the northeast this is tantamount to remaining a small group, highly suspect by the majority of the people who are very much under the thumb of police chiefs, political bosses, and landlords.

In some cases, by the initiative of pastoral agents, there is a mixture or a superimposition of both models. At least one social action group has also been put in charge of the religious activities of the area. Such *comunidades* generally generate a lot of conflicts. The activists monopolize the religious services and the more religious people do not accept their input. This causes endless controversies with Catholics and others who are still bound to tradition and dependent.

It is clear from these observations that implanting Base Ecclesial Communities is not without major problems. The *comunidades* are facing much resistance from the majority of Catholics — at times the resistance is overt and active, at others it is covert and passive. The more the religious activities — particularly those traditional services tied to Christian initiation — are linked to the BECs, the greater the opposition to them. There is a clash between two models of Christian lifestyle and ecclesiality. Confusion concerning the identity of the

BECs makes these tensions even more acute. If the BECs do not manage to resolve their tensions I do not foresee much of a future for them here. Any day now come ecclesiastical authority will come along to side with the "great silent majorities." At this place in time the local churches are marching to the beat of Western society; siding with the conservative majority against the "progressive minorities." One can easily predict the outcome of a showdown.

The Essentials of Base Ecclesial Community

What are the essential elements of the BECs, when we consider their history and their present sociological situation? What is contingent and what can be set aside? What do we have a right to expect and to look for? Should we question a utopia that may generate dangerous reactions? I believe that two elements are indispensable and necessary in the BECs.

The milieu of the BECs is poverty. They are committed to liberation — *comunidades* of the poor who are involved in the liberation process (with infinite variety of approaches and forms). In this the BECs reflect the situation of Latin America today. They are not imported. Puebla recognized that distinctive when it said: "The BECs embody the Church's preferential love for the common people" (par. 643).

Now, when it comes to ecclesiality there was and always has been an underlying dimension that does not appear in the documents of the magisterium because it does not fit into the way the magisterium understands ecclesiality. But it does fit the ecclesial understanding of the people. The goal of the Base Ecclesial Communities is to encompass all of the Catholic poor of Latin America. They differ from Catholic "movements," which are groups of the elite and vanguard that carry out specialized or specific tasks.[3] In contrast, the BECs aim to mobilize the mass of the Catholic poor.

This goal immediately establishes certain preconditions. The BECs will never be able to carry out their project if they become sectarian, elitist, or if they identify with particular social and political projects. If they identify with a labor union slate or with a political party they will never be able to bring together the bulk of the Catholic poor. They will not attract the masses with inside jargon and elitist party symbols. The BECs will never be accepted if they insist on the highest membership standards for everyone. These are all great dangers.

Quite frequently one hears objections such as, "I don't like that *comunidade*." Or, "that community is very soft, or very weak." Or again, "I don't even want to hear about that *comunidade*." And even, "Those BECs divide the people," and so on. The fact is that the BECs have a political project (in the broadest sense) that prohibits sectarianism and isolation. Evangelicals can practice their sectarianism and isolate themselves from the people because they do not have a political project. But Catholics cannot proceed simply by multiplying small elitist groups. The Catholic Church follows a different path. What strategy should the BECs use to penetrate and be accepted by the Catholic masses? We are quite aware of the problem because it has been discussed, at least since 1988, in several articles by Clodovis Boff.

It would, however, be equally hazardous to think that the entire church should adopt the BEC model. If they are communities of the poor, then it is impossible for the Catholic Church to become only a church of the poor. It always has been and will continue to be multiclass. Even a socialist revolution cannot suppress social classes, and least of all the cultural aspects. The very mention of a church made up of BECs, or only of the poor, would arouse very strong opposition, setting in motion very strong pressures by the middle classes and rejection by the hierarchy.

It sometimes happened in the past — for example in the history of the brotherhoods — that the poor managed to have their own institutions, which made their life bearable and helped them to attain recognition within their own culture of poverty. Most of the time, however, the poor were not recognized in their own culture; they had to be content with remaining subordinate and anonymous within institutions that were formed, maintained, and carried out in more rarified cultural environments. In contrast, today the outcasts can find a place in the BECs and can become a church of the poor. In the BECs they are integrated, not separated, isolated, and cut off from the universal Church. They become the beneficiaries of a privileged but not exclusive position — that is, if the Church remains faithful to the spirit of Medellín and Puebla.

It is possible to have a clearly-defined church of the poor without fear of schism or heresy, because the poor are not, by inclination, schismatic. Church history shows that schisms and heresies are usually caused by bishops and priests. The most recent schism, by Bishop Lefevre, confirms this fact. From the church of the poor one should only expect respect and submission to the Church hierarchy. And the poor have a right to expect the same kind of recognition of their identity that the Church grants to individual cultures.

The BEC leadership style is collegial. Their aim is to adopt the shared leadership model of church instead of the traditional paternalistic model, which has a very long ecclesiastical history. It is the monarchical model that was instituted by canon law in the Latin Church during the Middle Ages. The present Code maintains this structure, at least in regard to juridical matters. The bishop gives orders in the diocese and the vicar in the parish. Everything flows from the top down — pastoral initiatives, planning, appointments, and decisions. Of course, neither the bishop nor the vicar make decisions without seeking advice. But this counts for very little in the decision-making process. More important is the ecclesiastical "court." Vicars have their courts, and so do the bishops. In monarchic regimes the most important instrument is always the court. If subjects want to influence the monarch they must go through the court.

Nonetheless, today many things have changed in monarchic authoritarianism. The regime of fear that prevailed before Vatican II is no longer with us. The authoritarianism of fear has been substituted by benevolent authority. The priests are low-key — they listen, ask questions, show a lot of patience and kindness; they take part in meetings, and remain silent when they are in disagreement; people feel free to speak up. Priests practice every kind of dialogue; they have every intention of being dialogical. Nonetheless, there is generally not much dialogue, or else dialogue does not come easily.

The obstacles to dialogue — at least four — are very great. (1) The poor suffer an inferiority complex, which paralyzes them in the presence of people with education and causes them to leave all of the talking to the priest. (2) Priests are prestigious. They are often the only educated persons in the locality, the only ones who know how to speak well, the only persons whom the authorities respect and fear. (3) Priests are prisoners of an incomprehensible language, which comes from their theological formation. The moment a priest starts using the jargon that was forced upon him in seminary, communication is cut off. Very few of us manage to forget the theology that we were taught for so many years! (4) Priests are very mobile; they do not stay in one place long enough to become integrated. As a result of all of this, *padres* suggest rather than command. They may propose or not respond to some proposal; but even a priestly silence counts as an order. In sum, what we have here is a paternalistic culture.

Benevolent authoritarianism is ingrained even in the Base Ecclesial Communities and causes confusion. The people of the *comunidades* are always awaiting the opinion of their pastoral agents. Nothing is decided, nothing is invented, nothing changes without his approval. And that approval is taken as an unchallengeable order that the people accept with enthusiasm and devotion. The other side of benevolent authoritarianism is benevolent submission. What this means is that no one learns to take initiatives, to accept risks, to debate and deliberate, and to arrive at conclusions. No one learns how to be dialogical and fraternal in community. Everyone remains passive and expects everything from the priest, who has solutions for every problem. This is a very profound malaise in northeastern Brazil. Wherever the priest fails to take the initiative, nothing happens. The laity have become accustomed to receiving everything on a platter, with bowing and scraping.

Pastoral agents of this kind homogenize the communities. They promote to leadership persons who are compatible with them — those who think alike, do the same things, and are perfect reflections of the priest. They are perfect mirrors, because they project into the community the image of their pastoral agents. By so doing the *comunidades* do not learn to live with diversity and to overcome conflicts. There are no conflicts in these communities because whoever does not think like the *padre* does not stand a chance. Nonconformists learn to put up and shut up. Many communities cannot abide even the slightest of internal conflicts.

Benevolent authoritarianism forces priests to work overtime. They are always exhausted because they have to do everything. Priests are also limited as to the number of *comunidades* they can shepherd, and the communities do not multiply. Clearly, the BECs have multiplied much less than the evangelical communities, at least during the past decade.

In the collegial model of BECs, however, we must look at both the internal and external relationships. Within these communities there is room for close association between people of very diverse tendencies. But diversity is not easy in a society such as the one in northeastern Brazil. For example, quite frequently rural BECs do not make room for young people, simply because adults do not like the same things that attract the youth and reject all of their proposals. They insist that young people adapt to adult ways. Similarly, there is a tendency in rural *comunidades* to overlook the men. Once the women take charge of the chapel, there isn't much room for men, who are usually put off by completely religious activities. Some will say that the high participation of women in the *comunidades* — frequently in excess of 80 percent — is a sign of progress. This is not necessarily true in a society such as that of northeastern Brazil. It could simply be a continuation of the tradition that makes religion the preserve of women. Both of these extant examples reveal the very human inclination to impose homogeneity. True collegiality begins the moment that we recognize and accept our differences.

The collegial model is fraternal. Decisions are discussed and debated, not on the basis of opinions, hunches, and personal family and group rivalries, but with objective facts in hand. The fraternal communities have learned to discuss and to decide. Unfortunately, many BECs have not learned about the decision-making process — how to tie up loose ends and to reach conclusions. They seem unable to make collective decisions when a patriarchal authority figure is not around.

Collegial communities will accept criticism, unlike traditional authoritarian societies in which every criticism is a form of rebellion with a potential for anarchy and physical stress. Collegial BECs do not take criticism as a personal affront, but as a challenge to improve. The most frequent criticism made of the BECs is when they close in upon themselves; when their members choose to remain in small homogeneous groups in which everyone knows everybody else and the risks are few. Authoritarian societies abhor risks, the kind of risks we take every time we open ourselves up to people who are unlike us. In contrast, collegial communities practice their own self-criticism, and are most true to their mission when they denounce their own lack of concern for the poor. Poor communities need to remember this as well, because, to protect themselves, they tend to forget those who are poorer than they are.

For *comunidades* to gradually learn a collegial way of coming together they must first break with their authoritarian tradition, even when it is tempered by love. This will open the way for them to acquire a certain autonomy. This has nothing to do with autonomy from the magisterium, the dogmas of our faith, or sacramental liturgy — nor from papal, conciliar, and episcopal decrees. We are referring here to autonomy vis-à-vis the pastoral agents to which the BECs are immediately subordinated. We are speaking about their freedom to take initiatives and make decisions; to program their activities, overcome their internal conflicts, and elect their own leaders. Officially the *comunidades* already have this freedom. But, in fact, their autonomy is relative so long as the shadow of the pastoral agents looms omnipresent over the BECs — if they remain the de facto movers and shakers. Actually, the communities are not asking for this autonomy because they are afraid of it. But they need to be gradually educated in this direction.

Conclusion. Part of the "novelty" of the BECs has been their horizontal and collegial style in which fraternal relationships predominate over authoritarian relationships. That is, they are novel because of their acceptance of the poor, and

also because of the collegial style of their leadership. There is a close relationship between these two aspects of what is new in the BECs. The dominant
culture in Latin America has established and maintains an authoritarian and
vertical society, with the appearance of democracy. Our governments are weak
imitations of the so-called Western democracies. Yet among the poor, community and fraternity are more spontaneous. Life is shared in common, no matter
how precarious the existence; everybody can count on the help of everyone else.
Lack of ambition removes the causes of jealousy, envy, and competition. There
is more equality among the poor than among the rich — fewer rivalries, more
opportunities for sharing.

The Councilor Foundations of the Base Ecclesial Communities

Both dioceses and parishes are institutions that have been created by the hierarchy, and they remain under the immediate jurisdiction of the hierarchy. But the
BECs do not need to be created by the hierarchy, even though they might need
some kind of hierarchical recognition. They are, of course, under the general
hierarchical jurisdiction that applies to all Catholics. Neither are the BECs subdi-
visions of parishes. They are not so juridically, and neither should they be treated
as if this were the case. To find the basis for the *comunidades* we must look to the
councilor texts that proclaim the freedom and relative autonomy of the laity.[4]
Since the Council of Trent, an authoritarian church structure had prevailed; the
laity, however, always found ways to develop horizontal structures. Today, with
parishes that had once been small now grown to unmanageable proportions, the
BECs and not parish subgroups would seem to be the answer.

We have today an opportunity to allow another kind of Church to arise in the
vacuum that the crisis in the parish system is causing. Vatican II encouraged this
new ecclesial model, even though it did not get around to defining it. This, in
any case, is not a council's responsibility. It is not enough for the BECs simply
to exchange a fear-based authoritarianism for the benevolent authority that we
have today. The spirit of Vatican II, of Medellín, and of Puebla opened new
horizons. A church is being formed by the fellowship and coordinated action of
communities that owe their existence to Christian initiative — communities that
are motivated and directed by the people.

The role of the clergy changes in this new church model. Instead of directing
everything — lovingly, of course — from the top down, priests should walk
alongside the communities. Rather than always initiating, we should be facilita-
tors, keeping our channels of communication open to all the groups and communities, near and far, and to the entire Christian Tradition. We can share with
them our rich spiritual heritage, as well as help provide links with other churches
at home and abroad. After all, the role of the successors of the apostles is first
and foremost to transmit the testimony of the apostles about Jesus Christ, with
discernment of spirits. The priests exercise the ministry of unity, uniquely
through the Eucharist, bringing together all of the groups and communities in a
parish or diocese. The Eucharist is the sign and sacramental means of unity of
the whole people of God.

The BECs: Alternatives or Instruments of Parish Monopoly?

In the Brazilian northeast, priests are turning more and more to a single Base Community to service their parish for them, thus effectively blocking the multiplication of *comunidades*. One community then begins to monopolize all of the parish functions, from liturgy to alternative projects. Their point of reference is no longer people as such but, like in parishes and dioceses, a particular territory wherein priests define the meaning of community. Any wonder, then, that many Catholics operate under the authoritarian presupposition that as they were born into a diocese or parish, so they do not have a choice in BEC, no matter what their personal feelings? This is probably one of the principal causes for the problems of genuine BECs and for the popular resistance against them. So it is no good to blame this resistance upon the "ignorance" or "alienation" of the people. The Church, with all of its problems, has to shoulder a portion of the responsibility.

Lessons from Tradition. In the above situation obedience to ecclesiastical tradition is the watchword! However Church tradition points in a different direction. The city-based diocese structure formalized by the Council of Nicea was the next step in an ecclesiastical process that had begun with numerous ecclesial communities in each city. For a long time, ecclesial communities responded neither to territorial, geographical, nor administrative constraints, but to human needs. Going against the weight of tradition, it was fairly recently that parishes evolved as an unconscious, yet uncalled for, extension of the authoritarian principle. The traditional way is for city-dwelling Christians to gather in communities, by choice. The Church in the city is the fellowship of all the communities. The unity of the Church in each city does not negate the possibility of Christians being able to found their own sharing communities.

Lessons from History. History shows that Christians always resisted the monopoly of the parishes. The greatest resisters were the monks and the friars, who eventually acquired the well-known "exemption privilege," which allows them to carry on their own lives completely separate from the parishes. Monks started the first Base Ecclesial Communities. Although the autonomous status of the monastic orders in the Middle Ages was harshly opposed by powerful bishops, the popes defended them vigorously. The battle was easier for the laity who were able to achieve ample autonomy for their spiritual lifestyle in the Third Orders and brotherhoods that multiplied during the thirteenth century. Membership in them remained high until this century. Despite the creeping authoritarianism in them and in the newer associations, the laity managed to preserve considerable freedom and autonomy from the parishes.

Again, after Vatican II, many of the laity acquired considerable freedom of action. Take, for example, the Opus Dei, which has virtual autonomy vis-à-vis both parish and diocese. The Charismatic Renewal, Focolari, Neochatecumenate, Schönstatt, etc., have achieved somewhat less autonomy, but with the exception of initiation rites, these movements maintain their own independent community activities. Paradoxically, it is the BECs that remain most under the thumb of benevolent authoritarianism. This is probably due to their social status. Middle-class movements tend to find acceptance and autonomy more easily, while the poor tend to submit to dependence more readily because autonomy requires more effort than they are capable of putting out.

After Vatican II, the Church has tended to move toward lesser dependence on the clergy — starting with upwardly mobile and more aware lay Catholics. This does not mean that the clergy is ceasing to be functional. On the contrary, priests are freed up from the administrative responsibilities that have isolated them from the people. They can now dedicate themselves more to the fundamental task of witnessing to the "real Christian tradition," which is the witness about Jesus. Their new role is to stimulate, exhort, teach, communicate, and coordinate unity.

Missiological implications. Privileged monopoly has the same deleterious effects upon BECs as on any institution or enterprise. It takes away the stimulus for creativity, energy, and inventiveness, and in the end destroys the very missionary spirit.

Parishes have never been missionary-minded, despite unfruitful attempts to make them so here and there during the twentieth century. Priests blame the people when interest in their parishes declines and they lose members. We are treated to litanies and lamentations on the sins of the world. "It is the spirit of the age, secularization, unbelief, or the indifference of the people." The hierarchy blames anticlerical propaganda, liberalism and rationalism, naturalism or Marxism, and on and on. Always it is others who are to blame. Because of this tendency to blame the world for their problems, parishes do not foster a missionary spirit. They do not see a world that needs to be called to conversion. In the Western Church, the missionary spirit was present, down through history, in the Mendicant Orders, the missionary institutes, the Jesuits, Lazarists, Redemptorists, Salesians, and others. None of these movements let the parish structures interfere with their missionary vision — nor did certain diocesan priests who were involved in industrial mission (the worker priests). The long and drawn-out struggle between the parish structures and Catholic Action also confirms this observation.

But what happens to the BECs that are set up to strengthen the parishes? More often than not they lose their missionary thrust. They do not try to grow, convert, expand, and multiply; nor do they send out missionaries. They close in upon themselves and turn into small cliques of friends who grow accustomed to thinking of themselves as "the community." And when BECs in the northeast do not grow, they blame the people: they are not interested, they are ignorant and alienated. The BECs sit back waiting for the people to come to them. If they don't come, it is the fault of the people and not of the BECs! Persons or groups that enjoy a privileged monopoly are not open to criticism. But when the *comunidades* do not try to regain their people they lose their missionary dynamism.

However, for the BECs to regain their missionary spirit, they must be free to be themselves. Yet very few *comunidades* in northeastern Brazil have any notion of what this is all about. Most of them think of themselves as "the people" — when they discuss the needs or wishes of the people, they mean themselves. They see non-BEC Catholics as "alienated," "traditional," and even incorrigible, abandoning them to their own fate. BECs show little interest in adding new members; they are self-contained, a world unto themselves. There is no dialogue with the masses; their programs reflect their own self-interests rather than the real needs of the people. Communities become monopolies when they impose and make demands upon Catholics without offering anything in return.

In contrast, what allows for the very strong missionary spirit of the pentecostals is precisely their freedom of action. No group has exclusive claim its own turf. Every community must work to win a following.

The inertia of monopoly maintains a goodly part of Catholics in a situation of passivity and of resistance to change. Too many BECs are in the hands of a handful of leaders. BECs become identified with this or that person, some of whom may be even disliked by the community membership for any number of reasons: personality, conduct, poor leadership abilities, imposition, etc. Since the only way to take part in church activities is to work through these BEC leaders, many Catholics simply opt out of the system. The so-called community writes them off and vice versa. Occasionally, dissatisfied Catholics manage to get around the monopoly by finding priests who will offer them the sacraments. This creates resentment all around.

The need for freedom to be themselves is even more acute in those *comunidades* which see themselves as popular movements, because they are more elitist. These BECs move ahead so rapidly that they lose contact with the people. Because their own internal dynamics separate them from ordinary men and women, they show no concern for the Christian development and growth of the masses. Their predetermined program absorbs all of their energies. When this happens, other communities will spring up in their place to care for the general public. If this did not happen, the people would be abandoned.

Whether the BECs follow the quasi-parish model or the elitist model, their future seems very uncertain. It will take a long time for these outmoded church models to disappear. Four centuries were necessary for the parish model to be generally accepted. A Church made up of freely-born communities may need as long to succeed. Meanwhile, the parish model should free itself up to provide a transition into the future. But little is presently being done along these lines. It is a long way between theory and practice in the BECs. The elitist *comunidades* share many of the problems of Third World elites, particularly in communicating with the masses. Because of their lack of a missionary drive they remain a minority, out of contact with the people, and show no signs whatsoever of being aware and concerned about this fact.

When communities grow old and lose their dynamism, they pull into their own shells and become incapable of opening themselves up to others. It is better to let them die a slow death and to encourage parallel communities to develop.

Conclusions. What is the reason for this lack of missionary drive — the will to expand and grow? It cannot be blamed upon some kind of "*nordestino* psychology," because evangelicals in northeastern Brazil demonstrate an extraordinary capacity for expansion and missionary drive. Besides, the Catholic Charismatic Renewal does have a missionary dynamic. Why do the BECs show less drive than the Charismatics? In my opinion it is because the *comunidades* are part of the traditional Catholic monopoly. When one feels that one has a monopoly, one waits for others to come to "us" instead of going to "them."

The Institutionalization of the Base Ecclesial Communities

BECs are stated priorities of the National Conference of Bishops of Brazil (CNBB), as well as in a number of dioceses. Officially, the *comunidades* occupy a privileged position in many local churches or parishes. Yet, despite the fact that it is often proclaimed that the parishes are based upon the BECs and function on their behalf, few of them really seem to know what they are about — nor are the dioceses willing to be any more specific. This lack of definition is causing a great deal of misunderstanding as well as concern in BECs within dioceses that have begun to change direction.

So far, the position of the BECs depends a lot on the personal charisma of certain bishops and pastoral agents who fully identify with the cause of the *comunidades*. This charismatic support, which is less than institutional, still allows the BECs to have preferential treatment, but it remains precarious. A change of bishops or vicars can throw everything off balance. At the same time, not even those dioceses in which the communities have achieved the greatest measure of identification (e.g. the Crateús diocese, which is the most identified of them all) have the BECs affected every aspect of diocesan life and structure. Parishes maintain their own activities and so do the BECs. And other dioceses sponsor a variety of programs besides the BECs.

We have been afraid of defining the BECs to avoid their becoming just another movement alongside others. But in actual fact, that is exactly what they are: just another movement. It is no good to hide the facts. It is inconceivable that the BECs might someday encompass all Catholics. The present status is, therefore, fraught with dangers. The situation is precarious, especially when we realize that the new generation of bishops will be very different from those who have supported the BECs. The *comunidades* cannot simply be banned by more conservative prelates, because they have been publicly recognized by popes and officialized by episcopal conferences. But they can be quietly ignored, while other movements step into their privileged position. But is that necessarily bad? In point of fact, the support of charismatic bishops and pastors is just another form of benevolent authoritarianism — less evident perhaps, but nonetheless present. But there will be no more paternalism when a loving father is replaced by an indifferent parent.

What, then, are the alternatives? One alternative is to go ahead and make the BECs branches of the parishes, i.e. to institutionalize the virtual parish model. This would, of course, institutionalize the authoritarian church. The other alternative is to affirm outright what the BECs really are by canon and natural law — associations of the laity that preserve all of their freedoms, including the right to make their own decisions, even while they preserve natural morality and theological orthodoxy. They could also perform a lot of the functions the clergy is increasingly delegating to the laity, such as baptisms, initiation, and marriages.

If this were to happen, the relationship of the BECs with the particular or local church would not be along the parish model. It would be more analogous to what is the case with religious associations, monastic communities, and new movements. This would require a new kind of institutionalization.[5]

WHAT WE CAN LEARN FROM PENTECOSTALS

Do the pentecostal churches have something to teach us? It is customary in the Catholic world to look down our noses at pentecostals, calling them "alienated" or "inferior." Meanwhile, they are growing overwhelmingly and at an ever increasing rate. Pentecostals can be found in every village in northeastern Brazil, even in the remotest areas. There are even cities in which the majority of the population is evangelical. Their chapels and communities multiply and their rate of growth far surpasses that of the BECs. It is as overwhelming as a tidal wave that nothing can stop. And they are conquering precisely the popular classes to which the Catholic Church has invested most of its efforts in recent decades. What are the reasons for the Pentecostal success?

But first, a clarification. I shall refer specifically to Pentecostal churches. The story of the so-called historical churches, which belong to a somewhat older protestantism, is different. Neither am I talking about the "revelation churches," which appeal to different sources of revelation than the Bible — such as Jehovah's Witnesses, Mormons (they work with the middle class, lots of resources, and trained personnel), or the Seventh Day Adventists. None of these groups has been very successful. Nor shall I discuss the so-called "mission societies" that are almost always from the United States or Scandinavia, with mission stations scattered throughout the Amazon region. They are made up essentially of foreign missionaries who do not start national churches, but maintain their foreign character. What stands out is the phenomenon of the Pentecostal churches, all of which were born in this century.

There are dozens of Pentecostal denominations in Brazil. The better known are the "Assambleia de Deus,"[6] "Congregaçao Crista do Brasil,"[7] "Brasil para Cristo,"[8] and the Church of the Foursquare Gospel, which is the only one with U.S. ties. All of these churches are led by Brazilians. They fit right into the cultural context of Brazil and even more so of the northeast. Not dependent upon foreign funding, they operate with the relatively high contributions they solicit from their members.

My evaluation of Pentecostal growth is, admittedly, subjective. It is based largely upon hypotheses that are based upon probabilities and possibilities, comparisons and differences. Such is the stuff of the social sciences, and in particular of the study of religious phenomena. But hypotheses are not to be sniffed at — better a tentative hypothesis than to stumble along in the dark without knowing where we are going. As I describe the pentecostals I shall rely on what they say about themselves, the studies of social scientists, and firsthand observations by Catholics. I shall highlight only their more obvious and incontestable characteristics, avoiding potentially tendentious interpretations.

Some Observations about Pentecostal Churches

Personal caring. What one immediately notices in any of the Pentecostal churches is the warm personal concern. At a time when the Catholic Church — alleging a paucity of priests — has reduced to almost nothing its personal attention for the vast majority of Catholics, Pentecostal caring provides a very attractive alternative for many people. An educated guess, after some spot checking, is that many conversions can be explained by the solicitous attitude of pentecostals, particularly in response to personal need. One notices this from the first moment of contact between pentecostals and persons in need. Those who seek out a Catholic parish expect to be treated more or less as in a government office. They will be told that they have come at an inopportune time, that they lack some document, that the letter should have been written differently, and so forth. The visitor is treated as a pain in the neck and a nuisance. When in need, many people do not seek out their parish for this very reason. They will forego the rites of baptism and of marriage because they are afraid of being made to feel unwelcome. A maid answers the door at a parish house, while in the churches of the *crentes* it is a *missionária*[9] who welcomes them. This accounts for the different quality of the reception. Among the "believers" a visitor is received as a brother or as a messenger from God. Such a person is already a potential convert, someone who is capable of accepting Jesus.

Personal caring stands out in house-to-house visitation. *Crentes* are looking for lost sheep, and not only in homes but also on the street, in jails, parks, hospitals, and schools — in point of fact, everywhere. They visit the sick; actually, this is the way in which the majority of people are won by the pentecostals. In contrast, sick Catholics are virtually abandoned by their church; they are not visited in hospital. But Protestants offer support, assistance, prayers, and blessings for the sick.

Fraternal community. The communities of Pentecostal believers are usually small. They make up for their feeling of isolation by reinforcing their fraternal bonds. In *crente* churches no one remains anonymous, as is the case in many Catholic churches. Every effort is made to foster human warmth and to make new members feel part of a family that has adopted them into their midst. They are truly "brothers" and "sisters." This fraternal experience is also one of the most frequently cited reasons for conversion to the Pentecostal communities.

Personal worth. This is expressed in many ways. (a) A new believer is expected to evidence an overwhelming conversion experience, with a lifelong impact, in most cases. This is the center force of a personality that has been reclaimed. Frequently the new converts come from an unstable environment. Personality deterioration is caused by migrations, unstable lifestyles, insecurity, and collective moral disintegration. (b) Conversion includes moral recovery. Believers renounce vice and turn to traditional moral values — sexual, familial, and social. They overcome the crisis of modernity by returning to tradition, with a new capacity to distinguish between right and wrong. (c) Conversion leads to intellectual improvement. Pentecostals learn how to read so that they can understand the Bible. They go to Sunday School and acquire intellectual knowledge that enhances their self-worth, so they no longer see themselves as ignorant, lazy good-for-nothings. (d) Moral and intellectual renewal makes for increased social prestige. Believers are esteemed in the workplace for their honesty, faithfulness, organization, and reliability — qualities that are also recognized and appreciated in civil and political society.

Religious expression. Pentecostal religiosity is fairly simple, but nonetheless decisive. Their services are essentially expressions of praise and thanksgiving to God, in the Spirit and accompanied by manifestations of joy. These evidences of joyfulness and praise seem to compensate for the sadness of lives that are full of trials and tribulations. Some Catholics complain that after going through an entire week of tragedy, they have to sit and listen to a chorus of sad tales at mass on Sunday. It is different for the *crentes* — one hears only hallelujahs in their churches. Such expressions of hope and of a will to live and to overcome help them triumph over suffering.

Missionary outreach. This may be the most decisive factor: every believer is a missionary. Converts all feel called to witness to their conversion. They share their faith on the streets and city squares, in homes and buses, while standing in line, in public buildings and schools — in fact, everywhere. Pentecostals do not do this out of a sense of obligation but because of an inner compulsion. Their testimony wells up inside of them and they can do no less than speak, in season and out of season. They are not worried about being a nuisance; they speak out anyhow. *Crentes* are not timid — they witness even to people who are socially a cut above them. It is as if Jesus himself were speaking through their mouths with temerity and confidence. All of these people were once Catholic. When they were Catholics they remained inert and passive, timid and withdrawn. They did not dare to speak in public. What happened to them? Did Jesus change them, as they say? Are they, indeed, inspired by the Holy Spirit?

Pastoral leadership. The central figures in Pentecostal churches are the pastors. Without them Pentecostal success cannot be explained. They are the key to the whole question. Pentecostal pastors feel very comfortable in their role. In our day, many priests feel somewhat uncomfortable — almost as if they were not fully convinced of the role that they are fulfilling. They act as if they are unsure of themselves and of their message. Pentecostal pastors have no such doubts.

Pastors are numerous and multiply amazingly. Why are there so many who are being called to the Protestant ministry and so few Catholic priestly vocations? A different approach to pastoral formation is one reason. The training of Pentecostal pastors is more summary than what priests are given. Pastors learn exactly what they will need in their ministry, and nothing more. Their training is neither critical nor philosophical, more practical than intellectual. Pentecostal pastors are never taught to doubt but rather to hold to deep convictions. Beyond this, the pastoral life is very fulfilling because it usually signifies a step upward, with at least some social prestige. Yet becoming a pastor is not beyond the capabilities of the average northeastern Brazilian. There is no need for exceptional prior training. The great majority of *nordestinos* could become pastors.

Pentecostal pastors must be missionaries. They must reach their people. But once reached, converts are free, they enjoy a great deal of autonomy. Grassroots Protestants depend very little on the dictums of their leaders. Everything is done so that the greatest possible number of young people can have pastoral experiences. Not everyone will make it, but everyone can have a try at it.

Surprisingly, some Pentecostal characteristics that at first might seem negative turn out to be positive, or at least coincide with the interests of many people.

(1) *An apocalyptic understanding of the relationship between faith and world.* For most pentecostals the world is evil and their beliefs are good. The frontiers between good and evil, between good and bad people, are clear-cut. The world is to be judged and condemned and divine judgment will not delay. Pastors preach obedience and submissive acceptance of earthly trials because salvation will be attained in the other life. It is a doctrine that separates Christians from social and political tasks. Because of this, this doctrine is rejected by the more "aware" sectors of society. It coincides in the world of the poor with an endemic and latent apocalypticism and with a generalized rejection of politics. The general perception is that politics are totally corrupt and that honest persons will not get involved in such things. Because it confirms popularized convictions, this Pentecostal view of the world must seem very appealing to many people.

(2) *The authoritarianism of pastors could be negatively interpreted.* In fact, pastors are very authoritarian — an authority that seems based more on fear than upon love. However, the people are accustomed to this leadership style because it is the only kind that they know. Poor people will also accept authoritarianism if it seems to give them certain advantages. Traditional people neither understand nor have been taught democracy. And when simple folk are given some authority they almost automatically become authoritarian, because they never learned another way.

(3) *The extreme diversity and multiplicity of churches* appears to be a scandal and an obstacle to their acceptance. But this is certainly not the case. The world of the poor is very small, so that religious communities of twenty or thirty people are sufficiently ample for them. They are not upset if their neighbors chose to live their Pentecostal faith differently. In fact, they are probably not much aware of the other groups. They have no idea of universality and catholicity in the world because they have no concept of the earth's size. Earth is what they know firsthand — their land, their shanty, Rio de Janeiro, Sao Paulo, perhaps some city or shrine they may have visited, and that is the extent of it. Strangely enough, these negative aspects do not seem to limit the Pentecostal expansion. Thirty years ago many critics were saying that protestantism would never take hold in Latin America because the people were too attached to Our Lady. Their devotion to Mary, which does not seem to be as strong as we once believed, has not hindered the conversion of grassroots Catholics to protestantism. Likewise, adherence to traditional family religion has been greatly weakened. Quite frequently, Protestant converts are able to win over their traditional parents.

A Comparison with the Catholic Church

What we Catholics also have. Some of the characteristics of pentecostals can also be found in the Catholic Church. For example, in the Base Ecclesial Communities we find a pastoral concern that is similar to that of the *crentes*. We find a community of sisters and brothers where individual persons are respected. Conversion may not be as intense as in the Protestant communities, but it is present nonetheless. BEC members can all remember the ways in which their lives were changed when they joined the *comunidade* — even though the change may not have been as spectacular as, for example, no more smoking and drinking, etc.

The problem is more a matter of quantity than of quality. Fewer baptized Catholics (between 1 and 2 percent) take active part in Base Ecclesial Communities. But for all the rest, there is not even this. For the great majority of Catholics there is only one vast desert. This leaves an open field for pentecostals, while Catholics do not multiply sufficiently to fill the vacuum. Catholic growth, when it does occur, is very slow. In many regions, the BECs are simply not growing. A seeming exception, the Catholic charismatic renewal movement with its religiosity of praise and joy, is largely limited to the middle classes and does not reach the masses.

What Catholics do not have. We do not have pastors and we lack the missionary drive of the Protestant believers. There is no lack of Protestant vocations — there are thousands upon thousands of them. In fact, the tens of thousands of pastors who have sprung up in recent years were once Catholics — Catholics with a pastoral vocation. But that vocation or calling did not find an echo in the Catholic Church. At this point we Catholics are swamped in absurdity and drowning in surrealism. Enormous investments are being made in priestly vocations, yet ordinations do not even keep up with the present level of priests, which is already absurdly low. This situation has been going on for a hundred years. With a stubbornness that is worthy of a better cause, the clergy perseveres in its blindness. When the blind lead the blind . . . , as the saying goes. And there is none so blind as they who will not see. There are, in fact, tens of thousands of Pentecostal pastoral vocations and barely dozens of priestly vocations. Are we to continue in this way for another hundred years? We will not be given the chance because it will not take much less than a century for northeastern Brazil to become entirely Protestant. We have wasted a hundred years in vain attempts; we can no longer afford the luxury of wasting the next hundred. The solution is to accept the pastors that God is sending us and to grant them their place in the Church. Are not a hundred years of stubbornness enough?

Secondly, we do not have a missionary motivation. Why is this so? It is not at all difficult to awaken this motivation among BEC animators. But they are not given the freedom of action to move ahead. Someone who feels a prisoner, hamstrung and tied, cannot be a missionary. A missionary spirit can be awakened, then slowly strangled to death. Why? The fault lies in the monopoly of the virtual parish type of BECs, which ends up stifling enthusiasm.

It is a fact that, despite the personal authoritarianism of Pentecostal pastors, there is more actual freedom to be and to act than in the Catholic Church.

Pastors feel free — they have the entire world to save, that is, to win to Jesus. BEC animators never achieve this sense of freedom and responsibility. The believers feel free to initiate a new life, to live in a new world, and to look forward to the dawn of the great day when they will witness the new heavens and the new earth.

Can this kind of experience happen in catholicism? It could if there were more freedom and more responsibility; if the old structures did not interfere, imposing criteria that are beyond the reach of the common folk. The Catholic Church is burdening the shoulders of the poor with twenty centuries of history that hinders their contact with the Gospel of Jesus.

The poor have very little opportunity to really experience the life of the people of God, because diocese and parish are right there to remind them of what the structures demand. The hierarchy can undo with one word all of the BEC plans. They are like the law of Moses that the doctors wanted to impose upon the early Christian communities. But back then the apostle Paul was around to defend the freedom of the new converts against the legalists who wished to force them into prefabricated models. Who will be the Paul today, who will raise a voice in defense of the animators and their *comunidades*? The clergy insists on maintaining control because it is afraid. Have they not yet discovered that they should really fear themselves, because, historically, only bishops and priests have caused schisms and heresies? But the clergy is fearful. The fundamental relationship between the clergy and the BECs is one of fear. Despite all of the celebrations to calm things down and set people at ease, the hierarchy and most of the priests are afraid. The fearfulness of the authorities generates fear on the part of the animators and of their communities. Fear feeds upon fear; it is a vicious circle. But the *crentes* are not afraid of anything. This is their great strength.

A Different Social Context

Pentecostals belong to a single class. Catholics belong to many social classes. The working conditions are therefore different. Pentecostals live in a small world. Their own pastors have not turned their backs on their traditional popular culture. They have learned a traditional theology, in the sense that it is neither critical nor scientific, and it does not face up to modernity. Pentecostal theology is not aware of a world view that takes modernity seriously. Pentecostals do not see themselves as makers of history, in fact, they do not have a concept of history. For this reason, their understanding of society, politics, and collective action remains medieval. Though they cannot avoid modernity, Pentecostals have yet to come to terms with it. They see the modern world as something alien. It belongs to the devil, as do politics and modern culture. In the modern world they see nothing but moral corruption and the destruction of traditional values.

This does not mean that pentecostals cannot involve themselves in social works, tasks, and struggles. Much to the contrary. They can in fact become involved in transformational politics, as has been the case in Nicaragua, Chile, and in certain regions in Brazil. But in these cases, the value of their commitment stands out at the practical level. One gets nowhere with them discussing social and revolutionary theory — they do not want to be ensnared by atheism. For engaged pentecostals, the value of social action lies in its concrete manifestations.

Whatever the case, we cannot continue to live in mutual ignorance. Pentecostal churches are poor and of the poor. A large part of the poor are already there. Their cooperation in social tasks — although the process will be long and difficult — is essential. Pentecostal pastors will always suspect that the Catholic Church is trying underhandedly to win them back by the social action route. Since they do not feel comfortable in this role, they are afraid of losing control of their congregations. This is a normal reaction on the part of religious leaders when they learn that the competition is opening up new horizons to their members. Pentecostal pastors also fear rejection by their own people as "antiquated," "redundant," or "alienated." For this reason, the road to ecumenism requires a great deal of patience.

The Catholic Church is multiclass, and has been so since the time of the Pauline churches. From the time of Constantine, however, the dominant social class also provided the dominant class within the Church. A good indication of this is that the *Ratio Studiorum* [Study Guidelines] requires that priests be trained within Western molds, and in accordance with upper-class standards. No one can become a priest without belonging culturally to the middle class. The poor occupy a subordinate position. They have been made to be receptors, not creators — molded by the Church, without being able to mold it. Only a few marginal openings have been available to the poor in Western history; the more recent examples are John XXIII and Medellín. These are prophetic signs — but they are the exceptions, not the rule. The day after the 31 August 1988 death of Leonidas Proaño (the activist bishop of Riobamba, Ecuador), a fellow bishop commented: it is time to begin to *deproañise* the church. Actually, the Ecuadorian church had never been *proañized,* but whenever a prophet dies, the system moves quickly to reestablish equilibrium.

There will always be the spontaneous and unconscious tendency in a multiclass church to keep the poor where they are — forgotten and on the periphery. It is their allotted role to be forgotten — not out of any ecclesiastical ill will, but because the rich speak louder and occupy every space in the Church.

The challenge that we face, then, is how to set aside room in the Church for the poor. How can we value their culture and allow them to be the church without forcing them to remain at the tail end of the church of the powerful? If the BECs are not protected by free structures, if their legitimate autonomy is not recognized — in the same way that religious orders, bourgeois movements, and the great Catholic multinationals are recognized — they simply will be absorbed into the system without a complaint or a murmur.

Being a multiclass church is not entirely a disadvantage for the BECs. Thanks to the pastoral agents who come from the upper class, the poor learn how to move around in modern society. They learn to understand what is taking place and to use available tools such as how to play politics and how to play off the social forces. It is, of course, a difficult initiation for them, which is why the pastoral agents are undertaking these tasks. Social and political leadership has not reached down to the poor in the northeast. But in a pluralistic church, the poor have the privilege of communicating with other social levels. This is often the only way in which the poor have access to the modern world — that global society in which they live without even being aware of it.

Some people think that they can hasten this evolution. They would like to force the poor to become involved in social and political movements. It may perhaps be not too difficult to convince the minuscule *comunidades*. But how are they to convince the masses of the poor? Our experience in recent years shows how much the BECs can cut themselves off from the majority of people when they get ahead of themselves and accept commitments that the people do not understand.

At such times, pastoral agents become irritated because the poor cannot understand what is best for them, choosing to remain on the side of their oppressors. They consider the poor to be "alienated" because they vote for the most reactionary candidates and support the most demagogical leaders. But, in fact, the poor are interpreting the situation within their own frame of reference, using the knowledge that they have of their social milieu. They do not understand history as a society in transformation, because in their own world everything remains the same and, after all is said and done, things revert to where they were at the beginning. If this is the case, we cannot introduce people into the modern world merely with high-sounding words, discourses, and reason. The poor will gain confidence only after they have experienced the value and possibilities in a particular way of doing. Pastoral agents should not think that they can force their own awareness upon the traditional cultural consciousness of the masses. To destroy all of our bridges to the masses can be counterproductive and dangerous; it amounts to leaving them entirely in the hands of demagogues. A Base Community, however committed, that does not have the confidence of the masses will not make an impact on the people and their history. This is a conclusion that we could only have arrived at after reflecting upon the lessons we have learned from the past thirty years of Latin American history.

It is yet possible for the masses of poor to become actors some day in their own history, through the mediation of the Base Ecclesial Communities. But this possibility is conditioned upon the BECs achieving sufficient freedom and autonomy within the Catholic Church. The alternatives to this ideal are either Pentecostal Christianity or, ten years from now, to sit back and watch the Lumen 2000[10] television programs! This could very well be where the poor might find themselves in a few years if the only other alternative — to set the BECs free — does not gain enough strength to become an historical reality.

NOTES

1. See John Eagleson and Philip Scharper, *Puebla and Beyond* (Maryknoll: Orbis, 1979).

2. Comblin was apparently one of those people. Cp. Cook (1985), p. 102. Cp. C. Boff (1987a).

3. *Editor's note:* Sociologically speaking, the BECs comprise a movement. However, their spokespersons are at great pains to insist that the BECs are not a *movimento.* This is probably because the term in Brazil has come to be particularly associated with mass political movements.

4. The BECs were not initiated by Vatican II but evolved as spontaneous lay movements. But the Council did affirm and encourage the right of the laity to initiate movements for the good of the church and humanity (*Lumen Gentium,* 37, 3; *Gaudium et Spes,* 55, *Apostolicam Actuositatem,* 19, 4). This is not privilege granted to the laity but their natural right, except in cases of schism or heresy (*Dignitatis humanae,* 4).

5. *Editor's note:* At this point, the original article enters upon a lengthy discussion of possible new forms of BEC coordination, support, leadership training, attributions, and relationships (both internal and external) to institutional catholicism.

6. *Editor's note:* The "Assembly of God," the largest Pentecostal body, is an idigenous Brazilian church that originated, in 1910, from the teaching of two Swedish-American evangelists. A loose confederation of large autonomous "mother churches" with "daughters" spread far and wide, this movement is virtually as old as the U.S.-based Assemblies of God with which it maintains loose fraternal ties.

7. *Editor's note:* The "Christian Congregation of Brazil" was founded in the early 1900s by Luigi Francescon, an Italian Waldensian by birth. The second largest Pentecostal denomination, the *Congregaçao,* has always maintained itself separate from other churches, including Pentecostals.

8. *Editor's note:* The third largest group, "Brazil for Christ," is the most ccumenical of the large Pentecostal churches. Founded in 1950 by Manoel de Mello, it boasts a "mother church" in the heart of Sao Paulo that can seat 26,000 people.

9. *Editor's note: Crentes* are Protestant "believers" and *missionários* are the fulltime church workers in Brazil.

10. *Editor's note:* Lumen 2000 is the "New Evangelism" program that the Catholic Church has launched to recover the faithful in Latin America. With considerable irony, Comblin is suggesting that the Catholic Church might have to resort to the "electronic church" to win over the masses.

18

Brazil: Church Growth, Parachurch Agencies, and Politics

Paul Freston

The parachurch agencies the author describes "fulfil the same role as Catholic entities that transcend parochial and diocesan boundaries." They "are typical of the denominational situation where there are no 'official churches,' and make it possible to bring together members of various denominations." Freston argues that "simplistic and polemical approaches have made it difficult to understand the relationship between Protestantism and Brazilian culture and politics." The author, a Briton who is married to a Brazilian, has lived in Brazil since 1976. He worked for a decade with the Aliança Bíblica Universitária, and is currently a research sociologist. He has degrees in Latin American studies, theology, and sociology from Cambridge and Liverpool Universities, Regent's College (Vancouver), and a Ph.D. from the University of Campinas. He is the author of books and articles in Portuguese and of a chapter on Brazilian Protestant Politics in *Rethinking Protestantism in Latin America* (Burnett and Stoll 1993). This chapter from his dissertation on Protestants in Politics in Brazil is used with permission.

Two things have characterized protestantism in Brazil in recent years: enormous numerical growth and an unprecedented penetration of the public sphere. Even at a conservative estimate, there are now more than 20 million Protestants. The Pentecostal and Charismatic segment (perhaps 70 percent) has shown an impressive ability to adapt culturally, forming a genuinely popular protestantism. Since the return to democracy in the mid-1980s, there has been unprecedented Protestant political activity, allied to a penetration of the mass media that is probably second in the world after the United States.

Aspects of this numerical growth and public visibility have created controversy, in part about the role of organizations that can be variously described as "parachurch," "interdenominational," or "ecumenical." Often divided manichaeistically by analysts into "fundamentalist" and "ecumenical," there is no doubting the ideological importance of these parachurch organizations. I shall argue, however, that simplistic and polemical approaches have made it difficult to understand the relationship between protestantism and Brazilian culture and politics. The traditional view of parachurch organizations is well stated by Mendonça: "Fundamentalism is not spread ecclesiastically, through the churches . . . but ideologically, through mainly foreign parachurch institutions. The rare national ones are imitations that sail in the same waters" (Mendonça and Velásques 1980, p. 142). This situation arose when the churches, tired of the principle of "he who pays the piper calls the tune," began to create problems for missionaries, obliging missions to change their strategy and work through parachurch agencies (Mendonça 1989, 50). The latter come "always from the theological far right" (ibid.) and act in total "independence of the official churches" (Bittencourt 1989, 29).

In fact, however, reality is more complex. Parachurch agencies are typical of the denominational situation where there are no "official churches," and make it possible to bring together members of various denominations. In the religious division of labor, they fulfil the same role as Catholic entities that transcend parochial and diocesan boundaries, such as religious orders, the lay movements of Catholic Action, specialized Pastoral groups (e.g. for students or for peasants) and the so-called "new movements" such as the Charismatic Renewal. This list of Catholic groups alerts us to the ideological diversity of the phenomenon, and it would be strange if the Protestant equivalents did not have the same potential for diversity. But there are two differences. On the one hand, Protestant parachurch agencies find it easier to survive, since they cannot be closed down by ecclesiastical hierarchies. On the other hand, Protestant segmentation makes it harder for them to have a reforming influence on the whole Protestant world in the way that Catholic Action movements did on Brazilian catholicism in the 1950s and 1960s. Protestant parachurch groups in Brazil are, in fact, quite varied, and their political influence has increased at all points of the political spectrum. There are various reasons why. One has already been mentioned: they can be shortcuts between the American religious right and Brazilian grassroots protestantism. But we must avoid reductionist conspiracy theories; some parachurch entities play in very different political teams.

Conservative foreign parachurch groups multiplied in Brazil from the 1950s onwards, especially in the areas of literature, Bible institutes, and camps for youth and pastors. There were several reasons for this. The United States' postwar international role, economic prosperity, and church growth stimulated the export of religious manpower. After the closing of China in 1949, a large part of this flow was redirected to Latin America. But, on the Brazilian side, the churches were reaching organizational maturity, Protestant competition was fierce, and the country was passing through a nationalistic phase. No foreign denomination of reasonable size has managed to establish itself in Brazil in the last forty years. The parachurch model allowed missions to offer "services" without the approval of national church leaders. With their financial clout, they could bypass the churches and often entice away the most promising nationals with higher salaries. The relationship of foreign parachurch agencies to the American New Christian Right of the 1980s is well described by David Stoll as a series of concentric circles:

At the core were the groups promoting the . . . contra war in Nicaragua. . . . In the second ring were agencies which refrained from explicit support for the contras but identified so closely with North American interests that they made evangelism sound like a geopolitical insurance policy for North American churchgoers. . . . In the third ring were agencies that, like the first two, had definite ties to the religious right... but [who labored] to maintain an apolitical front. . . . In the fourth ring were equally conservative organizations who, owing to their long experience in Latin America, . . . [displayed] discomfort with the religious right. . . . In the fifth ring were those groups most likely to show signs of opposing the religious right. (Stoll 1990, 156-157)

In the Brazilian case, one can place influential American parachurch agencies like Open Doors in Stoll's second ring; Word of Life and Campus Crusade in the third ring; Youth for Christ and OC Ministries in the fourth; and World Vision in the fifth.

The parachurch model, however, is very flexible and can serve diverse ends. If it helped foreign organizations to bypass the congested ecclesiastical field of the 1950s, it also helped some Brazilians to avoid total exclusion from the Protestant camp in the 1960s.

THE ECUMENICAL PARACHURCH AGENCIES

The Ecumenical Movement of the 1960s and 1970s [in Brazil] looked toward society and politics. . . . It was restricted to a small group of people . . . [in] a few autonomous organizations that survived on foreign financing. . . . [It constituted] a tribe. . . . The Movement was founded on politics . . . but was not very given to personal piety.
Edin Abumanssur (1991, 8-9, 58, 85)

In the 1950s and 1960s the historical (i.e. non-Pentecostal) Protestant churches suffered a severe crisis in Brazil. Their rural mentality was unable to respond adequately to the impact of urbanization and new intellectual perspectives on their young middle-class members. A new lay leadership began to question ecclesiastical structures and to voice social concern.

The initial theological inspiration for this questioning came from neo-orthodoxy. The main figure in its (belated) introduction to Brazil was the American missionary Richard Shaull. In the Presbyterian Seminary of Campinas (where he sent his students to work in factories during their vacations) and in the Union of Christian Students of Brazil (UCEB), Shaull had a deep influence on a generation of young Protestants after 1952. The UCEB gradually abandoned its previous conversionist stance in favor of political action as the means to transform society. Shaull was also influential in the Sector for Social Responsibility of the Evangelical Confederation of Brazil.

In the 1960s this young Protestant intelligentsia was decimated by political and ecclesiastical repression. Even before the military coup of 1964, the main historical churches like the Presbyterians had begun to crack down. Some of the victims managed to regroup by founding parachurch organizations such as CEDI

(Ecumenical Center for Documentation and Information), ISER (Institute for the Study of Religion) and CESE (Ecumenical Service Coordination).[1]

CEDI illustrates the strategies adopted. The World Council of Churches (WCC) began to support these groups, making it easier to obtain international funding. CEDI is now a diversified institution, divided into "programs" (trade unions, Indians, ecology, and even "Protestant pastoral service").[2] Funds come mainly from Dutch, German, and British sources. The overtly religious side of the work, although limited, is useful for finding sponsors with the approval of the WCC. As the potential sources are limited in number, a "climate of subtle competition" is created between the organizations of the Ecumenical Movement (Abumanssur 1991, 67).

In this context, the use of the term "ecumenical" has two functions: abroad it helps in fund-raising, and at home it is a weapon in religious polemic. It is applied to these groups' own activities, whatever the degree of religious representativeness and the criteria of inclusion, and is denied to the activities of other groups. The first sociologist to study this phenomenon (being himself a product of it)[3] writes with irony: "The Ecumenical Movement ... [is] a homogeneous group of Christians, ... ["Ecumenism" has become] a tribal term ... which defines the 'insiders'" (Abumanssur 1991, 58).

Paradoxically, this "tribe" gave to ecumenism the widest possible meaning: the unity of the churches would result from the political transformation of society and not vice versa. "Religious discourse was just a working tool to explain reality" (ibid.). Following the theological fashion, the "tribe" spoke of Marxism, secularization, and the autonomy of the world. This discourse obviously distanced the "tribe" from the churches, but also reflected the estrangement that already existed.

The Movement was "more in tune with the position of the churches in the First World" (ibid., 51); in Brazilian protestantism they were outsiders and their political concept of ecumenism was the only one in which they could find a role for themselves. The distance from the churches was reinforced by the fierce ecclesiastical repression, the ideological polarization of the country after the military coup, and the hopes of an imminent revolution. Even today, the ecumenical parachurch groups have been unable to close the gap with the Protestant masses of the country. Their elitist attitude is demonstrated in a letter sent by several leading ecumenical figures to a major daily newspaper in 1989. Repudiating the generic way in which the newspaper usually referred to the action of "the Protestants" in the presidential election campaign, they affirm that "Protestant pastors should be people who have done a university level course and been ordained. Anything short of this is a downgrading and insult to pastoral dignity.... We represent many thousands of pastors, people who are officially pastors."[4]

On this basis, the popular classes would be forever unable to produce their own religious leaders. It is an attitude that condemns ecumenism to being conservative (by freezing the current balance of power in the religious field) and elitist (by using socially exclusive criteria of legitimation).

In the mid-1970s, the "ecumenical tribe" attempted to work more within the churches. The change in strategy was motivated by events in the Catholic Church after the Latin American Bishops' Conference in Medellín in 1968, which showed that churches could, after all, be reformed; and also by the coup d'état in Chile, which made radical social change seem a more distant prospect. But the attempt came to very little (ibid., 133).

To understand this failure, we need the help of the sociology of theological currents. A phrase by Richard Shaull serves as an introduction to the problem: "I could never identify with those who treat the faith as a religion of salvation: salvation from sin and guilt" (Shaull 1983, 48). This position not only creates a huge distance from the mass of Brazilian Protestants, but it also creates a sociological instability for its very defenders. As sociologist of religion Steve Bruce says, "the church in the modern industrial society has superior credentials in only one area: the mediation of the supernatural. . . . When churches move away from [that], they face competition from other organizations which are taken to be better qualified and which, having narrower goals, are seen as more likely to succeed" (Bruce 1990, 145).

The crisis of the Ecumenical Movement in Brazil was not only external (political and ecclesiastical repression) but also internal. By the 1960s, neo-orthodoxy was declining in the face of secularizing neoliberal theology. Student movements gave a dramatic example of the sociological problems. Although the coup d'état undoubtedly quickened the demise of the UCEB in Brazil (it folded up in 1966), most of its sister movements abroad (in the World Student Christian Federation) went into a severe crisis in the 1960s, regardless of political coups or ecclesiastical purges.

Bruce describes the sociological problem of theological liberalism:

> [It is] attractive to doubters on the fringes of the churches . . . [but has] no appeal to the thoroughly unchurched. . . . No large popular movement has converted non-believers to a liberal protestantism. . . . It was their own personal certainty [of the first generation of liberals] which made it possible for them [to abandon] creeds. . . . [They could] engage in liberal and ecumenical experiment because their personal past had been so firmly orthodox that it gave protection against anomie. . . . What no one involved envisaged was the wholesale capitulation to the agenda of the secular world which occurred in the 1960s. (Ibid., 109, 111, 113)

Liberalism, says Bruce, is organizationally precarious. As a diffuse belief system it lacks a strong "product-profile," and therefore suffers boundary-maintenance problems. Raising funds becomes difficult because a clearer identification of objectives always alienates a segment of its membership (ibid., 131-135). The British sister movement of the UCEB, the Student Christian Movement, exemplifies all this:

> The SCM's response to a decline of student interest in Christianity was to identify those things which students were interested in and present Christianity as being similar and complementary. . . . [But] the danger of building bridges . . . is that bridges can carry traffic in both directions. . . . The membership of the Edinburgh SCM commune house went off en masse to join the local Trotskyite party: a highly rational response to the then fashionable SCM claim that Marxism was really Christian. (Ibid., 144-145)

The Brazilian Ecumenical Movement sought in politics an integration point for its diffuse religious belief system. But at the end of the 1980s this model was dealt a blow by international changes: the fall of the socialist bloc and the electoral defeat of the Sandinistas. The religious situation also became less favorable. During the Brazilian military dictatorship (1964-1985), ecumenical Protestants had been given a warm welcome by the Brazilian Catholic Church, which was acting as a protective umbrella for many groups affected by political repression. In the late 1980s, however, the Catholic Church was no longer so receptive, partly because redemocratization had led it to adopt a different political stance, and partly because the Vatican was tightening its opposition to progressive currents. The ecumenical Protestants were left in an ever-tighter squeeze between the expanding "sects" (i.e. the Pentecostal groups) on the one hand and the increasingly conservative Catholic Church on the other.

The ecclesiastical purges of the 1960s and the failure of the Brazilian Ecumenical Movement had several religious and political consequences. The historical denominations (Presbyterian, Baptist, Methodist) are no longer so important either numerically or intellectually. Rapid Pentecostal growth has thus occurred in the context of feeble Protestant intellectual leadership and absence of any unifying pan-Protestant entity.

Despite the limitations mentioned, the ecumenical parachurch groups have made important contributions to Brazilian protestantism. They kept open a space for opposition to the military regime and have made notable contributions to the sociology of protestantism. There has also been some serious theological and biblical production, although this has come more from people associated with the ecclesiastical ecumenism of the 1980s. Today in Brazil there are two types of pan-Christian (as opposed to purely pan-Protestant) ecumenism: the political ecumenism of the parachurch groups, and the ecclesiastical ecumenism of CONIC.

THE NATIONAL COUNCIL OF CHRISTIAN CHURCHES (CONIC)

> *Would ecumenism be possible if all the churches were not in*
> *the process of realizing that they are in the same boat?. . .*
> *The hope for unity arises out of a common distress.*
> Quoted by Roger Mehl (1970, 195)

The National Council of Christian Churches (CONIC) was founded in 1982. It has fraternal relations with the WCC, whose credal declaration it has adopted. But despite financing from the WCC and from other foreign agencies, as well as from the member churches, CONIC is not very active. The location of the head office in the extreme southern city of Porto Alegre reflects its composition. The member churches are Catholic, Lutheran, Methodist, Episcopal, United Presbyterian, Christian Reformed (of Hungarian immigrant origin), and Syrian Orthodox. Protestant membership in CONIC is weak, the only large church to join being the Lutheran (which is composed almost exclusively of the descendants of German immigrants in the South). Of the historical churches of missionary origin, only the moderately-sized Methodist Church has affiliated. The other Protestant members are all tiny. No Pentecostal group (70 percent of Brazilian protestantism) has joined.

As a National Council of Churches, CONIC's activities are limited. Its composition leaves it excessively dependent on the Catholic Church, where ecumenism is going through hard times. Although useful, CONIC is hardly vital to the Catholic hierarchy's objectives. It is not difficult to see why ecclesiastical ecumenism is so restricted in Brazil. The quote from Mehl (above) gives us the clue. In Brazil, secularization is limited and all the churches are definitely not in the same boat. On the contrary, many Protestant churches are growing rapidly and are confident. But CONIC is structured around two Christendom churches (the Catholic, for the vast majority of the population, and the Lutheran, for the people of German descent in the South), both of which are losing their members rapidly. This imbalance leaves CONIC heavily dependent on Catholic strategy.

If ecclesiastical ecumenism in Europe is an attempt to achieve economies of scale in the face of the common enemy of secularism, in Brazil it has the aspect rather of an attempt by the older (stagnant or declining) churches to form a cartel against the advance of the "sects." This attempt, however, has not yielded the desired results. Therefore, while maintaining its ecumenical contacts, the Catholic hierarchy has developed an ambiguous strategy based on the distinction between "churches or ecclesial communities" (with whom one practices ecumenism) and "sects" (who are attacked as being foreign-financed "invaders" and "exploiters of the people"). In this way, the Catholic Church manages to live, so to speak, on both sides of Vatican II. The current president of CONIC recommended that his pastoral agents read the book *Devils Come Down from the North*, an extreme example of the "invasion of the sects" conspiracy theory (Della Cava and Montero 1991, 127). The result of all this can only be a crippled ecumenism that denies the very legitimacy of the enormous segment of Brazilian Christianity constituted by the Pentecostals.[5]

Having looked at the characteristics and limitations of the two types of pan-Christian ecumenism in Brazil (the political and the ecclesiastical), it is time to examine other Brazilian parachurch groups that have influenced Protestant participation in politics.

EVANGELICAL PARACHURCH AGENCIES

*A new current of theologically but not politically conservative
evangelicals has emerged [in Latin America] since the mid 1970s.*
David Stoll (1990, 5)

*The growing concern to break with . . . theological dualism and a
conservative ideology . . . [is producing] an "evangelical social
ethic" which [instead of Liberation Theology] proposes an
alternative linked to classic Biblical evangelical theology.*
José Míguez Bonino, former president of the WCC (1977, 173)

The historical denominations like the Presbyterian Church of Brazil have, since the 1960s, lost their intellectual leadership and capacity to be at the forefront of reform movements. This has increased the theological and political importance of parachurch groups that are neither "ecumenical" nor "fundamentalist." Usually led by members of historical churches but with a certain degree of penetration in the Pentecostal world, they represent the main channel by which perspectives from historical protestantism influence pentecostalism and vice versa.

The study of these Evangelicals[6] has been made difficult by the manichaeistic typologies of some analysts who divide Latin American Protestants into "fundamentalists" and "ecumenicals."[7] Any current that, at first sight, does not seem to fit this dichotomy is treated either as a disguised fundamentalism or as an unstable transitional stage. Virtually the only more nuanced sociological studies of Latin American Evangelicals are those by Fernandes (1981) and Stoll (1990). Even so, Fernandes speaks of "left-wing fundamentalism," under the mistaken impression that the people concerned refer to themselves as fundamentalists. In fact, they see themselves as heirs of a different tradition.

Contrary to Velasques's statement that "the Evangelical movement originates at the same time and in the same circumstances as fundamentalism" (Mendonça and Velasques 1980, 150), evangelicalism is in fact a much older and broader tradition. In the words of a British historian, "evangelical religion is a popular Protestant movement that has existed in Britain since the 1730s" (Bebbington 1989, 1). Despite many changes over time, Bebbington finds four qualities that allow us to speak of an Evangelical tradition: conversionism, activism (in evangelism), biblicism, and crucicentrism (ibid., 3). Biblicism means simply a "particular regard for the Bible" and should not be conflated with inerrancy. In British evangelicalism, says Bebbington, neither belief in inerrancy nor dispensationalist eschatology (with its literalistic reading of Bible prophecies) ever came to predominate.

Bebbington also shows that the cultural affiliation of evangelicalism is with the Enlightenment and with Locke's doctrine of the validity of human experience.

> Consequently, there was in the eighteenth century and long into the nineteenth no hint of a clash between evangelical religion and science. . . . [In the second half of the nineteenth century] evangelicals rapidly learned to live with Darwin's discoveries. Theologians took account of it in their schemes; [Evangelical] scientists treated it as an assumption in their work. (Ibid., 57, 207)

Needless to say, the fundamentalism that emerged in America in the early twentieth century has different cultural affiliations. As Marsden says, "fundamentalists were evangelicals . . . who in the twentieth century militantly opposed both modernism in theology and the cultural changes that modernism endorsed" (1980, 4).

Fundamentalism as a militant defense of a cultural tradition has no basis in Brazilian protestantism. Likewise, the militant rational defense of a concept of biblical inerrancy has little appeal among Brazilian Pentecostals. The majority of these are fundamentalists in a naive and unreflective way: they agree with the fundamentalist creed when it is explained to them, but give it little importance.

What matters is not whether the biblical miracles happened as reported, but whether the same miracles happen today. Precise doctrinal definitions are much less important than the dynamic communication of a strongly supernaturalistic message. Besides, Brazilian Pentecostals are not on the defensive; they have no nostalgia for a glorious past, but the hope of conquering the country in the not too distant future. Their naive fundamentalism, encouraged by the literalistic reading of the Bible that dispensationalist eschatology requires, is functional for this expansion. As Steve Bruce points out, fundamentalism is a very democratic philosophy, being a critique of society's intellectual hierarchy and of theologians as the snobbish defenders of a new priestcraft (1989, 23).

The point of this digression into worldwide currents within protestantism is to show that a large part of the sociology of Latin American protestantism has used "fundamentalism" in an elastic and sometimes polemical way, ignoring the fact that there is a whole theologically conservative tradition that cannot be equated with it. It is older and broader,[8] and has a different relationship to culture.

Worldwide evangelicalism has gone through changes since the 1960s, principally with regard to social and political questions. It has come to revalue the Evangelical tradition of the nineteenth century in which personal evangelism and support for social reforms were not seen as mutually exclusive (Bruce 1990, 103). Most importantly, sociopolitical concerns received the green light from the Lausanne Covenant of 1974. This major congress in Switzerland was organized by the Billy Graham Association but took turns that went beyond the intentions of its American idealizers. A leading Brazilian Evangelical theologian describes what happened.

> By speaking of "socio-political involvement," Lausanne placed itself in tune with a sort of British vein of evangelicalism which . . . had never gone fundamentalist. . . . And by speaking of social justice and against "every form of alienation, oppression and discrimination," Lausanne revealed the significant presence of a Third World evangelicalism. (Steuernagel 1990, 7)

Latin American Evangelicals Rene Padilla and Samuel Escobar had an important role in the Lausanne Covenant. But the task of interpreting it became a battlefield. There is a parallel here with the Catholic Church after Vatican II. Like the Vatican Council, Lausanne represented an opening up to the modern world. It had great symbolic importance in legitimizing certain concerns as Evangelical. It broadened evangelicalism's frontiers and influenced Brazilian protestantism. But in many ways the Brazilian trajectory is the opposite of that of the worldwide Lausanne movement. At the international level, conservative American groups regained the ascendancy on social questions during the 1980s. This turn to the right parallels that of the Catholic Church under Pope John Paul II. The Brazilian Evangelical theologian quoted above criticizes the "liberal and idealistic/individualistic ideology" of the current Lausanne leadership and its "unwillingness to let its agenda be co-determined by the poor South of the world" (Steuernagel 1990, 13).

Latin American Evangelicals are linked to the renewal of world evangelicalism, especially in the sociopolitical arena. Just as, in the Catholic world, Liberation

Theology innovated in the only Christian continent of the Third World, so also in theologically conservative protestantism the nearness to poverty and oppression and the influence of Liberation Theology led some to take up positions that were not on the horizons of First World Evangelicals. After the conflicts of the 1960s, a new Evangelical leadership slowly developed in the 1970s and 1980s, heavily influenced by a few parachurch groups. In the late 1980s, as a subproduct of this trend, an Evangelical Progressive Movement emerged in politics.

The self-image of the Evangelicals is expressed in the words of Robinson Cavalcanti, leader of the Evangelicals who supported the Workers' Party candidate, Lula, for president in 1989, and now one of the key figures in the Evangelical Progressive Movement:

> Pressured on the one hand by the fundamentalist tradition, with its one-sided verticalism, and on the other hand by the liberal and liberationist tradition, with its one-sided horizontalism, we [Evangelicals] represent a commitment to sound doctrine and godliness, a commitment to those who suffer and a struggle against unjust structures. (Cavalcanti 1990, 35)

This is a recipe that permits greater penetration of the Pentecostal world than that of the Ecumenical Movement. The key is the epistemological unity of the Evangelicals with all Pentecostals, with regard to the status of the Bible as the "single unchanging source of authoritative salvational knowledge" (Bruce 1990, 156). Hans Tennekes's conclusion to his sociological study of Chilean pentecostalism is instructive.

> Whoever does not speak with enthusiasm . . . of salvation through the blood of Christ and does not have a clear conviction of the will of God in his personal life, is a person who can say nothing to the Pentecostals. . . . In order for the Pentecostal movement . . . to contribute its enormous revolutionary potential to the process of transforming Chilean society, there must be people who, while adopting a very orthodox view of God and man, are ready to proclaim the importance of not leaving the world as it is. (Tennekes 1985, 108)

When we analyze the trajectory of those Latin American Evangelicals who influenced the Lausanne Covenant, and of many Brazilian Evangelical leaders, two parachurch groups are frequently in evidence: the Latin American Theological Fraternity (FTL) and the International Fellowship of Evangelical Students (IFES), whose movement in Brazil is known as the Aliança Bíblica Universitária (ABU). Open to the contribution of the social sciences, these two organizations exemplify the way in which some parachurch groups have been focal points for the integration of historical protestantism into Brazilian culture.

The ABU, which began in 1957, was initially a theologically and politically more conservative alternative to the UCEB. When the latter folded up in 1966, the ABU was left alone in the student field. In the 1970s, and especially after 1974 when the military regime initiated its slow process of opening up, the ABU began to put more emphasis on sociopolitical involvement. In part, this was due to the stimulus of the sister movements in IFES in Latin America, and was facilitated by the fact that there was no longer any need to distinguish itself from a liberal competitor such as UCEB. While maintaining internal political pluralism, ABU leaned to the left, filling the gap left in Protestant ranks after the purges of the 1960s. The first repercussion in Brazil of the Lausanne Covenant and its emphasis on holistic mission (i.e. "the whole gospel to the whole person") was in an ABU congress in 1976, after which various social projects in slums and poor rural areas were started by student and professional groups.

Since there was no longer any liberal Protestant student movement, the Evangelical identity of the ABU was challenged in moments of political effervescence in the universities (1968-70 and 1982-85) by some participants who wished it to occupy the theological vacuum. But ABU had a more clearly defined theological position than the UCEB had had, and was also helped by its international affiliation to IFES. The internal battles were therefore won by the more theologically conservative elements, with a temporary retreat from sociopolitical questions, especially in 1986-87.

At its height in the early 1980s, ABU had over two thousand participants in some sixty cities.[9] Today, several ex-members are in the forefront of Protestant political involvement. There is a notable ideological dispersion (the center-right Liberal Party in Paraíba state was founded by ex-ABU people), but the majority are on the left and center-left. Cavalcanti, leader of the Evangelical Pro-Lula Movement in 1989 (supporting the leftist Workers' Party candidate) had been a student leader and then a staffworker of ABU. The leader of the Workers' Party caucus in the Federal District legislature had the same trajectory. He says ABU "gave me a questioning faith, a biblical basis for identification with the marginalized, and contact with authors who emphasized the prophetic dimension of the church."

Why was ABU able to follow a course that was different from the stereotype of a "conservative parachurch agency"? In the first place, because the IFES, to which ABU is affiliated, is a conglomerate of autonomous national movements and not a mission "multinational." The movements are united by a common basis of faith, and not a uniform methodology. This has allowed the national movements to be spearheads of theological contextualization in Latin America.[10] In the second place, the style of work is low-key, avoiding large expenses and consequent economic dependence. Resources come mostly from former participants and other sympathizers within the country, allowing relative freedom to define emphases.

Thirdly, each local student group is autonomous in planning its activities. This emphasis on student initiative means that the intellectual ferment of the university world makes itself felt, to some extent, within the movement.

Lastly, the international contacts are diversified. North American influence (through personnel and literature) is smaller than the British influence. In fact, the ethos of IFES is historically European; the first movements arose there (Cambridge, 1877; Norway and other Protestant countries, early twentieth century), whereas the North American movement only dates from 1940. Other influences on the ABU have come from Continental Europe and, especially, from Spanish-speaking Latin America.[11]

The history of the ABU in Brazil shows that a theologically conservative movement tends to withdraw from sociopolitical questions when it competes with a theologically liberal alternative. But when the liberal camp is inoperative, the theologically conservative movement may come to incorporate these questions, maintaining an internal political pluralism that stretches largely from the center to the non-Marxist left. However, as soon as it feels theologically threatened from within, there occurs a new sociopolitical retreat, until the theological identity is once more guaranteed. This illustrates how internal competition in the religious world can influence the positions adopted in the political field.

The case of the ABU also exemplifies the way in which an organization that does not define its identity in expressly political terms can have a substantial political influence within the Protestant world. This contrasts with the Ecumenical Movement, which defined itself in overtly political terms (Abumanssur 1991, 85) but was not actually very successful in producing Protestants with a left-wing political involvement. A former leader once remarked that only a handful of the fifty or so people with whom he began some years ago are still in the church. On the other hand, a group like ABU, which does not include a definite political stance as part of its basic identity but whose political orientation comes as part of a package of religious teaching, seems able to produce, in the middle run, a greater political effect within protestantism, enjoying wider acceptance and producing people who are aware of the religious specificity of their worldview. This last item is important, as it frees a segment of conservative protestantism from liberalism's difficulty of defining agendas and keeping members.

Another key parachurch group in the career of many leading Brazilian Evangelicals is the Latin American Theological Fraternity (FTL), most of whose founders were products of the IFES movements. The FTL was founded in 1970 as, at one and the same time, an alternative to ISAL (Church and Society in Latin America) — a proto-Liberationist Protestant theological movement (Bastian 1984, 57) and an alternative to American-imposed theologies and agendas (Smith 1983, 11). Its intention was to develop a theology that would be Latin American and also "biblical," i.e., different from Liberation Theology.

> Like liberation theologians, FTL's members defined sin in social as well as individual terms. . . . They recognized that . . . one's reading of the Bible was shaped by history and culture. . . . But they were also critical of Liberation Theology. . . . Instead of "liberation" as a paradigm, the Fraternity chose another term: "contextualization." (Stoll 1990, 132)

The FTL was characterized by European influence (where many of the leaders had studied) and by the presence of members with training in the social sciences. Breaking with pietist tradition, questions of social structure were incorporated in theological reflection via the biblical theme of the "powers." The themes of the first meetings (hermeneutics, the Kingdom of God, social ethics) are indicative of the opposition to dispensationalist eschatology[12] and to the fundamentalist use of the Bible.

All this had implications for funding. The inclusion of thinkers connected to the WCC, such as José Míguez Bonino, "signaled a decision to break away from

North Atlantic sources of funds that would not tolerate [such] fellowship" (Smith 1983, 29). In the 1970s, some funding came from a foundation created by a Greek-American millionaire[13]; after the latter's death, the widow channeled donations to more fundamentalistic groups. Other important sources of funding for FTL have been European churches and organizations (some of which also fund the Brazilian ecumenical parachurch groups) and World Vision.

The importance of the FTL in Latin American protestantism can be gauged by the congress it convoked in 1992, attended by more than a thousand people from all points of the theological spectrum, and which included the first dialogue ever held between the two entities supposedly representative of Protestant churches in Latin America.[14]

In the 1980s, the FTL came into growing conflict with the leaders of the Lausanne Movement regarding Christian mission and its sociopolitical implications. One can see a parallel with the conflict in the Catholic Church between the Vatican and the ecclesiological line of people like Leonardo Boff: i.e. "whether a culturally polycentric Christianity is really possible" (Cox 1988, 138). This is related to the rise of a worldwide church and the need to make theology less a monopoly of the rich North. In both cases (in the view of the Latin American dissidents), the work of *aggiornamento* (Vatican II, the Lausanne Covenant) is being silently undone by the very curias (Roman and Californian) who are supposed to be its guardians.

The strength of the FTL is also its main limitation: an agenda closely tied to the church. It "was not so convinced about acting prophetically in the extra-ecclesial, socio-political arena. . . . Political protest against government oppression of non-Evangelicals, and practical support for exploited workers, were virtually shunned by FTL personnel" (Smith 1983, 283). This was in part due to the social distance between non-Pentecostal Protestants and the poor (ibid., 276), a limitation that also affects the ecumenical groups (Mendonça and Velasques 1980, 154).

The lack of this sort of parachurch group in the 1960s contributed to the exit from protestantism of much of a generation of young leaders, and to the isolation of the Pentecostals. Only in the last few years has it been possible partially to overcome this qualitative loss. By the mid-1980s, however, the size of the Protestant community and the political context were very different, as can be clearly seen in the founding of the Brazilian Evangelical Association (AEVB).

THE BRAZILIAN EVANGELICAL ASSOCIATION (AEVB)

What do you gain by becoming a member of the AEVB: (1) You gain
credibility . . . a public attestation of your personal, organizational
and financial seriousness; (2) You gain the certainty of seeing evangelicals
speaking in your name to Brazilian society in a moderate manner
. . . . This means not having to be ashamed anymore.
Leaflet of the Brazilian Evangelical Association, 1992

As there have been Protestant churches in Brazil since the nineteenth century, it may be thought strange that the Brazilian Evangelical Association (AEVB) should only be formed in 1991. In fact, it is not the first attempt to form a representative organ of Protestants. With the transplanting of foreign denominations, Brazilian protestantism started life divided, but a Brazilian Evangelical Confederation (CEB) was finally created in 1934, partly as a reaction to Catholic attempts to restrict religious freedom in the new Constitution promulgated that year, and to identify Catholic faith and Brazilianness.

For thirty years, most of the historical churches (except the Baptists) cooperated in the CEB, especially in the area of religious education and the defense of freedom of religion. As the CEB was the link with international ecumenism, it felt the impact of the latter's thought. In 1955, the Sector for Social Responsibility was created; but the reaction soon made itself felt, even before the military coup d'état of 1964.

In the 1960s, the precarious unity that maintained the CEB disappeared. The political situation deepened ideological divergences among Protestants, weakened the CEB's ability to act as spokesman for the nation's Protestants. The churches began to pull out, and it survived into the early 1970s as a mainly social service agency.

Never having been officially dissolved, the CEB was reactivated in 1987 by a group of mainly Pentecostal federal deputies who were taking part in the Constituent Assembly to restore democracy after the military regime. The new CEB was repudiated by most historical churches, since its only raison d'être was to receive public funds in exchange for votes favorable to the government in the Constituent Assembly. A scandal erupted in 1988; as a leading daily paper said, "a good number of the Protestant deputies are making a profitable trade out of preparing the new Constitution, by negotiating their votes in exchange for advantages for their churches, and often for themselves." [15]

This scandal (the Brazilian equivalent of the television preachers' scandal in the United States) hastened the move by some Lausanne-line leaders to form another representative body. After fruitless attempts to persuade the CEB directors to submit to public auditing of their books, it was decided to found a new entity, the Brazilian Evangelical Association, in 1991. Its statutes emphasized the need to improve the public image of Protestants, much battered after the scandal of the politicians and media criticism of the money-raising techniques of some of the newer Pentecostal churches. The AEVB promised not to accept any public funding and not to allow its directors to stand for political election.

From the results of a survey held at the inaugural meeting, the founders of the AEVB represented the political center and left of the theologically conservative Protestant world. The idealizers were young and modern clergy from the historical churches and leaders of some parachurch organizations. This base was too small for an entity that intended to be representative.

The first president and key figure in creating a wider base for the AEVB was Caio Fábio D'Araújo Filho. Although a Presbyterian pastor, he is personally influenced by the charismatic renewal. Still under forty years of age, he has an independent base and is well known for his books, evangelistic crusades, television programs, and retreats for pastors. His career has been atypical. His grandfather was once interim governor of Amazonas state, and his father, a prosperous lawyer and businessman, was owner of the first television station in the same state. The latter afterwards suffered financial difficulties, which resulted in his conversion to protestantism and a new career as Presbyterian pastor. Meanwhile, Caio himself had a turbulent adolescence in the drug world before a dramatic conversion. At just twenty years of age, he began a career as a television preacher. Becoming nationally famous in the Protestant world, he founded his own parachurch entity, VINDE (National Vision for Evangelization).[16] The title of his television program, Stop and Think, indicated a different style from that of most tele-evangelists. VINDE is now supported largely by donations from Brazilian businessmen and from the American evangelist, Leighton Ford. Caio Fábio has made many forceful pronouncements on the behavior of most Protestant politicians:

> We have been on the wrong side of history in the last few years. . . . I am fed up with Protestant politicians who worry about putting the name of God in the Constitution. Politics is something to do in the name of man, not in the name of God. We need a politics that is verbally atheistic but practically Christian.

On taking office as first president, Caio Fábio said that the AEVB was being created "to prophesy the Word. . . . The only hope for Brazil is to be saved by a profound outpouring of the Spirit. And this has nothing to do with an ideology of the right, of the left, or of the center." This idea of "non-ideological prophecy" is evidently functional for the AEVB in consolidating its position within the Protestant world.

The original proposal contained a tension between the desire to be representative and to promote the concept of holistic mission defended by the Lausanne Covenant. The short history of the AEVB suggests that the achievement of greater representativeness will take precedence.

Circumstances have contributed to this. The scandal of the CEB meant that the proposal to create the AEVB attracted adherents from a broader range of theological positions than would otherwise have been the case. Even so, there was still serious opposition. But the events of 1992 helped to consolidate the AEVB's position. It needed events of national importance in which it could appear before the public as the legitimate representative of the Protestants, and two such events appeared. The AEVB had prepared a "Manifesto to the Nation," and its publication coincided both with the preventive detention of Bishop Macedo, leader of the fastest-growing Pentecostal church in Brazil, the Universal Church of the Kingdom of God, on charges of charlatanism, quackery, and fraud, and with the eruption of the corruption scandal surrounding President Collor, which would lead a few months later to his impeachment. In these events, the media looked for an official voice of the Protestants, a role the AEVB was able to fill. After that, some politically conservative church leaders who had supported the CEB began to participate in the AEVB, showing that the latter had become a coveted power base. With the CEB extinct (public funds dried up once the Constituent Assembly had finished) and CONIC unable to expand because of Catholic domination, the AEVB will have a clear field.

In its "Manifesto to the Nation" (May 1992), the Association presents itself as "the legitimate representative of the Protestant community of the country," i.e. it claims to represent not only its actual members but all Protestants. Such usurpation is only possible because, in the words of an AEVB leaflet, the lack of "an official voice has told against the Protestants . . . because in the last six years we have been the object of public scandals." For the time being, a self-proclaimed "legitimate representative" seems the lesser of two evils. But probably not for long. The more it manages to establish itself, the more it will become the center of dispute between conflicting projects in ecclesiastical and national politics. In the Protestant, unlike the Catholic, world, there is no unifying hierarchy capable of reconciling such conflicts. With the political and economic potential of Brazilian protestantism today, the leadership posts of AEVB could become political trampolines. Already, in less favorable circumstances, the president of the National Protestant Council of Peru was elected second vice president of the republic (although later deposed by his own president).

PROJECTIONS

In conclusion, I would return to the words of Hans Tennekes: if there is any chance of influencing the growing masses of popular protestantism (which means largely Pentecostals) in the direction of transforming Brazilian society, it lies with those who speak with enthusiasm of salvation through the blood of Christ and have an orthodox view of God and man. The Evangelical Progressive Movement may be able to play a key part in this in the coming years; it is certainly better placed to do so than the Ecumenical Movement. There is a sociological parallel in Brazilian catholicism, in which the "popular church" of the 1970s managed to avoid the ecclesiastical isolation suffered by the "Catholic left" of the 1960s, and was able to make profound changes in the Brazilian Catholic Church as a whole. Scott Mainwaring (1986) explains the difference. The former, unlike the latter, took care not to transform the church into a political institution; did not abandon the church impatiently, even though this meant accepting a slower pace of change; showed more respect for popular religiosity, rejecting a secularized radical theology; emphasized the unity of the transcendent and imminent aspects of religion; and worked for the reform of other areas of pastoral practice. Brazilian protestantism, which is already one of the largest Protestant constituencies in the world and may reach 20 or 30 percent of the population in the first decades of the new century, does not have a predetermined political destination and may yet have a key role in the social and cultural transformation of the country.

NOTES

1. CEDI began life as CEI in 1964. ISER later became more directed toward the academic than the religious world, and is today one of the main centers for the sociology of religion in Brazil.

2. The "Protestant" in the title has since been removed.

3. *Editor's Note:* Edin Abumanssur has worked for several years for CEDI.

4. AGEN, 164, 10 August 1989.

5. It is estimated that on an average Sunday there are more people in Protestant churches than in Catholic ones. At current rates of growth, there will soon be more practicing Pentecostal Christians in Brazil than practicing Catholics.

6. The word *evangélico* has traditionally been used in Brazil as a synonym for *protestante*, without any theological specificity. For this reason, a segment of Protestants influenced by these parachurch groups has come increasingly to refer to itself by the term *evangelical* [eh-vahn-ge-li CAHL], which is a neologism in Portuguese.

7. For example, Bastian (1984), Bittencourt (1989), and Mendonça and Velasques (1990).

8. More than half the new ordinands into the Church of England are now evangelical (Bebbington 1989, 270).

9. This compares with the roughly 5,000 the Catholic university movement, JUC, had in about 1960, when it shared power in student politics with the communists and had a large influence on the changing Catholic scene. There had, however, been a big expansion of the overall student population between 1960 and 1980.

10. Even during the Cold War, there were movements functioning openly in Cuba, Angola, and Eastern Europe, because they were not seen by the governments as purveyors of anti-communist ideology.

11. These diversified links have sociological consequences. As Bruce says of Britain, for example, evangelicals there have less freedom to create alternative subcultures than their American counterparts. The size of Britain and its centralized media and public life mean that pluralism affects the ordinary person much more. It also has a longer history of urbanization (Bruce 1990, 171, 182-183). Because of this, the ethos of British evangelicals takes pluralism and metropolitan life more into account.

12. Which treated the Kingdom as totally future, with the result that "verses about the Kingdom — often quoted to agitate for social improvements — could be . . . put into storage" (Stoll 1990, 48).

13. Arthur DeMoss, insurance magnate.

14. These are the Latin-American Council of Churches (CLAI), linked to the WCC, and the Latin-American Evangelical Confraternity (CONELA), which is very conservative.

15. *Jornal do Brasil* (7 August 1988), B6-B8.

16. *Editor's Note: VINDE* is also the plural imperative of the verb "to come" in Portuguese.

PART FIVE

THE FUTURE OF THE
LATIN AMERICAN CHURCH

19

Challenges to Liberation Theology
in the Decade of the Nineties

Pablo Richard and Team

"The main question is not what will happen to liberation theology but what will happen to the lives of the poor and to human life. What is to become of their liberation, and of the commitment of Christians to their lives and to their liberation? Liberation theology will not continue to be by mere inertia or by dint of repeating old formulas. We must recreate and reprogram it, with an eye to the future." The content of this theology is the concern of this chapter by a group of liberationists. It was published as "La Teología de la Liberación en la nueva coyuntura," in *Pasos*, no. 34 (March/April, 1991), Costa Rica, Departamento Ecuménico de Investigación. It is used with permission.

Many people believe that with the fall of historical socialism in Eastern Europe — the crisis of marxism and the imposition of the New Economic Order — that Liberation Theology (LT) no longer has a future. We are, it is said, living the End of History, the final triumph of capitalism. Any alternative ideas, any hope for a different world, all liberating utopias are irrelevant and condemned to failure. It is said that theology of liberation no longer has meaning. The expectation of all those who enjoy the privileges of the New Economic Order is that never again there shall be a people motivated by hope. This triumphalism and this expectation of the oppressors brutally flies in the face of the reality of poverty, misery, and oppression that continues to dominate a huge majority of the human race. The historic rationale for LT is still in place. As long as the scandal of poverty and oppression exists — while there are Christians who live and reflect their faith critically in the struggles for justice and life — there will be a liberation theology.

The main question, however, is not what will happen to LT. More importantly, it is what will happen to the lives of the poor, to human life. What is to become of their liberation, and of the commitment of Christians to their lives and to their liberation? We do liberation theology to keep their future alive, to keep our commitment alive. Yet, LT will not continue to exist by mere inertia or by dint of repeating old formulas. We will also need to reconceptualize LT at this juncture in history. We must recreate and reprogram LT, with an eye to the future.

During the past three years the world has changed drastically. In Central America we experienced the invasion of Panama (December 1989) and the defeat of the Sandinista government (February 1990). The Berlin Wall fell, which was a positive sign to the entire world. But shortly after that, there was the massacre of the six Jesuit priests in El Salvador (16 February 1989). These were contrasting signs which demonstrate to us the contradictions of the history we are living today. Then followed *perestroika* in the U.S.S.R. and the crisis of the historical socialisms in Eastern Europe. The rich world then vented a veritable ideological orgy, proclaiming, as we said before, the definitive triumph of capitalism and the End of History (Fukuyama 1972; 1990). Neo-liberal capitalism responded, with renewed vigor, with an avalanche of structural adjustments, in reaction to the non-development and increasing poverty of the Third World. Finally, in 1991, there was the horror of the Gulf War. It was a war of extermination against Iraq, as well as the First Great War against the Third World.[1] Through this conflict, the government of the United States has tried to impose its political and military hegemony over the entire world, with the acquiescence, for now, of Europe and Japan. This signifies for the Third World a veritable New International Disorder and a very real threat of death. The government of the United States and its Western allies may have won a battle. But they have also set in motion a process, only dimly recognized as yet, of conscientious resistance throughout the world against their imposition of death.

If the world has changed so profoundly, the theology of liberation must also change. In faithfulness to its original spirit and methodology, we must recreate it. In response to the present challenge, we need a new theology of liberation to follow upon that which we have known. Furthermore, this reconstruction of LT should be an essential part of a new process of resistance and of affirmation of life. In spite of the idolatry of Western Christianity we need to renew our faith in the God of the poor and the God of Life. In order to rebuild our solidarity and hope, we need to find new ways of doing liberation theology. This article, which is the fruit of the collective reflection of several theologians within the framework of the Ecumenical Research Department (DEI), was written with this objective in mind.[2] Let us consider the subject in two steps: the theology of liberation in the new historical context; and new themes and challenges for LT during the decade of the 1990s.

LIBERATION THEOLOGY
IN A NEW HISTORICAL SITUATION

Continuity with the Past

Liberation theology was born in the 1960s and 1970s as Christians became involved in the historical processes of liberation. It was born as we reflected — theologically, critically, and systematically — on our experience of God in the practice of liberation. The content of this theology has always been our experience of God. But we live, celebrate, and reflect upon it in the context of a liberation practice.[3] We were not dealing with a new theological subject matter, but rather with a new way of doing theology. The object was not liberation, but God himself. As a matter of fact, the theology of liberation (LT) was never feared merely because it spoke about liberation or because it was political. It was feared because the starting point of its reflection concerning God were the poor and the threat to life and justice in the Third World. Liberation theology was able to discover the unsettling presence of God in the lives of the oppressed and in the liberation struggles. Conversely, it denounced the unsettling absence of God in the oppressors' world and in Western Christian culture. The concept of "practice" helped LT to understand history critically, from the perspective of the oppressed. While classical theology used Aristotelian and Thomist philosophy, liberation theology made use of the more critical and liberating stream of the social sciences. Oppressors hide their oppression behind abstract and universal themes. In marked contrast, LT discovers oppression in history and reflects upon it with a view to overcoming it. It goes beyond radical discourse to become transforming practice. This is its only logical rationale.

The basic structure of liberation theology — a critical and systematic reflection on the experience of God in the practice of liberation — remains unchanged at this crucial juncture in history. To be sure, the LT structure and the rationale have not changed because today, more than ever, God is present in a special way in the world of the oppressed. He reveals himself in their struggles for liberation. But having said this, we must also recognize those elements which are new in the present historical juncture, making it necessary for us to *re*think and *re*create LT.

New Historical Situation: Changes in Liberation Theology

The crisis of historical socialism in Eastern Europe and the advent of human-face *perestroika* in the Soviet Union ended the cold war. The worldwide confrontation between East and West — the so-called socialist block and the so-called democratic block — ceased. Now capitalism is being touted as the only alternative for all of humanity. When capitalism was forced to compete with socialism, it was concerned with showing a human face, with carrying out development policies in the Third World so that poor nations would not opt for socialism. Now that capitalism has no competitors it no longer needs to keep up a humanitarian façade. Nor must it concern itself with Third World development. It can definitely impose itself as the only solution. So that we now have a savage totalitarian World Order. The government of the United States, as international policeman, imposes its political and military hegemony upon the entire world in order to ensure the acceptance by all of one capitalist system. The Third World has no other alternative but to submit or perish.

During the 1960s and 1970s, which saw the birth and maturation of LT, capitalism was promoting a development policy for poor nations that in the process made them more dependent. The liberation concept was used, then, to construct a model for autonomous or non-dependent development, even substituting the term "liberation" for "development." A "theological break" took place as we moved from development theology toward liberation theology. Dependence theory made it possible for us to develop both a theory and a strategy for liberation and revolution in the Third World. "Developmentalism" and "reformism" were radically critiqued as dependency models and the "ideological break" was expressed by the term "liberation." This new all-embracing concept pointed to many new breaks. It expressed a new theory and a new praxis. It became the reference point that defined a new culture, new ethics, and a new spirituality, as well as a new theology.

As things now stand with capitalism, the appositions development–liberation, reform–liberation, and dependence–liberation are no longer operational. Today, the radical apposition is between Life and Death, because capitalism has virtually given up everywhere on its policies of Third World reform and development. Only very limited sectors of the Third World benefit from the reforms and development that capitalism promotes in its own interests. Meanwhile, the vast majority of people have been given over to death. The Third World is no longer even dependent, but simply nonexistent. Where we were once dependent we are now expendable. In fact, it is now a privilege to be dependent, when the majority of our people have been given over to oblivion and death.

No longer are we even the Third World. We are now the Last World, the Non-World — the accursed world of those who have been excluded and condemned to death. Because of this, attempts to bring about life-giving reforms and development for everyone in the Third World are today profoundly revolutionary and liberating. Thus, the real alternatives are not development vs. liberation but life instead of death. Capitalism proposes to save the lives of a privileged few, even if this means the death of many. It is an option for death. But we cannot accept that many must die so that a few may live. This will ultimately lead to the death of all. The only legitimate choice is life for everyone. The option for development, for liberation, for the poor, etc., is at this juncture an option for life. LT becomes then a theology of Life. Life — for every human being and for the entire cosmos — must become our new rationale — our new way of thinking, our culture, ethics, spirituality, and theology, all of which are diametrically opposed to capitalism at this point in time.

There is a further and a more profound change in capitalism today. Not only has it ceased to be capitalism with a human face, having left behind its policies of reform and development for the Third World. It has now become a sacrificial capitalism, offering up the lives of the poor in order to save the free-market system. The laws of private property and of contract obligations are considered absolute and in their name human life is sacrificed. The clearest example of this mindset is the foreign debt. It must be paid even while millions of Third World poor are being sacrificed. This is considered necessary sacrifice in order to safeguard the law of the marketplace and to uphold the spirit of capitalism. Whoever defends human lives against market law and against the human sacrifice it demands is written off as a millennialist, a utopian, or a terrorist. We are accused of wanting to build heaven on earth by making this earth a hell. People who believe that human life is an absolute that should never be sacrificed, and that the law is to serve human beings and not the contrary, are seen as a cancer that must be excised from the body politic of capitalism, even at the cost of pain and bloodshed. The liquidation of the six Jesuit fathers in El Salvador is probably the best evidence of the "sacrificial aggressiveness" of the capitalist system. It explains the hostility toward LT as a theology of life-for-all. In this spirit, a U.S. bishop showed his hostility by labeling liberation theologians "flies that infect the mystical body of Christ."

The challenge to liberation theology — all of these profound structural changes in the dominant system challenge us both theoretically and practically. We need to develop new concepts to help us acquire a better grasp of the new historical reality, and the possibility of its transformation. With the so-called crisis of marxism, attempts have been made to undermine our capacity to theorize — to destroy the theoretical space that we need to resist and to continue struggling. Our right to think alternatively is under threat, as are our hopes and utopias. Countering this, LT must again engage in dialogue, both critically and creatively, with the social sciences — particularly with economics, ecology, and anthropology. At this new juncture we must repossess our historical rationale in order to think critically and systematically about our faith in the God of Life.

A New Meaning of "Poor": A Challenge to Liberation Theology

During the past decade LT has deepened and broadened the concept of "poor" by applying the term "oppressed" to racial, cultural, and sexist discrimination, as well as to economic oppression. The concept of class was replaced by race, nation, and sex. The world of the poor and oppressed is the world of those who are economically poor. But it is also the world of native and Afro-Americans, of women (above all Third World women, who are twice exploited, as poor and as women). We also speak today of oppressed and marginalized nations and peoples. The concept of "Third World," in itself a misnomer (we are not a "third" world, but rather the underdeveloped and exploited portion of one and the same world), is nonetheless significant. It includes not only the poor nations, but the poor in all the nations, as well, i.e. the exploited minorities in the First World.

Meanwhile, there has been a qualitative and profound redefinition of the reality of the poor and oppressed within capitalism. It is a fact that the rich and industrialized world needs the population of the Third World less than ever. It needs our natural environment — to exploit our natural resources, to attract tourism, and as a dumping ground for toxic wastes; but it does not need our population — although it may need a portion of it for cheap labor and as potential consumers. Nonetheless, a majority of the Third World inhabitants are considered expendable. Ironically, as things now stand, to be "exploited" is to have a certain measure of privilege. It means that one continues to be taken into account by the system. But the redundant population, because it has been written off by the system, is bereft of power. It can no longer bring pressure to bear by such measures as strikes, etc., because, as far as the system is concerned, this population does not exist, either as a producer or a consumer.

Exclusion leads to social breakdown and dispersion. Because the system is not interested in a superfluous population, it does not invest in its most basic needs, such as work, health, housing, education, affordable foodstuffs, etc. This has contributed to a process of impoverishment that can only end in death. The breakdown is total — economic, social, corporeal, human, familial, religious, moral, etc. The system treats this redundant and degraded population as rubbish, as little better than rats that must be exterminated. Cities need to be cleansed of the poor. In several countries (e.g. Colombia) death squads maraud nightly, killing off street children, tramps, beggars, prostitutes, homosexuals, unemployed, the homeless, etc. In other countries (as in Santo Domingo) cities are cleansed of the poor and their bodies are disposed of in remote gullies and garbage dumps. Furthermore, this redundant population is considered dangerous. It is a threat — a hotbed of thieves and of contagious disease (such as cholera, leprosy, tuberculosis, and AIDS). These redundant poor die silently, uselessly, and perhaps for them desirably. In this new and deadly form of poverty children, young people, and women are particularly hard hit. And when they are native and Afro-Americans as well, they are in double jeopardy.

It goes without saying that such a profound change in the situation of the poor challenges LT radically at every level — terminology and worldview, commitment and pastoral practice, as well as moral and spiritual depth. The preferential option for the poor has now acquired a qualitatively different radicality. Beyond the struggles for justice within the system, the option for the poor is committing us to a struggle for life, at times dramatic, on behalf of that majority population which has been condemned and excluded, and who are in an accelerated process of degradation and dispersion. Faith in the God of life is forcing us to confront this system more radically. With every passing day, we discern with increasing clarity that this a legalized system of sin and death.

Transforming Liberation Practice: New Role for Liberation Theology

Liberation theology, we have said, is a critical and systematic reflection upon faith within a practice of liberation. The concept of "practice" is therefore crucial to LT. The changes we have described in the dominating system and in the situation of the poor also modify liberation practice and the way in which we think about it. This is, to be sure, a challenge for LT.

Liberation practice interprets reality while it seeks to transform it. It focuses upon the alienated and ideologized forms that the dominating system has created in order to overcome the inherent historical contradictions. Liberation practice, then, is all about transforming historical realities whose principal victims are the poor, the oppressed, and the excluded. It therefore challenges us to work toward a new historical reality where there need no longer be any people who are poor, oppressed, or excluded, and where everyone can enjoy life to its fullest. In sum, LT does not reflect — alienatingly — on abstract tenets. We are not in the business of interpreting universal principles, but of living and celebrating our Christian faith within specific historical transformations, which in turn impact upon both the rationale and the spirituality of LT.

We cannot consider here all of the transformations in liberation practice at this new historical juncture. We will concentrate only on two dimensions that affect and challenge LT. We are referring to a double displacement: from political to civil society and from political and military confrontation to cultural, ethical, and religious confrontation.

First: from political to civil society. We do not want to abandon political society. Power and the State continue to be important dimensions. The State must play a decisive role in civil society, in economic planning, and in protecting nature. Once it is divested of its repressive apparatus, the State can play a positive role for the Common Good and at the service of the poor and marginalized. But at this juncture neo-liberalism is attempting to dismantle the State in order to impose its own totalitarian market economy. Meanwhile, liberation practice has moved into civil society and the popular movements, from where it can point out the problems of political power and of the State. The popular movements are proposing societal renewal from below, from the base of society. Such is the case with the new expressions of "people power" that offer alternatives to the dominant system. They are attempting to restructure work, production, the marketplace, technology, health, education, habitat, and recreation, etc. Certain movements — such as Amerindian, Afro-American, women's liberation, children and youth movements, along with ethnic and solidarity movements — have gained new impetus at this time. Many of these popular expressions are also involved in significant regional and international solidarity movements. Such is the case with the successful Amerindian, womens movements, and with the growing North-South solidarity movement.

Second: from political and military to cultural, ethical and religious confrontation. It has become very clear — particularly after the defeat of the Sandinista government and the Persian Gulf War — that Third World peoples cannot afford to confront the Western powers militarily. On its own turf, the Empire[4] is invincible. For this reason, the Empire must be confronted on a different battlefield, at the point where the Third World is strongest, in particular at the level of culture, ethics, and spirituality. The Third World is poorest in financial, technical, and military resources, but it is rich in humanity, in culture, in moral and religious values. We must overcome our tendency to be violent, warlike, and militaristic so that we can discover wherein lie our strength and identity. The cultural, moral, and spiritual strengths of the Third World can be a source of life for ourselves, as well as for all of humanity.

At the cultural level, the Third World must confront culture of militarism, the violent culture of the dominant Empire, as well as its culture of materialism, consumerism, and individualism. The Third World can go on living and resisting, fortified by its ancestral cultural values of peace and respect for life, nature and community. At the moral level, the Empire imposes upon us an ethic of absolute law (of private property and of contract obligations), and to it sacrifices the lives of nations and of the poor. During the Gulf War, the Western Empire showed us its double standard — one was applied to Iraq and the other to itself, its allies, and Israel. The West showed its capacity to distort the truth and to manipulate the media. The Third World is capable of life and resistance at a higher moral level armed only with the ethic of truth in which human life, and not the law, is considered absolute. Law is at the service of life rather than life being at the service of law. At the religious level, the Third World is especially strong. The great religions of the world come from the Third World. In them entire peoples find meaning, identity, and strength to resist on behalf of truth and life. The First World, wrapped up in positivism and liberalism, in secularism and materialism, believes only in the power of money, of arms and technology. The Third World must not fall into that trap, but instead it must develop all of its own spiritual and religious potential, which is its greatest strength. On this ground all of the religions of the world can join around a common faith in the God of Life, and in a common struggle for life and for justice.

The last two points are intimately joined, because it is clear that the cultural, moral, and religious struggle is not abstract and ideological. It is a historical struggle that takes place within social movements and in the practice of liberation. The cultural struggle is a struggle for life ("agriculture is culture," said a Guatemalan Indian); moral and religious struggles are an essential dimension of civil society. The cultural, moral, and spiritual spheres are dimensions of the same historical practice of liberation.

True to its methodology — faith that is lived and reflected upon while practicing liberation — LT must accept the changes and transformations that this practice requires in the present historical juncture. Liberation theology will find a field for action in civil society, as well as in the cultural, ethical, and spiritual spheres. It will have a much wider scope than in the past when its energies were consumed by political and military struggles. Specifically, the Base Ecclesial Communities (BECs), the womb out of which LT was born, are a part of civil society and of the popular liberation movements. At the same time, LT will find a privileged field for creative development in the context of the cultural, ethical, and religious struggles of our people. In this sense, LT has, at this new crossroads in history, immense possibilities for growth and maturation that are far superior to what had been possible before. Today more than ever the theology of liberation has its own fertile field for development. However, LT will develop, both locally and internationally, to the degree in which it faces its task, critically and conscientiously at this crucial point in history, with its own ethos and methodology.

In this cultural, moral, and spiritual confrontation of the People of God[5] with the Empire, LT and the BECs are beginning to live the Apocalypse in a creative and liberating manner. Apocalyptic theology is a political and creative theology that lies within the scope of a history of hope and of utopia.[6]

NEW THEMES AND CHALLENGES
IN THE DECADE OF THE 1990S

We must analyze the new themes and challenges in each of LT's level of development of LT.[7] Liberation theology has three levels, which we liken to the image of a tree. The root of LT is culture, religion, and the spirituality of poor believers and of the social and popular movements.[8] The trunk of LT are the BECs and similar structures. The branches are the professional theologians, specialized journals, and centers of LT. Each level is different and has its own specificity and internal structure. The three levels interact. Professional theologians are linked to the BECs and rooted in popular culture and religion. At the same time, LT's cultural and religious roots are expressed in the BECs and in formal theology. Let us now look quickly at the themes and challenges of LT at each level.

Root Themes and Challenges

Liberation theology and social movements in general. Social movements, particularly those that are new and more creative, develop a culture within them, as well as an ethic, a mystique, and a spirituality. It is within such a context that LT has grown during the past decade, and within which it continues to grow and develop. It has produced, for example, a theology related to popular education and medicine, to alternative agriculture, as well as to movements for solidarity and human rights. Many of these movements were born within the BECs and many Christians take part in them, as well as many other profoundly religious people. In this way a theology of social and popular movements was born.

Special reference should be made to women's liberation theology, which was born as an organic part of the popular movements for women's liberation. In the same way, an Afro-American liberation theology came into being (especially in Brazil and the Caribbean). Most recently a theology has appeared that is related to youth movements. The impact of LT upon young people is something new and poses a new challenge to us as well. LT also is beginning to have a liberating impact upon middle-class movements, which could in turn make a very significant contribution to the popular movement.

Native American theology of liberation. While it is thousands of years old, the novelty is in the way in which it is recently being articulated and expressed at a continental level, as well as its relationship to TL. In a recent LT encounter a Mexican Zapotecan diocesan priest said more or less the following:

> Native American theology is indebted to LT, values it, and hopes to engage in dialogue with it. There is some fear that the crisis in the Church and contradictions in LT might affect our Native American theology. The subjects of this theology are the ancient peoples of this continent. Native American theology is very old; what is new is that the Church now recognizes it, as does LT. Native American theology is the strength of our peoples; it is an underground theology that expresses itself in the religious realm, by means of ritual and myth. Native American theology is not merely a reaction against the system, but a milleniar expression of its life and spirit.

On a Peruvian calendar we found the following witness from Native American theology:

> We caused our ideas germinate (that is, we did theology)
> in order to survive in the midst of so much hunger;
> to defend ourselves from so much scandal and attacks;

to organize ourselves in the midst of so much confusion;
to rejoice in spite of so much sadness and
to dream beyond so much desperation.

We have here a complete definition of Native American theology. It is the means by which a people, as it struggles against death, is finding a way to survive, to defend itself, and to organize, while rejoicing and dreaming dreams. There is little doubt that this native theology will be a new root source of future LT growth and a new field for its development, while respecting the autonomy and the rights of each.

Liberation theology and Latin American culture. LT is already part of the identity of our continent. It is part of our cultural heritage. This is the sense not only of Christians, but of intellectuals and cultural workers who do not profess to be Christian. There is no doubt that LT has gone beyond theology and ecclesiology. New literature, new Latin American songs and dances, are phenomena that are independent from LT, but they arise out of the same historical and liberating movement — which is why they are mutually influential. Liberation theology today expresses itself not only in concepts but with drums, myths, symbols, dances, as well as with stories and legends. Aside from the specifically indigenous and Afro-American cultures, there are also peasant and suburban cultures that have a direct influence upon LT and vice versa.

New Liberation Themes and Challenges from the BECs

The BECs, in spite of political persecutions and of the crisis of Christendom and of the conservative movement, continue to grow and to mature in Latin America. They also continue to provide space for theological creativity. The BECs are the collective subject of theological production and motivation, with both intellectual theological creativity and the creation of myths and symbols. They also demonstrate theological creativity in their spirituality and popular religiosity. Let us look at some examples of this productivity.

Popular Reading of the Bible. This is perhaps the BECs' most productive theological activity. It takes place in three steps. First, the Christian people, through the BECs' activity, make the reading and interpretation of Scripture their own. Second, the Christian people become a prophetic people when they discover the presence and revelation of God in today's reality, in the light of the Bible. Third, the Christian people lift up the Word of God — which has been discovered in Scripture and in reality, in the light of the Bible — as the Church's authority. In this way, through the popular reading of Scripture, a prophetic movement is born among the People of God, and in which the Word of God is recognized as authoritative and as a source of legitimization. In this popular reading the Bible is not an end in itself, but the prophetic movement that it creates. The BECs, of course, read the Bible in church, guided by tradition and the magisterium. It is a prayerful reading that maintains an intimate relationship with the life of the people and is in constant dialogue with professional exegesis.[9] The popular reading of Scripture is not in opposition to hierarchical church authority. It is, however, against the neoconservative movement that would like to make church authority a sacred and totalitarian power. This movement is a serious danger for the church because it destroys the meaning of faith and of the prophetic dimension of the People of God. The popular reading of the BECs lifts high the authority of the Word of God while it lends legitimacy to the prophetic movement in the church. In this way, the BECs create a source of legitimacy that gives them security and theological clarity. Through this popular reading, the BECs maintain a permanent and profound theological creativity "from below," from the People of God, in communion with the institutional and universal church.

Theology of evangelization of everyday life. This is another evidence of theological creativity in the popular religious sphere. The themes of everyday life — work, land, health, family, sex, children's education, culture, festivity, etc. — are being constantly reflected upon by the BECs in the context of their faith. Other central theological concerns, such as hope, encouragement, and comfort, arise particularly in BECs that are immersed in situations of extreme misery, among the most marginalized and deprived peoples. There is theological reflection as well on what it means for Christians to participate in movements of social change. The popular struggles for land, health, housing, schools, as well as the liberation of women and cultural reaffirmation, are the contexts wherein a new reflection upon the Gospel is taking place. The reflection is by no means abstract. It acts within the religious sphere through popular wisdom and piety, which is expressed conceptually, and above all by means of story-telling, symbols, and myths. We can say that the theological activity of the BECs is germane to an authentic evangelization of life. In the long run, the BECs are attaining a real evangelization of the structures and of the most fundamental dimensions of human life. In sum, the Gospel is gradually becoming a day-by-day reality in the life and thinking of peoples at the bottom of society, liberating and transforming them.

New Themes and Challenges for LT at the Formal Theological Level

There are also specific themes and challenges for liberation theologians who seek to do formal theology rooted in popular culture and religion, alongside of the BECs. We must tackle these themes with courage and responsibility.

Theoretical challenge. The structural transformations within the dominating system, in the situation of the poor, and in their resistance strategies — which we have already analyzed in the first section of this chapter — demand that liberation theology itself undergo a profound theoretical restructuring. In this new juncture, we need to work — critically and systematically — on new theoretical concepts, i.e. on a new theory or rationale to guide our thinking about the faith and practice. The very real crisis of marxism is one thing, but its ideological manipulation by capitalism is quite another matter. The crisis has been manipulated in order to repress any critical and liberating ideas of the oppressed against the capitalist system. Its aim is to destroy every thought that is founded upon hope and solidarity; to kill every alternative idea that dares to dream about a future different from that envisioned by the dominant system. More to the point, the crisis of marxism is being used to proclaim the end of

liberation theology. It is said — falsely — that marxism provided the deepest
rationale for LT. With marxism dead, LT also dies, so it is said. This is not the
place to discuss marxism and its relationship to LT. It is sufficient to underscore
the fact that liberation theology did not develop from marxism but from the
experience of God in the world of the poor and in the ongoing practice of
liberation.

Certainly, in its understanding of reality, LT uses the social sciences critically, including, it is true, some theoretical elements from marxism. Every kind
of crisis that is covered by the social sciences is of interest to LT, but this does
not signify the crisis of LT. Whatever the case, we should not be deterred by the
manipulations of ideological warriors who use the crisis within marxism in order
to kill any kind of critical and alternative thinking — in particular when it is
grounded in history, is liberating, and fosters hope. Liberation theology must
always be creating and recreating a theoretical space. It must go on developing a
rationale that is commensurate with its specific theological task, which is to
serve the poor and oppressed and contribute to their liberation.

New areas for theological development. To date, liberation theology has dealt
with the classical themes of theology — christology, ecclesiology, eschatology,
mariology, ethics, etc. Meanwhile, LT has deeply renewed other theological disciplines, such as biblical studies, church history, the social doctrine of the church,
and so on. Also, through its spirit and methodology, LT has created a social ethic,
as well as theologies of the land, of work, of women's liberation, and of
ecumenicism. LT has given precedence in its dialogue to sociology and philosophy. All of this work has been very fruitful and will continue in the future.[10]

In recent years, however, there has been a new and challenging development.
LT has begun to dialogue with three scientific disciplines — economics, ecology, and anthropology. In economics and theology, the book by Hugo Assmann
and Franz Hinkelammert[11] elaborates on the same concerns that were expressed
in earlier works by the latter.[12] Other liberationists who are working in this field
are Enrique Dussel, Julio de Santa Ana, Raúl Vidales, and several more. DEI has
published five books in ecology and theology,[13] and Leonardo Boff has made it
one of his top priorities, with several books in process. Much basic fieldwork
has already been done in anthropology and theology, especially on culture in
relation to our pastoral work with native American groups.[14]

New ecumenical and universal perspectives. Latin American and Caribbean
LT have intensified their dialogue with African and Asian theologians through
the Ecumenical Association of Third World Theologians. The EATWT held its
most recent general assembly, in January of 1992, in Nairobi, Kenya, around the
theme: "Cry for Life: Third World Spirituality." LT is also in dialogue with men
and women of the Black theology movement (James H. Cone and others),[15] with
women's liberation,[16] and with First World liberation theologians. And we are
currently engaged in a more universal dialogue with the liberation theologies
that are emerging within Third World religions. Dialogue is likewise in process
with Native American liberation theology, which has its roots in the native
religions of Latin America and the Caribbean. There are also very fruitful dia-

logues going on with Jewish[17] and with Palestinian liberation theologies.[18] More recently, several books have appeared on a Muslim theology of liberation with which LT has only begun to dialogue. The dialogue between LT and Hinduism and with Buddhism has a long history in Asia.[19] The dialogue of Christianity with other world religions in the spirit and with the methodology of LT should be very fecund and challenging at this crucial juncture — in the turbulent wake of the Gulf War, which was waged by the Western Powers against the Third World. It will be a liberating dialogue, which upholds life and justice, because the poor of the Third World are our point of departure.

CONCLUSION

The new world juncture demands new thinking about liberation theology. It challenges us with new concerns. We believe that LT has the maturity and the necessary strength to face up to this moment in history, with its concerns and challenges. This is not the end of LT, as some people had hoped, but rather a historical opportunity (the *kairos*) for its rebirth. The new juncture opens up uncharted paths for LT's growth. But this will require that it be seriously reconceptualized and reformulated in response to the new historical situation. This paper is a modest and tentative step in that direction.

Liberation theology has a future. This fact should be a source of hope for the poor and oppressed of this world. What ultimately matters is the future of liberation and the future of the life of the poor. LT's future is a function of the vital future that we desire for our entire threatened planet and cosmos. Let us continue resisting and constructing a future full of hope and, strengthened by this hope, let us continue to rethink and to recreate LT. We also need the solidarity of all of the oppressed, as well as of all conscientious women and men. With hope and solidarity we shall construct the liberation theology we need for the decade of the 1990s, and for the twenty-first century. Our faith in the God of Life will strengthen this our hope and energize our solidarity.

Translated by Guillermo Cook

NOTES

1. Cp. DEI team, "La Primera Gran Guerra contra el Tercer Mundo, capitalismo, aplastamiento y solidaridad en el final del siglo," in *Pasos*, Nº 33 (San José: DEI, January-February, 1991).

2. *Editors' Note:* A number of the topics dealt with in this article have been expounded more extensively by members of the DEI team and have been referred to in the footnotes of the original Spanish version. For further information, write DEI, Apartado 389-2070, Sabanilla, Costa Rica.

3. For a theoretical definition of Liberation Theology, see the first chapter of Richard (1980), "Theology of Latin American Liberation." Also, the chapter "How Liberation Theology is born, grows and matures," in Richard (1990).

4. When we speak of "Empire" we refer to the centers of economic, financial, political, military, cultural and social power that are fundamentally located in the

First World, although with branches in the Third. We do not include in that Empire those First World people who are also suppressed by the powers of death.

5. When we say "People of God" we include the Third World poor, as well as the poor and oppressed of the rich world — particularly those who are the most aware of their situation.

6. Pablo Richard has written several articles in Spanish on apocalyptic biblical themes. His book on revelation from a liberation perspective has recently been published (1990).

7. For a distinction of these levels, see Richard (1990), Second Part, Chapter III, "How LT is born, grows and matures," pp. 133-142.

8. *Editor's Note:* The rootedness of LT in popular culture, religiosity, spirituality, and political/civic activism gives it its radical (from *radix* 'root') character, to which the author frequently alludes.

9. For a more detailed description of the interaction between popular reading of Scripture and professional theology see Carlos Mesters, "The Use of the Bible in Christian Communities of the Common People," in *The Bible and Liberation: Political and Social Hermeneutics*, Norman K. Gottwald, ed. (Maryknoll: Orbis, 1983). Also by Mesters, *Defenseless Flower: A New Reading of the Bible* (Maryknoll: Orbis, 1989).

10. The Spanish-Portuguese "Liberation and Theology" project, which is published by Editora Vozes (Brazil) and Ediciones Paulinas (Spain) and several Latin American publishers, including DEI (Costa Rica) is an example of the wide ranging interests of LT theologians. The largest and most recent systematizing of LT is Ellacuría (1990).

11. Assmann and Hinkelammert (1989).

12. Hinkelammert (1981; 1994)

13. The most recent work is by Fernando Mires (1991).

14. A good example of writing in this field is Marzal et al. (1991). The same publishers have put out more than thirty volumes on theology and anthropology on occasion of the five hundred years since Columbus.

15. Cp. James H. Cone, *A Black Theology of Liberation* (Maryknoll: Orbis, 1990). See also Theodore Walker, Jr., *Empower the People: Social Ethics for the African-American Church* (Maryknoll: Orbis, 1991); Dwight N. Hopkins and George Cummings, *Cut Loose the Stammering Tongue: Black Theology in the Slave Narratives* (Maryknoll: Orbis, 1991); Bénézet Bujo, *African Theology in its Social Context* (Maryknoll: Orbis, 1992); Mercy Amba Oduyoye and Musimbi B.A. Kanyoro, eds., *The Will to Arise: Women, Tradition and the Church of Africa* (Maryknoll: Orbis, 1992).

16. Cp. Gebara and Bingemer (1989).

17. Marc Ellis, *Toward a Jewish Theology of Liberation* (Maryknoll: Orbis, 1989).

18. Cp. Naim Stifan Ateek, *Justice, and Only Justice: A Palestinian Theology of Liberation* (Maryknoll: Orbis, 1989). See also Naim S. Ateek, Rosemary Radford Ruether and Marc Ellis, eds., *Faith and the Intifada* (Maryknoll: Orbis, 1992).

19. Cp. Virginia Fabella, Peter K. H. Lee, and David Kwang-Sun Suh, eds., *Asian Christian Spirituality* (Maryknoll: Orbis, 1992).

20

The Condition and Prospects of Christianity in Latin America

José Míguez Bonino

"I am presupposing that the dominant social and religious tendencies which prevail today in most Latin American countries will continue for the immediate and perhaps mid-term future. But should we not be more concerned with the purpose of Christianity in Latin America? How do we intend to offer to our people in message and life an authentic testimony of the Gospel? It is no more a question of what will happen to Christianity in Latin America but of what will Christianity do here. This demands not so much an analysis as a confession and a commitment." Dr. Míguez is a an Argentinian Methodist pastor-theologian who has served as president of the WCC, has written extensively on Liberation themes, and was a prominent speaker at the Third Latin American Congress on Evangelis (CLADE III). This chapter is used with permission of the author and of *Jahrbuch Mission 1992: Fokus Lateinamerika*, Evangelisches Missionswerk, Hamburg.

It takes a certain "irresponsibility" to attempt to draft even a few tentative and general comments on a topic such as this. The very word *Christianity* is a generic and imprecise term. Should we include in it the Afro-American cults (Umbanda, Candomblé, voodoo, etc.), the new religious movements (like the Unification Church), or the renaissance of traditional indigenous religious symbols and ceremonies? Besides, the religious field has been changing so rapidly and radically during these last two decades at the impulse of social and cultural conditions and international relations that it is now as difficult to speak of the *condition* as it is of the *prospects* of Christianity in our Latin American world.

IN LATIN AMERICA

Naturally the present conditions and the future prospects of Christianity in Latin America cannot be analyzed as if Christianity were a self-contained and autonomous reality. The qualification, "in Latin America" has to be taken consciously, seriously, and responsibly as a conditioning framework for any significant reflection on this question. As I said before, to unpack what is contained at present and future in "Latin America" seems today such a theologically and sociologically risky enterprise as to be almost folly. We must, however, try to suggest some lines that we might explore, in order to point out some significant variables. We can propose some approaches — even while we are aware of the ambiguity inherent in this exercise, and consequently of the provisional and contingent nature of all the hypotheses that we may formulate.

As far as the social, political, and economic conditions, I am presupposing that the dominant tendencies which prevail today in most Latin American countries will continue for the immediate and perhaps mid-term future. Latin America will remain under the unifying hegemony of the United States and the neo-liberal economic orthodoxy proclaimed and supervised by the IMF and the international banking and financial system of the new world. It will continue under the security order which the UN seems to have taken on.

If such a hypothesis is valid, we can expect that there will be in Latin America a worsening of the *economic* condition of the large majorities — a growth in the gap between rich and poor. There will be a tendency to revert to two-class societies with small and very conditioned middle sectors and a large totally marginalized percentage of the population. *Politically*, this will mean formal democracies with different types and measures of control or repression. Possibly, there will be an increase of local social explosions and occasional violent confrontations, social and political protests, and certainly growth in delinquency. But I do not think that we should expect a revolutionary situation or profound structural changes. All of this means, of course, a *high degree of social anomie and marginality*.

CHRISTIANITY

"Christianity" has to be understood, historically and sociologically, as part of the religious field. Three brief observations seem to me particularly relevant to our concern.

The Growing Importance of the Religious Factor

This phenomenon manifests itself in different ways. As a subjective compensation in an increasingly objectified, depersonalized, and mechanized world, it appears in the form of charismatic communities, oriental religions, or new spiritualities, particularly in middle or higher class sectors. As religious legitimation of authoritarian governments and repressive measures or as theological vindication of the neo-liberal economic rationale, it has played and continues to play an important role in political life. As a refuge from social anomie and uprootedness, it is recruiting millions among the poor. Over against the growing secularization and the decline of the gods that were so greatly feared or expectantly celebrated in the first half of our century, an observer could well summarize our situation in St. Paul's exclamation: "I see that in every way you are very religious" (Acts 17:22).

Dispersion in the Religious Field

The "assured religious clienteles" (the religious homogeneity of the people of a nation, culture, or language group) tend to disappear. In the central square of Quito, Ecuador, on a beautiful Sunday afternoon, we saw at least four religious groups peacefully competing for followers. A Pentecostal brother was calling people to accept Christ as Savior. A Krishna group danced and invited to a lecture that would take place in the evening. Some people listened attentively to a discussion by a small group of Seventh Day Adventists and Jehovah's Witnesses on the signs of the final times. And a fortune teller, at the door of the Cathedral, was offering the little cards where people could read their future. A survey of religious TV or radio programs would offer the same or similar spectrum of choices. It is the new "religious free market" where each group can define its purpose, its message, its methodology. There is no reason to expect that this dispersion will disappear or diminish in the near future.

A Conflictive Religious Field

Not all plurality, however, is so peaceful. Social contradictions, ideological differences, conflictive historical projects are also reflected in the religious world. They evoke religious and theological responses which create tension and conflict, not only between different religious groups but, perhaps even more, within them. Thus we are not only facing "a return of the gods" but "a conflict of the gods."

Is it possible to devise a topology so as to organize a religious map of Latin America? What kind of projection should we use? Should we draw groups along denominational lines, by socio-political options, by cultural origin, by social location? I think that such typologies would require a much more careful theoretical and empirical knowledge and reflection than what we have at present. Even classical categories such as "church," "sect," or "cult" prove insufficient and even misleading. I prefer, therefore, simply to group my observations about the present conditions and prospects of Christianity under the large and general labels of "Roman Catholic" and "Protestant." Other distinctions will have to be drawn within these two.

LATIN AMERICAN ROMAN CATHOLICISM

"Latin America is a Catholic continent." The sentence, so frequently used, does not accurately describe the religious scene in Latin America. But it does characterize its background. It is not mainly a question of numbers and percentages but of the mark that five hundred years of Catholic presence — however resisted or conflictive at times — has left in all Latin American life. Roman Catholicism is not today — if it ever was — a monolithic, totally homogeneous reality. Therefore we must briefly notice some of the trends and dynamics within it.

The Secularization Process

Since the 1940s and 1950s the Catholic Church in Latin America has become acutely aware of the increasing process of secularization, the presence of other social and religious forces in Latin America, and the inadequacy of the religious life of Catholic people to face this new situation. Several books and congresses held in those years dared to ask the question whether Latin America could still be called — either quantitatively or qualitatively — "a Catholic country." This questioning led to a new self-understanding: Latin America is for the Catholic Church a mission field. Expressions like that, which recur on the lips of many bishops and in Church meetings, and even from the pope, do not mean that Latin America is a "pagan" or "non-evangelized" area. It means that a re-evangelization, a "new evangelization," or a new phase of evangelization must take into account the history of what that Church has meant and means for Latin America. *The basic point, however, is this: The Catholic Church has to be in Latin America a missionary church.* How to interpret such "mission" and how to carry it out? It is at this point that we see differences of understanding and projection.

Traditional Popular Catholic Religiosity

In the countryside and among indigenous populations — and even to some extent in poor urban *barrios* — traditional Catholicism has remained basically unaltered. Liturgical and theological changes following Vatican II have not radically affected the piety that turns around pilgrimages, patron saints' celebrations, *cofradías* [religious guilds], vows, and local devotions. Curiously enough, a similar resistance to change — although perhaps for different reasons — exists at the other end of the social scale: in Catholic aristocratic circles where the resistance to change has been militant and at times even violent (cp. for example the influence of "Lefebvrism" in some Latin American countries).

Social Changes

However, what internal renewal has not accomplished, social changes tend to produce. The "habitat" of that popular piety — the traditional society with its strong ties, its regularity, its carved "niches" for everybody — tends to disappear. Peasants, indigenous people, and poor in the cities are thrown into anonymity, marginality, and social anomia. Traditional religious practice in the new shanty towns or marginal sectors tends to diminish. New religious movements dispute — sometimes quite successfully — the place that Catholic religiosity used to hold. Catholic aristocratic circles, on the other hand, are caught in the ideology of the new world economic trends, and their religiosity tends to become more "modern" — subjective and individualistic. Some traditional "Catholic nationalism" with fascistic tendencies does survive, but it clearly has no future.

The Second Latin American Bishops' Conference

The Medellín Conference of Bishops in 1968 gave official expression to a different understanding of mission. CELAM II stated that Latin America is a continent trying to come out of a situation of economic dependence, poverty, and injustice; of underdevelopment and ignorance. The Church's function is to accompany, to strengthen, and to dynamize with the truth and the power of the

Gospel this transformation. The *option for the poor* and *liberation*, though the words do not appear in Medellín, have been the key expressions to name this movement. The Base Ecclesial Communities and the Theology of Liberation are the most important instruments for the mission of the Church thus understood. The growth of the Base Community Movement, particularly in some countries, with its emphasis on people's active participation, a committed and contextual reading of the Bible, an openness to the problems of the total society, and an active participation in its struggles for freedom and justice, has made a strong impact on the religious life of the people. The Theology of Liberation has articulated at the level of ecclesiology, Christology, Biblical interpretation, as well as ethics and *pastoral*, a coherent doctrinal support for the renewal of the Church in the direction of the Medellín perspective.

The Episcopal organization in Latin America (CELAM) and the Vatican have, meanwhile, interpreted Medellín in a different direction. The new evangelization is seen as the recreation of a Christian (fundamentally a Catholic) civilization, inspired in the Social Doctrine of the Church and actualized to the conditions of the urban industrial modern world. Internally there is an emphasis on discipline, obedience to authority, and a centralized definition of plans and procedures. The preparatory documents for the Fourth General Episcopal Conference that was held in Santo Domingo in 1992 (the fifth Centenary of the coming of Christianity to this continent), the papal address on the occasion, and the Final Document, are representative of this project, which I would call "neo-Christendom."

Future Trends

It seems to me that this last tendency, which no doubt will be the official line of the Roman Catholic Church, at least in the immediate future, has no historical possibility of realization. Internally, there are contravening projects, generated and dynamized from within the Church itself. Ecclesial Base Communities and Liberation Theology might be partially marginalized and partially co-opted but they can hardly be eliminated. Traditional popular piety, to the extent that it can survive the social crisis, is more likely to find its place in the Base Communities than in a neo-Christendom project. Consequently, I think that we can foresee the prospect of a Catholic Church conducted by its hierarchy along the lines of the "official" project but with considerable internal debate, dissent, and conflict (with significant losses both at the popular and at the leadership levels) but probably without schisms.

On the other hand, the social, economic, and political reality of Latin America, as it is more and more incorporated into the world economic system, with its cultural and ideological consequences, will hardly accommodate itself to the social doctrine of the Catholic Church. The Church, therefore, may find itself tied to the dominant social and economic structures and serving, in spite of its progressive discourse, as religious legitimation of hegemonic sectors, both at the international and Latin American levels. This will mean very limited insertion in the world of the poor and the popular — although it will formally remain the majority Church and popular Catholic religiosity will subsist.

PROTESTANTISM

The word "Protestantism" covers different things for different people. I will, however, use it as a generic term for all the churches, movements, and communities which have originated at some point in the Protestant religious field. Latin Americans call them *evangélicos* or *evangelistas.* We have, nevertheless, to introduce some distinctions. I will try to do it in a pragmatic way, not according to denominations or sociological distinctions, but in terms of their place in society, ideological tendencies, "missionary" perspective and religious ethos as I find them today in Latin America. The names I use are conventional, and I would happily entertain suggestions for a better terminology.

Historical Churches

I am grouping here both the churches which resulted from Protestant immigration and those originating in Protestant (mostly Anglo-Saxon) missionary work: Reformed, Lutherans, Presbyterians, Anglicans, Waldenians, Methodists, Disciples of Christ, Baptists, etc. They are at present predominantly middle-class churches (although some of the missions began as working-class or poor people's churches). There has been a growing ecumenical openness and forms of cooperation among these churches. Most of them would recognize themselves as sharing a common ethos, understanding of mission, and fundamental theological stance. They can be characterized as "progressive" or "liberal" (in the way the word is used in the United States) in ideology and non-fundamentalist in their theology. They have developed a diversity of services to society (education, health, and care for children and the aged). More recently some have been in the forefront of the struggles for human rights and social justice.

The membership of these churches has in the last fifty years barely kept pace with the growth of the population, with the exception of Baptists, who are perhaps the least integrated in this group. They have developed a significant "evangelistic" activity in middle-class sectors. All of these churches are deeply affected by the crisis of the middle classes in the present situation. Two opposing tendencies are present in these churches, and frequently lead to internal tension and conflict. On the one hand, to react with bitterness and to look to the churches for refuge as their middle-class dreams fade or are frustrated. On the other, to see the situation as a challenge to solidarity with the lower or even more impoverished groups. Some of these churches have begun to develop a new Evangelical witness in popular sectors and some base communities are emerging among them. I don't think one should expect any spectacular growth among these churches but, in the best of situations, they can provide a valuable theological and spiritual service to the larger Protestant movement.

Indigenous Pentecostal Churches

These churches have been present in Latin America for more than half a century. Their growth has always been notable, but it has reached in the last ten to fifteen years extraordinary proportions in most Latin American countries.

This growth has taken place almost totally among the poor and socially marginalized or uprooted sectors of the population — though some of the older Pentecostal churches already have a significant middle-class constituency. Usually these churches have not developed a systematic theological thought but have retained and reinterpreted the Methodist, Baptist, or Reformed doctrine of their origins. It is in the expressive (charismatic) worship and in the fraternal, solidary, and closely integrated community where one finds the elements which make Pentecostalism distinct.

The traditional stance of these churches has been a total separation of church and world. They try to avoid as much as possible any close contact with the world, which they consider to be under the control of Satan. However, some of the indigenous Pentecostal churches have begun to develop a new social awareness and to look for social and political participation. In recent elections in Perú, Brazil, Guatemala, and Venezuela, there have been candidates from Pentecostal and other Evangelical communities, in some cases with the explicit support of their religious communities. I think we can expect this tendency to increase and, while realizing the ambivalence of motivations, ideologies, and social projects that are present in these trends, I think we should see in them the signs of a positive development that Protestantism should critically own and help to develop. At the same time, a younger leadership is providing for these churches, from within their own traditions, a theological understanding that can widen their missionary horizon and strengthen and clarify their social commitment.

Transnational Churches and Religious Movements

Under this heading I shall have to group different religious associations whose characteristic in common is that they have been more or less recently constituted. Organized in many cases on the model of modern transnational enterprises or corporations, they come with organized teams, mass communications media, and certain standard features such as modern music, elaborate staging, a strong emphasis upon the "charismatic" personality of the "evangelist," etc. Although the basic evangelistic "outline" of their message is that of classical fundamentalist theology, its emphasis (and I would add, its impact) seems to hinge on other things. A key factor seems to be the offer of "health and prosperity" as goals attainable by belief, through the personal gift of the evangelist and as a consequence of their personal conversion to the message. Originating mainly in the "new religious right" in the United States, the number of such groups, movements, and organizations has multiplied during the last decade. But they are now also originating in Latin America (in Brazil, Colombia, Puerto Rico, etc.). They are not all necessarily connected with the religio-political religious right in the United States, although they frequently share their ideological positions.

We should, however, make distinctions within this grouping. There are some recently arrived Pentecostal missions who organize churches. There are also evangelistic corporations that are mostly interested in the use of mass media and mass meetings around "traveling evangelists," but which do not constitute churches. And we have the more traditional para-Protestant groups like Mormons, Jehovah's Witnesses, Christian Science, and more recent ones like the Unification Church (Mr. Moon) or the Children of God.

It is still too early to gauge the significance of this phenomenon. On the one hand, we should be careful to distinguish the message, purpose, or intended result of these movements and what the people, particularly the poor people, do with it. On the other hand, frequently the people who are attracted to these groups through the mass media are ultimately looking for a more permanent and full religious life in the more established churches. Meanwhile, others are doubtless more or less permanently "immunized," because of these experiences, against all religious concern. I think that, as long as the present social conditions and the networking of nations through business, travel, and media continues and increases, we can expect this type of religious force to grow and multiply as part of what I have already referred to as "a diversified religious market." We can like it or deplore it. But we must recognize the human and religious need which their presence and success reveals, however much their action may not fulfill these needs or even function as an alienating factor.

Theological and Ideological Conflict

The difficulty of characterizing in absolute and unequivocal terms the different groups and churches in Latin America results from an important phenomenon that we must take into account. Some of the more acute tensions and conflicts on the Latin American religious scene have to do with theological interpretations, social commitments, and visions of the mission of Christianity which do not correspond to confessional or denominational divisions but cut across them. The result is that we have — and I think we will increasingly have — forms of association which will bring together Christians from different churches for common tasks and witness without, in many cases, breaking the ties with their own communities. But this, no doubt, will be potentially conflictive. Or it may introduce a ferment for change, even as it opens up the possibility of new unities.

PROSPECTS AND PURPOSES

We have been speaking about the "prospects" which the situation opens up for Christianity in Latin America. Should we not be more concerned with the purpose of Christianity in Latin America? How do we intend to offer to our people in message and life an authentic testimony of the Gospel? It is no more a question of *what will happen to Christianity* in Latin America but of *what will Christianity do* here. This question does not so much demand an analysis as a confession and a commitment. I will not attempt to answer these questions. But speaking from within my own community — one of the Protestant churches mentioned in the first group — and also as my own personal concern, I ask myself and my church some questions in terms of the challenges and options I think we confront as Latin American Christian churches and communities in the immediate — and perhaps mid-term — future.

1. Will my church opt to accompany the growing marginalized and oppressed

majorities in their religious and human quest? Or will it be satisfied with a "stable clientele" in the middle and high-middle sectors of society, with perhaps some "social service" to the poor on the side?

2. Will my church limit itself to entering the "religious market" with an offer of "salvation products" — health, inner peace, earthly prosperity, and a happy hereafter? Or will it be an invitation to the discipleship of a Lord who offers forgiveness, joy, peace, and eternal life, but who also demands prophetic courage, active solidarity, and the building of a different world?

3. Will my church offer closed communities of refuge or will it recruit for open communities of evangelizing witness, solidarity, and service?

4. How will my church define the center of its message? By "reduction" — whether sotereological, ethical, pietistic, or social — or by the integrity of the wholeness of the Biblical message?

5. Will my church give preference to the "success" of a narrow, self-concerned, and aggressive confessional or denominational militancy, or privilege the witness of a Gospel that creates a spirit of cooperation and unity?

21

The Many Faces of the Latin American Church

Guillermo Cook

The foregoing study makes it fairly clear that there is not one "face of the Church in Latin America." There are many faces — the several faces of catholicism and of protestantism. What we have, in fact, are facets (small faces) that reflect the light off of each other in complex and unpredictable ways. The groupings that are represented in this book — Catholics, Liberationists, Ecumenists, Pentecostals, and Evangelicals — can be hyphenated with each other in a variety of ways. The book's contributors demonstrate that, despite the dramatic changes in ecclesial reality in Latin America, many things remain unchanged, or continue to function, albeit with sometimes surprisingly different actors.

As José Míguez Bonino and Pablo Richard have pointed out in the concluding chapters, the tragic social reality of Latin America, if anything, will worsen. In the words of Samuel Escobar, "For the vast majority of the poor, the situation is, indeed, hopeless. There would be no hope at all if the expectation of a significant number of the poor were not placed upon the God of integral salvation and liberation."

But there are changes, especially at the ecclesial level. The most significant change, of course, is that it is now the *Latin American* churches, warts and all, that have taken their destiny into their own hands. Traditional holdouts in Roman Catholicism and in North American and European mission structures, one is tempted to say, will go the way of the dinosaurs — except that it is now possible to bring back the dinosaurs, in fantasy, and perhaps even in fact. And it is the grassroots churches, more than the local ecclesiastical heirs of the traditional churches, that are shaking the trees of well-entrenched vested interests.

But some of the key actors, even at the grassroots level, have changed.

CATHOLICISM: BETWEEN TRADITION AND CHANGE

These are some of the issues that have struck me as I have compiled this book.

Popular Religiosity

Catholic popular religion, which Maria Clara Bingemer Luchetti explains so eloquently, remains a problem for most Protestants. In the Latin American Protestant tradition, criticism of Roman catholicism is based on

> the great Reformation themes of *solo Christo* (vs. the mediation of Mary, saints, and priesthood), *sola gratia* (vs. sacramentalism), *sola fides* (vs. papal authority), and *Sola Scriptura* (vs. Word of God, weight of tradition, and interpretation by magisterium). These issues stand out in Latin America where both traditional or medieval catholicism and fundamentalist protestantism remain strong. (Cook 1993c)

Protestantism, as Stanley Slade shows, also has its own brand of popular religiosity. His argument, that popular protestantism maintains a traditional Catholic attitude toward the magical effects of the *cultus*, is not limited to El Salvador. How to relate to popular religion, both Catholic and Protestant, is part of what anthropologist Paul Hiebert calls "the unfinished agenda in the lives of young churches around the world." These beliefs and practices need to be studied "without rejecting them outright in order to understand them and the questions they answer," then tested "in the light of biblical teaching" (Phillips and Coote 1993, 258).

A Counter-Reformation

This is what Winn (1992, 372f.) calls the present Vatican policies toward the Catholic renewal movements, and in particular liberation theology and the base communities. Nonetheless, he states (referring to Brazil, but extrapolating to all of Latin America):

> Progressive Catholics may be on the defensive in the final decade of the millennium, but they have made their mark on the world's largest national Church. As a result, there is a consensus in Brazil in favor of a strong Church stand on human rights and democracy, and even conservatives talk of the need for social justice and a special concern for the poor. . . . Grassroots organizations such as the base communities have proliferated throughout the region and established a popular participation that the Vatican may want to redirect into more exclusively spiritual channels but is reluctant to reverse. (1992, 377)

While "progressive theologians might trim their sails to accommodate the changed winds from Rome . . . 'people have been touched by the message of liberation theology and that is consolidated,'" in the opinion of a lay missionary. The people "themselves tell us that, and you can see it in the connections that they make between life and faith — even in what they sing. . . . They love to sing that song about the Exodus that goes: 'We are the people of God' — and, when they reflect on that line, they say: 'We *too* are the people of God. Now that won't go away'" (ibid., 377-378).

Tradition in Crisis

What comes as a surprise is that liberation theology is one of the traditions that is in crisis. This is apparent not merely because of Vatican opposition (nor even because of its over-reliance upon a now defunct Marxism), but because it somehow strayed from its original vision as a movement "from the bottom up." It was also on the way to becoming a tradition (as Richard indirectly recognizes). What was once a movement with considerable promise is in danger of becoming a monument to aging theologians. Sadly, liberation theology lost touch with the masses that it thought it represented. Historian Winn observes that, to conservatives "progressive base communities were part of the problem, not its solution, because they offered 'sociological support,' not the 'human support' that the Protestant sects provided." This critique needs to be taken seriously. But more than that:

> the problem was not the social concerns of the base community, but the character of its members and the burdens of its theology. The BECs, with their stress on Bible reading and the analysis of the written word, emphasized a literacy that many poor Brazilians did not possess. (1992, 383)

An illiterate woman who left a base community in a Rio shantytown to become a Pentecostal explained that "I used to be a Catholic. But when these Bible circles came, all they did was read, read, read. There was no more prayer. I felt they only liked those who could read." This raises an interesting historical question. The MEB, or Basic Education Movement, which was pioneered by an "intellectual, idealistic, and radical" young Catholic Action elite in the 1960s, was one of the sources of the Brazilian BECs. It gradually developed from a literacy program into "a movement that had a growing stake in changing the basic socio-economic structures of Brazil." The MEB leadership debated over the relative merits of a non-directive vs. a directive methodology and eventually chose the latter, "more efficient" way of achieving their goals (Cook 1985, 65-67). Today, Fr. Comblin, a Belgian missiologist who had identified closely with those "young radicals," decries the passivity and top-down mentality of today's BECs in Northeastern Brazil. The following statement, from a leading Brazilian daily, sums up the problems of Brazilian, and in varying degrees, Latin American Catholicism:

> The decline of the so-called historical churches . . . and the growth of the Pentecostal sects can be seen as the consequence of the disillusionment of urban Brazilians who do not find in them where and how to spiritually compensate for the bitterness of their daily lives. Disillusionment largely explains why five churches from "new denominations" appear in Rio de Janeiro every week. This is a religious phenomenon of great consequences, if one pays attention to the recently converted mother who remarked: "We grab whatever religion is closest to us." The more dehumanizing that life becomes in urban spaces it would seem that the less space there is for acceptance of historical religions. . . . The poorer the population of Rio becomes the less Catholic it is. (*O Estado* 1993; cp. *Veja* 1991, 32-38)

A great deal of the problem with liberation theology and its appeal (or lack of it) to the churches is language. Fernando Quicaña has reminded us of the admonition of St. Paul: "If I do not grasp the meaning of what someone is saying, I am a foreigner to the speaker and he is a foreigner to me. . . . I would rather speak five intelligent words to instruct others than ten thousand words in a [strange] tongue" (1 Cor. 14:10, 11, 19). Reminiscent of old-time Protestant fundamentalism — where one's orthodoxy was often judged by the "biblical" language that one used — liberationists often evaluate the commitment of other Christians to social change and integral liberation by the "in-house" language that they use. Going completely counter to the Freirian method that they once espoused, liberationist Catholics and Protestants continue to rely too much on technical terminology when they discuss social issues. Aside from being largely incomprehensible to many, this idiom creates an unnecessary inferiority complex among those that do not belong to the intellectual elite. It can all too easily be dismissed as "so much marxist jargon." I see no signs of change in this respect in much of the liberationist literature that I have read since the fall of the ex-Soviet Union. This also happens in theological discussions.

> The question that must be raised at this point is methodological. Is there not an inherent contradiction between the use of the categories of an erudite 'higher' criticism and the development of a 'theology from below' based upon . . . popular wisdom? (Cook 1985, 111)

Theological questions need to be raised as well. Evangelical Protestants have not been speaking solely out of ideological conservatism when they point out the small emphasis in liberationist literature upon personal conversion. Granting that Evangelicals have often made conversion an individualistic and vertical experience, they have valid Scripture-based concerns. In reacting against this imbalance, liberation theology leaned overmuch in the direction of horizontalism. Thousands of persons, including not a few who once participated in the BECs, have turned to grassroots protestantism in search of forgiveness and freedom from sin and peace with God. The hope of everlasting life, here and in the hereafter, is very much a part of popular — and biblical — faith. Liberation theology neglects this at its own peril.

These observations are not meant to question the value of liberation theology. It has made the entire Church, including many erstwhile conservative Evangelicals, aware of structural sin, and has moved many into active solidarity with the poor. Perhaps the greatest contribution of liberation theology has been — and will continue to be — its "new way of doing theology." Scripture is being read in community by the poor and marginalized "from the bottom up." It is when liberation theology and some of the base communities started to move up and away from this methodology that they lost contact with their roots. It is a phenomenon akin to the upward mobility of the historical Protestant churches that moved them from the great majority of Latin Americans.

The BECs in Central America may have escaped some of the problems of their Brazilian counterparts because of the virtual absence of priests, as a result of the wars, and also the input of grassroots protestantism. It is probably because of this that Fr. Richard insists on the continued viability of the BECs in the region. A decade ago I wrote that the Catholic base communities were the hope of the church (Cook 1985, 251). What I could not foresee is that the major beneficiaries of their vision of social transformation may turn out to be grass-roots Protestant churches and a new breed of ecumenical base communities!

PROTESTANTISM: BETWEEN TRADITION AND CHANGE

Native American Cultural and Religious Revival

Speaking from his Quechua ethnicity, Quicaña asserts that ancient cultural traditions are being revived and celebrated in Native American Protestant churches, as well as in the Catholic context. In Guatemala, "the emergence of a broader pan-Maya identity . . . is a striking development of the past decade." A vigorous Mayan studies movement has developed that transcends the ancestral rivalries of the various tribes. "Particularly striking," says Winn, "is their stress on transmitting a sense of Mayan culture and identity to the younger generation, subjected to the lures of modern *ladino* society, international popular culture, and evangelical Protestantism" (1992, 268, 269). The missing article by a Protestant Maya in Central America would have shown just how radical this cultural and religious revival can be — among Protestants as well as Catholics. Sr. Judith Noon comments on this fact, even as she is critical of the sociocultural insensitivity of her Protestant missionary colleagues. Our assessment of nativistic religions will have to await a more serious study lest we be guilty of premature judgments.[1] Rather than throwing stones, we need to recognize our often insensitive and culpable practices in the evangelization and discipling of native peoples. Hiebert's assessment is correct.

> Christian converts found in the gospel the way of ultimate salvation, but the church often had few answers to their immediate questions about sickness, witchcraft, spirits, guidance, and success. So they returned to their old ways for answers to these questions, even as they went to church for forgiveness and fellowship with God. When the missionaries and church leaders condemned them for doing so, they simply continued in secret. (Phillips and Coote 1993, 258)

New Popular Majorities and New Sects

The poor sink deeper into poverty and can never be forgotten by the Church. But the agents of hope and transformation may have changed. There is a noteworthy and unsettling fact about radical Protestant agencies and churches in Central America, and perhaps elsewhere. The bewildering alphabet soup of small activist organizations has entered into a profound identity crisis. Within months of the downfall of the "communist menace," they fell to squabbling among themselves, and breaking apart. Lacking a clear theological focus, when the sociological realities seemed to change, they lost their sense of direction.[2]

Escobar argues that the new protagonists of ecclesial renewal are now grass-roots Protestants, and in particular the Pentecostals. Curiously, those erstwhile champions of radical change and ecumenism, liberationists — both Catholic and Protestant — have been the slowest in recognizing the fact that the baton may have passed to "conservative" grassroots Pentecostals. Pentecostals have been accepted by them only to the degree that they fit into a particular social agenda. The rest are written off as "sects." However, as a Brazilian ecumenical activist points out in Paul Freston's chapter, "ecumenical/liberationist" protestantism, at least in Brazil and probably in other places as well, became a short-lived sect. Meanwhile, some of the "sects" (i.e. the Pentecostals) have become more ecumenical — in the real sense that they do encompass the Latin American *oikomene*, and also in their approaches to other Christian confessions (Westmeir 1993, 133). The Roman Catholic Church, however, backed off from its past attempts at ecumenism, as was demonstrated by the handful of Protestant observers who were invited to Santo Domingo (Cleary 1993).

Ms. Bingemer, Fr. José Comblin, and the Catholic missiologists quoted by Escobar must be commended for debunking the conspiracy myth. While critical of the Pentecostals, they take them seriously. Unfortunately, many other liberation theologians are unable to recognize their ideological blindness. A case in point is the concluding paper by Fr. Pablo Richard. I find no recognition of the significance of the Pentecostals as a factor in social as well as spiritual liberation. Pentecostals, however conservative they may seem to many of us, cannot be excluded from the "popular majorities" that are the principal focus of liberation theology. Pentecostals, as Juan Sepúlveda, Escobar, Comblin, and others point out, are not all the introverted and quietist "sects" that we took them to be. They must be taken into account as a factor in social liberation and integral transformation. A recent article by a conservative missiologist asserts:

> Pentecostal social assistance programs are often extensive. . . . Pentecostals are concerned with providing immediate help for people in need. However, the desire of Pentecostals to ease present suffering goes beyond the urgency of the moment. In the midst of a society that delegates the poor to inner slums and shanty towns, the Pentecostals endow their followers with a sense of identity and dignity and give them hope for tomorrow. In surveying a Brazilian slum, it became clear that, after a few years, the believers had achieved modest improvement in their social conditions through sacrifice and hard work." (Westmeir 1993, 29)

Pentecostal involvement in social change does not stop at providing aid for suffering people. There is an increasing awareness among Pentecostal leaders of the structural nature of evil and involvement at the grassroots in "such grassroot revolutionary activities as an *invasión* — an occupation of largely unoccupied lands by landless peasants and homeless city dwellers." These activist Pentecostals argue "that landowners who had more land than they needed were obligated by the Gospel to share it with others" (ibid., 30).

A New Reformation

Stoll suggests that grassroots Protestant congregations may be going through the same slow process of awareness raising as did the Catholic base communities in the 1950s (1990, 182). This is because there is more opportunity for radicalization when Protestant growth collides with increasing sociocultural impoverishment. Anthropologist Rubem César Fernandes adds another perspective.

While he "is skeptical of Protestantism's ultimate power to change Brazil," he identifies its focus on individual self-determination as a potentially powerful cultural force. He states:

> Both the Catholic Church and the Afro-Brazilian religions say you don't really control yourself. You belong to the spirits. They haunt you, they guide you, they follow you around. But the Protestants have this image of self-control. They are secure, strict, ethical. (Marcom 1990, 64)

Middle-Class Responses

Tradition and change are also vying with each other among middle-class Protestants. Extreme poverty and the gospel, both growing, now overlap. This has produced a new set of factors on the Latin American religious scene.

A superficial theology and a poorly-trained clergy are hindering Protestant responses to the social crisis. Fewer Protestants today are achieving social betterment. Nonetheless, by the sheer force of numbers, Protestants may be making a positive impact upon society. But those Protestants who manage to move upward by dint of discipline and hard work have more to lose by rocking the boat, and have become more politically conservative.

Both Martin and Stoll argue that conservative religion is capable of becoming an agent for change. Was this not the case with the Catholic Church in the 1960s and 1970s? Martin warns us not to underestimate the transformational potential of the Pentecostal "social strike *from* society" (as opposed to the marxist "strike *against* society"). Once marginal Protestants gain a greater feeling of security in numbers, mature, and improve their social lot, they can become more aware of their civic responsibilities. There are indications that this is beginning to take place.

Social Awareness and Activism

Because they are now part of the mainstream of Latin American life, Protestants partake of the same problems, challenges and responsibilities as their non-Protestant neighbors.

Protestant responses reflect the major tensions in society rather than a coherent position. Latin Americans — the churches included — are experiencing a crisis of ideology and of identity, as they search for new utopias and role models. The "prosperity gospel" competes with grassroots hopes. By nature creative and adaptive, the poor may pick and chose from among the political and religious options those that best seem to meet their immediate needs. Among those options are the Pentecostal churches and the more radical base communities.

Meanwhile the middle classes, having finally attained some status and power, are seeking to cut their losses. While social betterment as a result of the gospel and hard work seemed to be an option, the small Protestant middle class was not tempted to change the existing social order. But their perceptions have begun to change as a result of the social and religious crisis in the region. Although Protestants now have high political visibility in several countries, their political involvement is still a divisive issue among many of their coreligionists. Indeed, this involvement is not without dangers. It has tended to be self-serving, instead of acting out of a concern for the general welfare of the people — especially the most disadvantaged. There is a growing disillusionment with both the institutional churches and the traditional political processes. Christians are looking for new models of church and civil society that are more responsive to the needs of the majorities. Protestants can make a solid contribution to integral transformation to the degree in which they follow the way of the crucified God. The Catholic BECs and grassroots Pentecostalism would seem to point the way.

Zeal for Evangelization and Mission

Protestants in Latin America are renowned for the untiring zeal with which they witness to their faith and hope in Jesus Christ (chapters 5 and 6). Although not originally a grassroots movement (the original impetus came from North America), increasingly the middle class, and particularly Pentecostal and Charismatic churches, are sending missionaries from Latin America to every continent. The question was asked at a major evangelical missions conference, COMIBAM 1987, "How can we Latin Americans avoid the same mistakes committed by Western Missions?" (Philips and Coote 1993, 132) An increasingly vocal group of Latin American missiologists is questioning "the managerial missiology that stresses verbal proclamation and numerical growth of church affiliation as the main component of Christian mission, and is reluctant to criticize the imperialistic nature of its ideological assumptions." This questioning is based upon "a clear commitment to the enterprise of mission and evangelism, but also a conscious search to carry on that enterprise according to biblical standards" (133).

WHATEVER HAPPENED TO BIBLICAL CHRISTIANITY?

What place does the Bible have in the Latin American churches? How does Holy Scripture fare in the tension between tradition and change? One of the more troubling aspects of what is happening to the churches in Latin America is the marginalization of the Bible, not only in catholicism but also, increasingly, in protestantism.

Catholics and the Bible

Because of the Vatican-approved Biblical Renewal, the Charismatic Renewal, and Base Ecclesial Communities, Scripture in the common language became available to the people. Catholics began to read the Bible with new eyes, unencumbered by the centuries of overlay from our various Protestant traditions. This was a very exciting and challenging new phenomenon, which even some Protestants were capable of recognizing. It was likened to "a new reformation." However, something happened on the way to the institutionalization of the renewal movements. Biblical hermeneutics seems to have been coopted — by the hierarchy, by middle-class Charismatics, and by some liberation theologians.

Protestants and the Bible

This phenomenon is not limited to the renewal movements within Catholicism. Protestants are also losing sight of the Bible, and for the same reasons. "The gospel people" that Mike Berg and Paul Pretiz write about have been called "people of the book" —the Bible. Yet they call themselves "biblical and Christian, with no idea of what these words mean" (quoted in Stoll 199C, 173). Despite the reformational *sola scriptura* doctrine, Protestantism also has its traditions through which we interpret Scripture and magisteriae who interpret it for us — at times with pretensions of inspired infallibility. The latter is particularly true in those churches stressing "the prophetic gift." However, "prophecy from above," when not anchored in the prophetic Word of God and in concrete historical events and realities, becomes nothing less than false prophecy (cp. Dt. 18:17-22; Jer. 28). As John Stam, a knowledgeable Central America observer, evaluates the situation:

> Evangelicals . . . have every reason to be thankful to God for the great tradition of which they are heirs, but little reason to feel triumphalistic. . . . [They] have been repeating all "the saved by faith" formulas, but in general have tended to fall into nonevangelical legalisms . . . [reflecting] all too faithfully the individualistic, competitive, success-oriented elements of their society. (Stoll, 172)

If the Church in Latin America is truly to show "a new face" as it turns to a new millennium, if it is to maintain a healthy equilibrium "between tradition and change," it must rediscover the Bible. Rather, we must allow Scripture to act freely, without encumbrances. Like a lion, God's Word does not need to be protected. It must be freed from its cage so that it can fulfill the divine purposes in history. The "new reformation" that Latin America cries for will begin, as all reformations throughout history have done, from the grassroots churches — Pentecostals, base communities, house churches, local congregations — that open themselves up to the action of the Holy Spirit. Churches, Protestant and Catholic, that let themselves be freed up by the Word of God in order to act as responsible agents of radical change for persons and society. If this does not happen, we are in danger of repeating the tragic mistakes of the first five hundred years of evangelization in Latin America. Despite all of the positive changes in the churches, it might be said that in Latin America: "The more things change the more they are the same."

San José, Costa Rica
Sunday, 18 July 1993

NOTES

1. Shortly after turning in the manuscript for this book, I had the opportunity to spend two weeks in a number of Maya communities, some of them quite remote, where some Protestant churches are very much a part of a cultural awakening and resistance movement. The implications of this for Protestant mission must be the subject of another study.

2. The Baptist Association of El Salvador and the Presbyterian Church of Guatemala are two recent examples.

BIBLIOGRAPHY

Abumanssur, Edin. 1991. *A Tribo Ecumênica: Um Estudo do Ecumenismo nos anos 60 e 70*. Master's thesis, Pontifícia Universidade de São Paulo.

———. 1987. "Pentecostais e trabalho comunitário." *Comunicaçoes do ISER*, vol. 6, no. 24.

Adriance, Madelaine. 1986. *Opting for the Poor: Brazilian Catholicism in Transition*. Kansas City: Sheed and Ward.

Aguilar, Edwin Eloy, et al. 1992. "Protestantism in El Salvador: Conventional Wisdom versus Survey Evidence," *Latin American Research Review*, Research Reports and Notes.

Alvarez, Carmelo. 1990. *People of Hope: The Protestant Movement in Central America*. New York: Friendship Press.

AMERINDIA. 1989. "Povos indígenas antes da chegada do branco," *Tempo e Presença*, no. 242 (Rio de Janeiro, June).

Anderson, G. H., Phillips, J. B., and Coote, R. T. (eds.). 1991. *Mission in the Nineteen 90's*. Grand Rapids: Eerdmans.

Anis, Sheldon. 1987. *God and Production in a Guatemalan Town*. Austin: University of Texas Press.

Arbunckle, Gerald A. 1990. *Earthing the Gospel*. Maryknoll: Orbis.

Arévalo, Juan José. 1963. *Anti-Communism in Latin America*. New York: Lyle Stuart.

Arns, Paulo Evaristo. 1992. "Brazil: Social Justice and Ecumenism," *SEDOS Bulletin*, no. 24.

Arroyo, Victor, and Paredes, Tito. 1992. "Evangelicals and 'The Fujimori Phenomenon,'" *Transformation: An International Dialogue on Evangelical Social Ethics* (July-Sept.), pp. 15-19.

Assmann, Hugo, and Hinkclammert, Franz. 1989. *A idolatria, do mercado: Ensaio sobre economía e teología*. São Paulo: Vozes.

Aubry, Mgr. Roger. 1990. *La misión siguiendo a Jesús por los caminos de América Latina*. Buenos Aires: Ed. Guadalupe.

Baez Camargo, Gonzalo. 1981. *Genio y espiritu del metodismo wesleyano*. México: Casa Unida de Publicaciones (second ed.).

———. 1959. "Evangelical Faith and Latin American Culture," in Edward J. Jurji (ed.), *The Ecumenical Era in Church and Society*. New York: Macmillan.

Barbieri, Sante U. 1961. *Land of Eldorado*. New York: Friendship Press.

Bastian, Jean Pierre. 1993. "The Metamorphosis of Latin American Protestant Groups: A Sociohistorical Perspective," *Latin American Research Review*, vol. 28, pp. 3-61.

———. 1992. "Protestantism in Latin America," in Enrique Dussel (ed.), *The Church in Latin America: 1492-1992*. Maryknoll: Orbis, pp. 313-351.

———. 1990. "Popular Groups, Popular Culture, and Popular Religion," *Comparative Studies in Society and History*, vol. 32, pp. 718-764.

———. 1990. *Historia del Protestantismo en América Latina*. México: Casa Unida de Publicaciones. First published in 1986.

_____. 1989. *Los Disidentes: sociedades protestantes y revolución en Mexico 1872-1911*. México: Fondo de Cultura Económica.

_____. 1985. "Para una aproximación teórica del fenómeno religioso protestante en América Central," *Cristianismo y sociedad*, no. 85.

_____. 1984. "Protestantismos Latinoamericanos entre la Resistencia y la Sumisión: 1961-1983," *Cristianismo y sociedad*, no. 82, pp. 49-58.

_____. 1983. *Protestantismo y sociedad en Mexico*. Mexico: CUPSA.

Bebbington, David. 1989. *Evangelicalism in Modern Britain*. London: Unwin Hyman.

Berger, Peter L., and Luckmann, Thomas. 1966. *The Social Construction of Reality*. Garden City: Doubleday.

Betto, Frei. 1980. *O que é a comunidade eclesial de base*. São Paulo: Editora Brasiliense.

Bingemer, Maria Clara Luchetti. 1992. "The Laity in Today's Latin American Church," *SEDOS Bulletin*, no. 24.

Bittencourt Filho, José. 1989. "As Seitas no Contexto do Protestantismo Histórico," in Leilah Landim (ed.), *Sinais dos Tempos: Igrejas e Seitas no Brasil*. Cadernos de ISER 21, Rio de Janeiro, ISER, pp. 27-32.

Bobsin, Oneide. 1984. "Produção religiosa e significação social do Pentecostalismo a partir de sua Prática e Representação." Masters thesis, Potifícia Universidade Católica de São Paulo.

Boff, Clodovis. 1987a. *Feet on the Ground Theology*. Maryknoll: Orbis.

_____. 1987b. *Theology and Praxis*. Maryknoll: Orbis.

_____. 1979. *Sinais dos tempos: principios de leitura*. São Paulo: Ediçones Loyola.

Boff, Leonardo. 1990. *New Evangelization: Good News to the Poor*. Maryknoll: Orbis.

Bogenschild, Thomas E. 1991. "The Roots of Fundamentalism in Northwestern Guatemala — 1900-1944," *LASA* (4 April). Center for Latin American Studies, University of California, Berkeley.

Boletim Teologico. 1991. Vol. 23, no. 41. Buenos Aires: Fraternidade Teológica Latinoamericana.

_____. 1990. Vol. 22, no. 39.

_____. 1989. Vol. 21, no. 36.

Boletim Teologico. 1980. São Paulo, Brazil: Fraternidade Teológica Latinoamericana, no. 12 (August).

Borah, W., and Cook, S. F. 1985. *The Aboriginal Population of Central America on the Eve of the Spanish Conquest*. Berkeley: University of California Press.

Borges Morán, Pedro. 1987. *Misión y civilización en América*. Madrid: Alhambra.

_____. 1960. *Métodos misionales en la cristianización de América—Siglo XVI*. Madrid: Consejo Superior de Investigaciones Científicas.

Boston Theological Institute. 1988. *One Faith, Many Cultures, Annual Series*, vol. 2. Maryknoll: Orbis; Boston: Boston Theological Institute.

Boxer, C. R. 1978. *The Church Militant and Iberian Expansion 1440-1770*. Baltimore and London: The John Hopkins University Press.

Brandao, Carlos R. 1980. *Os Deuses do povo: um estudo sobre religiao popular*. São Paulo: Editora Brasilense. (See Cook 1982.)

Bruce, Steve. 1990. *A House Divided: Protestantism, Schism and Secularization*. London: Routledge.

_____. 1989. *God Save Ulster! The Religion and Politics of Paisleyism*. Oxford University Press.

Bruno-Jofré, Rosa del Carmen. 1988. *Methodist Education in Peru. Social Gospel,*

Politics, and American Ideological and Economic Penetration, 1888-1930. Waterloo: Wilfrid Laurier University Press.

Bühlman, Walbert. 1986. *The Church of the Future*. Maryknoll: Orbis.

Burgos-Debray, Elizabeth, ed. 1984. *I, Rigoberta Menchú*. London: Verso Editions.

Cajas, Marco Tulio. 1985. "La tarea política de los evangélicos: Ideas para una nueva Guatemala." Guatemala: Grupo Cristiano de Reflexión. Unpublished paper.

Calder, Bruce. 1991. "The Response of the Catholic Church to the Growth of Protestantism in Guatemala." Department of History, University of Illinois at Chicago.

Campbell, Tim. 1980. "Resource Transformation in Squatter Households: Testing a System Model of Urbanism." Ph.D. dissertation, University of California at Berkeley.

Canales, Palma, and Villela. 1991. *En Tierra Extraña II. Para una sociología de la religiosidad popular protestante*. Santiago, Chile: SEPADE.

Carmack, Robert M., ed. 1988. *Harvest of Violence: The Maya Indians and the Guatemalan Crisis*. Norman and London: University of Oklahoma Press.

Cartaxo Rolim, Francisco. 1979. "Pentecostisme et Societé au Brasil," *Social Campass*, vol. 26, no. 2/3.

Castro, Emilio. 1990. "Mission in the 1990s," *International Bulletin of Missionary Research* (IBMR).

Cavalcanti, Robinson. 1990. "Lausanne: Caminhos e Descaminhos do Evangelismo," *Boletim Teológico*, pp. 29-36.

CEDI. 1990. "Pentecostalismo Autônomo, uma inversao sedutora?" *Aconteceu no mundo evangélico*, Suplemento especial Nº 548. São Paulo, Centro Ecuménico de Documentacao e Informacao (December).

CELAM (Consejo Episcopal Latinoamericano). n.d. *Elementos de pastoral ecuménica*, no. 52. Bogotá.

Cenami, A. C. 1993. *Teologia india mayense: Memorias, experiencias y reflexiones de encuentros teológicos regionales*. Quito: Abya Yala.

Clawson, David L. 1984. "Religious Allegiance and Economic Development in Rural Latin America," *Journal of Interamerican Studies and World Affairs*, vol. 26. no. 4 (November), pp. 499-524.

Cleary, Edward. 1993. "El maltrato de la jerarquía católica a los pentecostales," *Pastoral Popular*, no. 26 (March), Santiago, Chile, pp. 15-17.

Cleary, Edward, and Stewart-Gambino, Hannah, eds. 1992. *Conflict and Competition: The Latin American Church in a Changing Environment*. Boulder: Lynne Rienner Publishers.

Coleman, M.M., William. 1958. *Latin American Catholicism: A Self Evaluation*. Maryknoll: Orbis.

COMLA IV. 1991. Cuarto Congreso Misionero Latinoamericano. *Memorias del COMLA IV*. Lima: Obras Misionales Pontificias.

Conceição, M. 1980. *Essa é nossa terra*. Petrópolis: Vozes.

Cook, Guillermo. 1993a. "Évangélisation, Repentir, Conversion," *Spiritus: Monde Noveau, Création Nouvelle*. Trimestral Review, Missions étrangères de Paris (May), pp. 163-177.

_____. 1993b. "Protestant Presence and Social Change in Latin America: Contrasting Visions," *The Church in Latin America*. In press.

_____. 1993c. "Santo Domingo through Protestant Eyes," in Alfred T. Hennelley, ed., *Santo Domingo and Beyond*. Maryknoll: Orbis.

_____. 1993d. "The Church, the World, and Progess in Latin America, in Light of the Escatological Kingdom," in Sepúlveda (1993).

_____. 1992a. "Christian Conversion: A Perspective from Latin America." Paper presented at the Conference of the International Association for Mission Studies (IAMS), Hawaii (August).

_____. 1992b. "Growing Pains," *Christianity Today*. CT Institute.

_____. 1992c. "Von der religiösen Sehnsucht und Energie der Armen," *Jahrbuch Mission 1992*. Hamburg: Evangelische Missionswerk, pp. 115-132.

_____. 1991a. "Entstehung un Praxis der evangelischen Bassisgemeinden in Mittel- amerika," *Evangelisches Theologie*, no. 61. Tübingen, pp. 543-550.

_____. 1991b. "The Church in Latin America after 500 Years." Paper presented to the Overseas Ministries Study Center (OMSC) Study Group (April).

_____. 1990. "The Evangelical Groundswell in Latin America," *The Christian Century* (12 December).

_____. 1985. *The Expectation of the Poor: Latin American Base Ecclesial Communities in Protestant Perspective*. Maryknoll: Orbis.

_____. 1982. "*Os Deuses do Povo* [The Gods of the People]. A review of the book by Carlos Rodrigues Brandao," *Missiology: An International Review*, vol. 10, no. 2, pp. 3-6.

Costas, Orlando E. 1976. *Theology of the Crossroads in Contemporary Latin America*. Amsterdam: Rodopi.

_____. 1974. *The Church and its Mission: A Shattering Critique from the Third World*. Wheaton: Creation House.

Costello, Gerald M. 1979. *Mission to Latin America*. Maryknoll: Orbis.

Coward, Harold. 1985. *Pluralism: Challenge to World Religions*. Maryknoll: Orbis.

Cox, Harvey. 1988. *The Silencing of Leonardo Boff*. Oak Park: Meyer-Stone.

CT Institute. 1992. "Why is Latin America Turning Protestant?" *Christianity Today*, vol. 26, no. 4 (April 6).

Damen, Franz. 1987. "Las sectas ¿avalancha o desafío?" *Cuarto Intermedio*, no. 3, Cochabamba, May.

Darry, Claudia. 1989. *El Protestantismo en Guatemala*, no. 2-89. *Cuaadernos de Investigación*. Guatemala: Universidad de San Carlos.

Dayton, Donald H. 1991a. "Algunas reflexiones sobre el pentecostalismo latino- american y sus implicaciones ecuménicas," *Cuardernos de Teología*, vol. 11, no. 2, pp. 5-20.

_____. 1991b. "El pentecostalismo está encontrando su destino en América latina," *Evangelio y Sociedad*, no. 11 (Nov.-Dec.), pp. 15-17.

_____. 1991c. *Raíces Teológicas del Pentecostalismo*. Buenos Aires: Nueva Creación; Grand Rapids: Eerdmans.

_____. 1988. "The Holy Spirit and Christian Expansion in the Twentieth Century," *Missiology: An International Review*, vol. 16, no. 3.

Dayton, Edward, and Fraser, David A. 1980. *Planning Strategies for World Evangelism*. Grand Rapids: Eerdmans.

DEI Team. 1991. "La Primera Gran guerra contra el Tercer Mundo: capitalismo, aplastamiento y solidaridad en el final del siglo," *Pasos*, no. 33. San José: DEI (Jan.-Feb.).

Deiros, Pablo Alberto. 1992. *Historia del cristianismo en América Latina*. Buenos Aires: Fraternidad Teológica Latinoamericana.

_____. 1986. *Los evangelicos y el poder político en America Latina*. Buenos Aires and Grand Rapids: Nueva Creación.

Dekker, James. 1985. "Conversion and Oppression: A Case Study on Guatemalan Indians," *Transformation*, vol. 2, no. 2.

Della Cava, Ralph, and Montero, Paula. 1991. *E o Verbo se Fex Imagem: Igreja Católica e os Meios de Comunicação no Brasil: 1962-1989*. Petrópolis: Vozes.

Domínguez, Enrique, and Huntingdon, Deborah. 1984. "The Salvation Brokers: Conservative Evangelicals in Central America," *NACLA Report on the Americas*, vol. 18, no. 1.

Douglas, J. D., ed. 1975. *Let the Earth Hear His Voice*. Minneapolis: Worldwide Publications.

Duarte, Laura M. S. 1963. *Isto nao se aprende na escola: a educação do povo nas CEBs*. Petrópolis: Vozes.

Dulles S.J., Avery. 1992. "John Paul and the New Evangelization," *America* (1 February).

Duque, José, ed. 1983. *La tradición protestante en la teología latinoamericana*. San José, Costa Rica: DEI.

Dussel, Enrique. 1981. *A History of the Church in Latin America. Colonialism to Liberation (1492-1979)*. Translated and revised by Alan Neely. Grand Rapids: Eerdmans.

Eagleson, John, and Scharper, Philip. 1979. *Puebla and Beyond*. Maryknoll: Orbis.

Elizondo, Virgilio. 1983. *Galilean Journey. The Mexican–American Promise*. Maryknoll: Orbis.

Ellacuría, Ignacio. 1990. *Mysterium Liberationis: Conceptos fundamentales de la Teología de la Liberación*, vols. 1, 2. Madrid: Editorial Trotta.

EMQ. 1979. *Evangelical Missions Quarterly* (Oct.).

Escobar, J. Samuel. 1992a. "A New Reformation," *Christianity Today*. CT Institute.

_____. 1992b. "Mission in Latin America: an Evangelical Perspective," *Missiology: An International Review* (April).

_____. 1991a. "Catholicism and National Identity in Latin America," *Transformation*, vol. 8, no. 3 (July-Sept.).

_____. 1991b. "Se revisa la nueva leyenda negra," *Edificación Cristiana*, nos. 145-146 (Madrid).

_____. 1991c. *Los Evangélicos ¿Nueva leyenda negra en América Latina?* México: CUPSA, 1991.

_____. 1989. "Nuevos estudios sobre la historia del Protestantismo en el Perú," *Boletín Teológico*, vol. 21, no. 36.

_____. 1987. *La fe evangélica y las teologías de la liberación*. El Paso: Casa Bautista de Publicaciones.

_____. 1982. "Beyond Liberation Theology: Evangelical Missiology in Latin America," *International Bulletin of Missionary Research*, vol. 6, no. 3 (July).

_____. 1978. "Identity, Future and Mission of Latin American Protestants," *Theological Fraternity Bulletin*, nos. 1-2. Buenos Aires.

_____. 1976. "The Return of Christ," *The New Face of Evangelicalism*. Downers Grove, IL: Intervarsity Press.

_____. 1975. "The Kingdom of God, Eschatology and Social and Political Ethics in Latin America," *Theological Fraternity Bulletin*, no. 1. Buenos Aires.

Espoz, Renato. 1990. "Los cristianos frente a la dependencia económica y la deuda externa," *Boletín Teológico*, 1990, pp. 219-228.

Falla, Ricardo. 1980. *Quiché rebelde: Estudio del movimiento de conversión religiosa, rebelde a las creencias tradicionales en San Antonio Ilotenango*. Guatemala: Editorial Universidad de San Carlos.

Fernandes, Luiza Beth A. 1985. *The Contribution of Basic Ecclesial Communities to an Education for Social Transformation in Brazil*. Ed.D. dissertation, Harvard University.

Fernandes, Rubem César. 1981. "Fundamentalismo à Direita e à Esquerda," *Tempo e Presença*, no. 29 (August), pp. 13-55.

Field, Alexander J., ed. 1987. *The Future of Economic History*. Norwell: Kluwer-Nijhoff.

_____. 1970. *City and Country in the Third World*. Cambridge, MA: Schenkman.

Freston, Paul. 1989. "Teócratas fisiológicos, nova direita e progressistas: Protestantes y políticos da Nova República." Paper presented at the twelfth AN-POCS, Caxambú, Brazil.

Fried, Jonathan L., and Gettlemen, Marvin, eds. 1983. "Religion and Revolution: A Protestant Voice," *Guatemala in Rebellion: Unfinished History*. New York: Grove Press.

Fry, Peter, and Howe, Gary H. 1975. "Duas resposas à aflição: Umbanda e Pentecostalismo," *Debate e Crítica*, no. 6, pp. 75-94.

Fukuyama, Francis. 1992. *The End of History and the Last Man*. New York: Free Press.

_____. 1990. *A Look at "The End of History."* Washington: United States Institute of Peace.

Galeano, Eduardo. 1973. *The Open Veins of Latin America: Five Centuries of the Pillage of a Continent*. Trans. by Cedric Belfrage. New York: Monthly Review Press.

Garrard-Burnett, Virginia. 1987. "Onward Christian Soldiers: The Rise of Protestantism in Guatemala: 1954-1984." Paper presented at SECOLAS Conference, Mérida, México.

Garrard-Burnett, Virginia, and Stoll, David, eds. 1993. *Rethinking Protestantism in Latin America*. Philadelphia: Temple University Press.

_____. 1989. "Protestantism in Rural Guatemala," *Latin American Research Review*, vol. 24, no. 2 (Nov.).

Gebara, Ivone, and Bingemer, Maria Clara. 1989. *Mary Mother of God, Mother of the Poor*. Maryknoll: Orbis.

Gibson, Charles, ed. 1971. *The Black Legend: Anti-Spanish Attitudes in the Old World and the New*. New York: Knopf.

Goldin, Liliana, R. 1991. "An Expression of Cultural Change: Invisible Converts to Protestantism among Highland Guatemalan Mayas," *Ethnology* (Oct.).

Gomes, José Francisco. 1985. *Religiao e política: Os Pentecostais no Recife*. Masters dissertation, Universidade Federal de Pernambuco.

González, Justo L. 1990. *La evangelización de la religiosidad popular andina*. Quito: Ediciones Abya-Yala.

_____. 1992. "The Christ of Colonialism," *Church and Society* (Jan.-Feb.), pp. 5-36.

_____. 1987. *From the Protestant Reformation to the Twentieth Century*, vol. iii of *A History of Christian Thought*. Nashville: Abbingdon.

Goodpasture, H. McKennie. 1989. *Cross and Sword: An Eyewitness History of Christianity in Latin America*. Maryknoll: Orbis.

Greenleaf, Richard E., ed. 1971. *The Roman Catholic Church in Colonial Latin America*. New York: Alfred A. Knopf.

Gutiérrez, Gustavo. 1992a. "New Evangelization: A Theological Reflection on the Latin American Church — Santo Domingo," *SEDOS Bulletin*, no. 24, pp. 182-197.

_____. 1992b. "The Quincentenary," *SEDOS Bulletin*, no. 24, pp. 169-176.

_____. 1982. "The Irruption of the Poor in Latin America," in Torres and Eagleson (eds.), pp. 107-123.

_____. 1981. "En busca de los pobres de Jesucristo," *Mensaje*, no. 302 (Lima, Perú), pp. 506-510.

Hallum, Anne M. 1993. "Mission Strategy and the Political Consequences of Evangelical Growth in Guatemala." Public Justice Report, Background Paper #93:1. Washington, DC: Center for Public Justice.

Hanke, Lewis. 1949. *The Spanish Struggle for Justice in the Conquest of America.* Philadelphia: University of Pennsylvania Press.

Hawkins, John. 1984. *Inverse Images: The Meaning of Culture, Ethnicity and Family in Guatemala.* Albuquerque: University of New Mexico Press.

Hewitt, W. E. 1986. "Strategies for Social Change Employed by the 'Comunidades Eclesiais de Base' (CEBs) in the Archdiocese of São Paulo," *Journal for the Scientific Study of Religion*, vol. 25, no. 1, pp. 1-30.

Hill, Robert M., and Monaghan, John. 1987. *Continuities in Highland Maya Social Organization.* Philadelphia: University of Pennsylvania Press.

Hillman, Eugene. 1989. *Many Paths: A Catholic Approach to Religious Pluralism.* Maryknoll: Orbis.

Hinkelammert, Franz. 1994. *La deuda externa y América Latina.* San José, Costa Rica: DEI. (First edition 1989.)

_____. 1981. *Las armas ideológicas de la muerte: democracia y totalitarismo.* San José, Costa Rica: DEI. (First edition 1977.)

Hoffnagel, Judith C. 1978. *The Believers: Pentecostalism in a Brazilian City.* Ph.D. dissertation, Indiana University.

Hollenweger, Walter J. 1986. "After Twenty Years' Research on Pentecostalism." *International Review of Mission (IRM)*, vol. 75, no. 297.

_____. 1972. *The Pentecostals: The Charismatic Movement in the Churches.* London: SCM Press, Ltd.

Horner, Norman A. 1965. *Cross and Crucifix in Mission.* Nashville: Abbingdon Press.

Hourton, Jorge. 1993. "Poco ecumenismo en Santo Domingo," *Pastoral Popular*, no. 26 (Santiago, Chile), p. 13.

Howard, George P. 1944. *Religious Liberty in Latin America.* Philadelphia: The Westminster Press.

Hurtado, Alberto. 1941. *¿Es Chile un país católico?* Santiago: Ediciones Esplendor.

IBMR. 1990. *International Bulletin of Missionary Research.* New Haven: Overseas Ministries Study Center (OMSC).

Ireland, Rowan. 1986. "Comunidades eclesiais de base, grupos espíritas e a democratização no Brazil," in Kirsche and Mainwaring (1986), pp. 151-184.

Itioka, Neuza. 1991. "Recovering the Biblical Worldview for Effective Mission," in Anderson et. al. (1991).

Johnstone, Arthur. 1978. *The Battle for World Evangelism.* Wheaton: Tyndale House.

Kessler, Jean B. A. 1990. "A Summary of the Costa Rican Evangelical Crisis: August 1989." Translated and updated from "La crisis evangélica costarricense en cifras." Pasadena: IDEA/Church Growth Studies Program, Research-in-Progress Report, Central American Series.

Keyes, Lawrence. 1983. *The Last Age of Missions: A Study of Third World Mission Societies.* Pasadena: Wm. Carey.

Kirkpatrick, Dow, ed. 1988. *Faith Born in the Struggle for Life.* Grand Rapids: Eerdmans.

Kirshke, Paulo J., and Mainwaring, Scott, eds. 1986. *A igreja nas bases em tempos de transição.* Porto Alegre: L&PM-CEDC.

Klaiber S.J., Jeffrey. 1990. "Toward a New History of the Church in the Third World," *IBMR*, vol. 14, no. 3 (July).

Kliewer, G. U. 1982. "Assembléia de Deus e eleições num município do interior do Matto Grosso," *Comunicaçõ do ISER*, no. iii.

Lalive d'Epinay, Christian. 1969. *Haven of the Masses: a Study of the Pentecostal Movement in Chile*. London: Lutterworth.

_____. 1968. *El refugio de las masas: estudio sociologico del Protestantismo chileno*. México: Casa Unida de Publicaciones.

Lancaster, Roger N. 1987. "Popular Religion and Class Consciousness in Managua's Working-Class Barrios." Paper presented to the annual meeting of the American Ethnological Society, San Antonio, Texas.

Latin American Council of Churches. 1991. *500 Years*, no. v. Quito, Ecuador: CLAI.

Latourette, Kenneth Scott. 1941. *The Great Century: History of the Expansion of Christianity*, vol. IV. Harper: New York.

Leeds, Anthony and Elisabeth. 1970. "Brazil and the Myth of Urban Rurality: Urban Experience, Work and Values in Squatments of Rio de Janeiro and Lima," in Field (1970), pp. 226-276.

Lernoux, Penny. 1989. *People of God*. New York: Viking.

Lopetegui, Leon. 1965. *Historia de la iglesia en América española desde el Descubrimiento hasta fines del siglo XIX*. Vol. 1 of *México, América Central, Antillas*. Madrid: Biblioteca de Autores Cristianos.

Macedo, Carmen Cinira de A. 1986. *Tempo de Gênesis: O povo das Comunidades Eclesiais de Base*. São Paulo: Editora Brasilense.

Mackay, John A. 1928. "The Power of Evangelism," *Addresses and Other Records. Report of the Jerusalem Meeting of the International Missionary Council*, vol. 8 (London: Oxford University Press), pp. 121-125.

_____. 1932. *The Other Spanish Christ*. New York: Macmillan.

Mackensie, Maud Worcester. 1951. *The Book of the Jaguar Priest: A Translation of the Book of Chilam Balam of Tizimim with Commentary*. New York: Henry Schuman.

Maduro, Otto. 1982. *Religion and Social Conflict*. Maryknoll: Orbis.

Mainwaring, Scott. 1986. *The Catholic Church and Politics in Brazil 1916-1985*. Stanford: Stanford University Press.

Manz, Beatriz. 1988. *Refugees of a Hidden War*. Albany: State University of New York Press.

Marcom, Jr., John. 1990. "The Fire Down South," *Forbes Magazine* (Oct.), pp. 56-71.

Marsden, George. 1980. *Fundamentalism and American Culture*. New York: Oxford University Press.

Martin, David. 1991. "Otro tipo de revolución cultural. El protestantismo radical en Latinoamérica." Santiago: Estudios Públicos.

_____. 1990. *Tongues of Fire: The Explosion of Protestantism in Latin America*. Oxford: Basil Blackwell.

Martínez, Carlos. 1991. "Secta: un concepto inadecuado para explicar el protestantismo mexicano," *Boletím Teológico*.

Martínez Peláez, Severo. 1970. *La patria del criollo: Ensayo de interpretación de la realidad colonial guatemalteca*. Puebla, México: Universidad Autónoma de Puebla.

Marzal, Manuel M. 1985. *El sincretismo iberoamericano*. Lima: Pontificia Universidad Católica del Perú.

_____. 1983. *La transformación religiosa peruana*. Lima: Pontificia Universidad Católica del Perú.

Marzal, Manuel M. et al. n.d. *Rostros indios de Dios*. Quito: Editorial Abya-Yala.

McCoy, John. 1989. "Robbing Peter to Pay Paul," *Latinamerica Press*. Lima (29 June).

McGavran, Donald. 1970. *Understanding Church Growth*. Grand Rapids: Eerdmans.
Mecham, J. Lloyd. 1963. "The Church in Colonial Spanish America," in A. Curtis Wilgus (ed.), *Colonial Hispanic America*. New York: Russell and Russell.
Meeking, Basil, and Stott, John. 1986. *The Evangelical–Roman Catholic Dialogue on Mission 1977-1984*. Grand Rapids: Eerdmans.
Mehl, Roger. 1970. *The Sociology of Protestantism*. London: SCM.
Mendonça, Antônio Gouvêa. 1989. "Um Panorama do protestantismo Brasileiro Atual," in Leilah Landim (ed.), *Sinais dos Tempos: Tradições Religiosas no Brasil*, Cadernos do ISER 22 (Rio de Janeiro: ISER), pp. 37-86.
Mendonça, Antônio Gouvêa, and Velasques Filho, Prócoro. 1980. *Introdução ao Protestantismo no Brasil*. São Paulo: Loyola.
Meyer, Jean. 1969. *Historia de los cristianos en América Latina Siglo XIX y XX*. México, D.F.: Ed. Vuelta.
Míguez Bonino, José. 1983. *Toward a Christian Political Ethics*. London: SCM Press.
_____. 1977. "Visao da Mudança Social e de Suas Tarefas por parte das Igrejas Cristãs Não-Católicas," *Fé Crista e Transformação Social na América Latina*. Petrópolis: Vozes.
_____. 1975. *Doing Theology in a Revolutionary Situation*. Philadelphia: Fortress Press.
_____. 1974. "Popular Piety in Latin America," *Concilium*, no. 96. New York: Herder and Herder.
_____. 1964. "Latin America," in M. Searle Bates and Wilhelm Pauck (eds.), *The Prospects of Christianity throughout the World*. New York: Scribners's Sons.
Mires, Fernando. 1991. *El discurso de la naturaleza: Ecología y politica en América Latina*. San José, Costa Rica: DEI.
_____. 1987. *La colonización de las almas: Misión y conquista en hispanoamérica*. San José, Costa Rica: Departamento Ecuménico de Investigaciones.
_____. 1986. *En nombre de la cruz. Discusiones teológicas y políticas frente al holocausto de los indios (período de conquista)*. San José, Costa Rica: DEI.
Mondragón, Rafael. 1985. *De indios y cristianos en Guatemala*. México, D.F.: COPEC/CECOPE.
Muratorio, Blanca. 1981. "Protestantism, Ethnicity and Class in Chimborazo," in Norman E. Whitten, Jr. (ed.), *Cultural Transformations and Ethnicity in Modern Ecuador*. Urbana: University of Illinois Press, pp. 506-634.
Neill, Stephen. 1986. *A History of Christian Missions*. Harmondsworth: Penguin Books, rev. edition.
Noll, Mark. 1991. "The Scandal of Evangelical Political Reflection, 1896-1991," unpublished lecture, on "Ethics and Public Policy Center" (3-5 April).
Novaes, Regina Reyes. 1985. *Os escolhidos de Deus*. Rio de Janeiro: Marcozerol ICER.
Nuñez, Emilio A., and Taylor, William D. 1989. *Crisis in Latin America: An Evangelical Perspective*. Chicago: Moody Press.
Nuzzi-O'Shaughnessy, Laura. 1988. "Onward Christian Soldiers: The Case of Protestantism in Central America." Paper presented at the Conference on Religious Revivalism and Politics in the Contemporary World, North Texas State University, Denton, TX (5-6 April).
O Estado. 1993. "A religiao que passa," *O Estado de São Paulo* (21 February, São Paulo).
Obermüller, Rudolf. 1957. *Evangelism in Latin America: An Ecumenical Survey*. London: Lutterworth.

Oppenheimer, Andrés. 1992. "Catholic Church Losing Followers to Protestants," *The Miami Herald* (12 Oct.), p. 8A.

Orozco, Samuel Calel. 1992. "Protestantismo y Política en Guatemala." Unpublished paper. Part of the Iglesia y Represion project (July).

Ossa, Manuel. 1991. *Lo ajeno y lo propio. Identidad pentecostal y trabajo.* Santiago: Edit. Rehue.

Padilla, René. 1992. "Whatever Came of 'The People's Church'?" *Christianity Today.* CT Institute.

_____. 1991. "Toward the Globalization and Integrity of Mission," in Anderson et al. (1991).

_____. 1987. "Hay lugar para Dios en la política?" *Misión*, vol. 6, no. 1 (March), p. 4.

Pate, Larry D. 1987. *Misionología: Nuestro cometido transcultural.* Miami: Editorial Vida.

Paul, Benjamin D. 1987. "Fifty Years of Religious Change in San Pedro de la Laguna, a Mayan Community in Highland Guatemala." Prepared for a panel on "Dios, Mundo, and Jehovah: Religious Change in Guatemala," American Anthropological Association Meeting (Chicago, Nov.), pp. 18-22.

Perez Guadalupe, José Luis. 1992. *Por qué se van los católicos: El problema de la "migración religiosa" de los católicos a las llamadas "sectas."* Lima: Conferencia Episcopal Peruana. Colección de Teología Pastoral.

Peters, George W. 1970. *Saturation Evangelism.* Grand Rapids: Zondervan.

Petrini, Giancarlo. 1984. *CEBs em São Paulo: Um novo sujeto popular.* Pontifícia Universidade Católica de São Paulo.

Phillips, James M., and Coote, Robert T., eds. 1993. *Toward the 21st Century in Christian Mission.* Grand Rapids: Eerdmans.

Picón-Salas, Mariano. 1962. *A Cultural History of Spanish America: From Conquest to Independence.* Berkeley: University of California Press.

Piel, Jean. 1989. *Sajcabajá: Muerte y resurrección de un pueblo de Guatemala, 1500-1970.* México D.F.: Centro de Estudios Mexicanos y Centroamericanos.

Pneuma: The Journal of the Society for Pentecostal Studies. 1992. Charles E. Self, "Conscientization, Conversion, and Convergence: Reflections on Base Communities and Emerging Pentecostalism in Latin America," vol. 14, no. 1, pp. 59-72.

_____. 1991. Roger Cabezas, "The Experience of the Latin American Pentecostal: *Encuentro*," pp. 175-188.

_____. 1991. Adoniram Gaxiola, "Poverty as a Meeting and Parting Place: Similarities and Contrasts in the Experiences of Latin American Pentecostalism and Ecclesial Base Communities," vol. 13, no. 2, pp. 167-174.

_____. 1991. Dennis A. Smith, "Coming of Age: A Reflection on Pentecostals, Politics and Popular Religion in Guatemala," vol. 13, no. 2, pp. 131-140.

_____. 1987. Everett A. Wilson, "Latin American Pentecostals: Ecumenical and Evangelical," vol. 9, no. 1, pp. 96-98.

Poblete, Renato. 1969. "Sectarismo portoriqueño," *Sondeos*, no. 55. New York: Centro Intercomunal de Documentación.

Poblete, Renato, and Galilea, Segundo. 1984. *Movimiento Pentecostal e Iglesia Católica en Medios Populares.* Santiago: Centro Bellarmino.

Portilla, Miguel León. 1984. *El Reverso de la Conquista: Relaciones aztecas, mayas e incas* (Series, "El legado de la América Indígena"). México: Editorial J. Mortiz. Reprinted in 1987 and 1990.

Prien, Hans Jürgen. 1985. *La historia del Cristianismo en América Latina.* Salamanca: Sígueme.

Ramalho, Jether Pereira. 1977. "Algumas notas sobre duas perspectivas de pastoral popular." *Cadernos de ISER: O Pentecostalismo*, no. 6, pp. 30-37.

Reina, Rubén Edward, and Schwartz, Norman B. 1974. "The Structural Context of Religious Conversion in Petén, Guatemala: Status, Community and Multi-community," *American Ethnologist* 1: 1 (Feb.), pp. 157-191.

Reinsberger, David. 1988. *Overcoming the World: Politics and Community in the Gospel of John*. London: SPCK, 1989, 168 pp. First published as *Johannine Faith and Liberating Community*. Philadelphia: Westminster Press, 1988.

RIBLA. 1988. "Lectura popular de la Biblia en América Latina: Una hermenéutica de liberación," *Revista de Interpretación Bíblica Latinoamericana*, no. 1. San José, Costa Rica: DEI.

Ricard, Robert. 1966. *The Spiritual Conquest of Mexico*. Berkeley: University of California.

Richard, Pablo. 1990. *La fuerza espiritual de los pobres*. San José, Costa Rica: DEI.

_____. 1987. *Death of Christendom, Birth of the Church*. Maryknoll: Orbis.

_____. 1985. *The Church Born by the Force of the Spirit in Central America*. New York: Circus Publications.

_____. 1984. "The Church of the Poor within the Popular Movement (*Movimiento Popular*)," in Leonardo Boff and Virgilio Elizondo (eds.), *La Iglesia Popular: Between Fear and Hope*. *Concilium*, no. 176. Edinburgh: Clark, pp. 10-16.

_____. 1980. *La Iglesia latinoamericana: Entre el temor y la esperanza*. San José, Costa Rica: DEI.

Rivera Pagán, Luis N. 1992. *A Violent Evangelism: The Political and Religious Conquest of the Americas*. Westminster: John Knox.

_____. 1991. *Evangelización y violencia: La conquista de América*. Puerto Rico: Ediciones SEMI.

Rodriguez, Richard. 1989. "A Continental Shift: Latin Americans Convert from Catholicism to a More Private Protestant Belief," *Los Angeles Times* (Sunday, 13 Aug.), *Opinion*, pp. 1, 2, 6.

Rojas Lima, Flavio. 1988. *La cofradía: Reducto cultural indígena*. Guatemala: Seminario de Integración Social.

Rolim, Francisco Cartaxo. 1987. *O que é Pentecostalismo*. São Paulo: Editora Brasilense.

_____. 1985. *Pentecostais no Brasil: uma interpretação sócioreligiosa*. Petrópolis: Vozes.

Rose, Susan, and Schultze, Quentin. 1993. "The Evangelical Awakening in Guatemala: Fundamentalist Impact on Education and Media," in Martin Marty and R. Scott Appleby, eds., *Fundamentalists in Society*, pp. 415-451.

Salinas, Maximiliano. 1990. "The Voices of Those Who Spoke Up for the Victims," in Leonardo Boff and Virgilio Elizonda (eds.), *1492-1992: The Voice of the Victims*. *Concilium*, pp. 101-109. *Concilium*. 1990/6. London: SCM.

Samandú, Luis E. 1988. "Estrategias evangélicas hacia la población indígena de Guatemala." San José: CSUCA.

_____. 1987. "La Iglesia del nazareno en Alta VeraPaz, su historia y presencia en el Mundo Kekchí." San José: CSUCA.

Santa Ana, Julio de. 1990. "Through the Third World Towards One World," *Exchange*, vol. 19, no. 3 (December).

Schwartz, Norman B. 1990. *Forest Society*. Philadelphia: University of Pennsylvania Press.

Segundo, Juan Luis. 1978. *The Hidden Motives of Pastoral Action*. Maryknoll: Orbis.

_____. 1973. *Masas y minorias en la dialéctica divina de la liberación.* Buenos Aires: La Aurora.

_____. 1970. *De la sociedad a la teologia* Buenos Aires: Ed. Carlos Lohlé.

Sepúlveda, Juan. 1993. "Pentecostalism and Liberation Theology: Two Manifestations of the Work of the Holy Spirit for the Renewal of the Church," in H. D. Hunter and Peter D. Hawkins (eds.), *All Together in One Place: Theological Papers from the Brighton Conference on World Evangelization.* England: Sheffield: Academic Press.

_____. 1992. "Die Pfingstbewegung und ihre Identität als Kirche," *Jahrbuch Mission 1992.* Hamburg: Missionshilfe Verlag, pp. 145-153.

_____. 1992a. "El aporte socio-cultural del movimiento pentecostal chileno," Segundo Encuentro de Diálogo Pentecostal, Angostura de Paine, Chile (Dec.).

_____. 1992b. "El crecimiento pentecostal en América Latina," *Pentecostalismo y Liberación: Una Experiencia latinoamericana.* San José, Costa Rica: DEI.

_____. 1989. "Pentecostalism as Popular Religiosity," *IRM*, vol. 78, no. 309 (Jan.).

_____. 1988. "Pentecostal Theology in the Context of the Struggle for Life," in Kirkpatrick (1988).

Sharp, Brett S. 1993. "Protestant Church Growth in Central America: Sociopolitical Consequences of Evangelical Expansion." Paper presented at the Conference on "Church and Society in Latin America: Sociopolitical and Economic Restructuring since 1960." Villanova University (March).

Shaull, Richard. 1983. "Entre Jesus e Marx (Reflexoes sobre os Anos que Passei no Brasil)," *Religiao e Sociedade*, no. 9 (June), pp. 47-58.

Shorter, Aylward. 1988. *Toward a Theology of Inculturation.* Maryknoll: Orbis.

Simon, Jean-Marie. 1987. *Guatemala: Eternal Spring —Eternal Tyranny.* New York: Norton.

Smith, Carol A. 1990. *Guatemalan Indians and the State.* Austin: University of Texas Press.

Smith, Anthony Christopher. 1983. *The Essentials of Missiology from the Evangelical Perspective of the 'Fraternidad Teológica Latinoamericana'.* Doctoral thesis, Southern Baptist Theological Seminary, Louisville.

Souza, Beatriz Muniz de. 1969. *A esperiencia de salvação: Pentecostais em São Paulo.* São Paulo: Duas Cidades.

Spykman, Gordon, Cook, Guillermo, et al. 1988. *Let My People Live: Faith and Struggle in Central America.* Grand Rapids: Eerdmans.

Steigenga, Timothy J., and Coleman, Kenneth M. 1992. "Protestants and Politics in Chile: 1972-1991." University of North Carolina at Chapel Hill, Department of Political Science and Institute of Latin American Studies. Unpublished paper.

Steuernagel, Valdir R. 1991. "Social Concern and Evangelization: the Journey of the Lausanne Movement," *IBMR*, vol. 15, no. 2 (April).

_____. 1990. "Responsabilidade Social e Evangelização: A Trajetória do Movimento de Lausanne," *Boletim Teológico*, pp. 5-14.

Stoll, David. 1990. *Is Latin America Turning Protestant? The Politics of Evangelical Growth.* Berkeley: University of California Press.

Stoll, Sandra J. 1986. *Púlpito e palenque: religião e política nas eleições da Grande São Paulo.* Master's thesis, UNICAMP, Campinas, São Paulo: UNICAMP.

Strachan, R. Kenneth. 1968. *The Inescapable Calling.* Grand Rapids: Eerdmans.

Suro, Roberto. 1989. "Tide of Catholic Hispanics Floods to Protestant Sects," *Miami Herald, International Edition* (Monday, 15 May), p. 5A.

Taber, Charles R. 1991. *The World Is Too Much with Us.* Macon: Mercer Press.

Taylor, William D., and Núñez, Emilio A. 1989. *Crisis in Latin America*. Chicago: Moody Press.

Tennekes, Hans. 1985. *El Movimiento Pentecostal en la Sociedad Chilena*. Iquique, Chile: Centro de Investigaciones de la Realidad del Sur.

Thornton, Russell. 1987. *Indian Holocaust and Survival*. Norman: University of Oklahoma Press.

Tippett, Alan R. 1970. *Church Growth and the Word of God*. Grand Rapids: Eerdmans.

Tormo, Leandro. 1962. *Historia de la Iglesia en América Latina*. Madrid: OCSHA.

Torres, Carlos A. 1992. *The Church, Society, and Hegemony: A Critical Sociology of Religion in Latin America*. Westport: Praeger.

Torres, Sergio, and Eagleson, John, eds. 1980. *The Challenge of Base Ecclesial Communities*. Maryknoll: Orbis Books.

Transformation. 1985. *An International Dialogue on Evangelical Social Ethics*, vol. 2, no. 2.

Turner, Victor. 1975. "Symbolic Studies," *Annual Review of Anthropology*, no. 4, pp. 145-161.

Vaccaro, Gabriel O. 1991. *Aportes del pentecostalismo al movimiento ecuménico*. Quito: CLAI.

_____. 1990. *Identidad pentecostal*. Quito: CLAI.

Valcárcel, Luis E. 1972. *Tempestad en los Andes*. Lima: Ed. Universo (second ed.).

Vallier, Ivan. 1970. *Catholicism, Social Control and Modernization in Latin America*. Englewood Cliffs: Prentice Hall.

Van Elderen, Marlin. 1990. *Introducing the World Council of Churches*. Geneva: WCC Publications.

Veja. 1991. "Fé em desencanto," *Veja* (Rio de Janeiro, 25 Dec.).

Vergara, Ignacio. 1962. *El protestantismo en Chile*. Santiago: Editorial del Pacífico.

Wagner, Peter. 1973. *Look Out! The Pentecostals Are Coming*. Carol Stream: Creation House.

Waldrop, Ricardo. 1990. "Experiencia pentecostal: realidad y posibilidades," *Vida y Pensamiento*, vol. 10, no. 1. San José, Costa Rica, pp. 67-70.

Walls, Andrew. 1985. "Culture and Coherence in Christian History," *Evangelical Review of Theology*, vol. 9, no. 35 (July).

Warren, Max. 1967. *Social History and Christian Mission*. London: SCM.

Weber, Max. 1958. *The Protestant Ethic and the Spirit of Capitalism*. New York: Scribners.

Westmeier, Karl-Wilhelm. 1993. "Themes of Pentecostal Expansion in Latin America," *International Bulletin of Missionary Research*. New Haven: OMSC, pp. 129-136.

Willems, Emilio. 1967. *Followers of the New Faith: Culture Change and the Rise of Protestantism in Brazil and Chile*. Nashville: Vanderbilt University Press.

_____. 1964. "Protestantism and Cultural Change in Brazil and Chile," in William V. D'Antonio and Frederick B. Pike (eds.), *Religion, Revolution and Reform* New York: Praeger.

Winn, Peter. 1992. *Americas: The Changing Face of Latin America and the Ca bean*. New York: Pantheon Books.

Woodward, Ralph Lee. 1976. *Central America: A Nation Divided*. New York: ford University Press.

Wright, Ronald. 1992. *Stolen Continent: The Indian Story — 1492*. London Murray.